Herman Ruiz

December 2005,

AIRBALL

The Complete and Unvarnished
Account of Louisville's 30-Year
Odyssey to Acquire an NBA Franchise

J. BRUCE MILLER

JBM PARTNERS, LLC

ISBN 0-9761748-0-4

This book is dedicated to the many who dared mighty things with no fear of the unknown, and who were willing to embrace life's inexorable change, all the while refusing to take rank with those timid souls who daily exist in the grey twilight, never experiencing either victory or defeat and who thrive in the warmth of mediocrity's comfort zone that's found in the middle-of-the-herd. They are the Champions.

TABLE OF CONTENTS

The credit belongs to the man who is actually in the arena, whose face is marred by dust and sweat and blood, who strives valiantly; who errs, and comes up short again and again, because there is no effort without error and shortcomings, who does actually try to do the deed; who knows the great enthusiasm, the great devotion and spends himself in a worthy cause; who, at worst, if he fails, at least fails while daring greatly....

Far better it is to dare mighty things, to win glorious triumphs even though checkered by failure, than to take rank among those timid souls who neither enjoy much nor suffer much, because they live in that grey twilight that knows not victory nor defeat.

Theodore Roosevelt

Author's Note

When the group or a civilization declines, it is through no mystic limitation of a corporate life, but through the failure of its political or intellectual leaders to meet the challenges of change.

The Story of Civilization
Will and Ariel Durant

This is the complete and unvarnished account of a thirty-year odyssey—Louisville, Kentucky's effort to acquire a major league professional sports franchise in the National Basketball Association. It represented an enormous economic opportunity, one that has been grasped by seventeen American cities[1] since 1970 and that, by the Millennium, has vaulted those cities past Louisville into the pantheon of the world's economically vital cities.

Repeatedly over those thirty years all that was required for Louisville to seize this opportunity was the simple opening of a previously locked door. The ease of the door's opening was astounding. Louisville's inability to simply walk through it was alarming. It didn't, and the odyssey failed.

To succeed, Louisville's political and intellectual leaders were required to heed the Durants' observation "...to meet the challenges of change" and through progressive leadership repress the city's long-lived fear of the unknown and its debilitative yearning for the status quo. They were required to pilot the plane by looking through the windshield into the future instead of through the rear-view mirror's reflection of the community's past. Other virtues were necessary, too, like a vision of how things ought to be and a willingness to reach beyond what the community inherently felt was the limit of its grasp. In sum, civic leadership was required to reverse a mindset that had retarded Louisville's economic growth for a century.

In the process of attracting a major sports franchise Louisville competed against other cities—and itself. Each of those other cities also had its fair share of citizens who abhorred change and feared the unknown. However, through effective public and private leadership they were able to control their destiny by forward-looking and selfless public decision-making that eventually accepted the challenge of change. They overcame their fear of the unknown and didn't beat themselves. In the end, if Louisville hadn't beaten itself, it would have won—but it didn't.

The inside story of how Louisville defeated itself is disturbing. The ineptitude and lack of vision of its political leadership should be clear to everyone. As the world moved into the 21st century, particularly distressing was the overwhelming desire of the city's elected leadership to recoil from the cutting edge of economic progress, favoring instead the comfort and warmth of the middle of the road and a self-indulgent satisfaction with being average. The virtues of Louisville's sedate lifestyle and its small-town traditions are authentic and legitimate virtues, but such parochialism represents the manifestation of an observation (rendered a half century ago) by John Gunther—that Kentucky's major economic impediment is its steadfast unwillingness to distinguish between "...fruity myth and brutal fact."[2]

Louisville's continued disregard of the difference between fruity myth and the brutal facts of economic reality in the 21st century will inescapably result in the forfeiture of significant future economic opportunities for its children and grandchildren.

Thus, the mantra of the underlying message of this book: if Louisville really wants to be what it knows it ought to be, and can be, it must change the way it thinks.

There's never been an up-close and personal examination like this written about decision-making in Louisville and the debilitating forces that repress the city's leadership in that process. Some Louisvillians will say that I shouldn't have written this book because it doesn't reflect a totally positive view of Louisville, some of Louisville's prominent citizens, and certain of its local politicians. Some will choose to believe that a good citizen shouldn't dwell on his city's failure to accomplish something and is better off letting bygones be bygones. Others will prefer to rationalize by concluding that it's been written out of anger buttressed by my desire to get even with those who don't fare well herein. None of them are correct.

One would be far more correct to observe: "There's more to learn from defeat than victory," or as Carl Sandburg said, "Nothing happens unless first a dream." From the panorama of facts surrounding these defeats there's much to learn about life itself and the role that change and aversion to change play in it. While the achievement of an NBA franchise for the city may have been a personal dream of mine, this dream was an easily obtainable reality—with only a modicum of effective local political leadership.

On more than one occasion I thought, "What difference does it all really make to anyone?" I have ceased writing several times, only to begin again, realizing that the story of Louisville's NBA odyssey had to be told.

In the end, the decision to publish was made because the time has come for Louisville to demand real leadership from its elected political leaders. While its laid-back lifestyle has been the subject of conversation at countless cocktail and dinner parties over the years, little has really changed in Louisville, down deep.

So this book will tell the whole story of Louisville's—and my—NBA odyssey, warts and all. Its purpose is to record for posterity the inside drama of the good, heroic work done by some, and the miserable failure and oversight of others, that was played out on the national stage for three decades. I'm afraid that mostly it is a story of ineptitude. It is my hope that Louisville's citizens, once informed with the truth, will become more demanding of its leadership, asking it to "lead, follow or get out of the way."

The cast of characters in this saga is a virtual kaleidoscope of American life. There were those with wonderful qualities of strength, courage, determination and loyalty who sincerely wanted to see Louisville move beyond the middle tier of American cities. They were countered by those whose self-serving actions were designed to protect their turf within Louisville's comfort zone and those whose incompetence seldom allowed them to rise to the challenge. The glorious truth, pride, and honesty of many were rivaled by the lies and duplicity of others. High-minded cooperation confronted unrestrained negative positioning and psychological gamesmanship. It included the efforts of many well-intentioned people to gather a community together and enable it to reach beyond its grasp, and the attempts of others to sink the ship.

Some of the crew were aboard that ship in the beginning, others at the end. But only one sailor was aboard for the entire three decades—me. The information for this book comes from my extensive contemporaneous notes, calendars, letters, e-mails, and written chronologies of the events while on the thirty-year odyssey. In some instances, thoughts, conclusions and feelings have been attributed to the participants. These attributions come from either the person himself, a secondary source, the written record, or my impressions of events. Extensive Endnotes, arranged numerically, are provided at the text's conclusion. Many books and news accounts have been read and utilized in the fact-gathering for this book. There are a multitude of references to them in the Endnotes, and the books are listed alphabetically, by author, in the Bibliography.

Credit for this book must be shared with the many people who participated with me and dedicated themselves to this challenge, and who attempted to change the community vision that was required if Louisville was to move forward. Many of them will be mentioned in the book.

I would be remiss in not expressing a special thank you to the hundreds of people who have written, phoned, or come up to me all over Louisville, southern Indiana and throughout Kentucky to express their personal appreciation for the effort chronicled in this book. More than once these expressions of kindness have brought a lump to my throat.

There are others who, in their loving way, have been instrumental in allowing me to circumnavigate the deep waters of Louisville's perplexing exigencies. My wife, Norma, was the loving steel rod, who stood by my side as the most recent portion of the odyssey played forth. Never wavering in her support and encouragement, she held the sextant that allowed me to find our way through the storm. My adult children, Jamie, Alexis (and her husband, Darrell) and Sarah; and my adult stepchildren, Gavin and Mitch Osborne and Carter Gaw, along with her husband, Brevin, each gave their love, encouragement and hope for success at a multitude of family gatherings, Christmases and birthday parties. A particular thank you must go to Brevin, who helped with so much of the research, fact-gathering and the odyssey itself.

Then there's my granddaughter Anna, who frequently e-mailed Grandpa Bruce from Murfreesboro, Tennessee with words of encouragement. At the time she was a brand-new teenager who had become a vigorous Tennessee Titan fan and because of that understood why something like the impending challenge for Louisville was important in the life of a city. Now Anna is a high school senior who has just been elected president of the student body at one of the largest high schools in Tennessee. Even at the age of 17 she could teach a few of our local politicians a lesson or two about leadership and bold vision.

Last, but by far not least, is my six year-old grandson, Tristan (the T-man). The T-man had just turned two when the most recent odyssey began and was a little past four when it was over. The T-man and I are best buddies. Sometimes we're even best friends. When he comes to our home he runs up to me and gives me a big hug. Always glad to see me was the T-man, whether things were going well or poorly. It's unconditional love and it's priceless. As we went through the odyssey together, we shared other things as well—beginning with Barney, gravitating to Buzz Lightyear and Wrestlemania, then to Scooby-Doo, ending with Sponge Bob Square Pants and Jimmy Neutron. They were his love and my release. Somewhere in the middle we both had Power Rangers and Rescue Hero action figures. Mine were Christmas presents from the T-man. Today, they proudly sit in my office, mementos of a very special time spent with an absolutely precious little guy.

Throughout the three years of the last NBA quest, the unabashed love and wide green eyes of my dear best friend, Tristan, enabled me to do something I might not have been able to do—to see clearly into the future two generations out, and realize the utter importance of thinking young, thinking proud, thinking big about growth and change, because all that happens every day in the life of a pre-kindergartener. Through this little guy's unrestrained joy of life, his love and happiness with everything around him, along with his acceptance of his own growth and development, it becomes easy to see what Louisville needs so desperately.

So welcome to the odyssey. Despite the unease that periodically accompanies the telling, it is hoped that the reader will find the adventure as thought-provoking, challenging, interesting, and as incredible as it has been to live through, and its underlying message as important as I deem it to be. When my days come to an end, as they shall, it will be even more sad if nothing is learned from all this by those who remain—and care.

J. Bruce Miller
Louisville, Kentucky
2004

PART ONE
Basketball: The Religion in Kentucky

You gain strength, courage and confidence by every experience in which you really stop to look fear in the face. You must do the thing you think you cannot do.

Eleanor Roosevelt

CHAPTER ONE

When the Saints Come Marchin' In

Shall we begin at the end?

Known as "The Buccaneer from Barataria Bay," Jean Lafitte was a legend, renowned for his ferocious gang of seafaring smugglers who lived on an island called Grande Terre and marauded Caribbean ships—selling the gang's bounty in the Louisiana bayous to indigent Cajuns and Creoles. He was their hero. They owed their meager existence to his Robin Hood-esque villainy. General Andrew Jackson also owed something to him (along with the Kentucky long-riflemen)—his 1815 victory over General Pakenham's 15,000 British troops at the Battle of New Orleans. For nearly two centuries the legend has grown. Today, there's even a national park named in his honor.

New Orleans was Lafitte's city—a strange city, situated on an impossible site below sea level. Today it is known for many things, from its compelling voodoo witchcraftery to its bustling seaport, from its culinary delights to the Mardi Gras, where *laissez les bons temps rouler* is the order of the day, the week and the month. Among the many others are instant festivals and celebrations that bewitch and bewilder.

It was one of those celebrations—a picturesque festive jazz band-led parade, often doubling as a funeral dirge, that escorted North Carolina multi-millionaires Ray Wooldridge and George Shinn, guests of the New Orleans mayor and Louisiana's governor, on a flower-bedecked winding path through the Vieux Carre, eventually ending up in the New Orleans Arena, where on Thursday, January 18, 2002, it was formally announced that their Charlotte

Hornets NBA franchise was transferring to New Orleans.

The celebration was New Orleans'—the funeral dirge was Louisville's. It had lost, again, for the fourth time—this time not because of a 19th century Jean Lafitte-like act of piracy, but because of the sheer ineptitude of its own political leadership.

The front-page headline of the next day's *The Courier-Journal* precisely observed: "Louisville deal was too slow, Hornets say." Wooldridge was further quoted as saying: "Louisville was the front-runner on this. But what happened was there was time pressure. They had certain things they had to get done in a certain time frame. And things just didn't happen. I don't know if it was a political thing or if it was UofL or if it was about who was going to operate the arena. All of that had to be decided in a certain time frame, and they didn't do it."[3]

In response and not missing a beat, Louisville's long-practiced post-failure political spin geared up, immediately passing the blame for failure elsewhere—anywhere but where it belonged.

Mayor Dave Armstrong was quoted saying Wooldridge had never mentioned a time lag when they last spoke several days prior. But this spin wasn't a reason. Instead it was just another in a long list of fabricated excuses designed to justify failure. For it was known by everyone involved that time had been of the essence for the four months since early October of the previous year. Had Mayor Dave acted promptly and decisively when, *at his insistence*, the responsibility was turned over to him, the Hornets application for transfer to Louisville would have been submitted to the NBA by December 31, 2001—*because on September 14, 2001, the Hornets ownership had signed a written agreement committing the team's transfer to Louisville.* Instead Mayor Dave simply blew it.

Nick Anderson's editorial cartoon in *The Courier-Journal* on January 19th said it all—depicting a goofy-looking guy wearing a "Dave" button running helter-skelter into a meeting room where the conference table bore a sign read "Arena discussions" and saying, "I've got another starting point for discussion" while everyone was leaving the meeting out another door.

Others, fashioning themselves as leaders, entered the justification game with the incredible observation that the loss was really a win, because Louisville was "in the hunt." It was "in the race!"—another of Gunther's fruity myths—ignoring the reality that the eighth-place horse in the Kentucky Derby was also "in the race" but had accomplished nothing.

There's no other way to describe it except to say it was simply and utterly pitiful. To comprehend just how pitiful, one must examine what was lost.

The Opportunity

The immense economic power of the twenty-eight American cities that are home to an NBA franchise is astounding.

By the year 2000, these twenty-eight cities produced a combined metropolitan gross product (value of all goods and services produced) of $4,232.83 trillion, representing 41.5% of the entire $10.208 trillion gross national product of the nation.[4]

Over many years, leaders of these cities had paid homage to the Durants' advice delivered in *The Story of Civilization*:

> "When the group or a civilization declines, it is through no mystic limitation of a corporate life, but through the failure of its political or intellectual leaders to meet the challenges of change."

Those leaders in those cities had entered the arena, striving mightily, caring immensely, daring relentlessly and risking greatly through dynamic and forward-thinking effort, with no fear of the unknown, to achieve prodigiously for their cities.

In the process, these twenty-eight American cities became the integral and relevant urban hub of world commerce. The magnitude of their economic success has been staggering.

If these twenty-eight American cities were a single nation, it would possess the world's second largest economy, with a gross national product of $4,232.83 trillion, ahead of Japan's $4.145 trillion. As a single nation, its gross national product would nearly equal that of all the nations on the continents of Asia, Africa and South America combined.

Diverse in virtually every respect, these cities span the four corners of our nation, from Seattle to Miami and from Boston to Los Angeles. Some are among the nation's oldest cities and others were mere outposts at the time of America's 100th birthday. Some have an industrial economic base and others are technical and service industry centers. Some are comprised of significant immigrant populations, others are not. Some suffered as the nation's rust-belt economy disintegrated and others didn't even miss a beat.

Some experienced great upheaval during the nation's racial integration in the mid-20th century and others didn't. Some developed in primarily rural states and others did not. Of the twenty-eight cities, only seven are state capitals, yet since the U.S. Supreme Court's one-man, one-vote decision, each city had been accepted by their state's more rural citizens as the unquestioned economic engine in their respective state. As the Millennium turned, they daily competed with each other for increasing portions of the world's economy. The competition was relentless. Few things brought them together.

But in the last thirty years, despite the diversity of their development and the inter-city competition between them, thousands of times annually they became interconnected by virtue of one common product—the NBA. That product is internationally televised by global satellite to 212 nations[5] and annually generates an average of $248.9 million in economic activity for each of the twenty-eight cities. It is headquartered in the Olympic Tower on New York City's Fifth Avenue, next door to St. Patrick's Cathedral, with international regional offices in London, Paris, Toronto, Barcelona, Hong Kong, Melbourne, Tokyo, Taipei, Miami, Beijing and Mexico City.

From the barrios of Rio to the inner-city playgrounds of Beijing, from sub-Saharan Africa to the King's palace in Nepal and throughout the European continent to the Ural Mountains of central Russia, that product, while invented in America, has become one of only two true international sports.[6] Each of those twenty-eight American cities possesses an exclusive franchise for the right to contract with the world's most highly-skilled professional athletes in that sport. Those franchises have experienced worldwide licensed merchandise and apparel sales increase of 57% in 2003 and are estimated to exceed $3 billion in 2004.[7] Its fastest-growing market is the nation of China, where the regional television arrangements serve 300 million viewers.[8] The owners of those franchises are collectively worth nearly $75 billion and are among the giants of American and international commerce with other wide-ranging business interests, many of which are located in those twenty-eight American cities.

So over the last thirty years, Louisville has lost four distinct and realistic opportunities to join these twenty-eight cities and become a part of the hub of the world's urban economic engine.

You ask — how and why did all this happen?

Since the mid-1920s, major league baseball was impossible to accomplish in Louisville because of the existence in Cincinnati of the historic Reds and their territorial prerogatives that were protected by the sport's 1924 congressional grant of immunity from anti-trust laws. Major league hockey was never even considered, and the concept of an NFL team in Louisville became economically futile after the league's expansion to Cincinnati in the 1970s, to Indianapolis in the 1980s and to Nashville in the 1990s.

Left was the National Basketball Association and the game that Kentuckians adored and worshipped—basketball—a fact not unrecognized by the NBA. Louisville, like most mid-sized American cities, would be pursued by the league as a logical candidate.

The years 1967 to 1978 presented Louisville with its first opportunity, as a dozen mid-sized American cities joined the NBA. It was real and existed on the very edge of Louisville's fingertips. The effort was legitimate and exhaustive. In the end, it was lost solely because of one person's decision. The perplexing vicissitudes of this episode are explored in Chapters 4-6.

For the next two decades Louisville didn't even pursue admission.

As the Millennium turned from 1999 through January, 2002, Louisville was presented with three additional opportunities. They are examined in Chapters 9-13. Each was to be primarily sponsored by an international corporation headquartered in Louisville, with over 840,000 world-wide employees and nearly $24 billion in worldwide annual sales emanating from store locations in over 100 nations. Along with this company's enormous financial commitment and three NBA franchise owners desirous of transferring to Louisville, all that was required was the creation of a public/private vehicle to bond, fund and construct a downtown, multi-purpose, state-of-the-art arena with fiber optic and cable-ready facilities capable of instantly transmitting a televised signal worldwide.

In 2000 the financing of such an arena would have been a snap. With bond interest rates at their lowest levels in over forty years, the state and local taxes generated by an NBA team meant the actual cost to taxpayers was virtually nothing. The day-to-day operation of the arena would have been guaranteed by the NBA tenant and the arena's operation, resulting in virtually no future financial exposure to the city's taxpayers. The net result would have been a $250 million city-owned asset generating hundreds of millions of dollars a year in revenue streams throughout Louisville's economy and replacing its near-fifty year old arena, Freedom Hall. A same or similar thing had been done in the 1990s by Denver, Los Angeles, Portland, Seattle, Salt Lake City, Sacramento, Chicago, San Antonio, Phoenix, Dallas, Minneapolis, Indianapolis, New Orleans, Miami, Atlanta, Philadelphia, Washington, D.C., Boston and Cleveland. Action templates were aplenty and a modern Daniel Boone trailsman wasn't required to lead an excursion across the Appalachians into a fearsome no-man's land.

One would think that this change wouldn't be a particularly earth-shattering event. But in Louisville, Kentucky, it was!

Despite the reality of a supportive, home-based, international corporation offering active participation in the effort; despite the Kentucky Governor's full support and encouragement; and despite the existence of three NBA teams whose owners were willing to move to Louisville (one of which, the Charlotte Hornets, had even signed a written agreement to do so), Louisville's political leadership repeatedly failed to accept the challenge of change and rejected the opportunity to join the National Basketball Association.

The story is nothing short of mind-boggling, particularly when one considers that in 1950 Louisville was the 30th largest American city with a population of 369,129, behind Portland for 29th place by only 4,499 persons and followed by the now-NBA cities of Atlanta (33rd with 331,314), Miami (42nd with 249,276), Salt Lake City (52nd with 182,121), Sacramento (67th with 137,572), Charlotte (70th with 134,042), Phoenix (99th with 106,818) and with Orlando not even listed among the largest 100 cities.[9]

But some Louisvillians would disagree that it was mind-boggling, believing that it's just fine and probably preferable for the city to reject an open door to the world's economic hub.

If you had to make up something like this, you couldn't.

The amazing thing is that it wasn't always this way. There was a time when Louisville was a dynamic, forward-thinking and economically venturistic city, with political and community leadership that understood the importance of a city sustaining its economic progress at a rate faster than its competitors. There was a time when Louisville was a highly relevant participant in the nation's economy. It was a time when competitor cities were required to take note of Louisville and its actions.

Let's look at that moment in time and examine the astounding series of events that befell Louisville over a period of 100 years, gradually dulling the initiative and confidence of the city and its leaders before turning to one of the results of its lost purpose and tenacity—Louisville's failed NBA odyssey.

Only in growth, reform and change, paradoxically enough, is true security to be found.

Anne Morrow Lindbergh

CHAPTER TWO

Louisville Becomes Infected With Kentucky[10]

Winston Churchill once observed that Russia was "...a mystery, wrapped in a riddle, around an enigma." In a far smaller geopolitical context, his observation finds application in Louisville's 19th century ordeal over economic progressivism, Kentucky's 19th-century yearning for a return to provincialism, their collective 20th-century predicament, and 21st-century challenge.

Kentucky Economic Development

The magnitude of America's economic development in 19th century was incalculable and, arguably, has never been equalled in the history of mankind. But Kentucky's was virtually unnoticeable, as described by the state's noted historian, Dr. Thomas Clark: "Kentucky's historical shame was the fact in its first century and a half of its existence....they and their children were handicapped in trying to take their place in a rising urban-technological society because they were functionally illiterate and incapable of performing with intelligent human efficiency.[11]

During the 19th century Louisville's economic development, while initially so dramatic and strikingly different from that of rural and agrarian Kentucky, began to level off by 1900. By the mid-20th century, Louisville's national economic prowess had deteriorated to a point of virtual economic non-relevance.

Fifty years ago John Gunther, writing in *Inside U.S.A.*, defined the affliction as Kentucky being infected with Kentucky.[12] Here, it is defined as Louisville becoming infected with Kentucky. The astounding events that caused this reversal is a tragic chronicle about what was once the shining City on a River, with so much promise.

A shining City on a Hill (River)

In 1800 Louisville was an inconsequential 359-person mosquito-infested river hamlet[13] with its lone noteworthy moment occurring across the Ohio River. There, on October 14, 1803, Meriwether Lewis met William Clark and formed one of the most famous and successful partnerships of "undaunted courage" in American history.

Meanwhile, seventy-five miles east, Lexington, graced with exceptionally fertile soil, had become the commercial center for trailsmen crossing the Appalachians. It thrived, primarily due to the region's hemp crop that was used for rope and textiles—both necessary staples for the western adventure. Many of its agrarian families had become wealthy, overnight. Wealth generally breeds culture and Lexingtonians, seeking it, built printing houses and a two thousand book library. Its university, Transylvania, was graduating students with bachelors degrees, had chairs of learning in law and medicine. The university's president, Horace Halley, was one of the nation's premier educators. The educational prowess of Transylvania was not better reflected than by Thomas Jefferson's statement when founding the University of Virginia:

> "...unless something is done we must send our children to college in Kentucky or Cambridge."[14]

Lexington's leaders, thinking far ahead, created an unusual place in the sun for their burgeoning city by organizing the Kentucky Jockey Club in 1797, and by sponsoring match races between great thoroughbred horses. Soon the city was to become one of the nation's leading thoroughbred horse centers.[15] Then known as the "Athens of the West", Lexington had a population in 1800 of 1,795[16] —five times that of Louisville, the river hamlet to the west.

Even in the first generation of their existence there was conflict between these two places and their most prominent citizens. January 19, 1809 found Lexingtonian Henry Clay waging a duel to the death in southern Indiana (still a part of Canada) with Louisville's Humphrey Marshall. In the state legislature, Clay had proposed a resolution requiring legislators to wear clothes made in central Kentucky, but the Federalist and more worldly

Marshall preferred imported cloth. In the legislative debate that followed, Marshall had called Clay a 'liar.' Clay retorted that Marshall was a 'poltroon' (coward)—hence the duel to the death. No one won. Clay was wounded in the thigh and Marshall the abdomen.[17]

But soon would come another duel, and this time there would be a victor. Virtually overnight, everything about these two places was to change. On October 28, 1811, Captain Nicholas Roosevelt docked his steamboat, the *New Orleans*, in that river hamlet.[18] The resulting torrent of river commerce was, literally, overwhelming. Within several years, sixty-eight steamboats were making regular stops, turning Louisville into a bustling commercial city. Received were exports from the American south of beef, pork, bacon, flour, whiskey, lard, rope, hemp and tobacco, along with a Santa Claus sack full of manufactured products.[19] It became Louisville's turn to seek culture and refinement.

By 1816, the Louisville Library Company had opened the city's first public library—twice as large as Lexington's. Dr. Charles Caldwell left Transylvania's medical school and founded the Louisville Medical Institute, which merged with Louisville Collegiate Institute—to be subsequently merged with a law school to form the University of Louisville, becoming the nation's first municipally-owned university.[20] Paul Skidmore began manufacturing steam engines in 1812, and the six-story Merchant's Manufacturing Mill, built in 1815, was the tallest building west of the Allegheny mountains. The Hope Distillery was one of the largest in the country.[21] By 1820 the river hamlet had grown by 1,100+% to 4,012; and ten years later Louisville had grown 3,160% to 11,345[22], passing Lexington's population by more than 2,000. This was only the beginning.

You had to deal with Louisville in 1830. It was becoming a distinct and highly relevant factor in America's swiftly developing commercial and industrial economy. To be sure, Mother Nature had been kind to Louisville. She placed it alongside the Ohio River through which funnelled steamboat-borne commerce that by 1850 had reached an annual dollar value of $37 million (the rough equivalent of $4 billion dollars in today's economy) with 14,820 tons of steamboats registered in the Louisville port.[23] Longer than Europe's Rhine or Seine rivers, the Ohio's 981 miles had only one navigable barrier—the Falls at Louisville, the traversing of which required cargo to be unloaded and portaged by land. As a result the city became an overnight stop-over for river transporters and their goods.

During the pre-Civil War steamboat era, the cotton planting and agrarian south had become economically dependent upon Louisville's Ohio River facilities and New Orleans' Mississippi River port. Wealthy southern plantation owners frequented these cities to purchase goods and supplies, returning to the rural south as middlemen to distribute their purchases.

The economy of Lexington had been severely damaged by Louisville's spectacular growth, as has been described by Dr. Clark: "The Athens of the West was completely shorn of its commercial glory and its merchants were casting about aimlessly in search of some means of satisfying ... commercial discrimination.[24]

Winds of change

Often such quick growth can be bipolar for a city. It was for Louisville as it became two separate cities. One part was sedate, enjoying the sophisticated gentility of beautiful homes around Central Park and Fourth Avenue, literary societies, theater and other amenities, which made that part of Louisville an elegant replica of Philadelphia's Main Line.

The other part was a polar opposite—a lusty waterfront town, replete with brothels, taverns and wide-open gambling. Mike Fink became that part's legend, a symbol of the hard-drinking keelsman. His boast: "half horse, half alligator [I can] could out-run, out-jump, out-shoot, out-drink, drag-out and lick any man in the country."[25] Any man except one—Fink was shot dead, through the heart, in 1823.

In 1828 the Mike Fink part of Louisville was cleaned up when the legislature granted 'city' status for Louisville, authorizing a local government and police department. Further strides occurred in 1833, with the completion of the Louisville and Portland Canal around the falls and the 1834 opening of the largest hotel west of the Appalachian mountains—the Galt House Hotel, which brought refined east-coast hostelry to the waterfront. While still a lusty riverboat city, winds of change were blowing.

A faster and more economically-productive means of commercial transportation was on the horizon—the railroad. The idea of a railroad revived Lexington's hopes. With the steamboat era declining, maybe its economic significance could be re-established.

Between 1830 and 1850 Lexington desperately tried to generate more effective economic competition with Louisville. Its patron, Henry Clay, succeeded in obtaining a railroad charter for Lexington and it was quickly built all the way to Frankfort by 1834.[26] Wealthy Lexingtonians then debated whether to build a railroad or a canal to the Ohio River. Along came Robert Y. Hayne and a group of southern planters and politicians, including Kentucky's Henry Clay and South Carolina's John C. Calhoun, with a $6 million dream[27]—a system of canals and railroads that would connect Charleston, South Carolina to Cincinnati through Lexington. The central Kentuckians grew even more hopeful. With a railroad connection to Ohio, Dr. Clark noted, "Lexington could deprive Louisville of much of its central Kentucky trade and she would not be dependent upon Louisville as her only outlet to the southern market."[28]

The Panic of 1837 shelved both the railroad to Frankfort and the Hayne dream. Upon its subsequent revival, Louisville's merchants and banking interests along with their political clout in the legislature killed Henry Clay's and Lexington's canal/railroad dream.

After twenty years of effort, in 1852 the two cities were finally connected with a rail line owned by two separate companies—the Louisville & Frankfort and the Lexington & Frankfort Railroad Companies. But nothing was solved, because the companies required passengers to change trains at Frankfort.[29] "The dream was realized too late to preserve Lexington's commercial supremacy."[30]

Louisville's growth explodes

With its population exploding to 43,194 by 1850,[31] in one generation Louisville had completely outstripped Lexington as a city of national economic prominence. It was the tenth largest American city, larger than Washington, D.C. (40,001) or even Chicago (29,963). Directly across the Ohio River was New Albany, then Indiana's largest city.[32] Quite an urban metropolis for mid-19th century America. The amenities of life in Louisville also exploded.

In 1851, Jenny Lind, known as the Swedish Nightingale gave three standing-room-only concerts at Louisville's Mozart Hall, with tickets costing $175 each. New York's famed Samuel Drake operated the City Theater, a majestic structure seating 700 patrons.[33] Louisville even stole a share of horse-racing thunder from Lexington when in 1839 10,000 cheering fans at its Oakland Race Course witnessed America's greatest match race to date—Wagner vs. Grey Eagle—with Wagner winning the $14,000 purse.

Louisville's economy accounted for one-half the value of manufactured goods produced in Kentucky and paid twice as much into the state treasury as the rest of the state combined.

Despite its economic success, all wasn't well for Louisville, as Squire Turner, a flamboyantly and fiery rural legislator from Madison County, impassionately spoke to Kentucky's 1849 legislative redistricting convention, which had been necessitated by the passage of Kentucky's second constitution. After asking the rhetorical question, "Shall we allow one city, if it grows large enough, to govern the whole state?" Turner proposed Louisville be granted only one of the state's thirty-eight state senators.[34] The Squire's ploy failed and Louisville was given even larger representation in the legislature than before.

With the legislature's power over Louisville substantially curbed,[35] the economic result for the river metropolis was immediate. The value of Louisville's industrial output nearly doubled in the ten years between 1850-1860 from $21,710,000 to $37,931.00.[36]

But old Squire had succeeded in delivering a prophetic message. An agrarian revolt had begun against the 'big city' and its yearning for economic growth and change, as Dr. Clark observes: "Kentucky entered into the new industrial and economic age shackled to the past in which agrarian interests attempted to maintain as fully as possible a legal status quo, which would eventually hold the state in social and political thraldom."[37]

Louisville's leaders ignored the Squire's warning, as another urban competitor on a much smaller river appeared. Nashville, on the Cumberland River, was seeking commercial opportunity with southern Kentucky. With unsatisfactory access to Louisville through the Barren and Green Rivers,[38] Glasgow and Bowling Green petitioned the Volunteer state's legislature for a railroad. To prosper economically they had to get their goods to market, and real movement was afoot in Tennessee to build a railroad from southern Kentucky through Nashville to Memphis and its Mississippi River port.

The aggressive and venturous political, economic and business leaders of Louisville were determined to remain ahead of the curve. They rose, together, irrespective of their personal or political interests, to meet the challenge.

The L&N

Despite Squire Turner's continuing diatribe about Louisville's growth and importance, the new state legislature further enabled the city's economic growth on March 5, 1850, by chartering a railroad between Louisville and Nashville. Both cities "...saw the road as their chief weapon in the battle not only against each other but against such potential outsiders as Cincinnati...."[39]

Soon the L&N's ownership convinced two extremely far-sighted men to assume positions of leadership. One was a Jacksonian Democrat, James Guthrie, who had been elected president of the constitutional convention, where Squire Turner sought to frustrate Louisville's economic growth and state-wide influence. Born in Bardstown, after practicing law in Louisville he had been appointed the Secretary of the Treasury under President Franklin Pierce. A skilled, dynamic and forward-thinking leader, Guthrie became the L&N's vice-president. The other man was even more talented. The six-foot, seven-inch German-born Albert Fink (nicknamed the "Teutonic Giant") was hired as the L&N's chief railroad construction engineer and superintendent. He enjoyed national renown for his engineering expertise. For the next thirty years, Guthrie and Fink would lead the L&N into a premier position in America's railroading industry.[40]

Louisville's city council, long-known for its progressive thinking, promptly acted. On June 17, 1851 it appropriated $1 million of venture capital to be invested in the L&N for the purpose of building the L&N Railroad[41]—a sum the reasonable equivalent to $150 million in today's dollars.[42] In the next eight years, Louisville's city council would contribute an additional $1 million.[43] The railroad construction to Nashville had drawn national attention, enabling Louisville to become the host city of the American National Convention that nominated Millard Fillmore for the presidency on June 27, 1856. On October 27, 1859, "...a special train with 200 passengers, including local and state political notables, travelled the newly-opened rail to Nashville—amid much celebration."[44]

Costing a total of $6,674,249[45] (nearly nine billion dollars in today's money) with a start-up debt of $4,705,000 and an annual interest payment of $279,830,[46] the Louisville-led project was far-sighted in its vision, tolerance of risk and with absolutely no fear of the unknown. In an economic sense, it was even more noteworthy—reflecting the willingness of Louisville's leadership in the 1850s to accept the challenge of change by making a direct frontal strike for regional economic supremacy.

L&N and the Civil War

When completed, the L&N was unique. No other railroad connected the Ohio River to the south. As the Civil War progressed, Union forces began using it to transport soldiers and supplies to their front lines. Louisville became a major war-planning center as General William Tecumseh Sherman, Commander of the Army of the Cumberland and General Ulysses S. Grant planned Sherman's invasion of the South ('March to the Sea') at Louisville's Galt House Hotel.

Despite the Civil War's devastation of the south's plantation society, the steamboat-era distribution system remained unchanged in New Orleans. Southerners, placing a high value on tradition, were determined to continue the economic development of the Ohio and Mississippi river valleys by the use of traditional steamboat transportation.[47] But this economic stagnancy in New Orleans was not replicated in Louisville. By 1863, the L&N had paid off its entire $4.7 million debt, declared 10.25% in stock dividends, 14% cash dividends and experienced a net earnings increase of 500%.[48]

The L&N had become an overnight economic mega-success and the impact of that success on Louisville was remarkable. Between 1840 and 1865, the city's manufacturing capital investment increased from $5,945,000 to $20,256,000 and its trade increased from $37 million in 1860 to $61 million in 1865.[49] At that time, being far less tied to the ways of the past and considerably less affected by the economic dislocation of the Civil War, Louisville had vaulted into the position as the leading and most progressive economic/transportation center south of the Ohio and east of the Mississippi rivers.

Great leaders and great cities never rest on their laurels. They pursue, with continuing vigor, the next mountaintop. At the war's conclusion, the L&N's leaders, Guthrie and Fink, established two new goals—the completion of the Ohio River Bridge at Louisville's 14th Street to connect the railroad across the river into the midwest; and a rail connection between Louisville and Cincinnati that would require Cincinnati to use Louisville as its transfer point to the south.[50]

The city's merchants also devised a significant change in Louisville's distribution economy. Traveling salesmen (referred to as "drummers," as in drumming up business), most of whom were former veteran Confederate officers, were hired by the hundreds. Traversing the south by horseback, taking orders for shipment to southern community stores from Louisville, these drummers were extremely effective. As Dr. Thomas Clark writes: "The Louisville drummer's two-horse rig was a familiar sight at the hitching rack of every crossroads from Columbia, South Carolina, to Shreveport, Louisiana....They shrewdly realized that no one would sell a bill of goods to an indifferent southern merchant like a veteran of the Chickamauga or Vicksburg campaigns.[51]

By 1870, Louisville's population had grown to 100,753[52] and that growth was accompanied by noteworthy racial progress. An African-American, Nathaniel Harper, was admitted to the local bar association in 1871, and Dr. Henry Fitzbutler became the first black Kentucky physician. African-American families lived among whites on three of four Louisville city streets.[53] From a national perspective, Louisville appeared on its way to becoming a post-Civil War model for southern integration.

Other events made Louisville the talk of the nation. One of America's most grandiose City Halls was constructed in 1873, along with Macauley's Theater that was soon to present the national premier of *A Doll's House*.[54] In 1876, the Louisville Grays became a charter member of the National League, remaining in baseball's major leagues until the Millennium and the first Kentucky Derby was run in 1875 at Churchill Downs and won by Aristides. Its newspaper was the most influential and important southern daily paper with the largest circulation in the south.

Despite remarkable economic advances in Louisville, peculiar and competing forces were emerging throughout the rest of Kentucky.

Kentucky, following the Civil War

Kentucky's world in 1865 was comprised of a dichotomy — the end of antebellum society with a new and uncertain national economic structure soon to be constructed upon the Civil War's wreckage. Amidst this catharsis of economic change, rural and central Kentuckians became increasingly obsessed with fear and distrust. "While some places and certain communities embraced new ideas and different outlooks almost immediately, others would remain virtually unchanged for more than a century."[55]

In an astounding reversal, Kentucky's rural and agrarian political leaders began to sympathize with the south. The notion began to grow that the state's future economic advantage was greater with the south than the north, which prompted a series of stunningly regressive actions.

In the early summer of 1865, the state legislature refused to ratify the

Thirteenth Amendment by votes of 56-18 in the House and 23-10 in the Senate.[56] The nation was undeterred by Kentucky's aberration, as the Amendment became the law of the land, freeing the former slaves, on December 18, 1865.[57] Kentucky's return to the past and an antebellum mindset continued.

Four years later, in January 1869, the state legislature rejected the Fifteenth Amendment that conferred the right to vote upon the former slaves. With the overwhelming tallies of 80-5 in the House and 27-6 in the Senate,[58] Kentucky's future as a progressive state that could serve as a model for the post-Civil War south was seriously jeopardized. Kentucky would not ratify these federal constitutional amendments until 1976.[59]

The absence of adequate leadership on the state level was striking. Leaders were needed who could fire people's imaginations with visions of what was possible and could inspire them to do what was necessary to attain these goals.[60]

This political regression brought unwanted attention upon Kentucky from across the nation, as the state's motivations were being critically analyzed. In this process one of Kentucky's greatest liabilities (and a largely-held secret to that time) became exposed—namely, in 1870 one fourth of all Kentuckians were illiterate. Instead of challenging this enigma and taking proactive measures to improve the state's educational level, rural Kentuckians reverted to the agrarian ideal—to the days of the Appalachian trailsmen when oral traditions of the past and rural life were passed to subsequent generations. Resistance to change was dramatically infecting rural Kentuckians. Even the landed gentry in central Kentucky felt "...little need to re-examine the basic arrangement of their lives."[61]

In many ways, Kentucky of the 19th century resembled some of the third world countries of the late 20th century.[62]

This confusing anomaly between economically adventuresome Louisville and rural Kentucky provided an opportunity for a new economic competitor with Louisville. Cincinnati's businessmen, who operated its Ohio River port and rail facility that served the swiftly growing Illinois/Indiana grain belt, envisaged the expansion of its midwest railroad distribution center into the south. Immediately to its south was Lexington and a rural state that many Cincinnatians felt might be "easy pickins" to entice into a business deal. The astute Cincinnatians knew that "Baltimore merchants retained a firm hold on Virginia and the southeastern region, and the L&N's monopoly over rail connections through Kentucky threatened to drive Cincinnati merchants from the trade altogether. Unwilling to lose that lucrative prize, the Queen City's merchants...plotted a new invasion of central Kentucky."[63]

Viewing Cincinnati's move as a potential economic challenge, the L&N's Albert Fink insisted that the Louisville, Cincinnati & Lexington Railroad (LC&L), be put back on the drawing board. It was, but an engineering dilemma would prove to be as dramatic as it was large. Railroads from Cincinnati to the north used the 4-foot 8 1/2-inch gauge. All southern lines utilized a 5-foot gauge.

Another inter-city economic war broke out.[64]

The quandary: if the L&N constructed the normal southern 5-foot gauge to Cincinnati, all rail traffic from Louisville to Cincinnati would have to be unloaded/reloaded in Cincinnati. But if the rail line between Lexington and Louisville were converted to 5-foot gauge and the rail between Louisville and Cincinnati was the 4-foot 8 1/2 inch gauge, then everything would be unloaded/reloaded in Louisville and its warehousemen would be able to further prosper, because all rail freight would be portaged at Louisville, just like the river traffic. The ever-aggressive Louisville city council agreed to pay for 60% of the gauge's changing costs, and it was done.[65]

Thus began an economic war between Louisville and Cincinnati as did the climactic battle in Louisville's fifty-year long economic duel with Lexington.

Cincinnati's counter-attack

Cincinnati's answer to Louisville's railroad portage gambit was to nurture personal relationships with Lexington's beleaguered business leaders along with their rural Kentucky associates and encourage the construction of a railroad into Kentucky. To be called the Cincinnati & Southern, it would connect Lexington north to Cincinnati's Ohio River port and travel south through Knoxville to Chattanooga. The rivalry between the Louisville-Nashville and Cincinnati-Lexington-Knoxville axis intensified. The editorial page of Henry Watterson's *Courier-Journal* vehemently opposed the Cincinnati gambit.[66] For the next twenty-five years, the inter-city economic warfare raged.[67] The unrestrained competition turned bad. Branch line trains were sabotaged, food spoiled on trains deliberately delayed and discriminatory pricing was rampant. It cost more to transport goods from Frankfort to Louisville than from Louisville to New Orleans. In the process

Louisville became further estranged from Lexington and the rural central Kentucky farm belt. The L&N increased the ante.

The irrepressible Albert Fink, looking north, completed the 14th Street bridge in Louisville on March 1, 1870. It was the first railroad bridge linking the north with the south, and it was the L&N's.[68] At the same time, looking south, Louisville businessmen played the Civil War/southern loyalty card by sending financial aid to Atlanta to support its rebuilding after Sherman's march to the sea. Then an even bolder move was made. Louisville created the 1869 Southern (economic) Exposition—a week-long party with free entertainment, lodging and various other licit and illicit offerings that was visited by 700,000 people and the U.S. President.[69]

Despite Louisville's determination, Cincinnati enjoyed several significant advantages. As the nation's 7th largest city in 1870 with a population of 216,239 it was twice as large as Louisville (100,753.[70]). However, Louisville's leaders were emboldened, because it had grown faster than Cincinnati since 1850, by 223% vs Cincinnati's 187% (Cincinnati from 115,435 to 216,239 and Louisville from 43,194 to 100,753.[71]) Additionally, due to its already-developed northern window, Cincinnati's prices were generally higher than Louisville's and its rail system into the north connected it with the swiftly expanding grain belt of Indiana and Illinois. The Queen City was, indeed, 'in the game.'

It continued courting central Kentuckians and Lexingtonians by providing economic assistance (bribes) to local county fairs, to Kentucky legislators and even conducted its own business/commercial exposition. Gradually, the tide began to turn in Cincinnati's favor — as Dr. Clark writes: "Louisville made the mistake of doubting Cincinnati's ability to stem the tide of competition against her....The Falls City had grown haughty in its attitude toward the rest of the state without realizing the dangerous political possibilities."[72]

Cincinnati/Lexington win

Once the Ohio businessmen felt they had sufficiently assuaged Lexington and rural/central Kentucky, they completed their plan and made their checkmate chessboard move.

Aligning with prominent central Kentucky and Lexington businessmen, they proposed the long-sought railroad charter to the Kentucky legislature —the Cincinnati & Southern—to unite Cincinnati through Lexington to

Knoxville, connecting with the Central of Georgia to Chattanooga, Atlanta and Savannah.

Replicating Cincinnati's intrepid use of legislative bribery and other intrigue, the L&N successfully prevented C&S from being chartered.[73] Federal congressional intervention was requested by Cincinnati—then suspended—while Kentucky's legislature reconsidered the C&S charter. Louisville upped the ante. Steamboats to and from Cincinnati were delayed at the Louisville portage site. When Cincinnati sent officials to break the delay, Louisville's city council assessed a tax on them for their presence.

After repeatedly failing, eventually the C&S charter passed when the senate's presiding officer and the state's Lieutenant-Governor from Covington, John G. Carlisle, broke a 19-19 Senate vote. With the governor's signature on February 13, 1871, "...the L&N's rail monopoly into the south was officially broken."[74]

Great was the rejoicing throughout central Kentucky, with mass meetings and firing of cannon in Lexington, Danville and other towns. The struggle had been unique in the annals of Kentucky. It required the breakup of one of the most complete monopolies ever enjoyed by an American city.[75] The C&S was completed through Knoxville and Chattanooga to Atlanta and Savannah. What had been proposed to cost $9 million was completed in nine years, on March 8, 1880, for a total cost of $28 million. Despite the enormous cost overrun, the C&S quickly became profitable. Money was being made by both cities and their railroads. But problems grew for the L&N, despite its profits.

The L&N's continued expansion and competition with Cincinnati produced a perplexing irony—the larger it became, the greater the competition. In order to match Cincinnati's financial power in the competition, the L&N was required to gain access to larger capital sources. New York City financiers gradually moved into the company's management and then its ownership. By 1884, the L&N was experiencing a financial and ownership debacle.[76]

In addition to the L&N's lost rail monopoly to the south and its adverse financial effect on the L&N — another and far more tragic consequence of the fifty year inner-state economic warfare between Louisville and Lexington reared its head. Irrevocably, the state of Kentucky had become socially and economically divided right down the middle—Louisville and western Kentucky vs. Cincinnati, Lexington and central Kentucky. The seeds that had been planted by Cincinnati/Lexington's success in the state legislature were beginning to flower into a series of events that would turn this division into a permanent chasm, even to today.

Rural Kentucky goes haywire

L&N's new president, Milton Hannibal Smith, was determined to regain the railroad's legislative clout in Kentucky, believing it to be essential for survival. Legislators and lawyers throughout Kentucky were placed on the payroll. Free passes for rail trips were dispensed in return for local and legislative support. Gradually it began to appear that the L&N's fortunes were rebounding.

But despite appearances, the gulf between Louisville and the rest of Kentucky continued to widen as the state continued to regress. Regress may be an understatement.

Rural Kentucky, literally, went haywire with its return to antebellum ruralism and unrestrained lawlessness. When the state's Ku Klux Klan was revived with another name—"the Regulators," illegal lynchings recurred (166 between 1875-1900).[77] In addition to the infamous Hatfield-McCoy feud, eastern Kentucky exploded into a forty-year war among dozens feuding clans ([Carter County] Underwood-Stamper, Underwood-Holbrook, Kinney-Carter, [Rowan County] Martin-Tolliver-Logan, [Harlan County] Howard-Turner, [Perry County] French-Eversole, [Clay County] Baker-White, [Breathitt County] Amisted-Strong-Little.)[78] The noted historian Arnold Toynbee would later write, "...the Appalachian 'mountain men' at this day are no better than barbarians."[79]

By the mid-1800s tobacco had become the major agricultural crop of rural Kentucky. Dark burley tobacco was grown in western Kentucky, with the newly-developed lighter variety being primarily produced in central and southern Kentucky. Following the Civil War, Louisville remained the nation's largest tobacco market. Significant revenues for the city's economy were being derived from the crop's individualized marketing system—requiring the farmer to both deliver it to market and effectuate its sale. This all necessitated multiple trips to Louisville by tobacco farmers—further involving them in the expanding integrated life and economy of Kentucky's 'big city.'

Shortly thereafter the sales system was changed to an auction. At first auctioning produced better prices for the selling farmers, but the process quickly became controlled by the tobacco companies. Premier among them was Louisville's American Tobacco Company, soon to become the leading member of a newly-formed purchasing trust. The trust and its monopolistic purchasing drove prices into a downward spiral. Between 1894-95 tobacco prices dropped from 13.7 cents to 6.6 cents, per pound.[80] Dr. Clark observed: "The buying power of the American Trust and Tobacco Combine rested in few hands, and price control was easy. This system of controlled markets proved to be a source of agrarian revolution in Kentucky."[81]

The Kentucky 'big city', long-believed to be taking advantage of rural Kentucky interests with the railroad wars, was now being accused of directly affecting individual rural tobacco farmers. This dissension would continue into the 20th century. The 'big city' wouldn't go away and leave rural Kentucky alone.

It was inevitable—political ramifications would follow the economic disaffection. They did.

Beginning in 1882, the rural populists expanded their anti-big city fight by initiating an effort to control 'Demon Rum' in the state legislature. Even though the 1893 national depression decreased the production of distilled spirits, the temperance activity increased, finally succeeding a decade later.

In 1906 state legislation was passed providing for county-wide wet/dry elections. The 'drys' success was instant. One year later, 97 of Kentucky's 120 counties had voted to be dry.[82] The rural/populist prohibition war had just begun. It would spill over into the 20th century, along with other challenges to parimutuel wagering, the staple of Kentucky's horse-racing industry, along with a vituperative battle against the coal industry and their company towns. Regardless of whether the rural/populists goals were noble, one result was inescapable: Kentucky had regressed into an early 19th century agrarian economy as it entered the 20th century.

Louisville in 1900

Despite the decades-long challenge from Cincinnati and its central Kentucky allies, and despite the tobacco war and Goebel's rural/populist revolt, in 1900 Louisville was still a highly relevant player in America's industrial economy. Its population had again doubled in one generation to 204,731—the nation's eighteenth largest city.[83] The following chart reflects Louisville's 1900 population and ranking versus cities with whom it presently competes and other mid-sized cities which possess an NBA franchise in 2004:

Rank	City	Population[84]
12.	New Orleans	287,104
18.	Louisville	204,731
19.	Minneapolis	202,718
21.	Indianapolis	169,164
25.	Denver	133,859
36.	Los Angeles	102,479
37.	Memphis	102,320
42.	Portland, Or.	90,426
43.	Atlanta	89,872
48.	Seattle	80,671
70.	Salt Lake City	53,531
71.	San Antonio	53,321
85.	Houston	44,633
88.	Dallas	42,638

Charlotte, whose 1900 population was 11,555, wasn't even on the radar screen.[85] The Louisville/Portland Canal remained a major economic factor for the city, annually carrying 1,200,000 tons of freight in 2,000 vessels.[86] Since the Civil War, the annual value of Louisville's manufactured goods had increased from $15 million to $66 million; and clearing house records reflected an annual gross value of railroad-transported freight in Louisville totaled $360 million.[87]

At the turn of the century, Louisville was home to B.F. Avery & Sons, the world's largest plow factory, comprising a six acre building and employing 600 men annually producing 200,000 plows of 143 different varieties.[88] Turner Day & Woolworth Manufacturing Company was the largest hickory handle manufacturing facility in the world.[89] In addition, Louisville was the nation's chief producer and distributor of cast-iron pipe, whiskey and leather. Of the 1,271,000,000 pounds of tobacco produced worldwide, 280 million pounds were produced in Kentucky, with the nation of Turkey being the second largest producer.[90] The city's tobacco warehouses, fourteen in number, handled one-third of the tobacco raised in America, making it the largest leaf tobacco market in the world.[91] Louisville's cement mill product was larger than the combination of all cement mills west of the Allegheny mountains[92] and, even more amazing, the Kentucky Wagon Manufacturing Works, covering 30 acres with 8 acres under roof, was the precursor of

Henry Ford's assembly line.

It was the nation's largest paint and varnish manufacturing center and the largest textile manufacturing site west of the Appalachians. Louisville's medical school enjoyed an enrollment of 504.[93] Its premier public high school, Male High, annually provided routine college preparatory education for three hundred college-bound students in the disciplines of Latin, Greek, English, German, algebra, geometry, chemistry, psychology, logic, political economy with required reading including Cicero, Virgil, Homer, Herodotus, Chaucer and Shakespeare.[94] With only 10% of the state's population, Louisville's public school budget was 43% of the entire state's.[95]

Urbane and sophisticated with a substantial foreign (German/Irish) population and two of the three largest banks in the south, daily Louisvillians used over forty miles of inner-city electric train transportation as far east as Crestwood along with a telephone exchange, electric street lights[96] and such lavish amenities as a park system designed by Frederick Law Olmsted, home delivery of milk and fresh ice, and fine restaurants.

From the outside looking in, Louisville's future seemed unlimited. But by 1900 the disdain for it, held by rural Kentucky and Lexington's agrarian-leaning interests, had solidified. Elegant and swashbuckling Louisville had become their mortal enemy, to be controlled and limited—despite the enormous adverse impact on the state's economic future.

So Kentucky ended the 19th century in either ignorance of or in denial about the swiftly changing national economy and its position within it. The agrarian/populist interests that bellowed against the L&N, Louisville's American Tobacco Company, Louisville's distilled spirits industry and Louisville itself, had successfully gained legislative control over the city, which inhibited Louisville's ability to self-govern itself. The anti big city clique had won, but there were three brutal ironies.

Irony #1:
The premier foil of the rural/populist clique—the L&N—was soon to be decapitated. In 1902, J. P. Morgan purchased control of the L&N from John "Bet-a-Million" Gates and quickly sold it to the Atlantic Coast Line. Thus, even though for several decades the L&N's majority ownership had enjoyed no particular Louisville identity, most of its banking and financial transactions were still primarily undertaken in Louisville. With its sale to the Atlantic Coast Line, with its own New York financial connections,

Louisville lost the financial clout of the largest and most significant 19th century corporation in the state.

After decades of hostility Louisville's corporate and financial heart had been excised from it, and with no replacement capital or equivalent industrial presence, the city was rendered incapable of fighting back. Still, today, there has never been another corporation based in Louisville that even remotely approached the percentage of the gross national product that the L&N enjoyed in 1900.

Irony #2:

At the turn of the 19th century, a substantial portion of Louisville's existing industry—plows, hickory axe handles and wagon makers—were destined to become relics of the past. Its whiskey industry would soon be prohibited and, worst of all, its vaunted 19th century water and rail transportation system that had provided its window to the world for a century was soon to be eclipsed by all sorts of technological advances, such as the automobile, the airplane, the telegraph and a national highway system.

But little could be done by Louisville about it, because the rural state legislature controlled the 'big city.'

Irony #3:

Louisville's most significant 19th century asset, its highly-educated, forward-thinking and venturistic commercial and political leadership, had been muted. As the century turned, Louisville's leadership reverted to an Irish-Catholic boss/political spoils system controlled by the Whallen brothers, whose sole objective was to maintain political power instead of advancing and energizing the city. They were succeeded by Mickey Brennan, who was succeeded by Miss Lennie McLaughlin's 'Fourth Street Machine', which remained in power through more than half the 20th century. Within ten years of the start of the 20th century, the Whallen brothers would be responsible for such unmitigated political corruption that several Louisville elections were thrown out by the courts. Kentucky's leadership was also dominated by a political spoils/boss system.[97]

These three ironies rendered Louisville virtually helpless to tackle the 20th century challenges, ahead. Kentucky's long-drooping economic flower was soon to be joined in the proverbial vase by Louisville's swiftly wilting carnation.

Segue to the 20th century

Louisville, proudly standing as the shining City on the River only fifty years prior, was in the process of becoming infected with and morphed into Kentucky. The national economic relevance of Kentucky's biggest city was being subverted by Kentucky's rural and agrarian populist interests. The soon-to-occur explosion in the growth of industry and commerce across America was to pass Louisville with blinding speed—almost as if it were standing still.

Kentucky's 'fruity myth' prevails over blatant 'reality'

Kentucky's preeminent historian, Dr. Thomas D. Clark, has written about economic reality, which he found to be loathsome among Kentuckians. It deeply concerned Dr. Clark that a Kentuckian could be aware of his state's backwardness "...without expressing publicly any anger or revelation of griping concern."[98] In discussing this, he observed, "Throughout history Kentuckians opened avenues of escape from realities which confronted them. Pioneers faced with an Indian menace and the hardships born of nature were on the whole cheerful people who handed down traditional songs, partygames and competitive sports. The twentieth century native was true to his heritage. He developed an insatiable love for high school and college athletics. Athletic events in Kentucky became the essence of folk pageantry."[99]

As the Great Depression descended upon Kentucky and its third world economic mentality, escapism and the avoidance of reality was to become its reality. It had all begun 30 years prior.

After Kentucky Agricultural & Mechanical College (A&M), what was to eventually become UofK, split away from Lexington's formerly prestigious Transylvania, the sport of collegiate football found a home in Kentucky. At the time, football was a rough and tumble version of Australian rugby and began to be played by numerous southern colleges. In an effort to control the carnage, in 1894 Dr. William Dudley, the dean of Vanderbilt's medical school organized the Southern Intercollegiate Athletic Association,[100] which was also dedicated to controlling the importation of "ringers."

By 1898, the undefeated A&M team won the league's championship, and was honored by Kentuckians with the moniker, "The Immortals." Their success was ominous—A&M and its Lexington boosters had scavanged non-student veterans from the Spanish-American War to use as players, in total violation of the league's rules. Rural Kentucky, seeking an escape from reality, believed it had established the state's importance by football victories, but it was an escapist harbringer of much greater woes to come.[101]

That escapism manifested itself in another simple game that was soon to replace football and become a religion in Kentucky—and into the vortex of this escapist religion would enter a high priest. He quickly became an enormously successful larger-than-life hero. As the years unfolded, his personage would become worshipped and adored by Kentuckians. But as his success grew, so would his intransigence, aversion to change, and disdain for 'big cities.'[102]

He would capitalize upon the inherent need of rural Kentuckians to escape from reality. The escape he provided was amateur collegiate basketball. It was comfortable for Kentuckians, and since there is little economic relevancy in it, they were further enabled to continue turning their backs upon the state's economic and educational plight. That would continue throughout his tenure as high priest.

All the high priest had to do was win a multitude of amateur collegiate basketball games and fight to defeat the 'big city' in the game. The astounding success of this high priest's efforts would enable the yearning of Kentuckians to accept the 'fruity myth.' They began believing in earnest that their value and importance as individuals and their community's and state's national significance were being defined by those victories as they were broadcast to what was presumed to be an envious nation—despite the non-existence of any relevant economic benefit to the state.

Regardless of whether all this made any sense, amidst Kentucky's incredible economic retrogression a religion was about to be created.

CHAPTER THREE

Rupp Creates, Then Becomes "The Religion"

As the 19th century concluded, Dr. James Naismith, a Canadian graduate of Toronto's McGill University, who taught physical education at the International YMCA in Springfield, Massachusetts, invented the game of basketball. The story is as well-worn as it is well-known—off-season exercise for football players, peach baskets and all. Upon being imported to the University of Chicago by the famed football coach, Amos Alonzo Stagg, the game spread like wildfire throughout America's YMCA system, even to the south where Vanderbilt organized one of the first men's collegiate teams and played the Nashville YMCA in March, 1893. Meanwhile, the Yale Elis barnstormed the game into mid-America, and Indiana's little Wabash College claimed the national championship in 1908.[103]

Contemporaneously, the principal player in Kentucky's involvement with the sport that was to become the religion of the state was beginning his life at the dawn of the game's nationalization.

At the turn of the 19th century, on September 2, 1901, in the living room of a farmhouse on Harvey County Road, a few miles north of the Kansas prairie farmtown of Halstead, a boy named Adolph Rupp was born to an Austrian immigrant father, Heinrich, and a German immigrant mother, Anna Lichti.[104] His early life was rigorous with few frills or childhood pleasures. It was soon to be intersected by a tragic event.

Heinrich, a strict disciplinarian requiring silence after dinner,[105] died of pneumonia when the youngster was only eight years old, requiring him and his four brothers to become the father-figures of the family. While his older brothers ran the family's 163 acre land grant farm, the young lad worked odd jobs as a school janitor, drove tractors for neighboring farmers and assisted in operating a local grocery store to help his mother make ends meet. In the process this young Kansan became an inner-driven stoic, which fit in quite well with the 1,200 Mennonites who were the predominant residents of the southeastern plains of rural Kansas.[106] In that rural Kansas farmhouse, there was love, but little real joy, unless you gained joy from work. It was quiet and solitary on those Kansas prairies at the turn of the 19th century.

His teenage years were centered around individualized success and the work ethic. Both, at the highest level, would become his mantras. In high school he joined a German literary society, whose motto was "Practice makes the master."[107] About this time an outlet for his single-mindedness was discovered—the sport of basketball. It has been written that "...he took quickly to the sport that got him out of the house."[108] With above-average skill in the game, his personal confidence soared. In his senior year in high school he was elected as team captain. His response was a 19 point-a-game average.[109]

He had become a leader of men, learning to depend upon himself, and only himself, to do what had to be done. As he grew to manhood, the certainty of things never changing would become supremely important to him. Change could reflect weakness and doubt. You couldn't be weak around your mom when she depended on you and your older brothers to be strong and sure.

These early childhood experiences were to become of striking and deep significance as the rural farmboy grew older. His collegiate basketball days found him primarily sitting on the bench. While the end of the bench didn't foster his leadership capabilities, it did allow him to return to the tenets of his childhood upbringing—observation and contemplation. Then benchwarmers were called "meatpackers." Much later he would call them what he had been: "the Turds."[110] He would learn from others and intently absorb that learning—quietly and alone. The stoic Kansas upbringing would forever affect how he would approach life. His longtime assistant coach would write of him, "I think his personality was shaped when he was a small boy growing up in Kansas. He grew up very hard."[111]

Until the day he died, Rupp would conduct his life and everything about it with military precision. Life, for him, became a series of wars. You used people to win those wars. Life was a staccato-sound without a melody, in which everyone marched to the same drum—his drum—like a Prussian baron and his army. There was to be no such thing as change in his life. It was easier that way.

In time his inner-driven aversion to change would also affect the fabric of Kentucky, impacting the mind and spirit of those who would grow up in Kentucky worshiping the religion, regardless of whether they would ever step on a basketball court. It was all so mesmerizing that it would dramatically affect the attitudes and beliefs of subsequent generations in Kentucky, and play a large role in making the state what it is and isn't—today.

To be sure, "the religion" was in the process of being created in Kentucky and that young Kansan would soon march in the front of the parade—as the Baron, Adolph Frederick Rupp.

So long, Johnny—Heeeere's Adolph

On March 4, 1929, Herbert Hoover was inaugurated President of the United States. There were expectations of continued prosperity in the urban north and major change in rural America. Hoover had promised a swift correction of the decade-long agricultural recession.

But seven months later, on Wednesday, October 23, 1929, there was huge and unanticipated change—upheaval on the New York Stock Exchange. Six million shares of stock changed hands, wiping out what has been said to be $4 billion in paper value. The next day $9 billion was lost. But that still wasn't the worst. On the following Tuesday, Black Tuesday, the market slid even further, so that within a month—by mid-November of 1929—$26 billion in paper wealth had evaporated. America had changed and it was in trouble—really big trouble.

Back in Kentucky, not much was going right, either. As its agricultural economy teetered, John Mauer was the coach of the University of Kentucky men's basketball team. The year before he became its coach, UK had only won three games. Mauer had found success in Lexington in the form of three winning seasons in a row—40 of 54 games. Despite his success, Mauer was irritated because Kentucky's football coach had been offered a substantial raise, and his was only $300. Miami University (Ohio) lured Mauer north. So in the late winter of 1929-30, UK basketball was coachless. Seventy applicants sought the job opening.

In the spring of 1930 a meeting of the university's athletic counsel was scheduled. Its purpose was to select a new coach. Among the seventy applicants being considered was an Illinois high school coach. He had been encouraged to apply by the University of Illinois basketball coach, Craig Ruby, because many Illinois graduates worked in UK's athletic department.[112] He had won 80% of his high school games and learned the game as a reserve guard on Dr. Forrest (Phog) Allen's undefeated 1923 Kansas University team. As a student/athlete he also had met James Naismith, who was (sort of) the athletic director at Kansas. Pretty good pedigree, but he coached high school. He was surprised to get the offer.

The high school coach left Lexington to contemplate the athletic counsel's job offer. As legend has it, he sought advice from, among others, his high school principal and a local gas station attendant. The principal argued against the job, saying that his high school gym was bigger than Alumni Gym at Kentucky. The gas station attendant maintained he could always get a better collegiate job out of a college, but it was harder to get a college job if you were just an Illinois high school coach. The gas station attendant's reasoning prevailed.

So, on May 21, 1930, an announcement was made in Lexington, Kentucky. An Illinois high school coach, Adolph Frederick Rupp, the young, stoic Kansan with the Mennonite upbringing, would be hired for two years as the head basketball coach at the University of Kentucky.

Six months later, Louisville's National Bank of Kentucky (BancoKy), failed. Robert Worth Bingham's Burley Association, which had salvaged Kentucky's tobacco farmers for nearly a decade, had been primarily dependent upon BancoKy to finance the state's tobacco crop. When it crumbled, so did Kentucky's tobacco farmers.

Within a month the epidemic had spread to banks all over the midwest. Mobs of shouting depositors demanded their money, requiring the banks to call their loans to enable the return of their depositors' money. Within a few weeks, this roaring tornado had reached the ultimate. The financial heart of America was torn away—New York City's Bank of the United States closed. It was the largest bank failure in the history of America.

Rural Kentuckians, pre-conditioned for decades to dislike and distrust Louisville, would believe that "big cities" were the culprits of these bank disasters. In 1930, only 2.8% of their farms had a tractor (1/5 the national farm average), 4.3% had electricity (1/3 of the national farm average) and 25% had phones (1/3 of the national farm average.[113] In that environment, they would look at Louisville with contempt and envy because, in 1930, despite the impending depression, it still ranked 22nd nationally in value of manufactured product and still provided well more than half of the value added by the state's industries.[114]

Within a few years, rural Kentuckians' ingrained disdain for the north and "big cities," including Louisville, would find its way into the fabric of UK basketball. It was to become their "fruity myth" and their release from the economic reality of their dire condition.

On December 18, 1930, only a month after BancoKy failed, Adolph Rupp coached his first game at the University of Kentucky. It was against little Georgetown College, whose star player was Harry Lancaster. In the later glory years Lancaster would serve Rupp as his principal assistant coach. Within three seconds of the game's start, two points were scored by Kentucky. Before it was all over—42 years later—there would be 73,655 points scored by Rupp's UK teams. The final score of Rupp's first game was 67-19; Kentucky had won. That wasn't unusual. Kentucky's recent history under Mauer had been awash with victories—but 67 points in one game was unheard of. The score was astonishing and Kentuckians were yearning for happiness. Maybe things would be better now.

Adolph Frederick Rupp's career as the head basketball coach at UK began with a dramatic change—fast-break, precision basketball. An offense driven by screens, rhythm, repetition, quick precise passing and specific patterns —strictly Ruppian. But within such meticulousness loomed an inherent problem—that change would never come, either.

Soon the stock market crash turned into The Great Depression. But America's indomitable spirit remained unflagged. Kentuckians were no different. They literally fell in love with their state university, its basketball team and Adolph Rupp. UK was winning almost all the time. In the eleven years between his hiring and the start of WWII, Rupp won 177 games and only lost 45. Kentuckians had something about which to be proud. They were proving that Kentucky was—again—worthwhile, noteworthy and important. But it was being accomplished in non-economically-relevant amateur collegiate basketball.

Despite his success, Rupp had two lingering problems—he hadn't been out of the south to play the "big city" teams. They played a "different game" there. He also had difficulty winning games on the road. Of his 45 losses, 31 occurred away from Lexington.

Rupp Goes to The Garden

Enter Ned Irish, a sportswriter for the *New York World-Telegram*, who also ran the basketball program at New York's Madison Square Garden. In 1931, Irish had been asked by New York City Mayor Jimmy Walker to organize and promote basketball games at The Garden to raise money for the city's depression-ravaged unemployed. His games between New York City colleges had been a significant financial success. He yearned for more. Aware of Rupp and UK's southern rural success, and forever the promoter with dollar signs in his eyes, Irish invited Rupp's team to play NYU in one of his new-fangled Garden doubleheaders.

On January 5, 1935, with all Kentuckians expectant of another Rupp victory, 16,500 New Yorkers were worried and anxious awaiting the southerners' invasion. Irish billed it as the national championship. Rupp had been forewarned about "big city" officials. His favorite play, the inside screen, was considered a blocking foul in New York. But he had an All-American center, Leroy "Cowboy" Edwards, from the farmlands of Indiana. Rupp's homegrown rural farm boys would prevail and beat the "big city" boys—he thought.

But the warnings proved correct. The "big city" refs and Madison Square Garden prevailed. Cowboy drew three quick fouls and NYU won 23-22. Before the New York press Rupp became a star, loudly proclaiming he was robbed. But a brutal fact had been ignored. Up to that time, Kentucky had played 79 games under Rupp, and had never scored only 22 points.

It would not to be the last time that something would happen at the big city's Garden that would adversely impact Adolph Rupp's life and the growing Kentucky religion.

Steadfast and refusing to be conquered by the big city boys, Rupp went back to The Garden a year and three days later—same NYU. Kentucky scored 28 against NYU's 41.

He stayed away for a couple more years before going back to the big city to play Clair Bee's Long Island University. It was another frigid January night in the big city, January 4, 1939. During the Depression, Clair Bee was to New York City what Adolph Rupp had been to Kentucky. In the seven years before World War II, Bee won 223 games, losing only 20. And Clair Bee wasn't to lose that night, either. The final score was 52-34. Bee's LIU won the NIT (the national championship) that year and he would win it again in two years later in 1941.

Adolph Rupp was furious. Three times in four years he had been beaten by the big city boys. What did he have to do to defeat a New York City team? Whatever it took, his Halstead, Kansas upbringing meant he wasn't going to change anything—he'd just work harder.

Kentucky & Adolph Rupp—a match made in heaven.

By 1937, Rupp had become even more comfortable in Lexington. In that year the *Kentucky Leader* merged with the *Morning Herald*. For decades prior the *Morning Herald* had been led by its editor, Desha Breckinridge, who had championed economic progressivism along with women's and racial civil rights. He had fought the agrarian/central Kentucky economic disconnect for years. But with his death the battle was over. The merged paper's new owner, John G. Stoll, was far more provincial in his approach and thoughts.[115, 116] The merger was a significant step backward.

Little had changed in Kentucky. In 1912 the state had been ranked fortieth among the states in per pupil expenditure—forty-fourth in 1920 —and back to fortieth in 1930. The year before Pearl Harbor it spent $48 per pupil annually, for 46th place, when the nation's average was $94.[117] Fewer people lived in Kentucky's urban areas (29.8%) than a decade prior, yet one-third of Kentucky's 120 counties were near default on their debt and an additional twenty-five percent were overdue on payments.[118]

Despite the fact that the state had become an economic and uneducated basket case and regardless of Rupp's Garden and big city jinx, he was in the process of becoming a bigger-than-life figure back home in Kentucky. His victories quenched the rural state's thirst for pride—it was almost as if time had rolled back to the mid-19th century when Kentucky was the trail-blazing state, whose aura existed on the tips of the nation's tongues. While they had little economic prowess to brag about in those troubled times, Kentuckians did have Adolph Frederick Rupp. He was a winner, and like most Kentuckians, he distrusted the big city. That was fine with them, too, because long before Adolph Rupp arrived in the state they had set themselves apart from the big city. Since it was the natural outgrowth of his early life's upbringing, it was easy for Rupp to latch onto that mindset and become its band leader. He did it with gusto.

Rupp and rural Kentucky were fast becoming the proverbial "marriage made in heaven." They agreed on almost everything, particularly the belief that they didn't have to change. Rupp's life was like the plays he diagrammed —there was no gray, just black and white. Wearing a brown suit to every game since he coached in high school, he also wore red pajamas to bed and the same socks (washed every evening) unless he lost the previous game. Pretty much like most Kentuckians at the time. Both were winners all the way around.[119]

Adolph Rupp was growing to believe that he, himself, was the religion —and that, too, would never change. Rupp's personage, warring nature and omnipotence enabled his celebrity to become fixating and endearing to Kentuckians. It was almost as if rural Kentuckians were satisfied for UK to lose as long as Rupp was scowling and fighting against the 'big city.' Years later, Bill Spivey would say, "Rupp was unique, he wanted everybody to hate him — he succeeded."[120] Even more stark was the observation of the long-time UK game announcer, Cawood Ledford: "He [Rupp] just wasn't a warm person. I don't think he had a close friend."[121] This obsession of Kentuckians with Adolph Rupp was on the verge of becoming nearly psychotic.

Within a few years it would—but in the process things also got immeasurably worse. Indeed, ominous winds were on the horizon.

Something had changed in New York City. A "big city" Columbia law school graduate was unopposed in his candidacy for New York District Attorney. He would be re-elected and unopposed for the next thirty years. Soon, this Columbia law school alum would play a dramatic role in the near destruction of the religion that Adolph Rupp was creating in Kentucky.

Rupp Wins the World—and Loses It in The Garden, Again

After World War II, Rupp began cobbling together a host of former All-Americans returning from the armed services. To them he added high school all-stars and all-SEC players into what became, until UCLA's dominance in the mid-1960s and Duke's in the 1990s, the greatest collegiate basketball dynasty in history.

At the same time Rupp's former Kansas coach, Phog Allen, gave a prophetic interview in which he discussed a gigantic handbook agency in Lexington, saying, "As long as we have places like the one there in Lexington, the threat to our colleges and college boys will continue."[122] But Rupp wasn't paying attention to anyone, not even his former collegiate coach. Nothing had changed.

Beginning with forty-two players, Rupp narrowed the field to two young all-sports stars from Louisville and Harlan, Kentucky and a former Wildcat who had grown two inches and seventy pounds while in the Army. They— Ralph Beard, Wallace 'Wah-Wah' Jones and Alex Groza—joined Kenny Rollins from the Navy and Cliff Barker, a 27-year-old former German prisoner of war, and would be forever known and adored in the religion as "The Fabulous Five."

In the next three years, Beard and Groza became three-time All-Americans and twice Beard was chosen as the Collegiate Player of the Year. In the process, they would reverse Rupp's jinx at The Garden by winning the NIT there in 1946. They would win the NCAA championship in 1948 and 1949; and, along with the Phillips Oilers, became world champions by winning the 1948 Olympics in London, England. To appreciate the sheer power of The Fabulous Five, you only need to look at the score sheet of the 1948 NCAA semi-finals when Kentucky played Holy Cross. Their star player was Bob Cousy, the eventual Boston Celtic legend and Hall of Famer. Rollins held him to three free throws and Kentucky won 58-42. The record of Kentucky's 1948-49 Fabulous Five team was overwhelming—winning 14 of their 30 games by more than 30 points, six of which they won by more than 42 points.

Kentucky hadn't played UofL since 1921. Despite The Fabulous Five's success, Rupp refused to schedule a game with Kentucky's big city university. He wasn't going to change. He didn't care if Louisville played Western (as it had dozens of times), or Duke played North Carolina, or CCNY played Long Island U. It made no difference to Adolph Frederick Rupp. But as UofL's teams began to dramatically improve, the national tournament schedulers saw the intrigue. Change would be brought upon Rupp by others —the first of many changes that would be forced upon the reluctant Rupp in the years to come.

In March 1948, after UofL won the NAIB and Kentucky the NCAA, they were required to play each other in the Olympic Trials. The Fabulous

Five won 91-57. Finally, after all the battles, the Baron from Halstead had won the war. He had won the NIT, won in The Garden, won the NCAA, and now beaten Kentucky's "big city" team, UofL, with his star player, Ralph Beard, from Louisville. In Rupp's mind, Louisville was and would forever be the little sister—a nice small-college program. His vendetta against the big city hadn't changed—only another city had been added—and out-in-the-state Kentuckians loved it. For Rupp and them it wasn't a rivalry. It was sheer disdain, and by 1948, that attitude had existed for a long time.

At the end of World War II, Kentucky's "fruity myth" of escapism from its own economic reality, engendered and enhanced by Adolph Rupp, had continued to enable the lack of concern about the state's educational level. Kentucky ranked absolutely last, nationally, in the percentage of its population with a high school diploma.[123]

Regardless of the state's education crisis, in the minds of Kentuckians the 1946-49 years of The Fabulous Five were truly fabulous for them and Adolph Rupp. In the process, he had become the most powerful person in Kentucky, and financially secure—owning interests in land, prized Hereford cattle, a tobacco farm and a large tobacco warehouse. At that time, no basketball coach, whether collegiate or professional, had ever done better. The Fabulous Five lost only nine games out of 136 games played—a 93.5% winning percentage. But one of those nine losses was pretty bad—as a matter of fact, it was to be, eventually, cataclysmic.

Before winning the 1948-49 NCAA for the second time in a row, The Fabulous Five returned to The Garden to play in the NIT championship against Loyola of Chicago, one of those 'big city' northern schools. Rupp dearly wanted to become the first coach ever to win the NIT and the NCAA in the same year. It was not to be.

On March 14, 1949, even though prohibitive favorites, the mighty Fabulous Five lost to lowly Loyola 67-56. Groza scored only 12 points and the man he guarded (Jack Kerris) had 23. As an eight-year-old growing up on Lydia Street in Schnitzelburg, I have the game forever etched on my memory. My dad and I sat at the kitchen table and listened to UK's beloved broadcaster, Claude Sullivan, describe the disaster on our little red Philco radio to us and hundreds of thousands of other Kentuckians. I cried in utter disbelief. My little world that had been heroed by Adolph Rupp and his Fabulous Five was crushed that night. It was impossible. How could the

Fabulous Five lose to Loyola?

A few weeks later, the Fabulous Five supposedly made up for it all by beating Oklahoma A&M to win its second-in-a-row NCAA championship. But shortly it would be realized by all that they hadn't really made up for anything.

Despite the Loyola loss and the graduation of Ralph Beard and Alex Groza, the Baron's war continued. While Beard was irreplaceable, Groza wasn't, being immediately supplanted by a seven-foot recruit from Georgia named Bill Spivey. Rupp's 1949-50 team featured Walter Hirsch, Jim Line, Dale Barnstable and Spivey. After being spurned by the NCAA and not chosen to defend its two-season-in-a-row national championship, Rupp accepted an invitation to the NIT—back to The Garden. He would show 'em all—this time.

Rupp drew City College of New York (CCNY) for Kentucky's first game. New York scribes called it the Ego Bowl, Adolph Rupp's Wildcats v. Nathan "Nat" Holman's CCNY Beavers. The world of Adolph Rupp and that of the fourth son of the post-World War I Russian immigrant, who had grown up on the mean streets of New York City, had finally met.

Holman's career had been meteoric, resulting in his nickname, "Mr. Basketball." He had been the best player on the famed Original Celtics in the mid-1920's,[124] coached CCNY to over 300 victories and was the author of four major books on the game.[125] Mr. Basketball and The Baron were similar in many respects. Their practices began precisely at an appointed time (Nat's at 4:00 p.m. and Adolph's at 3:15 p.m.), they both drilled and redrilled their squads, ridiculed their players for mistakes, seldom played the second or third team players, and were tyrants with little interest in the lives or off-the-court behavior of their conscripts. Like The Baron, when Mr. Basketball blew his whistle in practice, "the terrified players would freeze while they waited for the wrath to descend on whoever was out of sync."[126] Like The Baron, when World War II concluded Mr. Basketball saturated his roster with returning GIs.[127] A former player described Holman as "a narcissistic bastard....[He] typified everything that was wrong with big-time college basketball."[128]

With mostly sophomore talent and three African-American players (Floyd Layne, Joe Galiber and Ed Warner[129]), Holman's CCNY wasn't even ranked in the top 20. Kentucky was ranked third. Rupp, waxing eloquent with the 'big city' scribes that this Kentucky team was better than the Fabulous Five, was so confident of victory he didn't even have CCNY scouted. But Mr. Basketball studied the Wildcats night after night. Instead of the expected slowdown and painstaking game replete with the 1-3-1 zone defense, Holman played "hell fer leather" fast-break basketball the entire game. The final score was CCNY 89, Kentucky 50.

Again, it had happened. Rupp had been gotten to by The Garden, and fooled by the "big city"—this time by that Russian Jewish immigrant's son, Nat Holman. Adolph Rupp never lost a game by more points, before or after. The Kentucky state legislature, responsible for the state's expenditure on education, ordered the state flag flown at half mast.[130]

Despite the CCNY disaster, the Baron's war lived on. His 1950-51 team was loaded. Now an All-American, Spivey was joined by Barnstable, Hirsch and two sophomore sensations from Kentucky high schools, Cliff Hagan and Frank Ramsey. Rupp and his warriors succeeded, winning another NCAA title in March, 1951—three national championships in four years. Surely The Baron had now prevailed. His success brought even more of the state's gratitude and allegiance. An 11,500 seat basketball palace was being built for him in Lexington—Memorial Coliseum. Resplendent with its imposing facade and marble foyer, it was the most luxurious collegiate arena in America.

By now, Rupp truly had become Kentucky's darling. He had proven to all Kentuckians that you didn't have to change—that all you had to do was to wage war. It didn't even need to be fun, as long as it was work and you beat the "big city" boys. At this point, a genuine psychosis had developed among Kentuckians, centering around Rupp's cult of personality and the disdain for anything resembling the big city, including Louisville. But such a cult is insular, defeating and enormously unrealistic. You couldn't then (and can't now) avoid or ignore the big city.

Hurricane Hogan and his big city storm clouds were gathering on the increasingly forbidding horizon. In the summer of 1951, like the Crash twenty-two years prior, a world was about to come apart. This time it would be Adolph Rupp's world.

The biggest city of all destroys Kentucky's "fruity myth"
Since his election in 1941, New York's Manhattan District Attorney Frank S. Hogan had successfully prosecuted Lucky Luciano, Dutch Schultz

and conducted a wide-ranging grand jury investigation of Mafioso Frank Costello that became the forerunner for Estes Kefauver's Senate-organized crime investigations. In the process, Hogan had become affectionately known as Mr. Integrity. Even though a Democrat, he was admired and fully-supported by New York's Republican Governor, future presidential candidate and fellow crime-fighter, Thomas E. Dewey.

New York City was a strange place in those days, no better typified than by the paradox of Manhattan College—named Manhattan but located in the Bronx. It was a strict college, run by the Christian Brothers, a Jesuit teaching order. Early in January 1951, with the encouragement of his coach, Kenny Norton, and the college's president, Brother Bonaventure Thomas, the star of Manhattan's team, Junius Kellogg, painfully reported to Hogan's office he had been offered a $1,000 bribe to dump a game in The Garden.

Mr. Integrity's subsequent fast-paced criminal investigation unearthed a mountain of evidence that numerous players for New York City schools (Manhattan as well as Nat Holman's CCNY and Claire Bee's Long Island University) had consorted with gamblers and fixed games. Frank Hogan was neither satisfied nor finished. As the collegiate players and gamblers confessed and ratted on each other, a gigantic line of dominos began to form and was about to topple, one upon the next. They began tumbling on November 19, 1951.

New York Supreme Court Justice Saul S. Streit sentenced Salvatore Sollazo, Edward Gard and Adolph Bigos to felony prison terms and ordered misdemeanor convictions upon thirteen collegiate basketball players from the New York City area. By virtue of Gard's cooperation, within a month, on December 7, 1951, pleas of guilty were received by Justice Streit from mid-America's Bradley University players Eugene Melchiorre, George M. Chianakas and Billy Mann. As with Gard, the Bradley players were totally forthcoming to the D.A.'s office, outing a whole host of additional fixers, including such human trash as Joseph Benintende, Jack Rubenstein, Saul Feinberg, Marvin Mansberg, Eli Kaye, Nicholas and Anthony Englisis—several of whom were ominously close on Rupp's horizon.

Mr. Integrity and his crime-stoppers were on a roll.

As the investigation moved nationwide, Adolph Rupp was obliquely obstinate, saying that his players were always under strict supervision[131] and that the gamblers couldn't touch them "with a 10-foot pole."[132] But unknown to the UK coach, the prosecutorial cooperation of the Bradley players and the gamblers had created an enormous problem for him and the University.

October 1951 was a month to remember. On its third day, Bobby Thompson hit the "shot heard round the world" off Ralph Branca to win the National League pennant for the New York Giants. Five days later, Rocky Marciano knocked Joe Louis out in the 8th round at The Garden.[133] But the biggest shocker was yet to come.

Within a few months of the Bradley players' arrest and shortly before their guilty pleas, the two greatest of the Fabulous Five (Alex Groza and Ralph Beard) went to an exhibition game at Chicago Stadium to watch Rupp coach the collegiate All-Stars against the NBA's Rochester Royals. Since leaving UK they had formed (and owned) the Indianapolis Olympians NBA team, upon which they had become first-string NBA All-Stars. It was to be a surprise party for Rupp. Was it ever![134]

On that night, October 19, 1951, Groza and Beard were arrested at Chicago Stadium, as was Dale Barnstable in Louisville, each for accepting a $1,500 bribe to shave points while playing for UK.[135] Even now, when the subject comes up, some Kentuckians try to minimize the crime by observing that $1,500 was a measly sum, ignoring the fact that in 1949 it was roughly the equivalent of nearly $20,000 in today's dollars. It is informing to note that in 1950 the average one-year teacher's salary in Kentucky was $1,014[136] —50% less than Groza, Beard and Barnstable received for their one night of point-shaving.

The arrests were affected pursuant to sealed indictments for the violation of Section 382 of the New York Penal Code, that criminalized the offering of a bribe to an athlete or for an athlete to accept a bribe. The law had been on the books since 1921, and was the legislature's response to the Chicago Black Sox baseball scandal.

When Beard and Groza were taken to the Chicago police station they were confronted with Nick 'The Greek' Englisis (a former UK football player who handed out towels on Rupp's bench[137]). Englisis was one of the fixers that the Bradley players had implicated. Upon seeing The Greek, Beard said, "I knew my life, the only one I ever knew, had changed forever."[138] The specific game that was fixed was the one in the NIT—that Loyola game in The Garden — the one that my Dad and I had listened to that sad night on radio. Mr. Integrity now had an eleven-foot pole.

Initially Rupp, exhibiting the teamwork he had demanded of his players, came to their defense observing that "The Chicago Black Sox threw ball games, but these kids only shaved points. My boys were the inexperienced victims of an unscrupulous syndicate."[139] But, to his surprise, this response was universally rebuked, no better exemplified by Dan Parker's writing in the *New York Daily Mirror*, "A coach who defends dishonesty of a type because it isn't as bad as dishonesty of another type is hardly the type to save basketball or mold a young athlete's character."[140]

As Hogan's nationwide investigation progressed, things were to get far worse. Now, it wasn't just one Kentucky game that was thrown. Young Barnstable, realizing the ramifications of his youthful mistake and gallantly trying to do the right thing, admitted that Eli Klukofsky, *aka* Eli Kaye, and Nick The Greek (both associates of convicted Sicilian-born mobster Salvatore Sollazzo) had paid Kentucky players for shaving points in games prior to the Loyola game and the bribery had gone on after Beard and Groza graduated.

Mr. Integrity was also Mr. Intrepid—his continuing work was becoming even more problematic for Adolph Rupp. Several Kentucky players, Walter Hirsch and Jim Line, told Hogan's prosecutors that Rupp frequently called a bookie to learn the point spread for Kentucky games[141] and they admitted shaving points in other games on the road. Hogan's eleven-foot pole was getting even longer, as was Rupp's swiftly-developing rap sheet. Hirsch and Line testified that they and Spivey were offered $2,500 (in today's dollars, about $33,000) to shave points in the New Orleans Sugar Bowl Tournament. Kentucky had lost that game to St. Louis (43-42) and only one other game en route to Rupp's third NCAA championship. The grand jury testimony of Hirsch and Line was all denied under oath by the grand jury testimony of Spivey, who was soon indicted for perjury.

The result of Spivey's perjury trial is disputed. Some say he was acquitted by a jury vote of 9-3, others say the jury hung, 9-3 for conviction, which resulted in a mistrial. Whatever the belief, it is known that UK's Athletic Board and the University's president went to the "big city", examined the evidence prior to his trial, determined that Spivey was involved in the conspiracy to shave points, and ruled that his "retirement" from the team was permanent.[142]

Heroes no more

The Fabulous Five and everything they stood for in Rupp's life and in the lives of Kentuckians was nationally tarnished. I was age eleven, and my heroes were no more. Several months later Beard, Groza and Barnstable entered pleas of guilty to misdemeanors and were given suspended sentences. Before it was all over, Hogan prosecuted 33 collegians for shaving points in 86 games in 33 cities and 17 states.

After his players' convictions, Rupp changed his tune. Trying to play the victim, he began blaming others, including the UK players themselves. He ordered all of the memorabilia and pictures of Groza, Beard and Barnstable removed from Memorial Coliseum.[143]

Regrettably, Rupp had turned his back on his players—the very human beings who had won his world for him. In Adolph Rupp's mind he, not his players, had become the religion. His players and their lives and careers were now expendable. It has been reported that until his deathbed Rupp never again spoke to Ralph Beard. But Rupp's blame-casting was false; Rupp's Time of Troubles wasn't to end with his players. Hurricane Hogan was now to bring the Time of Troubles right to Adolph Rupp's doorstep.

The New York D.A. knew that Adolph Rupp was familiar with Lexington-based Ed Curd—the bookie Hirsch and Line swore had received the point-spread calls from Rupp. The New York D.A. also knew that Curd had invented the concept of the point-spread and operated out of the Mayfair Bar at 224 Main Street in Lexington—complete with multiple banks of telephones and Western Union ticker tape machines.[144]

Without point-spread betting, you couldn't shave points. So Ed Curd was an integral part of the nationwide point-spread scheme used by the gambling Mafiosi. Ironically, Curd's Lexington operation was the very same establishment that Kansas coach Phog Allen had warned about in 1945, but Rupp wasn't listening then to anyone, including his own college coach.

Even more disturbing to Hogan, Curd was the bookmaker for Mafia kingpins Frank Costello, Meyer Lansky and Ben "Bugsy" Siegel. The relationship between the Mafia and Curd had been admitted by Costello during Senator Kefauver's 1950-1951 U.S. Senate's organized crime hearings. When asked to volunteer the name of his bookmaker, Costello testified that he wagered "with my little friend, Ed Curd, in Lexington, Kentucky."[145]

Hogan's noose around Rupp's neck had become a Gordian knot. Hogan's biography was entitled *Mr. District Attorney*. It carried the clever, but incisive epigraph, "The truth is the best swindle." Hogan provided Adolph Rupp the opportunity to come clean and tell the truth. Instead, Rupp defended himself by claiming that he only knew Curd by virtue of infrequent visits to obtain contributions for the Lexington Kosair Children's Hospital. Rupp's testimony was less than honest by a factor of two.

Rupp and Curd were partners in one of the largest mid-Kentucky tobacco warehouses. At Rupp's invitation, Curd frequently traveled with the Wildcats to games in New York and Chicago. New York criminal investigators also knew that, at least twice, when Kentucky was playing in The Garden Rupp had enjoyed private dinners with Curd in New York's notorious and show-girl laden Copacabana Restaurant[146] which was Costello's New York City hangout. Purely and simply the New York Crime Commission found Ed Curd to be the most significant gambler/handbook operator in America and something far more than a casual acquaintance of Rupp.

To make matters worse, Adolph Rupp's away-game statistics were a matter of record for the New York D.A. to easily examine. Every game Rupp's teams lost between 1944 and 1951, 23 in number, had been lost on the road. The D.A. knew that Rupp didn't supervise his players on the road[147]— the record spoke for itself.[148] He didn't supervise them, because he wasn't a "people person." From the beginning of his life and career to this point nothing had changed, and even the public's reconsideration of his greatness wasn't enough to create change in Rupp's mind. The best example of the difference between Rupp and Western Kentucky's coach Ed Diddle was observed by the chronicler of Uncle Ed Diddle's life when he wrote: "By the ever-present gamblers and fixers, men who eventually contributed to numerous basketball scandals, the Western Kentucky aggregation might have been considered easy pickings, a bunch of rubes from the sticks. However, years before the roof fell in on Adolph Rupp, Clair Bee and others, Coach Diddle, smart enough to recognize the danger, did something that thwarted such meddlers. Hilltoppers stuck together, exiting their hotel in pairs and large groups. The fact that players did not venture out alone discouraged any approach from the gamblers and fixers."[149]

On a cold, blustery February 25, 1952, Groza, Beard and Barnstable pled guilty before New York Supreme Court Justice Streit. They received suspended misdemeanor sentences on April 29, 1952. The proceedings from their sentencing hearing comprise sixty-seven pages. But the real heat was aimed directly at Adolph Rupp—the person responsible for their collegiate experience.

Beginning on page 38 of the hearing transcript, Justice Streit repeatedly quoted from Rupp's disjointed sworn testimony. Rupp denied trying out certain players prior to their enrollment at UK, but within a page admitted he did try out other players. Rupp admitted that he paid Hirsch money after one particular game, but denied that he gave him money after a different game. He admitted telling his players he would collect their payments for a Sugar Bowl game "with the boys who have the fund...." A companion admission was incredulous—that the Sugar Bowl payment money came from money left over from the Olympics, several years prior. He admitted knowing that Groza occasionally received money from a booster; admitted knowing the gambler, Ed Curd; admitted having dinner with Curd at the Copacabana in New York City: admitted taking UK players to the Copacabana and meeting Curd; admitted traveling on the train to New York with Curd, but justified it by testifying that "he didn't come with us, he was on the train when we came up here to New York;" admitted having a conversation on the train with Curd; admitted being aware of point spreads when his teams played in New York and elsewhere;[150] admitted going to Curd's Mayfair Hotel bookie joint, and with Nixonesque plausible deniability, testified, "We went there to solicit an ad for the Shrine Crippled Children's football game and he was not there;" and admitted going to Curd's home (twice). Rupp's testimony continues for fourteen pages, whereupon Justice Streit stated from the bench: "It is unnecessary at this time to decide the issues raised by the coach. The undisputed facts are that he aided and abetted in the immoral subsidization of the players. With his knowledge, the charges in his care were openly exploited, their physical welfare was neglected and he utterly failed to build their characters or instill any morals—indeed, if he did not impair them. In view of his conduct, Mr. Rupp's sanctimonious attitude before me becomes ludicrous and comic."[151] (Endnote 151 is of particular importance.)

While his players were indicted, pled guilty to misdemeanors and were damaged for life, Rupp was not indicted, even though admitting in his sworn testimony to indictable conduct. Ruppians would later marginalize Justice Streit by asserting that he was nothing more than a routine police court judge. However, the record reflects that not only was he a New York Supreme Court Justice, he was also a graduate of Brooklyn's Stuyvesant High School, which is known as the birthplace of the New York judiciary.[152]

About the same time Justice Streit was leveling Rupp and UK's basketball team, the implacable author, John Gunther, had completed his first revised edition of *Inside the U.S.A.*—a startling, comprehensive and controversial 1,014 page examination of our nation's states.

Gunther observed that while a border state, Kentucky also bordered "...between fruity myth and brutal fact." Some of those brutal facts were found in a then-recent study by The Committee for Kentucky, to wit: that Kentucky was next to last in literacy with only Mississippi having more illiterates; 42,000 Kentucky farms had no toilets of any kind and 97% of its farms didn't have indoor plumbing; 25% didn't have electricity and only 16% of Kentucky's farms had telephones. Among the 48 states it had the third highest rate of tuberculosis death; 100,000 Kentuckians had syphilis; there was an annual average of 50,000 cases of gonorrhea; 37% of Kentucky school children didn't finish elementary school; 41% of all Kentucky children between the ages of 14-17 attended school versus the national average of 67.9%; the average days in school of a Kentucky school child was 129 versus the national average of 150 days. Gunther, obviously perplexed, noted: Did the Bluegrass State rise in self-indignant shame on hearing these statistics and attempt to bestir itself? It did not. Instead, the general comment was only too likely to be, "Why worry about being progressive?"

Gunther closed by quoting a Kentuckian about Kentuckians: "Of course we [Kentuckians] don't know that the reason we're so backward is that Kentucky is infected with Kentucky."[153]

It is not known if Justice Streit had read or was aware of Gunther's best-selling book, but if he was it is even easier to understand how the Justice concluded that the Commonwealth of Kentucky had its priorities in a severe state of discombobulation.

Back home in My Old Kentucky Home

Once everyone got back home, removed from Justice Streit's jurisdiction, Kentuckians, even including the governor and the university president, Herman Donovan[154] (who had previously cooperated with the New York grand jury investigation and Justice Streit) vigorously rose to Adolph Rupp's defense.

They asserted the real culprits were the "big city" slickers and gamblers who prowled the halls of The Garden in New York City. How could the Fabulous Five be suspended for life from the NBA? It was all unfair, because the big city did it and was responsible for it. They even defended Rupp by noting that none of the Catholic schools in New York were implicated, overlooking the fact that the whole process had been initiated by the coach and college president of Jesuit-run Manhattan College, who had encouraged Kellogg to report a bribe to the proper authorities.

Nothing in Kentucky had really changed since BancoKy went under 30 years prior: the "big city" was the culprit. It was just that simple for Ruppians and most Kentuckians. Even though Rupp and Kentucky had gone national and won the world, it was still we versus them, and them were those nasty "big city" northerners. Their judges, their referees, their gamblers, the Madison Square Garden crowd were all out to get him. He couldn't get the big city stuff out of his system, having battled the big city with everything he had—nearly 20 hours a day, 7 days a week for nearly 50 years—and he hadn't changed.

Justice Streit's only response was, "All of my facts were obtained by me from the lips of the athletes, from coach Rupp, from UK's athletic director and from the officials of the University."[155]

Upon considering the wealth of evidence criminally implicating Rupp, along with the obstinate refusal of UK's and the state's political leadership to undertake dramatic corrective measures, university presidents across America were outraged. Immediate action was taken by the SEC university presidents who voted, unanimously, to ban Kentucky from conference play in the 1952-53 season, unless UK fired Adolph Rupp.[156] Rupp's answer was far from a contrite or apologetic response. He and Kentucky Athletic Director Bernie Shively began arranging games with industrial teams, athletic clubs, armed forces teams and Bible Schools.[157] The SEC presidents notwithstanding, Rupp and Kentucky would still play basketball.

Due to the continuing University-supported obstinacy and Rupp's complete unwillingness to accept any responsibility for his wholesale failure to control the UK basketball program, the NCAA quickly conducted its own investigation and prohibited UK from playing any games at all for the entire 1952-53 season.[158] It was the most severe penalty ever placed upon a collegiate team by the NCAA, and would remain so until the late 1980s, when SMU was given the "death penalty."

Typically, Rupp got mad, refused to change, and was determined to get even, publicly demanding, "I'll not retire until the man who said Kentucky can't play...hands me the national championship trophy."[159] During the entire suspended season, Adolph Rupp relentlessly coached his next year's team, morning, noon and night. The hero-worshiping Kentuckians were thrilled as they learned the Rupp game plan. Four intra-squad games were played during the suspended season to packed houses in the resplendent Memorial Coliseum. There would be no change. Again, UofK would prevail.

The next season, 1953-54, Cliff Hagan and Frank Ramsey, who had already graduated as fifth-year seniors, led Kentucky to an undefeated season with an average victory margin of 27 points a game. At the Tulane game, Rupp pointed to the Tulane coach, Cliff Wells, and told his players, "He's on the floor, now. The man that led the fight against you last year. For every blister, every bruise, every black eye, every tooth knocked out last year, that little runt of a coach owes you. Tonight you will pay them back for all of last year."[160] The final score was Kentucky 94, Tulane 43.

The Ruppian attitude still reverberated against him, his team and the state. When the NCAA declared Hagan and Ramsey ineligible for its tournament, as fifth-year seniors, Rupp wouldn't permit UofK to go to the tournament. But that didn't make any difference. While LaSalle would win the NCAA tournament, during the regular season Kentucky beat LaSalle 73-60. To Kentuckians that would forever mean UK was thirteen points better than the 'big city' team from Philly that won the NCAA. To them it meant that Adolph Rupp had won, again, beating the "big city." Things hadn't changed.

While the state's capital expenditure on public school education had increased by 214% since 1934, the south's had increased by three times more—by 667%.[161] Even though UK could win the SEC basketball championship nearly every year, Kentucky's school children remained one-third as advantaged as those in the other southern states of the same athletic conference.

More Change—No Change by The Baron
In 1956, Rupp had been out of the national spotlight for several years. That March he sat at the Kentucky state high school tournament and watched a cave-chested kid from the Kentucky mountains score 127 points in four games, leading his team to the state championship. That kid was Johnny Cox. Over the next four years, Cox would provide Rupp with 70 more wins and his fourth NCAA championship. As Rupp said of Cox, "I looked unto

the hills and from whence cometh my help."

Meanwhile, Peck Hickman's "big city" UofL teams were invited to The Garden and the NIT multiple times, winning it all in 1956, the year Rupp was watching Cox. But Hickman had changed things, including his recruiting strategy. While successful with regional players, he began looking to the north that Adolph Rupp despised. Peck's assistant, John Dromo, a master recruiter from New York, began assembling a collegiate powerhouse at UofL. Rupp's refusal to schedule a game with UofL continued.

In 1959 NCAA tournament schedulers forced another game between Peck and Rupp. It would be the last time their teams would compete during their coaching careers. UofL won 76-61, soundly defeating the nation's second-ranked team and defending NCAA champion. The All-American on the UofL team that year came from New York. This game was to disrupt Adolph Rupp's life for another half dozen years as he fumed at a post-game press conference about those "big city" slickers. By this time it was clear— Adolph Rupp simply wouldn't change.

But a far more dramatic change was occurring. It would confound Adolph Rupp, more intensely than anything in his life.[162]

The NBA is born

Professional basketball in eastern cities had existed for decades. From time to time there were a few loosely-structured leagues, but generally games were played by traveling teams that were matched by a promoter. Schedules, rosters, playing rules and sites continually shifted amidst an air of roughhouse disreputability.[163] Far to the contrary, the collegiate game with its famed coaches like Rupp, Diddle, Holman, and Clair Bee offered an organized game complete with league and post-season championship play. During the 1940s it had become far superior to the play-for-pay game.

With the conclusion of World War II and the arrival home of thousands of former athletes, some saw an economic opportunity of sizeable proportions, which resulted in a June 6, 1946 meeting at New York City's Commodore Hotel. It had been suggested by Max Kase, sports editor of New York's *Journal American*.[164] Kase was a leading national sports writer who soon would win the Pulitzer Prize for his reporting on the collegiate basketball gambling scandal. In attendance at the Commodore Hotel meeting were the owners of the largest big city arenas, among them the Boston Garden's Walter Brown and Ned Irish of The Garden.[165]

They formed the Basketball Association of America, with a total team salary limit of $55,000.[166] Its president was a 5-foot tall New Haven lawyer, Maurice Podoloff.[167] During the next three years, one of the league's top stars was a six-foot five-inch, 190-pound Marine veteran who had served on Iwo Jima and Guam in the Pacific. Hailing from Birmingham, Kentucky, he had played only one year at Murray State Teachers College in Kentucky before joining the armed services. His name was Joe Fulks, and in the league's first season he scored 1,389 points (463 points more than his closest competitor) for an average of 23.2 points per game. It was unheard of.[168]

To avoid impending anti-trust charges, Podoloff arranged for the merger of the BAA with the competing American Basketball League into the National Basketball Association.[169] Despite Fulks' talent and the majestic game of big man George Mikan, the NBA was still no match for the collegiate game. But the Manhattan D.A.'s actions in 1951 were to change everything.

The collegiate bribery scandals provided an opportunity for the NBA and its clean and heroic World War II veterans. It was seized upon by Commissioner Podoloff, as he perpetually banned from the NBA all the offending collegiate players, including Rupp's Fabulous Five and Bill Spivey, gaining much credibility for the NBA among the American sporting public. Credibility everywhere except in Kentucky and in Adolph Rupp's mind.

Over the next several years Podoloff undertook another far-reaching decision, one that would change the face of American professional sports: he encouraged the NBA teams to hire African-American players. Among these new players were Chuck Cooper from Duquesne (the first African-American drafted by the NBA, who had once played a game against Morehead in Louisville's Armory in mid-December, 1946—without incident[170]) and Sweetwater Clifton, the star center of the Harlem Globetrotters.[171] Chuck Cooper's draft selection by Boston Celtics coach Red Auerbach became the precursor to an American societal revolution of monumental proportions in major league athletics.

David Halberstam, author of *The Fifties*, a remarkable and exhaustive examination of what may have been the most dramatic decade of the 20th century, described it as "a dual revolution sweeping the country: in the quality of athletic ability of those able to play and in the number of people now able to watch. It was in basketball that the revolution most quickly took place and was most quickly completed."[172]

Most revolutions have a George Washington, and this one was no different. Its Washington was born in Louisiana. Unable to play collegiate basketball in the south, he was offered and accepted a scholarship to the University of San Francisco. There, Bill Russell led the Dons to two straight NCAA championships, only losing one game in the process. So utterly dominating was the six-foot nine-inch Russell that the NCAA changed the game's rules—widening the foul lane from six to twelve feet. It was called the Russell Rule.[173] Following his collegiate career, most pundits surmised that Russell would play for the Harlem Globetrotters and travel the world, starring in their zany performances. Most of the great African-American basketball players had done that and many had become highly-paid celebrities. The pundits were wrong.

Arnold "Red" Auerbach, whose Boston Celtics team was decent with a great team-leader in their guard, Bob Cousy, but certainly not a contender, decided he was going to change everything. St. Louis Hawks' attendance-conscious owner, Ben Kerner, coveted the Celtics center, Easy Ed Macauley, because he had starred as a collegian at St. Louis University. Auerbach saw an opportunity. He agreed to trade Macauley (and the Celtics draft rights for former UofK star Cliff Hagen) to the Hawks, for their second overall pick in the 1956 NBA draft. With his fingers crossed, Auerbach watched intently as the Rochester Royals exercised their first pick, choosing another African-American, All-American guard Sihugo Green. Auerbach, with a sigh of relief and knowing his plan had worked, then selected Russell. With Auerbach's decision, Bill Russell began his professional career as a Celtic and further began what Halberstam has described as "his tour as the most dominating team athlete of modern American sports."[174]

Bill Russell was hired to play defense and get rebounds. In his first professional game, he retrieved 21 rebounds in only 16 minutes of play. In his second game, he held the NBA's third leading scorer (Neil Johnston) to one basket in 42 minutes, retrieving 18 rebounds in the process. In his third game, Russell obtained 34 rebounds in 20 minutes. It went on from there, and for Celtic opponents it seemed like it would never end. Bill Russell changed everything.

With Russell the tempo of the game seemed to have no break. Now it was continuous, with offense flowing into defense, instantaneously. It was now a game for the swift and the agile.[175]

The 1956-57 season ended with the ultimate drama. The St. Louis Hawks faced the Boston Celtics for the NBA world championship. With

Macauley, Bob Pettit and UK's Cliff Hagan leading the Hawks against Russell, UK's Frank Ramsey and the Celtic guard combo of Cousy and Bill Sharman the series went to the seventh game in Boston Garden. At the half, St. Louis was winning 53-51 and the lead had changed 38 times. It was bedlam in Boston. With two minutes to play, Macauley fouled out, meaning that the Hawks coach, Alex Hannum, would have to play. The teams traded baskets and foul shots, and with two seconds left the Hawks had the ball and were behind 125-123. The balding coach, Hannum, threw a length of the court in-bounding pass, the purpose of which was for it to hit the backboard, with the Hawks star, Bob Pettit, rebounding it with a tap-in to tie the game. It was perfectly executed, bounced against the backboard into Pettit's hands, six feet from the goal. Pettit grabbed it, shot it, and the ball rolled around the rim, once, twice, and dropped out. The Celtics had won their first NBA World Championship. The Boston Celtics Dynasty had begun.[176]

Over the next thirteen seasons, the Russell-led Celtics would win 70.4% of their games and eleven world championships (including eight in a row). Russell would capture 19,854 rebounds and average 22.3 per game.[177] It was a professional basketball career with no prior equal, nor will its like ever happen again. The colossal battles between Russell and Philadelphia's Wilt Chamberlain became the biggest news in basketball.

For the first time, where a great high school player would play in the NBA became more important than where he would play in college. Now basketball fans could watch their favorite collegians mature and improve their game while playing for a dozen or more years in the pros. The superior talent of the fully-integrated play-for-pay boys had captured America's imagination.

Now Adolph Rupp was directly confronted with another challenge to his hegemony over the religion, this time from an economically-powerful professional league, headquartered in New York City, that had banned his Fabulous Five and Bill Spivey from participating, and from Red Auerbach, who was winning multiple world championships in Boston with the "big city" Celtics in a game increasingly dominated by African-American players, coaches and administrators.

That the amateur collegiate basketball world of Adolph Rupp and Kentucky's "fruity myth" was being challenged by the new economic juggernaut of the NBA became further compounded by the startling fact that Kentucky's legislature had still not ratified the Thirteenth and Fifteenth Amendments.

Rupp hated the NBA. Since he did, so did Kentuckians.

The Biggest Change challenges Kentucky's universities

America — sports and otherwise — was swiftly changing. Martin Luther King was demonstrating at lunch counters in Nashville. For years, since Arkansas Governor Faubus's obstinacy in Little Rock had been met by President Eisenhower's determination and federal marshals, children had attended integrated schools in the south. Since 1954 the city of Louisville had peacefully begun the integration of its school system. The Louisville Lip, Cassius Clay, had won the 1960 Rome Olympic Lightheavyweight Championship, astounding the world with his hijinx. The beginnings of America's racial integration in the 1950s was the biggest change of all.

The revolution had also mesmerized American sports. Jackie Robinson played for the beloved Brooklyn Dodgers and Jim Brown was the NFL's greatest running back. Along with Russell and Sihugo Green the mid-1950s found the collegiate All-America lists increasingly dominated by African-Americans—Walter Dukes, Wilt Chamberlain, Elgin Baylor, Guy Rodgers, Willie Naulls and soon by a phenom named Oscar Robertson from Crispus Attucks high school in Indianapolis. After annihilating the best Kentucky high school players in their annual all-star game with Indiana, he enrolled in the University of Cincinnati, across the Ohio River from Ruppdom.

Robertson's greatness wasn't a surprise to most people, but the completeness of it was. The three-time All-American led Cincinnati to collegiate supremacy, averaging 33.9 points a game over his three playing years, and for years thereafter was the star of Cincinnati's NBA team, the Royals. Just across the river from Ruppdom, Kentuckians had been confronted with the supremacy of the NBA talent and Cincinnati's economic benefits.

Robertson's impact on Kentucky continued even after his graduation, as the University of Cincinnati played in the NCAA finals the next two years, winning it in 1962 with four African-American starters. Then there was that Loyola again (that Rupp defined as that "gawd-damned Loyola") that had caused the demise of the Fabulous Five. Now, they were in Louisville's Freedom Hall, winning a national championship in 1963— with four African-American starting players.

Many realized the change and acted. Some of the many were Kentuckians. Other Kentuckians didn't.

Having integrated its football team in the late 1950s, in 1962 the UofL president and the African-American editor of the school newspaper insisted that the University integrate its basketball team. Peck immediately changed. He broke what had been referred to as the color-barrier at UofL, recruiting Eddie Whitehead, Sam Smith and Wade Houston. A year later, 120 miles down the road in Bowling Green, Uncle Ed Diddle changed, too, and did the same thing. Clem "The Gem" Haskins and Dwight Smith would lead Western back to the national collegiate spotlight, instantly.

Two years later in 1965, the Hickman/Dromo UofL combo successfully recruited an African-American, the two-time all-state center from Louisville's Seneca High School. His name was Wes Unseld. Before his basketball career was complete, he would become a two-time All-American at UofL, a perennial All-NBA star and would be inducted in the Naismith Basketball Hall of Fame.

For the forty years since, it has been claimed by Ruppians that Rupp tried to recruit Unseld, but lost due to the adverse racial climate in the south and Unseld's unwillingness to be the object of such racial hatred. Among UK aficionados there will be argument about this forever, but one thing is not debatable: the racial climate among Lexingtonians and rural/populist Kentucky agrarians, who had adopted Adolph Rupp's unchanging life as theirs, was clearly deplorable, and had been since the Civil War.

Lexington fans had booed Unseld when his high school team had won the state high school championship at UK's Memorial Coliseum. Unseld also had received hate mail from Lexington encouraging his enrollment elsewhere than UK.[178] In 1961, several years prior to Unseld's recruitment, a pre-season NBA charity game between the Boston Celtics and the St. Louis Hawks was arranged for UK's Memorial Coliseum. The Celtics (with former UK star Frank Ramsey) had five African-American players. The Hawks (with former UK star Cliff Hagen) had two African-Americans in uniform. It was a wonderful idea—the charity would be grateful for a soon-to-arrive financial windfall. But when the Phoenix Hotel, Lexington's largest, refused to serve the African-American players on the teams, they all took the next plane out of town. A year later, a UK vs. Temple game was canceled because the same hotel refused to admit Temple's African-Americans.[179]

Clearly Louisville, the big city of Kentucky, Peck Hickman and Uncle Ed Diddle were adapting to the thrombotic change racing through American society. Clearly, agrarian Lexington wasn't. It is also equally clear that elsewhere in the south the change had begun to be accepted, as the school year of 1965-66 found southern schools TCU, Florida State, Loyola of New Orleans, Memphis State, Vanderbilt and Duke receiving commitments from African-American recruits.[180]

Undeterred, Baron Adolph Frederick Rupp would march what may have been his greatest team—the 1965-66 Wildcats—to the NCAA finals. Ranked No. 1 and with no player taller than 6-5, they had been affectionately nicknamed "Rupp's Runts." They had only lost one game during the season and had beaten Michigan to reach the Final Four. In the prior game, Michigan had beaten Western by one point on a very disputed referee call involving a jump ball. Without that disputed play, Rupp would have played Western and its African-American All-American from Campbellsville, Kentucky, Clem Haskins, in the NCAA Regional Finals. But Rupp was lucky—he didn't have to do that. Instead, in the end he wound up playing another Western—Texas Western, for the national championship.

Who ever heard of Texas Western? No one. But as far as Rupp was concerned, it didn't make any difference. His thirteen players were outstanding (and they were all white), five coming from Langley, Graley, Ashland, Earlington and Lexington, Kentucky, seven hailing from little Southport, Brookville, Tell City, Anderson, Bluffton and Centralia, Indiana with one from Schenectady, New York. Things hadn't changed much in Lexington.

Texas Western's players were primarily African-Americans from the "big city" playgrounds. Its stars were Dave "Big Daddy" Latin from Houston, Willie Cager, Nevil Shed and Willie Worsley from New York City and Bobby Joe Hill from Detroit.

As the television camera panned the crowd in the green-roofed World War II quonset hut-like Cole Fieldhouse on Maryland's campus that March night, a confederate flag appeared among the UK fans, and the Kentucky pep band played Dixie.[181] No change there, either. While it wasn't The Garden, nor was it Loyola or CCNY, it was still a national stage upon which Adolph Frederick Rupp would prove to the nation he was right—he didn't have to change.

But what it really was was a night on national television that would forever change collegiate basketball. Kentucky lost. Noted sports writer David Israel would call it "the Brown vs. Board of Education of college basketball." Books would be written about it. One was titled, *And The World Came Tumbling Down*. It did. It was a sea-change.

After ten years of individual collegiate stardom by African-American players, after ten years of Bill Russell's dominance in the NBA, the credibility of the African-American basketball *team* was officially born, and Adolph Frederick Rupp had officially lost his war—for good—on the nation's stage. He had ignored change far too many times and his position in basketball's firmament was now relegated to antique status.

On that fateful and unusually-warm Maryland night, Rupp's center was sophomore Thad Jaracz. A perfectly nice and solid hometown player, Jaracz scored seven points and retrieved seven rebounds that evening. Meanwhile, Wes Unseld, as a sophomore at UofL, had averaged 19.9 points and 19.1 rebounds a game that year. Oh, what one change could have accomplished had Rupp and the agrarian Kentuckians heard and (more importantly) understood the message of Martin Luther King's "I Have a Dream" speech in August of 1963. With Wes Unseld at the center position on Rupp's Runts there would have been no loss to that other Western, from Texas, on that night in Maryland, and Kentucky would have finally exhibited the racial leadership that had been anticipated from it (and not delivered) after the Civil War a century prior.[182]

But it was not to be.

At the end of Adolph Rupp's coaching career, he enrolled his first African-American player, 7-foot Tom Payne, from Louisville's Shawnee High. Payne lasted one year at UK before turning pro. He did reasonably well, averaging nearly seventeen points a game. But the come-uppance of all come-uppances occurred.

On March 18, 1971, fourteen months after Uncle Ed Diddle had died, Rupp and Payne played Western, in the NCAA regional finals. It was to be the only time an Adolph Rupp-coached team ever played Western. That evening, Uncle Ed would look down from his bench in heaven and watch his beloved Hilltoppers take Adolph Rupp's team to the woodshed, beating them 107-83. The Hilltoppers were in the Final Four. The irony abounds. Western's star player was a home-grown African-American center from little

Scottsville, Kentucky, All-American Jim McDaniels, who scored 35 points that night[183] and was joined by four other African-American starting players. To make matters worse, the next night Adolph Rupp lost the consolation game 91-74 to Marquette and a host of African-American players coached by Al McGuire (another New York City-born villain in Rupp's and agrarian Kentucky's closet).

Rupp's last game as coach of Kentucky was the following year. Again, history would find him losing in the NCAA, this time to Florida State, with five African-American starting players, whose stars were two African-Americans from Louisville.

In Rupp's last year at UK four African-Americans played for Auburn and Florida, three for Vanderbilt, two for Mississippi and Tennessee, and one for LSU. There were none playing for Kentucky.

UK would not recruit an African-American basketball athlete to effectively represent the Lexington university until Jack Givens and James Lee, both from Lexington, led Kentucky to the national championship in 1978, a half dozen years after Rupp retired and two years after his death, and two years after the Kentucky state legislature finally adopted the Thirteenth and Fifteenth Amendments to the United States Constitution, 111 years and 107 years, respectively, after their original ratification by the nation following the Civil War (see endnotes 56-59).

The Glory Road and Beyond

Regardless of change, or no change, or aversion to change, or fear of the unknown, from 1922 (Ed Diddle's first year as Western Kentucky's coach), through 1971-72 (Adolph Rupp's last year) these two former high school coaches, together with UofL's Peck Hickman, had coached a total of 2,749 collegiate basketball games, winning 2,078 of them. The combined careers of these three giants totaled 106 years, meaning that they averaged winning 19.3 games a year for those 106 years! They were giants, each in their own right.

When Rupp retired, he thanked the many people who joined him down the Glory Road. His 876 victories would rank him #1 in the history of collegiate basketball. His record was unbelievable. Between 1930 and 1958 he only lost 110 games—3.93 a year. During the same years he would win 584 games—20.86 a year. In 15 of those 28 years Rupp's teams never lost more than three games. He would teach 23 All-Americans[184] how to play "the religion" he had created in Kentucky. The legend was astounding.

In the end, Ed Diddle's 759 victories would rank him #2 in the history of college basketball, behind only Rupp. When Diddle retired in 1964, after 42 years, his teams had won 32 Ohio Valley Conference championships, played in three NCAA's, eight NITs, played in the 1936 Olympic Trials (the first team from the south to do so, 12 years before Rupp would), and coached 13 All-Americans.[185] His Western teams won 759 games, losing only 302. In basketball, Western had reached the big-time, successfully, before UK had, and Uncle Ed had won more games than any coach in the history of basketball. It would take Adolph Rupp another year or so to pass Ed Diddle on that list. Like Rupp, Diddle would be inducted into the Naismith Basketball Hall of Fame.

Upon Hickman's retirement in 1967 he had won 443 games and lost 183, been to the NCAA tournament five times, had won the NIT and the NAIB, played in the NIT six times, in the Olympic Trials in 1948 and coached 5 All-Americans.[186]

In the process, amateur collegiate basketball became a religion in Kentucky—which it still is today.

The Fear of the Unknown in Kentucky

Not only was Adolph Rupp the undisputed high priest of Kentucky's religion, in his mind he had actually become the religion. UK president John Oswald observed that Rupp was "the biggest egotist I've ever known."[187] His unbridled ambition was once described by Ruth Shively, the wife of Kentucky's long-time athletic director, who said at age 90, "There are many people who let a little power go to their head. He got a reputation, and he thought he was the most important person in the world."[188]

Was Adolph Rupp a racist, as some have opined? I genuinely believe he was not. He was purely and simply afraid of change. The one person who would know and understand this better than anyone was his long-time assistant, Harry Lancaster, who for twenty-five years spent more time with him than any other person. He wrote in his memoir: "Oswald [Kentucky's president] was putting the pressure on us to integrate the black player into our program. Adolph would come back from those meetings and say to me, "Harry, that son of a bitch is ordering me to get some n_____s in here. What am I going to do?" I didn't see where we had much choice, but Adolph had never been around blacks and I think he worried about the unknown."[189] What a shame.

In my view Rupp's career-long intransigence to change, his inexplicable fear of the unknown and his disdain for anything "big city" have dramatically affected the psyche of Kentucky in the 20th century. This is an unfortunate legacy of Adolph Rupp, a legacy that has been handed down to those Kentuckians who grew up adoring him, or heard of his fame from their parents.

Like Rupp, there have been numerous Kentuckians during the 20th century who made enormous contributions to our nation, been in the forefront of change and refused the fear of the unknown. From noted jurists such as U.S. Supreme Court Justice Louis D. Brandeis, to U.S. Senator, Senate Majority Leader and Vice-President Alben W. Barkley, to politician-jurists Chief Justice of the U.S. Supreme Court Fred Vinson and Governor/Sixth Circuit Judge Bert Combs, to politicians, Governor/Senator Wendell H. Ford and A.B. "Happy" Chandler the list is long and distinguished. The average of their years on the national stage approached twenty-five. But none of their careers even remotely approached the raw and intense power over Kentuckians, their emotions, their psyches or their very beings that Rupp's career generated. Nor did any of them have careers that even approached the longevity of Rupp's forty-two years on the state and national center stage, during which time eleven different governors entered and left the Governor's Mansion.[190]

Nothing had changed with Adolph Rupp. No better example of Rupp's recalcitrance to change existed than his obstinate refusal to play a zone defense for over thirty years, and when finally done he would refuse to call it a zone. Instead it was jokingly called a stratified, transitional, hyperbolic, parabola defense.

Adolph Frederick Rupp was, unquestionably, the most powerful Kentuckian for nearly fifty years. It has been reported that his television show was watched by 83% of the television viewers in Kentucky.[191] During his career, change was happening everywhere except with rural/agrarian Kentuckians and Adolph Rupp. Sadly his intransigence allowed the tide of history to wash him aside and marginalize much of his storied success.

One would think such an adverse effect would have been eliminated by the simple passage of time, and that Rupp's utter disdain for the big city, adopted by rural/agrarian Kentuckians, would have lessened in the years since his death. But in Kentucky the religion's importance and the deification of Adolph Rupp apparently hasn't allowed a complete transition.

But "Once upon a time...."

Once upon a time, about forty years ago, Kentucky's century-long disdain for the big city was displaced. It was a time when something other than the Kentucky Derby at Churchill Downs made every Kentuckian proud of Louisville. It was a time when all the planets of Kentucky's solar system were pointed in the same direction and rotated in unison.

It was an exciting time in which to live—one of those unusual moments in the life of a city when common and ordinary young men accomplished uncommon and extraordinary results. A time when all across Louisville young people strove for greatness and excellence. The enthusiasm was catching. A young pizza maker with little family wealth joined with others and eventually became one of the regions's largest and most successful residential real estate developers. A time when a young man from Louisville's Highland Park neighborhood amassed enormous wealth out of sheer will, determination and endless hours of work. A time when business-changing concepts germinated in Louisville. A time when New York Stock Exchange companies were being created in the city's downtown and some even moved there. It was a time when the century-long influence of stodgy law firms was being challenged by new ones; when the century-old importance of old-line wealth was supplanted by action-oriented young people. It was a time when several young Louisvillians were selected among the ten "Outstanding Young Men" in America by the nation's Junior Chamber of Commerce. And a time when young men in their late 20s and early 30s were elected to leadership in the highest local political offices, while many of similar youth were demonstrating in the streets of American cities and burning the nation's flag. This whole host of young leaders made a loud noise about changing the city—a noise whose echo reverberates even today.

This Kennedyesque time caused something else to happen in Louisville, which literally shook the fabric of the city, the state and the major league sports world. What happened had never happened before—Louisvillians and Kentuckians coming together, no matter their collegiate preference, to cheer for the city and the state. It was a time when some of the greatest heroes of Adolph Rupp's Glory Road coalesced together under a single banner and helped lead a virtual revolution, becoming even greater heroes in Rupp's enormous pantheon of greatness.

It was the time of the Kentucky Colonels.

Louisville competed head-to-head with Indianapolis, San Antonio, Charlotte and a host of other cities on the field of professional athletic endeavor. It was a time when Louisville, *almost*, became a major-league sports city.

Yet, undeniably, it was also a time when one of those highly successful young people (not a politician) made a series of decisions (be they right or wrong at the time) that stymied the quickly-budding dream of Louisville's big-league status, eventually preventing it from coming true. Despite this bittersweet ending of that moment in time, its glory, its memory and its importance beg to be preserved, because they provide invaluable lessons about enthusiasm, hopes and dreams and how to accomplish something that seems nearly impossible—a revolution of thought and of action.

My little 6-year-old grandson, Tristan, and your own sons, daughters, grandsons and granddaughters need to know about the time of the Kentucky Colonels. Its replication by them may be important in salvaging Louisville's future in the 21st century.

It was a truly remarkable and glorious chapter of the religion of Kentucky, a chapter that every Kentuckian should hold dear as a moment in time when the state, as a whole, really did something right.

CHAPTER FOUR

Long Ago Days of Magic: The Amazing Story of the Kentucky Colonels

It was the year 480 B.C. as dawn was breaking over the strait of water that separates the small Greek islands of Salamis and Attica, just off the coast of Athens. Thousands of Athenians huddled and hid in a few slender wooden dingies clutching their weapons and oars. Facing them were 700 powerful ships, the majestic fighting navy of the great Persian Empire. Across the narrow strait, on a commanding hill, sat the great Xerxes, King of Persia. After his victory thirty years earlier at Thermopylae, Xerxes was eager to witness the final defeat of Greece and complete the capture of its prized jewel, the city of Athens.

For years Athenians had known the time was coming when their true mettle would be tested. Even though they were a rag-tag bunch, by the time dusk fell that fateful day the Persian king's dream was in ruins. The Athenians had successfully carried out a bold and innovative plan. Using the agility of their lighter ships and their knowledge of the local geography and weather, they outmaneuvered and defeated their far more powerful foe. Spurred by a deep sense of civic duty, they fought with special valor, superior ingenuity and motivation. Against all odds, the Athenians defeated their colossal foe. So began the storied democratic era of Pericles, resplendent with the Parthenon and its white-marbled Acropolis, built to honor Athena. The Golden Age of Greek civilization was born.

Louisville's recent NBA challenge during the Millennium wasn't exactly comparable to the historic importance of Athens' challenge of yore, but like Athens' challenge that took years to successfully meet, Louisville's didn't just begin in 1999. It started many years prior at a time that many alive today have only heard of. In the beginning that challenge was like that of the Athenians, comprised of a rag-tag bunch in battle with the Xerxes-like NBA. But from rather ignominious beginnings, it quickly grew into another facet of the religion in Kentucky.

Before beginning the story of Louisville's NBA odyssey, a visit to those long ago days of magic is essential to set the stage.

Alpha of the ABA[192]

The meetings were more than several, and tumultuous. From the Beverly Wilshire Hotel in Los Angeles to New York City, ideas, arguments, devil's advocacy and intrigue were in abundance. Finally, by February 2, 1967, in New York City's posh St. Regis Hotel, west coasters Dennis Murphy[193] and Gary Davidson, together with New Yorker Constantine (Connie) Seredin[194] succeeded in procuring tentative franchise commitments for a new ten-team professional basketball league.[195]

A month and a half later on March 31, 1967, thirty-seven years after Adolph Rupp was hired by UK, a press conference was held at the Summit Hotel in New York City. On that day the American Basketball Association[196] (ABA) was introduced to the American sports scene, with basketball icon, Naismith Hall of Famer and prominent Minneapolis attorney, George Mikan, as its Commissioner.

On June 17, 1976, the ABA died an ignoble death in a hotel conference room at Chicago's Hyatt Regency hotel, adjacent to O'Hare Airport.

For the 3,209 days in between, what had been formerly known by most Americans as that dull pro game of the NBA (often then-jokingly referred to as the National Brownball Association, and played in only ten American big cities[197]) was to be severely challenged by the raucous, zany, flamboyant and colorful ABA version of the sport. Over those days and against enormous odds, the ABA would change the game of basketball the world over—in the NBA and even in Kentucky. It would serve as the birthplace of the professional careers for dozens of eventual NBA superstars, NBA coaching legends, numerous Naismith Hall of Fame honorees, the 3-point shot, the 30-second shot clock, monstrous Afros donned by its African-Americans players and Prince Valiant-style hairdos for its whites, the red-white-blue basketball, slam-dunk contests and the above-the-rim game of basketball that we know and celebrate today.

And so that day in March, 1967, an outlaw league was formally announced that included a team called the Kentucky Colonels.[198] Maime Spears Reynolds Chinetti Gregory, an heiress to a family fortune[199] who once owned a ten-car auto racing stable while married to Luigi Chinetti of the Ferrari racing team, paid a reported $64,900 (which included a $50,000 performance bond) to put the Kentucky Colonels in the ABA. Her husband, Joe, an equally interesting character, trained show dogs and had met Maime when he was showing dogs for her father while she was still married to Chinetti. The Gregorys owned a premier show dog, Ziggy (a Brussels griffon). He became the Colonels team mascot. In those days of yore, Ziggy had a courtside seat and 39 different uniforms (one for each home game) including a tuxedo, sat at attention for the National Anthem, ate ice cream cones with the children of fans and joined the Gregorys at league meetings. To be sure, Ziggy was no slouch. A year prior he had won Best of Breed at the Westminster Kennel Club world championship in Madison Square Garden, along with nearly one hundred other similar honors. Season ticket holders were honored with The Ziggy Package, allowing them to spend halftimes in the non-resplendent Ziggy Room, and the team physician was a local pediatrician (and soon-to-be County Coroner), Dr. Richard Greathouse. It was an unusual and publicly-spirited group.

The Rag-Tag ABA, 30 Degrees Left of Sanity

The early years of the ABA have been lovingly described as being 30 degrees left of sanity. As teams shuffled between cities,[200] the Los Angeles Stars hired belly dancers to train the players in calisthenics; half-time of Pacer's games offered cow-milking contests in the decrepit Indiana Fairground's Fieldhouse; the Miami Floridians gave away pumpkin pies on Thanksgiving, Irish potatoes on St. Patrick's Day and vats of gefilte fish during Hanukkah, but became far more widely-renown for dressing their cheerleaders in mini-bikinis. Art Kim's Anaheim Amigos took a different cheerleader approach. Theirs was a man, dressed like a mustachioed Pancho Villa-type, pistol-packing Mexican bandido. While sitting on the team's bench, when the Amigos made a stirring play, the bandido would fire blanks in the air! Once in a St. Patrick's Day game at Madison Square Garden, each Miami Floridian player's name on his uniform was given an "O"— O'Jones, O'Calvin, O'Harge, etc. It was a time long ago, way before the avant guarde notion of political correctness. The standing ABA referee rule was "no blood, no foul."

During the ABA's first season, veteran NBA coach and Naismith Hall of Fame honoree, Alex Hannum, joked that the red-white-blue ball looked like a beach ball or something that ought to be on a seal's nose. A year later Hannum's opinion changed; he left his head coaching job with the NBA's Philadelphia 76ers, and joined the fun in the seal's league, to coach the Pat Boone-owned Oakland Oaks starring future Hall of Famer Rick Barry (who had bolted the NBA), Doug Moe and Larry Brown (who would eventually become one of the most successful coaches in the history of basketball). The Hannum-led Oaks consummated a regular season record of 60-18, winning the league's second-year championship.

To be sure, the Kentucky Colonels fully participated in that original zaniness. The team's never-explained original colors were literally awful— chartreuse green and white. Once the Colonels offered a tryout to a 42- year-old, 5-foot 4-inch college professor. Former Indiana high school all-state star, Jim "Goose" Ligon, released from the Pacers training camp, became a Colonel. Blessed with unusually long arms, a silky-smooth swooping hook shot and explosive rebounding skills, Ligon's playing style resembled that of a Harlem Globetrotter. An instant fan favorite, Ligon was once to be listed in a Colonel game program as being a graduate of PenStateU (because he had served a felony sentence out of high school). The game program was quickly changed. The Colonels first league playoff game was moved (due to prior commitments for a circus) from Teaneck, N.J. to Commack, N.Y., where goals were brought in from a nearby park and a carpenter was hired to nail plywood over the holes in the floor. Eventually, ABA Commissioner George Mikan forfeited the game to the Colonels due to the arena's condition.

The first woman to ever play on a men's professional basketball team was a Colonel. She was also the nation's first female-licensed jockey. Penny Ann Early was her name. Being incensed that male jockeys had boycotted the Churchill Downs races in which Early was entered, Maime Gregory inked Early to a Colonels contract. On November 25, 1968, after a timeout, Early reported to the scorer's table and entered the game. She inbounded the ball to Colonel guard Bobby Rascoe, who immediately called timeout—and Early retired to the bench—amid tumultuous applause.

A good time was had by all.

The Colonels, the Religion and the Gong Show

Something of greater significance than the Colonels' original zaniness occurred on June 7, 1967, several months after the ABA's birth announcement. One of Adolph Rupp's beloved Kentucky All-Americans —Louie Dampier—signed a player's contract for a $12,000 salary and a $3,000 bonus. Dampier's signature on that contract represented the beginning of a major change for the league. With his shotmaking and playmaking skills, the Colonels entry into the ABA began to legitimize. Little Louie would eventually become the league's all-time leading scorer and assist maker and be known to aficionados as the Bob Cousy of the ABA. The acorns from Rupp's oak had begun to fall and create new oak trees at the Kentucky Colonels. There were to be more.

The first three ABA seasons found the Colonels playing in the 5,700 seat downtown arena originally known as the Armory, then as the Convention Center, and finally as the Louisville Gardens) but only averaged 3,739 fans per game. In large measure local interest level was sustained through the excitement of the 3-point shot and the Gregory's ingenuity in contracting with many players and coaches with well-recognized tentacles to the state's collegiate basketball heritage.[201] Without question, in the early years the two Colonels who captured the fans' imagination were 3-point shotmakers, UK's Dampier and Western Kentucky's Darrel Carrier. During those first three seasons, they combined to average more than 50 points a game. A successful Colonels 3-point shot was met with the ringing of the Marathon Oil gong, piercing the ears of those present over an enhanced speaker system. The fans loved the "Gong Show" and when they weren't cheering for the dynamic guard duo, they were yelling for "Goooooose" (Ligon) and his Globetrotter-like exploits.

Despite the fun, the religion, the Dampier-Carrier led Gong Show and "Gooooose", Colonels fans were treated to a nondescript three-year record of 117 wins and 127 losses.

Toe in the Water

The Athenians of yore didn't begin their battle with a frontal onslaught against Xerxes; they first put their toe in the water, to test its depth and temperature. Within several years, the question began to be asked: "Is the

ABA going to really challenge the NBA?" In their second year of ownership, the Gregory's had failed to sign UofL's All-American, Wes Unseld. Spurning their offer, he joined the NBA's Washington Bullets.[202] But elsewhere in the ABA, big-time player personnel moves were being made successfully.

Eventual Naismith Hall of Famer Connie Hawkins led the Pittsburgh Pipers to the first league championship. NBA All-Star Rick Barry bolted to the ABA and won the second league championship for the Oakland Oaks, and New Mexico All-American Mel Daniels along with Roger Brown were in the infancy of creating a virtual Indiana Pacer dynasty. The ABA was gradually maturing, gaining bravado and élan.

Following the 1968-69 playing season, the ABA put its toe in the water. The first of many NBA-ABA battles was arranged. The ABA set out to purloin a highly-sought collegian from the NBA's hopeful grasp. The target was Lou Alcindor (Kareem Abdul-Jabbar), the three-time All-American from UCLA—unquestionably the most dominant collegiate player of the 1960s. Sensing a financial opportunity as a result of his unique bargaining position while equally-desirous of avoiding an untoward scene, Alcindor publicly declared he would accept one sealed bid from each league, with the highest bidder becoming the winner. The drama was intense. When it was announced the Milwaukee Bucks bid was higher, the ABA teams reportedly reloaded their offer with a one million dollar cashier's check ($600,000 more than had been paid to Joe Namath by Sonny Werblin's N.Y. Jets) — all to no avail.

Unflagged by the loss of Alcindor, the Denver Rockets owners, Bill and Don Ringsby, went to the bank and signed Spencer Haywood, an All-American from the University of Detroit and a member of the USA's 1968 Olympic championship team, who left college early under the hardship rule.[203] After two ABA seasons, Haywood would become an important player in the war games between the ABA and NBA, successfully litigating against the NBA to open its rosters for undergraduate collegians suffering provable financial hardship. His subsequent career with various NBA teams concluded with a lifetime average of 19.2 points and 9.2 rebounds per game. Not to be outdone, L.A. Stars new owner Bill Daniels acquired long-time NBA star center, Zelmo Beatty.

With the exception of the Oakland Oaks' Pat Boone and the Dallas Chaparrals owners (one of whom—Bob Folsom—was estimated to be worth $500 million), the owners of the ABA teams were neither wealthy enough nor sufficiently interested to wage this kind of dollar battle with the NBA. For most ABA owners the league represented fun and community involvement. But now, if the league was going to survive and prosper, a financial combat with the NBA was required.

From an attendance standpoint, at the end of the its first three years, the ABA's toe was barely in the water. While the Indiana Pacers average attendance ranked in the top 10 of the combined leagues' turnstile records, there also was instant success during the first year of the Carolina Cougars franchise (following its transfer from Houston) as its attendance approached reasonable competitiveness with the NBA. The following chart reflects the reported attendance figures for the combined leagues:

Combined NBA/ABA Average Attendance: 1967/68, 1968/69 and 1969/70 Seasons[204]

Rank	Team	67/68	68/69	69/70	AverageAttendance
1.	NY. Knicks	14,448	15,383	18,566	16,132
2.	LA Lakers	10,276	11,787	13,086	11,716
3.	Phil. 76Ers	8,704	10,622	8,210	9,179
4.	Boston Celtics	8,670	8,948	7,504	8,374
5.	Milwaukee Bucks	—	6,246	9,491	7,869
6.	Seattle SuperSonics	6,525	5,840	7,735	6,700
7.	Indiana Pacers	5,167	5,864	7,787	6,273
8.	Washington Bullets	4,754	7,635	6,096	6,162
9.	[Houston Mavericks	1,543	1,147		
	Carolina Cougars]	—		6,088	6,088
10.	Phoenix Suns	—	4,340	7,617	5,979
11.	Chicago Bulls	3,875	3,790	10,051	5,905
12.	S.Diego Rockets	4,606	6,054	6,123	5,594
13.	Detroit Pistons	7,005	5,301	4,412	5,573
14.	St. Louis/Atlanta Hawks	6,288	4,474	5,210	5,324
15.	Denver Rockets	4,128	4,302	6,281	4,904
16.	Golden State Warriors	4,520	4,748	5,268	4,845
17	Cincinnati Royals	4,156	4,065	4,869	4,363
18.	**Kentucky Colonels**	**3,225**	**4,157**	**3,834**	**3,739**
19.	N.J. Americans	2,054	1,108	—	
	New Jersey Nets			3,504	3,504
20.	Dallas Chaparrals	3,265	2,861	3,687	3,271
21.	Minn. Muskies/ Miami Floridians	2,473	3,197	2,724	2,798
22.	Oakland Oaks/ Washington Capitols	2,214	2,867	2,992	2,691
23.	N.Orleans Bucs	2,327	2,834	2,599	2,590
24.	Pittsburgh Pipers	3,143	2,183	2,009	2,445
25.	Anaheim Amigos/L.A. Stars	1,293	2,281	1,461	1,678

But all wasn't well. The general ABA fan interest level, as reflected by the league's attendance, was lackluster, at best. Inescapably, the attendance records told the story—the Colonels were little more than the leader of the all the rest. The Kentucky Colonels had a long way to go.

The Colonels (and the ABA) get down to business

As the decade of the 1960s inched to a conclusion, the ABA's bodaciousness in signing big name players for NBA-like salaries was met with an equally strong, but different, move in Louisville. On October 30 1969, five highly successful, dynamic, wealthy and young Louisville businessmen combined their resources to purchase the Kentucky Colonels from the Gregorys.[205] These five young men, all in their 30s, were remarkable, each in their own right.

Born and raised on Virginia Avenue in Louisville's west end with modest middle-class family resources, David A. Jones excelled in athletics and scholarship at Louisville's college preparatory high school, Male High. Having met this challenge with aplomb, Jones traveled to New Haven, Connecticut to become an Eli. With a prestigious Ivy League degree from Yale proudly in tow, he returned to Louisville, obtained a law degree from UofL and joined the city's leading law firm, Wyatt Grafton & Sloss. Meanwhile, from the northern end of Kentucky's cave country, Horse Cave, a high school basketball player, H. Wendell Cherry, matriculated to and graduated from UK's undergraduate and law schools. A brilliant student, Cherry led his law school class and served as the editor of the school's law review. Like Jones, upon graduation he gravitated to the Wyatt law firm. There they met J. David Grissom, a football and track (shotput) star at Louisville's Atherton High. Grissom had obtained his undergraduate degree at Centre College and his law degree, with honors, at UofL.

They were a determined, impatient and peripatetic trio desirous of implementing change in Louisville's still stagnant economy. While at the Wyatt firm, Jones, Cherry and four friends invested $1,000 apiece and formed a nursing home company called Heritage House. It began with one nursing home on Bardstown Road in Louisville. Within a few years Heritage House expanded to nine nursing homes, the company's name changed to Extendicare and became publicly-traded. In 1968, Extendicare acquired its first hospital, in Hunstville, Alabama. By the fall of 1969, Extendicare was a nationally-known "go-go" company.[206] During this period they left the

Wyatt law firm and joined with another young attorney, William C. Boone (who represented the Colonels owners, the Gregorys), and formed their own law firm, Jones Cherry Grissom & Boone. When Jones and Cherry left the active practice of law to give full-time attention to Extendicare, Grissom and Boone led a merger of their firm with the regional business and tax law firm of Greenebaum Doll. By the end of the decade, the merged Greenebaum Grissom law firm, representing Extendicare, Kentucky Fried Chicken and a host of other newly-developed businesses, was challenging Louisville's old-line law firms for local and regional primacy.[207]

The other two new owners were equally successful. One played a far less active role. Affectionately known as "Blue Jay", Stuart Jay had created and sold for a significant financial gain a national chain of state-of-the-art electronics schools. The other, but by far not least, was John Y. Brown, Jr., who had co-founded and developed what by 1969 had become the second largest fast food franchising company in the world—Kentucky Fried Chicken—and was instrumental in moving its world headquarters from Nashville to Louisville. While a relatively inactive co-owner in the beginning, Brown's participation, subsequently explored in depth, became cataclysmic in its proportion.

For a century, Louisville's public and private affairs had been controlled by what was commonly called old-line wealth—primarily second and third generation whiskey and tobacco money that was generally uninterested in any investment without a guaranteed income. This, inescapably, meant that old-line wealth was incapable of being an instrument of change in Louisville. Seldom, if ever, had a group of young Louisville businessmen, with no particularly demonstrable family wealth, ever taken such a bold move. It was a spectacular group of young and dynamic entrepreneurs, whose credibility and business acumen had an immediate impact on the ABA. There wasn't a city in America with five more capable, young and visionary businessmen. The stage and table were set to put Louisville and the Colonels on the nation's sports map.

The Colonels ownership change became a precursor to other ownership movement in the ABA. Within a year Roy Boe, the owner of Boe Jests, a multi-million dollar garment firm (and who reportedly owned the patent on the wrap-around skirt), purchased the New Jersey Nets from Arthur Brown. Carolina furniture magnate Ted Munchak acquired the Carolina

Cougars. The owner of the nation's first cable brokerage company and cable television system and the initial lead pilot for the flight team known as the Blue Angels, Bill Daniels, bought the Utah Stars. Ned Doyle, retired chairman of New York City's leading advertising agency, Doyle, Dane, Bernbach (renowned for their Volkswagen, Alka-Selzer and Avis ads), obtained ownership of the Miami Floridians, immediately changing the team colors and regionalizing the franchise.[208] East coast entrepreneur Earl Foreman purchased the Washington Capitals (formerly the Oakland Oaks) from Pat Boone by assuming their $500,000 debt, moving the team to Virginia and renaming it the Virginia Squires. The Squires, like the Floridians and the Cougars,[209] became a regional franchise playing in Norfolk, Hampton Roads, Richmond and Roanoke.

With these new owners, joining the five young Louisvillians and Bob Folsom's group that owned the Dallas Chaparrals, by 1971 the across-the-board wealth of the ABA owners may have approached a billion dollars.

Over the next several years, those young Louisville businessmen would change the Kentucky Colonels, the ABA, the sport of basketball in Kentucky and the religion of Kentucky itself. Alongside the collegiate sport would be added the ABA-version of the major league professional game. Into that version would soon be added another product of Kentucky's unfailing worship of Adolph Rupp.

ABA Athenians directly challenge Xerxes' NBA

The first ABA basketball season of the 1970s (1970-71) began with a bang. To alleviate the depreciating moniker of "no harm, no foul," the ABA bought the NBA's four best referees.[210] In Louisville, under the leadership of its new ownership group, the Colonels moved their games from a 5,700 seat, 70-year-old downtown arena to 16,613 seat (then) Freedom Hall. It was by far the largest and most significant ABA arena, having been the venue of six of the previous ten NCAA basketball championships. This progress was further magnified by a new Commissioner, Jack Dolph, the former head of CBS Sports, who facilitated the league's inking of a CBS television contract. Now the talent of the ABA would be exposed to the larger non-ABA public. In the 1970-71 season that talent level would be significantly enhanced.

The ABA's new owners outmaneuvered the old and tired NBA, just as the adroit Athenians had outfoxed Xerxes' Persian navy at the battle of

Salamis. Three-fifths of the Associated Press first team All-Americans joined the ABA: Rick Mount of Purdue (signed by the Pacers) and Charlie Scott from the University of North Carolina (contracted with the Virginia Squires).

The third was something extra special. Arguably, the most famous and revered of all Rupp's players—Dan Issel, UK's 6-9 two-time first-team All-American center—contracted to play for the Kentucky Colonels, despite interest from the NBA's Detroit Pistons. Issel was the highest scorer (and still is today 36 years later) in the storied history of UK teams. Realizing his importance to the Colonel's future, prior to the league draft, the new ownership obtained Issel's draft rights from the ABA's Dallas Chaparrals. The Issel contract drew considerable national attention with many varied values being placed upon it. Some claimed it was valued at $1.4 million and others were more bold with their conclusions.[211] But, regardless of its value, it was a coup for the Colonels, presaging even more of Rupp's acorns to fall on the Colonels.

Dan Issel's personal magnanimity would never be better exemplified than on the evening of his agreement to the Colonels financial package. Expressing his satisfaction, there remained one further requirement. His UK teammate, Mike Pratt, had to reach an agreement with the Colonels before Issel would sign. Shortly thereafter, the highly-stylistic rough-and-tumble Pratt joined Issel as a Kentucky Colonel. With Issel's signing, overnight the Colonels became a competitive ABA team. The five dynamic young Louisville businessmen had, yet again, stirred the pot and set the course of change.

The 1970-71 basketball season, beginning without initial won-loss success, was the subject of immediate corrective measures from the impatient young businessmen. Reaching back to the religion, two-time UK All-American, NBA Hall of Famer and Boston Celtic legend, Frank Ramsey, was hired to coach the Colonels. Now, there was real flash and splash.

The Kentucky Colonels exploded. With the rookie Issel averaging 29.9 points per game for the season, the Colonels reached the ABA championship finals against the Utah Stars. After Utah won the first two games in Salt Lake City's Salt Palace and the Colonels the next two at Freedom Hall, Game 5 at the Salt Palace was close, but the Colonels lost. Returning to Freedom Hall for Game 6, Dampier rang the Marathon Oil gong with one of his classic 3-point shots—tying the game at 100 each. Eventually, the Colonels prevailed, and traveled to Salt Lake City for the seventh and final game. Despite a 41-point performance from Issel, the Colonels lost to the Utah Stars for the ABA championship.

Clearly establishing himself as the key ABA player, Issel's initial season as a Colonel had been a roaring success. Being fully aware of Issel's impact in the ABA, the NBA made a Xerxes-like move during the ABA playoffs. Calls came from various NBA owners requesting immediate discussions about Issel's availability. While he authorized contact, Issel didn't want to know anything about the discussions, preferring to concentrate on the playoffs. Since the Detroit Pistons owned his NBA draft rights, the first call returned went to Fred Zollner, owner of the Detroit Pistons. A face-to-face meeting was requested and conducted on April 15, 1971, at the Zollner Piston Corporation on Bechter Road in Fort Wayne, Indiana. Wanting Issel immediately, Zollner orally committed to pay the full dollar value of his entire ten-year Colonels contract (including the deferred payments) in seven years. His salary was guaranteed during any legal proceedings as were his litigation expenses and any league fines imposed. Further, the Pistons agreed to negotiate Issel's draft rights with any other NBA team preferred by Issel. Stunning. He had a hard time concentrating on the drive back to Louisville.

Within several days other calls were received. Joe Axelson of the Kansas City Kings committed to the same offer, if Issel preferred the Kings. An identical commitment came from Seattle Supersonics general manager, Bob Houbregs, and their owner, Sam Schulman. Cleveland Cavaliers owner, Nick Mileti, dittoed the deal. Then came the blockbuster. On April 23, 1971, Jerry Colangelo, the young general manager of the brand-new Phoenix Suns called. Sun's owners Richard Block of Los Angeles and Donald Pitt of Tucson were willing to outbid the Pistons by reducing Issel's 10-year Colonels contract to a guaranteed five years, at the ten-year dollar amount and offering a cashier's check to Issel in the amount of $100,000 to be delivered at Phoenix's Sky Harbor airport if Issel and I (his attorney) would fly to Phoenix rather than to Salt Lake City for the final ABA championship game. How did they all know the Piston's offer? It was obvious—the NBA teams were working in concert with each other.

Since Issel couldn't be told of the developments, due to his prior instructions, discussions were entertained with Colonels co-owner David Grissom. Expressing his deep appreciation for the information, Grissom committed to a post-season restructuring of Issel's contract. He kept his commitment, adding Addendum II to Issel's player's contract later in the summer. Issel was appreciative for the way it was handled. He loved Kentucky and wanted his professional career home to be there.

The bottom line to all this was inescapable; there was a full-scale financial battle being waged between the ABA and NBA. It was reaching Salamis-like proportions.

ABA's and Colonels' challenge of the NBA intensifies

The bidding wars continued. The next year the young Louisville businessmen signed 7-2 Jacksonville University All-American, Artis Gilmore. Without question, he was the most sought-after graduating collegian that year. Surprisingly strong and with an enormous high-coiffed Afro rendering the appearance of his height to at least 7-6, Gilmore was a forbidding presence on the court that was unequalled in American professional basketball.

Following his playing days with the Celtics, Colonels coach Frank Ramsey had returned home to Kentucky and become a highly-successful businessman and banker. He loathed the travel demands of coaching. With his primary focus upon family, Ramsey refused to coach the Colonels for a second year. Nothing, not even Frank Ramsey's walk-off, would faze the team's new ownership. Without missing a beat, Joe Mullaney, who had just completed a two-year head coaching stint with the Los Angeles Lakers, was signed to coach the Colonels.

With the firm belief that their Colonels were now among the elite in professional basketball, their young ownership organized a series of preseason games with the best of the NBA teams. Scheduled were the NBA champion and runner-up from the previous season. The results were nothing short of spectacular.

On September 22, 1971, before 14,821 frenzied fans in Freedom Hall, the Colonels soundly defeated the 1970-71 NBA runner-up Baltimore Bullets, led by UofL's Wes Unseld. The score was 111-85. Gilmore's 16 point, 16 rebound effort and Issel's 24 point performance were devastating. Sixteen days later the Colonels lost 99-93 to the NBA defending champions, Milwaukee Bucks and their stars, Kareem Abdul-Jabbar and Oscar Robertson. A packed Freedom Hall witnessed Issel and Gilmore scoring 34 and 18 points, respectively, with Gilmore adding 16 rebounds and blocking 5 of Jabbar's shots. As great as they were, these exhibition games would pale in comparison to the upcoming 1971-72 regular season.

The Issel/Gilmore/Dampier-led Colonels improved from a 44-40 regular season record the prior year to a phenomenal 68-16. Gilmore averaged 23.8 points and 17.8 rebounds and blocked an astounding 422 shots on his way to be chosen as the ABA Rookie of the Year and Most Valuable Player. He won the honors over another soon-to-be rookie phenomena, the Virginia Squires Julius "Dr. J" Erving. Disturbingly, the regular season success wasn't replicated in the playoffs. Stumbling badly, the Colonels lost to Roy Boe's New York Nets, whose star player was former NBA superstar, Rick Barry.

Despite their playoff debacle, the Kentucky Colonels had officially arrived on the national stage of major league professional basketball. In the combined leagues attendance, the Colonels had moved from tenth in average attendance for the 1970/71 season (after the signing of Issel) to sixth in the 1971/72 season (after the signing of Gilmore), ahead of every ABA team as well as such other NBA luminaries as the Boston Celtics (who with a 56-26 record won the Atlantic Division), the Baltimore Bullets (who won the Central Division), Golden State (with a record of 51-31) and Phoenix Suns (with a record of 49-33).

The team's spectacular 235% attendance increase over the 3,739 average attendance in their first three seasons, combined with the preseason proof-in-the-pudding performances against the top two NBA teams and the season-long won-loss record, proved to be electric. The Kentucky Colonels were now a real franchise in the growing and real ABA. Things had really changed and the state of Kentucky's interest was electrified.

The following chart reflects the combined leagues attendance figures for the 1970-71 and 1971-72 seasons:

Combined NBA/ABA Average Attendance 70/71 and 71/72 Seasons[212]

	70-71 Season			71-72 Season	
Rank	Team	Av.Attend.	Rank	Team	Av.Attend.
1.	N.Y.Knicks	18,622	1.	N.Y.Knicks	19,154
2.	L.A.Lakers	13,808	2.	L.A.Lakers	16,301
3.	Milwaukee Bucks	10,503	3.	Seattle Supersonics	11,108
4.	Chicago Bulls	10,118	4.	Chicago Bulls	10,617
5.	Seattle Supersonics	9,315	5.	Milwaukee Bucks	10,346
6.	Phila.76ers	8,636	6.	Kentucky Colonels	8,811
7.	Indiana Pacers	8,187	7.	Phila.76Ers	8,804
8.	Phoenix Suns	8,121	8.	Buffalo Braves	8,557
9.	Boston Celtics	8,045	9.	Indiana Pacers	8,476
10.	Kentucky Colonels	7,375	10.	Boston Celtics	8,456
11.	Detroit Pistons	6,925	11.	Phoenix Suns	8,364

12.	Houston Rockets	6,775		12.	Utah Stars	7,998
13.	Portland T'Blazers	6,135		13.	Portland T'Blazers	6,988
14.	Baltimore Bullets	6,125		14.	Baltimore Bullets	6,642
15.	Utah Stars	6,106		15.	New Jersey Nets	6,204
16.	Atlanta Hawks	5,998		16.	Virginia Squires	6,124
17.	Carolina Cougars	5,579		17.	Golden State Warr.	5,740
18.	Golden State Warr.	5,156		18.	Atlanta Hawks	5,629
19.	Buffalo Braves	4,977		19.	Cleveland Cavaliers	5,222
20.	New Jersey Nets	4,636		20.	Carolina Cougars	5,077
21.	Memphis Pros	4,441		21.	Houston Rockets	4,966
22.	Virginia Squires	4,309		22.	Detroit Pistons	4,604
23.	Denver Rockets	4,139		23.	Denver Rockets	4,303
24.	Cincinnati Royals	3,992		24.	Cincinnati Royals	3,687
25.	Cleveland Cavaliers	3,518		25.	Memphis Pros	3,476
26.	Dallas Chaparrals	3,426		26.	Dallas Chaparrals	3,108
27.	Pittsburgh Condors	2,806		27.	Pittsburgh Condors	2,215

ABA goes 'a-courtin'

With the higher profile of its star players, the business and political clout and restless determination of its new owners and its surging game-style that was captivating fan interest, the ABA initiated an even more dramatic move—a merger with the NBA.

Antitrust litigation was filed against the NBA. Among most ABA owners, it was generally believed the case was reasonably solid. The proof behind the case was startling—a disgruntled NBA employee had leaked an explosive internal memorandum that clearly evidenced a conspiracy among NBA owners. They had agreed on the amount of money each team would pay each collegiate player in the 1968 draft[213] and how much money each team would contribute to a common pot to be shared, insuring that no NBA team would be outbid for players by the ABA. It just wasn't a one-year plan for 1968, either, because the offers to Issel were further proof that there was ongoing concerted action among the NBA teams. The memo was more than a smoking gun—it was a keg of dynamite.

The case progressed well and seemed to be achieving its purpose. By mid-1971, the NBA had tentatively accepted a merger plan that would have included the Kentucky Colonels and the other ABA teams (except the Virginia Squires unless they moved from the Baltimore Bullets' territory). The understandings included a dismissal of the ABA's anti-trust litigation, a $1.25 million payment ($125,000 annually) from each ABA team for ten years and no television money for two years. It was generally believed that when the NBA fans witnessed the talent level of the ABA teams, the merger's financial negatives would be more than compensated for by local increases in attendance plus local/regional television opportunities in the ABA merging teams market areas. Indeed, things looked promising.

Then Oscar Robertson and Bill Bradley, on behalf of the NBA Players Association, filed their own federal anti-trust action against both leagues alleging the merger would create an illegal monopoly. They reasoned that without the ABA as an alternative league, the NBA reserve clause bound an NBA player to his team for life. Further, they alleged that by conspiring to effect a merger and entering into an alleged non-competition agreement pending the finalization of the merger, the two leagues had engaged in a conspiracy to monopolize and restrain trade, in violation of federal anti-trust laws. The Players Association sought an injunction barring the NBA from compelling its players to sign the NBA Uniform Player Contract, enforcing the reserve clause and selling/trading players against their wishes. Additionally, they sought an injunction against the merger.

Despite the Robertson litigation, the collective political clout of the NBA/ABA owners was succeeding. In the fall of 1972, the antitrust subcommittee of the U.S. Senate approved the merger provided the NBA's reserve clause was removed in favor of an option clause permitting free-agency for the players and the NBA's $1.25 million entry fee was scratched. Change was on the horizon; it appeared that Louisville and its Kentucky Colonels would soon be in the major leagues.

However, in the real world nothing's easy; there always seems to be a thumb tack in the road. Now that tack was the octogenarian, Ned Irish of the New York Knicks, the impresario of the old Madison Square Garden where years prior Adolph Rupp and his Fabulous Five had met their Waterloo. The NBA was facing internal growth pains as the league's long-time domination by its New York, L.A., Philly, Boston and Chicago franchises was being effectively challenged. Prior to the ABA's advent, the Knicks, Lakers, Celtics and 76ers enjoyed at least 50% of the total league attendance. Since the advent of the ABA, new NBA expansion franchises had been awarded in Seattle, Milwaukee, Phoenix and Portland. By 1972, the new Seattle and Milwaukee expansion franchises were in the top 5 of all NBA franchises in attendance and they supported a merger. Determined to protect the hegemony of the old-line NBA franchises, Ned Irish and his Knicks refused give up the reserve clause. Between the Oscar Robertson suit and

Ned Irish's exercise of the Knicks clout, merger was dead. The NBA's battle with the ABA continued.

Refusing to yield, in 1974 the ABA upped the ante by filing cross-claims in the Robertson suit against the NBA, asserting more antitrust violations. The ABA also alleged the NBA had breached the merger agreement reached on May 7, 1971 and sought $3 million in liquidated damages and $97 million in compensatory damages. Finally, the ABA alleged that the NBA defrauded the ABA by entering into the merger agreement and asked for $100 million in actual and $100 million in punitive damages.

It was a lawyer's paradise, but hell for the ABA owners.

Unmerged, the ABA and the Colonels fight on

In 1972-73, with Gilmore, Issel, Dampier and coach Joe Mullaney, the Colonels enjoyed another fabulous regular season with a record of 56-28. The playoffs featured the Colonels again contesting the Virginia Squires. Three future Naismith Hall of Famers were on the floor in those games— Dan Issel, Julius Erving and George Gervin. The Colonels won in a five-game series. The next playoff series found the Colonels beating the Carolina Cougars and its own future Hall of Famer, Billy Cunningham. Were the Colonels going to finally win the ABA championship? Only if they beat their arch-rival, the Indiana Pacers. It was another seven-game marathon, featuring the Colonels trio and the hot-shooting, newly-signed former Pacer star, Rick Mount, against the George McGinnis-led Pacers. Success for the Colonels was not to be. They lost another final championship playoff game for the second time in three years.

Despite the playoff loss, the once-zany Colonels were at the apex of big-time sports, both in Kentucky and in the nation. The NBA was talking merger. In Louisville hopes were high, but in the early summer of 1973 Mt. Vesuvius erupted upon Pompeii.

Colonels sold to Cincinnati

The new Colonels ownership had grown understandably impatient. They were aggravated that merger legislation could be approved by a congressional antitrust subcommittee, yet become hamstrung in the labyrinth of arcane antitrust litigation. A lot of money in legal fees and enormous amounts of energy were being expended endeavoring to succeed. The effort was debilitating and exhausting. Attention to their young families, their other business pursuits and to Extendicare's well-being was mandated. The vicissitudes being experienced by the young Colonels ownership were greater than just local or personal concerns. Disturbing news was emanating from Dallas.

Since the league's inception, the Chaparrals had been owned by a group of enormously wealthy Texans led by Dallas Mayor Robert Folsom who, alone, was reputedly worth in excess of $500 million. While Folsom's group had never been particularly interested in utilizing their financial largesse to strengthen the Dallas franchise, their business, political and charitable involvement in Dallas had fueled a continuing hope among the other ABA owners that someday their interest could be enlivened. In the late spring of 1973, they stunned the ABA world by agreeing to an unusual business arrangement—leasing the Chaparrals for $1 a year for three years to a group of San Antonio businessmen with the option to buy or return the team to Dallas at the end of the three year term.

The San Antonio optionees had been organized by Angelo Drossos, whose business career had consisted of dabbling in the stock market, promoting boxers and boxing matches, buying and selling restaurants, bars and automobiles. Drossos' partner was B.J. "Red" McCombs, a then-46 year old entrepreneur who had assimilated one of Texas's largest automobile dealerships and begun organizing a group of radio stations known as Clear Channel Communications. McCombs was an interesting character who had begun his car-selling business in Corpus Christi. At the age of 25 he owned one dealership, but by the mid-1960s in southwest Texas, virtually any make of car one wanted could be purchased from a Red McCombs dealership and virtually every city in Texas contained a radio station owned by Clear Channel Communications. While Drossos and McCombs enjoyed a satisfactory reputation of business acumen, their combined wealth wasn't 1/50th of Folsom's ownership group. Of greater concern was the city of San Antonio itself. In 1973, San Antonio, Texas was to Dallas what the Sahara Desert was to an oasis.

Faced with a seemingly intractable set of problems, as usual, the young Colonel ownership acted. Bill DeWitt was the son of a prominent sports-personage in Cincinnati and St. Louis, and Brian Heekin's family-owned business in Cincinnati was one of the nation's major canning companies, The Heekin Can Company. They had quietly organized Cincinnati Sports, Inc.[214] In early June, 1973, within a month after the Chaparrals $1 lease with buy options to San Antonio interests, an announcement was made in Cincinnati by Heekin and reported by Byron Crawford of Louisville's WHAS Radio. The Kentucky Colonels fans and all of Louisville were stunned. The press release read as follows: "We have entered into a contract of purchase with the Kentucky Colonels, and while this is sort of an interim time, we are still negotiating with a group in Louisville to perhaps purchase the Colonels back or come into our group for some percentage of ownership, with the hope for conclusion that the greater majority of the games continue to be played in Louisville and some of the games to be played in Cincinnati."

The action had been quiet and quick. But there remained a rather large and looming problem. Issel's contract provided for his prior written consent to any sale or transfer of the team. There were two reasons for this provision: in the ABA, Issel only wanted to play in Louisville for the Colonels and his contract had been personally guaranteed by the five Louisvillians who owned the team. Issel's prior written consent to the sale had not been obtained.

For years many NBA teams had been seeking Issel. His contract provisions were no secret within the NBA. As a result of the Colonels surprise sale, calls began arriving from throughout the NBA, including a new and intriguing entry—the New York Knicks. The Knicks were the reigning NBA champions and there was a nagging concern about whether their center, Willis Reed, had suffered what appeared to be a career-ending injury in the NBA playoffs. With Issel in a Knicks uniform, along with guards Henry Bibby, Earl "the Pearl" Monroe and Dick "Skull" Barnett and forwards, Bill Bradley, Dave Debussschere and Jerry Lucas—even without Reed, the Knicks would remain virtually unbeatable. If the Colonels sale had actually taken place without Issel's consent, his contract had been clearly breached and he was a free agent. The Knicks wanted his services immediately and were willing to go to court to defend their and his actions in contracting with the Knicks.

A significant drama of rather large dimensions was unfolding.

Colonels re-purchased and returned to Louisville

Apparently, prior to the team's purchase Heekin and DeWitt had not examined the Colonels players contracts. Upon learning of Issel's contract provision, they were ashen. For sure, they wanted to own the Colonels but, to them, the Colonels meant Dan Issel. They were told, point blank, if the team was sold to Cincinnati interests, Issel would jump leagues to the NBA.

Intense around-the-clock negotiations were convened by John Y. Brown, Jr. to assure that Issel would stay with the Colonels if he re-purchased the team from Cincinnati Sports, Inc. Eventually an agreement was reached between Issel and Brown and a limited partnership was formed to repurchase the team. It was called Kentucky Colonels, Ltd.

A press conference was held on July 7, 1973. The shareholders of Cincinnati Sports, Inc. sold their controlling interest in the Colonels to Kentucky Colonels, Ltd., retaining a 40% limited partnership interest. The Gregorys joined as limited partners, increasing their ownership interest from 3% to 7 1/2%. Eleanor D. (Ellie) Brown, wife of John Y. Brown, Jr. owned 52 1/2% of Kentucky Colonels, Ltd. and became the general partner of the limited partnership. Her first act—the formation of an all-female board of directors—was announced at New York's Club 21, led by Billie Claire Kurfees, past president of the Younger Woman's Club of Louisville, Patsy Baker, president of the Younger Woman's Club, Faith Lyles, a prominent Louisville television hostess, Sissy Jenkins and Mary Baird, immediate past presidents of the Junior League. John Y. Brown stated: "These women are basketball fans and women amount to almost fifty percent of the sport's attendance, nationwide. Women are the most unused talent and resource in American industry today. We hope to present a program where they can broaden Colonel ticket sales substantially. The men have had their chance at it. Now it will be interesting to watch the women with this new undertaking. Who knows — we might be watching style shows or ballets at half-time. But whatever, it will be their show and team."

Interestingly included as an aside, the last paragraph of the carefully-crafted three page press release announced: "Dan Issel has signed a new three year extension to his remaining two year contract with the Colonels. Issel said, 'I look forward to playing the rest of my career with the Kentucky Colonels.'"

The prior written consent provision remained in Issel's contract and the now-Addendum III to his contract further mandated that any new owner of the Colonels would be required to play a minimum of 50% of the team's games in Louisville.

John Y. and Ellie Brown assume the battle
To rekindle fan interest in the Colonels, re-enter the religion and its

high priest. Ellie and John Y. Brown hired Adolph Rupp as the team Vice President. Rupp's imprimatur added additional credibility for the Colonels with the religion's UK parishioners. The all-female board of directors took the Colonels message out into the state. Up and down I-65 from Louisville to Bowling Green and back-and-forth along I-64 from Louisville to Lexington and from Louisville to Cincinnati along I-71 these intrepid ladies traveled with Adolph Rupp. The net result was spectacular—a near doubling of the team's season ticket sales. Other steps became necessary.

Three years prior, when the five young businessmen purchased the Colonels, they wanted a day-to-day manager to operate the venture in a businesslike fashion based on business principles. Mike Storen jumped at the opportunity, leaving the Indiana Pacers to become the Colonels general manager. As the Pacer's general manager, he had broadly promoted himself within the league (and beyond) as being singularly responsible for the team's early success. Storen was one of those people you run across in life who was fully capable of taking credit for virtually anything. He even bragged that it was his idea to pursue Dan Issel, when in reality the negotiation of the first Issel contract was undertaken exclusively with the new owners. The rumor had been passed that he "found" Frank Ramsey to coach the Colonels and he also reportedly discovered Artis Gilmore. Someone once joked, it was likely that if Storen had been a few years older, he might have taken credit for the parting of the Red Sea.

At the time, former UK Fabulous Five star, Alex Groza, worked in the Colonels front office. From Groza an interesting secret was learned about Storen. You could always tell when Storen was (to put it politely) fabricating —he wouldn't look at you. Instead, his eyes shifted to the corner where the wall met the ceiling. Apparently it was a long-running joke around the front office. It became very helpful, once. While negotiating with Storen for the extension of a player contract, he was asked if the dollars on the table were the Colonels "final" number, because if they were the free agent player was going to pursue offers from other teams. With a start his eyes went from his yellow pad to the corner of the ceiling and he said, "Yes, it's our best and last offer." Two days later, Louie Dampier signed his final contract with the Colonels. Later, when the occasion was shared with Groza, he roared with laughter.

Mike Storen simply hadn't fit in. Many of the players didn't like him, nor did the front office personnel. Storen aptly perceived that his influence with the franchise was being challenged by the Colonels all-female board of directors and the hiring of Adolph Rupp. He objected, profusely, but he had overstepped his bounds by privately challenging the wives of some of the most prominent Louisville business leaders. To make matters worse, he had placed himself in opposition with the religion's high priest, Adolph Rupp. There was no way to win such a battle. Storen's objections were rejected. He resigned. Everyone seemed happier, instantly. More changes were afoot.

The second coach of the Colonels, Gene Rhodes, highly admired locally, became the team's new general manager. Replacing Mullaney as coach was Babe McCarthy, the dean of ABA coaches. Before his tenure in the league, McCarthy had coached Mississippi State to a 169-85 record, winning or sharing four SEC championships—a unique achievement during Adolph Rupp's reign at UK. In the ABA's original season, he had coached a 48-30 record out of the New Orleans Buccaneers, losing to the Pittsburgh Pipers in the 7th game of the league championship. His nickname was "Ol' Magnolia Mouth," bequeathed him due to his southern-drawled witticisms. In defeat, his players were cajoled with, "My old pappy used to tell me the sun don't shine on the same dog's butt every day." Once when his team was on the verge of blowing out a game, he encouraged it by saying, "Now, let's cloud up and rain all over 'em." Babe McCarthy was a true classic.

Meanwhile, down in San Antonio the Spurs new owners Angelo Drossos and Red McCombs were quickly proving the former young Colonels ownership to have been in error over their concern about San Antonio as a basketball market. Coach Tom Nissaulke began winning with an exciting brand of basketball. With attendance nearly tripling by mid-season, Drossos and McCombs made their move, investing $1 million into the franchise. Using that money, they exercised their option to purchase the Spurs for $725,000 and used another $225,000 to acquire George Gervin from Earl Foreman's Virginia Squires. Mike Storen, the new-ABA Commissioner, rescinded the sale. Eventually, a federal court granted the Spurs a permanent injunction, finding Storen had no authority to rescind Gervin's sale. From that point forward, the San Antonio Spurs became a credible ABA power and George Gervin would average over 25 points per game during the remainder of his ABA (and eventual NBA) career—all capped by his selection into the Naismith Basketball Hall of Fame.

With McCarthy at the helm, the Colonels regular season record of 53-

31 continued to be inspiring and the attendance stabilized at an average of 8,201 per game. But when playoff time arrived, the Colonels had no answer for the now fully-grown phenomenon, Julius Erving. Dr. J had taken his aerial act from the Virginia Squires to the Big Apple and Roy Boe's New York Nets. In addition to Erving was the leaper, Larry Kenon, center Billy Paulz from Duke and guard John Williamson. Boe hired NBA veteran Kevin Loughery to replace Lou Carnesecca as coach. The new Nets were unbeatable. The Colonels lost four in a row. Winning 73% of their final 70 regular season games and only losing two playoff games, the Nets became the ABA champion.

Urgency arrives — the Championship follows

Pressure from the NBA prevented the ABA's national TV contract from being renewed. The clout of the NBA was proving awesome. Even without a national TV contract, the ABA star players were no longer a bunch of ragtag Athenians.[215] Urgency surrounded the Colonels franchise as the fans were demanding a championship. What else could or should be done to win a championship?

Prior to the 1974-75 season, suffering from poor health, Ol' Magnolia Mouth resigned and New Yorker Hubie Brown was hired as the seventh (and final) coach of the Colonels. Brown accepted the daunting task of creating a championship, with few requirements beyond insisting on coaching freedom to tinker with the Colonels style of play. There would be rigid, time-sensitive player substitutions. Everyone would agree to and understand their part of the puzzle, with their individual skills being captured into the game plan. Every conceivable player performance record was written in notebooks. Following each game, the statistical results were computed and recorded. No longer would Gilmore just post up near the basket, he would move in an intricate series of patterns. No longer would Issel average 27 points a game. He, too, would move in the pattern, pass and become a far more complete player.

In the early stages of the season, the change would be difficult for Issel. The natives were restless, longing to see "Issel Missiles" rain down upon Colonels opponents—and the Colonels weren't winning as regularly. Hubie Brown persevered. Gradually, the Colonels gelled. With Issel taking fewer but better shots and Gilmore becoming almost impossible to guard, and because of the motion offense Brown installed, victories began to occur in bundles. The Colonels tied Dr. J's Nets for the regular season division championship with 56-26 season records. The division championship was decided by a one-game playoff at Freedom Hall. It was won by the Colonels 108-99. The Colonels stormed their way to the ABA championship series.

Into Freedom Hall to compete for the ABA championship strode the Colonels' hated enemy—the Indiana Pacers. After winning three of the first four games, on May 22, 1975, before a capacity crowd, Gilmore's hook shot sealed the Colonels victory (110-105). The Kentucky Colonels had won the ABA championship. It was an amazing night—the roof came off the place. The towering Gilmore had scored 28 points and grabbed an astonishing 31 rebounds. In the five game series Issel averaged 22.6 points a game and 77,174 fans in Indianapolis and Louisville had witnessed the victory cup being transferred from the Indianapolis to Louisville in one of the then-great rivalries in professional basketball. For those who weren't born then—close your eyes and picture UK (as it did once) or UofL winning the NCAA championship at Freedom Hall—that's the best way to describe an otherwise indescribable evening.

For the Kentucky Colonels it was redemption. Twice in the previous four seasons they had lost the final ABA championship game. It was being asked: Are the Colonels chokers? The answer came that spring of 1975. The Colonels and their coach, Hubie Brown, were awesome, winning 22 of their last 25 regular season games and 12 of 15 playoff games to reach the finals and then demolishing the Pacers. At the time, it was described as one of the great runs in professional basketball history. The Colonels had reached the pinnacle.

When you're at the top, there's only one way to go—down.

Good-Bye Big Dan: The beginning of the end of the Kentucky Colonels [216]

The summer of 1975 was one of unrequited joy for the ABA champion Colonels. It was particularly joyous for Issel and his family; all the fame, success and glory he had achieved had not included a national championship until the Colonels won the ABA. Dan and Cheri had moved into a new white-columned home on Wolf Pen Trace in eastern Louisville. It had been built and designed to fit Dan, with higher than normal ceilings and doorways—the home of the young family's dreams. He had formed Dan

Issel Real Estate & Management Company that owned three large upscale Louisville apartment projects, and as a result of his re-negotiated contract with John Y. Brown, owned a 55% interest in the New Orleans Ollie's Trolley hamburger franchise (with Brown owning the remaining 45%). Since his collegiate days in Lexington, Issel had been mesmerized by horses and horse racing. For him it was more than a pastime. Busily planning his second career as a thoroughbred and harness horse owner, Issel religiously studied *The Racing Form* with the same determination given to his basketball career. The object—to learn and understand the complexities and intrigue of thoroughbred breeding. Several thoroughbreds had been purchased in partnership with then-prominent Lexington breeder, Tom Gentry,[217] as well as several harness horses. After the sale/re-purchase of the Colonels by John Y. and Ellie Brown and the 1974-75 championship season, the Issels had every reason to believe that Louisville and Kentucky would be their permanent home.

On Friday evening September 19, 1975, Dan, Cheri and their two year-old daughter, Sheridan, went to Louisville Downs, Louisville's harness racing track, for a family evening at the races.

There's an old adage—the trouble with the present is that the future always changes. That evening Dan Issel, his family and Louisville were about to find that old adage coming true. The passage of time would reveal that the next twenty-two days dramatically damaged Louisville's NBA odyssey. All hell was about to break loose.

September 19, 1975 /to/ October 11, 1975 [218]

At approximately 7:15 PM Issel called me from Louisville Downs. He had been paged over the loud-speaker with an emergency phone call. Such a paged phone call is always unnerving. Fears of health or life emergencies rush through one's mind on the way to the first available phone. Issel was no different. With concern and trepidation, he found a phone. The call was from Ellie Brown, advising him that arrangements had been made to sell his player contract to a team called the Baltimore Claws. Stunned, Issel reminded her that the contract required his prior written consent for any trade or sale. Apparently unaware of that provision, Ellie handed the phone to her husband. Issel got no satisfaction from John Y. other than an admission that he had not received Issel's prior written consent. My home phone was adjacent to the television. As Issel described the events to me, a trailer under the TV picture read: "News alert: Colonel Dan Issel traded to Baltimore Claws, details at 11:00 PM." In light of the fast-moving events, I suggested that Dan bring his family to my home to avoid the press.

They arrived at 8:00 PM. The next three hours were spent discussing the ramifications of the events upon his career and family along with his options. "Who are the Baltimore Claws?" Issel asked. Less than a month prior, the Memphis TAMS,[219] an abysmal franchise, had been sold to a group of Baltimore businessmen headed by David Cohan. The plan was to transfer it to Baltimore for the upcoming season. The best that could be determined that evening was that Cohan was a rock concert promoter in the Chesapeake Bay/Baltimore area. The 11:00 news led with the Issel sale story. Apparently the sale had actually taken place—in complete violation of Issel's contract. At that point only one thing was clear; we knew we were in for a long evening.

The Issel family agreed to stay at my home that evening. To go to sleep, Sheridan needed a pacifier. Dan wanted some beer. Neither being available, Issel accompanied me to the local Convenient Food Mart. I was dressed in bermuda shorts, a golf shirt and possessed a Nixonesque five o'clock shadow. After gathering the needed items and preparing to pay for them, a classic observation was made by the check-out person: "Mr. Miller, I don't know what kind of party you're going to, but it looks interesting!" Upon returning to the car and telling Dan of the comment, it was pleasing to see his enigmatic dry wit and sense of humor was still present. He roared with laughter.

With Sheridan and Cheri asleep, between 11:45 PM and 1:00 AM the next morning, we got down to serious discussion. While litigation was an option, Issel decided it was the last option. In categorizing those options, Dan determined he owed it to himself and his family to meet with the Claws ownership to at least see what they had to offer. Air flight time schedules to Baltimore and Washington, D.C. were obtained.

For the next twenty-two days, the Issels were subjected to a dizzying array of meetings, sleepless nights and red-eyed airplane trips. The comedy of errors was endless. While attending pre-season practice with the Baltimore Claws and awaiting the ultimate decisions about his career, Issel's Baltimore hotel reservation was canceled (no one ever knew why), Mike Curtis, an All-NFL linebacker with the Baltimore Colts was 'tire-ironed' and robbed in Issel's hotel parking lot, leaving considerable concern about the security of the hotel; a law suit and injunction against the Browns was prepared; a

Jefferson circuit court judge was readied as was the Jefferson circuit court clerk for a midnight filing, events eventually coming within several hours of the lawsuit's filing.

When John and Ellie Brown refused to reconsider their decision, negotiations began with Lee Silverman, Cohan's legal counsel, who had no authority and didn't know where he could find Cohan! Finally Cohan appeared in Louisville on September 24th. One of the age-old adages is "Don't judge the book by its cover." So I didn't, despite the fact that Cohan looked like Uncle Fester of the Munsters. Being reasonably sure his mother loved him, I was reminded of my father's observation when describing a less than attractive person—"Looks like he was made with some bad clay."

Finally, after twelve days of bi-city negotiations between Baltimore/Louisville with Cohan's Claws (jokingly referred to later as the Baltimore "Clause") an agreement was reached. Issel's signing by the Baltimore Claws was announced after a Colts/Raiders game at a dinner in the Pimlico Hotel, hosted by Cohan (but it seemed like few of the hundreds there knew who Cohan was). There were still two problems. "Uncle Fester" hadn't paid Brown his $700,000 sales price, and Issel's first Claws paycheck bounced.

On October 2nd, Denver Nuggets general manager, Carl Scheer, and coach, Larry Brown, called wanting Issel—immediately. After five days of negotiation between Scheer, Brown and me, at 3:45 AM on October 7, 1975, an across-the-board agreement had been reached. Issel's sale to the Baltimore Claws had been rescinded and he was a Denver Nugget, provided John Y. Brown's money (reduced to $550,000) was wired the next morning. It was, with Issel's sale from the Claws to the Denver Nuggets being announced in Louisville at 2:00 PM on the day after my 35th birthday, October 8, 1975. Brown pleaded with me to take him off the hook. I did.

The next morning the Issels and I left on a United Airlines flight, transferring in Chicago and arriving in Denver at 11:00 AM Denver time. With a few additions to the Claws agreement, Issel became a Nugget. After sharing a quiet dinner with the relieved Issel family at Denver's Stromberg's Restaurant, I flew back to Louisville and Issel flew to Oakland for an exhibition game, his first in a Nugget uniform.

At the time, there was no way to comprehend the enormous significance of those twenty-two days in September and early October of 1975. But on the flight back to Louisville, I was overcome with a feeling of despondence, unhappiness and unease. For sure, a dear and really special friend and his family had left Louisville to ply his career and spend their lives elsewhere. Another city would now become the beneficiary of a remarkable man and his family. Whatever was to happen, there was little question about one thing—a major chapter of the Kentucky Colonels history had ended.

During the next decade Dan Issel would play in nearly 1,100 games in a Nuggets uniform, giving 100% every moment and only missing 12 games, for which he was nicknamed "The Horse." He would be selected to the Colorado Athletic Hall of Fame, the Colorado Athlete of the Decade (1970s) and retire from the Nuggets with 27,482 points (including his ABA figures) as the then-fourth leading scorer in the history of the NBA. Seven years later he would receive the highest honor of his profession—membership in the Naismith Basketball Hall of Fame. And as the muse of history would indelibly etch on her granite tablet, thus began the first 22 days of the Kentucky Colonels death-march.

At the NBA All-Star game dinner in Milwaukee, the year after the ABA/ NBA merger, I enjoyed the honor of sitting at a table with *The Sporting News* columnist Jim O'Brien. He was the unquestioned guru of ABA columnists. Issel had been selected on the first post-merger NBA All-Star team. As the conversation turned to Issel, O'Brien inquired about Issel's sale to the Claws, then the Nuggets. Following my lawyer-like circumspect response, O'Brien made what would eventually be a rather prescient observation, characterizing the Issel sale by Brown as the third dumbest sale in the history of American professional sports. In O'Brien's mind Babe Ruth's sale from the Red Sox to the Yankees was unparalleled and would never be equalled as #1 on the "dumbest" list. O'Brien couldn't determine what the second dumbest sale was (but he was sure there had to be one that was dumber than the Issel's), so Issel's sale got the number three position on the list.

Considering the splendor that was to occur in Denver during Issel's professional basketball career there, in the context of the damage his sale brought upon major league professional basketball in Louisville and Kentucky, Jim O'Brien's opinion could gather considerable support among sports historians.

Gilmore-led Colonels

The Colonels' fans were utterly outraged with the loss of Issel. Two nurses even called from the Kosair Children's Hospital volunteering to organize a public demonstration. Apparently, Issel had frequented the hospital and had done many unpublicized favors for the children. Of all the things that I've participated in over the years that generated public comment, there isn't a single one that brought forth more. The volume of phone calls and letters was staggering. Daniel Paul Issel had become, and deservedly so, a hero to Kentuckians and Louisvillians.

John Y. Brown did his best to quiet the disaffection. Trades and swaps abounded. In the dispersal draft of the San Diego Sails, Brown acquired the All-Star center, Caldwell Jones. When Jones didn't fit into the playing scheme with Gilmore, he was traded to the Spirits of St. Louis for Maurice Lucas. Then came a trade of Colonels forward, Marvin Roberts, to the Virginia Squires for Johnny Newman and Jan Van Breda Kolff.

As the 1975-76 season advanced, the Colonels began to gel with the magnificent coaching of Hubie Brown. The regular season concluded with a record of 46-38 with an average attendance of 6,935—a huge drop. However, a season-ending victory run caused hopes to emerge for a successful defense of their ABA championship. With the hated Pacers being defeated in the first round, the semifinals for the league's championship presented the Kentucky Colonels with their final *coup de grace*—the Denver Nuggets, led by the Colonels' beloved Dan Issel and the new rookie phenomenon, David Thompson. It was a dramatic seven-game series, won by the Nuggets. Issel (at 6-9) was so keyed up that he would outjump Colonels center, Artis Gilmore, in the final game's opening tip. Gilmore later smilingly said to me, "Bruce, who said slow white guys can't jump!"

Though neither Artis nor I nor anyone else realized it at the time, there would never, ever, be another Kentucky Colonels game.

One shining and unforgettable moment

On Sunday afternoon, May 13, 1976, the ABA championship game was nationally-televised by NBC. The Nuggets rookie star David Thompson scored 42 points and the transplanted Colonel, Issel, bagged 20 rebounds to go with his 30 points. Despite this incredible talent display, few will remember this last ABA game ever played. It was, in reality, just another game, lost for the ages.

But the ninth and final ABA All-Star Game, played five months earlier on January 27, 1976 at the same Denver McNichols Arena will be remembered. It was the *sine qua non* of showcases. The NBA All-Star Game was always a dull, half-day event—but not the ABA All-Star Game. That year there was a week-long soirée that included parades, dinners and concerts by Glenn Campbell and Charlie Rich. The celebration was orchestrated to mask the dire straits of the ABA. The ninth (and last) ABA season had begun with ten teams, but by the All-Star break, the teams were reduced to seven.[220] With so few teams, the league decided that the entire Denver Nugget team would play the All-Stars from the remaining six teams—unusual, but workable. In an effort to divine how more tickets might be sold, Denver general manager Carl Scheer and ABA finance director Jim Keeler brainstormed. It had to be something dramatic that would grab the attention of the NBA, America's basketball fans and showcase the talent, star quality and greatness of the ABA's star players. What was it to be? The answer—a slam dunk contest—an atypical ABA moment and a stroke of genius.

The contestants were 7-2 Colonel Artis Gilmore; 6-7 George Gervin and 6-9 Larry Kenon of the San Antonio Spurs; Nuggets rookie, 6-4 David Thompson, and 6-7 Julius Erving of the Nets. There were no more colorful or explosive basketball players on the planet. The arena announcer was the Nuggets' Al Albert, the younger and less inhibited brother of the NBA's Marv Albert. The festivities were scheduled to occur at halftime. As the appointed time approached, Albert advised the fans that the dunks would be judged on artistic ability, imagination and crowd response. The ABA fanatics in Denver that evening had a premonition of what was about to happen—they had witnessed this collection of unearthly talent for several seasons—but the world outside the ABA had not. After the preliminary dunk-offs, the finalists were pared down to Thompson and Dr. J.

Thompson began with his patented windmill cuff slam. It was matched by Erving, who stood under the basket, held two balls like grapefruit and simultaneously dunked them both—in one jump. Then Thompson offered a two-handed jackknife reverse, which was mimed with equal flourish by Erving. Time for the last dunk. There was a rule—one of the three dunks had to begin by a jump at the bottom of the free throw circle. Thompson executed the first recorded 360 degree spinning dunk (later emulated by Darrell Griffith at UofL) by a running jump with the jump starting from the bottom of the free throw circle. Woooosh went the ball, and the hometown Denver fans erupted for David Thompson. The sound was deafening. Surely, this fan response would be a catalyst for his victory.

But now it was the Doctor's turn. What was to follow was one of the most dramatic things I have ever seen at a sporting event.

Erving walked to the free-throw line and began measuring his steps in long strides back to mid-court. All 17,798 in McNichols Arena stood. It was electric. It was a moment that others who witnessed it have said was a frozen moment in time. With confidence and quiet concentration, Dr. J turned around just past mid-court—paused—the crowd hushed—then began dribbling toward the basket with his long loping strides, reaching full speed at the free-throw line, from which he jumped, holding the red-white-blue ball in his right hand high over his head, and with his right arm fully extended easily dunked with a resounding flourish. No one could believe what they had just seen. Julius Erving had leaped and sailed to the basket five feet farther than had Thompson. No human being could possibly dribble a basketball at full speed, broad-jump 15 feet, reach toward a basket 10 feet in the air with the ball held in one hand like an orange, and casually dunk it. But Dr. J. did. Following the feat, there was a several-second pause as the crowd took in what had just happened, then there was an explosion of awed cheering and applause. Erving had done something that wouldn't be seen again for more than a decade, and then Michael Jordan could only match it, not exceed it.

The next morning, the most widely-watched morning television show, NBC's Today Show, featured a tape rerun of the Thompson/Erving slam dunk contest, and all America saw it. That evening, twenty-four hours after the event, another rerun of the drama was the lead-in for NBC News.

Within several months, the merger occurred. There are those who believed at the time that this single event mandated a merger; the NBA could not afford to allow this skill level to exist outside its environment. While I'm aware of no NBA or ABA official ever admitting that Dr. J's high-wire act that January afternoon in 1976 clinched the merger. But if a clincher was needed, that was it, without a doubt.

ABA—*sine die*

Prior to the start of the ABA's final season, the league had hired former New York Knicks star, Dave DeBusschere, as its commissioner. It was hoped his NBA connections would facilitate a merger. It has been written that before the season the Denver Nuggets and New York Nets secretly asked Colonels owner Brown to join them in a private request to become NBA expansion teams. Reportedly the NBA was willing to expand but required a fee of $6.15 million per team. It has also been written that Brown rejected the opportunity.[221] While Brown has consistently denied this overture, over time it was confirmed by Larry O'Brien during my later discussions with him in 1978, Denver's Carl Scheer and several old-line NBA owners.

During the final ABA year, the expansion/merger efforts continued. The ABA's public relations director, Jim Bukata, has reportedly said that the ABA made an offer for six of their teams join the NBA (Denver, San Antonio, Indiana, New Jersey Nets, Spirit of St. Louis and the Colonels), but the NBA didn't want Kentucky or St. Louis. Bukata has said that Brown was willing to move the Colonels to Cincinnati and St. Louis would move to Hartford, Connecticut, if they would be admitted. According to Bukata, the offer was refused by the NBA because the Bulls owners, the Wirtzes, wanted Gilmore and couldn't get him unless the Colonels folded and the Celtics didn't want a team in their geographic area of Hartford.[222] Brown has also denied this rendition, which denial was later confirmed in my discussions with Larry O'Brien and Bull's co-owner, Bill Wirtz.

During the last twenty-five years, basically everyone involved has denied any culpability in or direct responsibility for the Colonels extinction. The closest rendition of the truth I've ever been able to ascertain was that the financial aspects of the several NBA merger proposals were terrible and Brown had become fed up with it all believing he had a better deal in the wings (to be discussed later).

Regardless of what the truth really is, thirteen months after the Colonels won their first and only ABA championship, eight months after Brown's catastrophic Issel sale to the Baltimore Claws and four months after the incredible slam-dunk contest, four ABA owners[223] surreptitiously completed their negotiations with NBA commissioner Larry O'Brien and his new outside counsel, a then-35 year old David Stern, in Hyannis, Massachusetts.

In the end the NBA insisted that only four ABA teams would be accepted. The Colonels were excluded, even though the Colonels owner, John Y. Brown, was the only ABA owner who didn't need to borrow money to meet the financial requirements of the merger.[224] In essence, the deal called for the "expansion" (the NBA refused to call it a merger) of the four ABA teams into the NBA with the remaining teams to be folded. It was up to the ABA to deal with its two folding teams. The ABA expansion teams were each required to pay the NBA $3.2 million within ninety days and were denied television money for the first three seasons and participation in the first NBA draft. The player contracts of the four ABA teams entering the NBA became NBA player contracts with the Colonel and Spirit of St. Louis player contracts being placed in a dispersal draft. Additionally, the court approved the settlement of the Robertson/Bradley antitrust case by simply modifying the reserve clause and agreeing to pay former NBA players an aggregate of $4,300,000 over 8 years, all of which made Robertson/Bradley happy.[225]

June 17, 1976 — the approval of the Merger

Now the whole thing had to be approved by the ABA owners. John Y. Brown had publicly voiced his displeasure with the four ABA owners, who in clandestine fashion had operated behind his back. At his request, I undertook some complimentary legal research to develop the legal theories that might be at issue. With one change of clothing and several briefcases of documents and papers, I joined Brown in Chicago for the ultimate (and final) ABA meeting. Having never been in an airplane with Brown, I remember my surprise about his fear of flying. Here was a guy who'd made multi-millions and traveled the world in private and public jets for years. But as the plane rose from Louisville's airport on that calm June afternoon for a short hour-long flight to Chicago, he gripped the seat arm until his fingers were white with intensity.

The meeting was scheduled for the O'Hare Regency Hyatt Hotel, immediately accessible to the Chicago airport. We walked to the hotel and checked in. Less than an hour remained before the meeting was to begin. After freshening up Brown and I went to the second floor meeting room. The ABA owners and their lawyers were collected. We were the last to arrive. I would be less than candid if I didn't admit that the fifteen minute late arrival was designed. As we entered the room, tension was literally bouncing off the walls. It was 7:00 PM central daylight time. The body language in the room left no question, this was going to be a long night—and that it was.

The ABA renegade owners began by explaining their agreement with NBA Commissioner O'Brien. Denver's Carl Scheer initiated the discussion followed by Angelo Drossos of the Spurs. Scheer's personality and presentation were more staccato in style than Drossos', who was the kind of guy who wanted to be everyone's friend. The order of their presentations was clearly orchestrated. First, the hard facts; then upon them the Drossos chocolate syrup would be poured.

It was also clear that the leaders of the four renegade franchises were Denver and San Antonio. The Pacers' representatives said little and Roy Boe said nothing. Boe wasn't enamored with the merger deal because it treated his Nets far more harshly than the others. The Nets played on Long Island within the territorial rights area of the New York Knicks. As a result of the territorial prerogative, Boe was required to pay the Knicks an additional $4.5 million. This add-on was devastating to Boe's wallet and the Nets.[226] Boe couldn't afford the $4.5 million premium and later had to sell Erving to the Philadelphia 76ers to survive financially. Without Dr. J. the Nets would only win 22 games in the first year after the merger, and were later required to pick up stakes and move to New Jersey. When Drossos and Scheer finished their presentation, the floor was open. John Y. Brown seized it immediately.

After admonishing the four rebel owners for agreeing to the secret deal, Brown suggested what he considered to be a far better arrangement that, in his opinion, would cost less money and accomplish the same objective by the following playing season. Brown opined that unless all ABA teams were involved, the NBA expansion offer should be rejected and the ABA should expand to a full 10 teams, immediately. He had contacted wealthy individuals in other cities, including Minneapolis, Washington, D.C. and Ft. Lauderdale and they had expressed interest in quickly forming new ABA teams. Then, with 10 teams Brown felt that instead of asking for money from a national TV network, the ABA teams ought to take $1 million each and pay a network $10 million to put the league on national television directly opposite every televised NBA game. The theory was that the ABA talent level was so superior that in the following season the NBA would welcome the entire ABA, with open arms. Preliminary contacts with major network executives allowed Brown to believe there was significant interest in such a proposal.

The four ABA renegade teams rejected Brown's proposal outright. Two of them stated their bankers would call their notes and not permit another season unless they joined the NBA. This meant that there would be no ABA, and without the ABA's existence, its teams' legal entitlement to the contract rights of their players was questionable with the likelihood of the loss of enormous contract dollar value. There was to be no negotiating with Brown, television networks, or anyone. The ABA was clearly *sine die*.

By now it was 9:00 PM and John Y. was just getting started. Under no circumstances did he intend to accept a pre-arranged disposition of players that were legally contracted to play for his team. Since he wasn't party to the

NBA deal, Brown had no contractual privity with the NBA, and couldn't be legally bound by the renegades' agreement regarding his players. Therefore, to avoid further litigation, the disloyal ABA teams would have to purchase the Colonels players contracts from Brown. And since there was to be no negotiation about the number of teams entering the NBA, there wouldn't be any negotiation about the price Brown would set for the purchase of his players, either. His position was supported by my legal research. Brown had taken the departing ABA owners aback. The meeting adjourned for several hours, while the renegades conferred with their lawyers, their bankers and each other.

At midnight, they returned, in disagreeable agreement with Brown's legal position. They had no choice but to purchase the Colonels' player contracts from Brown, which would then be submitted to the NBA dispersal draft of ABA players.

The next question was—how much would Brown's players cost the renegades? Brown demanded $3 million, take it or leave it. If they didn't accept his demand, he would go to court and prevent the dispersal draft of his players that had been negotiated without his permission or agreement. For the second time during the evening, Brown had left them with no choice. They were beyond simply being irate. Having been born and raised in Louisville's Schnitzelburg, I thought I had heard (and spoken) every known curse word, but in the following ten minutes I learned a few more. The meeting adjourned for another hour or so, while their bankers were consulted to determine if they could obtain the requisite letters of credit to meet Brown's demand. They did.

At 1:30 the next morning Brown retired to his room. I spent the rest of the all-night stand in the hotel's offices with Scheer and Nuggets part owner/counsel, Gary Antonoff, typing the ultimate agreement on hotel stationery. We were finished by daybreak with the only matters remaining being everyone's signature and the acknowledgement of the transfer of funds to Brown's account.

At the time it was widely thought that Brown's negotiating ploy in picking up a check for $3 million and his subsequent (and virtually immediate) purchase of the NBA Buffalo Braves for only $1.5 million was a world-class business deal, because he became an NBA owner without paying the $3.2 million that saddled the renegade ABA teams; and since he owned an NBA team he shared, immediately, in the NBA television revenue *and* the player draft.

However, as events have borne out since, Brown's deal took a far back seat to the one struck that evening by the two New York businessmen who owned the Spirit of St. Louis. Instead of asking, as did Brown, for immediate and full cash on the table, Ozzie and Dan Silna agreed to receive 1/7th of all future television money that would be received by the ABA teams joining the NBA, in perpetuity.[227] At that time this seemed like a bad deal, since the NBA television package was minute, amounting annually to about $700,000 per team, and the ABA teams weren't to receive any television revenue for three years. The value of the Silna's deal was about $100,000 per year and wouldn't begin for several years. But after Stern became its Commissioner and with the arrival of Magic, Bird and Jordan, the NBA's national and international television rights increased exponentially—as did the value of the Silna's deal. It is believed that since that night in the Chicago O'Hare Regency Hyatt, the Silna's have received between $175 and $225 million dollars from their deal, without ever playing the first NBA game or incurring the first cent of liability or financial exposure. They and their families will receive this emolument in perpetuity.

On June 17, 1976, nearly thirty years ago, after that vituperative all-night meeting in a Chicago airport hotel conference room, the ABA was folded and the magic was lost for Kentucky.

During the life of the ABA, the Kentucky Colonels had won more games (448) than any team in the league, including the four that merged into the NBA. The Colonels were recognized across the nation as the class of the ABA. They easily co-existed in Freedom Hall with UofL. During the nine seasons prior to the Colonels existence, records reflect[228] that UofL's basketball team averaged 6,685 patrons per game, but during the Colonels nine year era, it averaged 12,200 fans per game—nearly a 100% increase. During the Colonels existence and playing in post-season tournaments every year, UofL recruited six players that became All-Americans.[229] Their won-loss record was 198-61 for a 77% winning percentage, whereas in the prior nine years it was 143-94 or 61% and in the subsequent nine years it was 220-77, or 74%.[230] Meanwhile, UK continued with its dominance of the Southeastern Conference and pre-eminence in collegiate basketball.

Some have said that the ABA wasn't any good. But the record speaks for itself. In the first year after the merger:

- four of the top ten scorers in the NBA were from the ABA;[231]
- The Pacers' Don Buse led the NBA in steals and assists, with Moses Malone ranking third and Artis Gilmore fourth in rebound average;
- Denver won the NBA's Midwest Division with a record of 50-32, while leading the NBA in average attendance;
- the first NBA All-Star game after the merger found 1 of the 2 coaches[232] and 11 of the 22 players being previously affiliated with the ABA;[233]
- the first NBA finals, after the merger, found five (5) of the ten (10) starting players previously affiliated with the ABA;[234]
- from 1971-76, ABA/NBA exhibition games found the ABA teams with 79 wins and the NBA with 76 wins; and
- thirteen (13) ABA-involved individuals would enshrined in the Naismith Basketball Hall of Fame (and over time there will be more)[235]

For those who weren't around or alive between 1967-76 — that's what the ABA and the Kentucky Colonels were. Over those raucous nine years, the ABA had become the equivalent of the NBA (and many would argue it had exceeded the NBA) and the Kentucky Colonels, festooned with icons and stars from Kentucky's religion, had become all of Kentucky's team in the ultimate kids' game.

It was an electric time, full of energy, youthful exuberance and community pride. It was a time when some of the most outstanding men I've ever known wore a uniform emblazoned with the words, Kentucky Colonels—and they were worn in Louisville.

One can only wonder what Louisville would be like now if the Kentucky Colonels had carried its banner into the NBA, with Dan Issel traded back from Denver, joining Artis Gilmore and Louie Dampier, with Hubie Brown as their coach. But in one all-night-stand, they and the ABA were deposited on the scrap heap of major league sports history. It was all gone for Louisvillians and Kentuckians, leaving only the memory of a grand, wonderful, shining moment in the sun. Or was it the stars?

...When he shall die, Take him and cut him out in little stars, And he will make the face of heaven so fine That all the world will be in love with night, And pay no worship to the garish sun.

William Shakespeare

CHAPTER FIVE

Dinner With the High Priest

Each of us experience a few electric, unexpected and cathartic moments, which often evolve into a chapter in our life's book.

I had one nearly thirty years ago. It occurred on the evening of March 29, 1975—fifteen months before the ABA died and nearly twenty-five years before the final stages of Louisville's NBA odyssey. The occasion was the NCAA Final Four at the San Diego Sports Arena. The contestants were UCLA, UofL, UK and Syracuse. It was a drama-filled turning point in the history of collegiate basketball. John Wooden had announced his retirement as UCLA's coach. He had broken Adolph Rupp's records for winning national championships and supplanted his position as history's greatest collegiate basketball coach. Adding to the drama, UofL was coached by Wooden's former assistant, Denny Crum, and UK by Adolph Rupp's successor, Joe B. Hall. It was a typically beautiful, calm and mild San Diego Saturday evening. Mister A's, a steakhouse restaurant atop a ten-story (or so) building called The Fifth Avenue Financial Centre on the corner of Fifth and Laurel Streets, had been recommended by an Islandia Hyatt Hotel bellhop as a quiet retreat perfect for finding a good meal, a few adult beverages, conversation and a wonderful view of the setting sun—something Adolph always tried to do, as often as possible.[236]

On that night, Adolph Frederick Rupp and I had dinner. His pre-dinner soup—a cup of chili!

I had first met Coach Rupp in the early 1970s when my law firm managed the four-week Rupp-Issel-Pratt Basketball Camps for 5-12 year-old boys at Louisville's Bellarmine College. We had shared some bourbons and branch water along with some good conversation in his dorm room and at Bardstown Road's non-elegant Bambi Bar. He called me "The Shyster." At that time those moments had been a life's highlight — the opportunity to meet and share time with my childhood hero. Later, I had gotten to know him even better when he began working for the Kentucky Colonels. That weekend, I was in San Diego to sign representation contracts with several players on UK's and UofL's squads after they completed their collegiate careers. Adolph Rupp was there, because that's where a Hall of Fame collegiate coach wanted and was supposed to be.

The national news of the day overshadowed the NCAA finals—President Gerald Ford had signed an Executive Order ending registration for the draft. A noteworthy day, with an even more incredible night ahead—an occasion of bittersweet emotions and personal conflict mixed with grudgingly brutal honesty. It was one of those unique times that turned out perfect for reflection and contemplation of one's life—an unusual occasion when someone you don't know particularly well, but who likes and trusts you, picks you out and decides to unbuckle and let it all (or at least some of it) hang out. It happened—and it should now be recorded for the ages. Why? Because it's important for Adolph Rupp and 'the religion.' That night The Baron quietly got off the grand stage of his life and modestly proved, despite his foibles, how great a man he really was.

The Coach was happy about the success of UK (or as he called it, The University), pleased with Joe B. Hall's accomplishment in getting to the Final Four and that of the UK senior class—the last one he recruited while coaching UK.

There was a restrained yet noticeable undercurrent of envy over John Wooden's success at UCLA, which had clearly surpassed his. It was aggravating to him that the press was willing to ignore the well-known recruiting largesse of Wooden's friend, Sam Gilbert, which Rupp felt was primarily responsible for UCLA's domination of collegiate basketball.

There was genuine surprise with the clever talent of the young UofL coach, Denny Crum, shortly followed by the remembrance of his own success at Crum's age. Coach Rupp expressed frequent irritation with his declining health that was becoming progressively more painful; yet there was full satisfaction with his life's work, which he elegantly described as "The Glory Road."

Knowing my involvement with the professional version of the sport and aware of my reason for being in San Diego, Coach Rupp waxed eloquent of his pride about the professional success of his players: Beard ("...better than Cousy."), Hagan ("Oh, what a hook shot—better than Houbregs'!"), Ramsey ("...surprisingly strong kid"), Riley ("highest-jumpin' 6-4 white kid I ever saw"), Dampier and Issel. But he was mystified why more of his players hadn't made it big in the pros. As the table discussion continued, it was obvious that this had privately disturbed Adolph Rupp for years. "All those All-Americans at The University and only five or six ever made it big in the pros. Shyster, can you figure that out?" He admitted over the years to frequently rationalizing that it might have had something to do with the team style of play he emphasized; but, then he quickly recalled that Red Auerbach's style of play with the Celtics, which featured team rather than individual style, debunked that rationale. Coach Rupp didn't seem to have an answer for his question.

His mention of Red Auerbach brought forth that famous Rupp scowl. "Did you ever want to coach in the NBA? Naw, couldn't live in an apartment in one of those damn big cities like Arnold Auerbach and have to deal with guys like him every day." Rupp admitted to near-lifelong disdain of the NBA, despising Ned Irish, "the Garden" and Maurice Podoloff for banning Groza, Beard, Barnstable and Spivey from the NBA. But a pause and some reflection tempered his remembrance—Podoloff hadn't only gone after The Fabulous Five. Coach Rupp recalled that several years later he had ordered a lifetime ban on former Columbia All-American and rookie NBA All-Star, Jack Molinas, after NBA private investigators had caught him dumping six NBA games while playing for the Fort Wayne Pistons. He admitted, later in life, to the realization that Podoloff and New York D.A. Hogan were just dedicated guys, determined to clean up the game.

The mention of Podoloff brought Coach Rupp to a rather rambling remembrance of The Fabulous Five—ending with a stunning observation: "We all made a lot of mistakes—I should have controlled that situation better and should've listened to Coach Allen about that gambling thing." Not understanding (at the time) what he meant by the Coach Allen reference, I asked and he replied that he was aware of Coach Allen's warning about (as he called it) the "gambling hall" in Lexington. Clearly, Adolph had mellowed in his golden years, observing that he had realized the NBA was changing and his earlier attitude about it had been too rigid. "There's some pretty good young guys over there in that thing, now, like that guy over in Phoenix [Jerry Colangelo]. John Y's son and some of these new ABA owners are nice young fellows, too."

The conversation turned to #44. I had long known he admired Dan Issel, but had no concept of that admiration's depth. As he told some (already known) Issel stories, it was as if, in his retirement, he was living through Issel (as a grandfather through a grandson) and knowing that the grandson's career and life would make up for the grandfather's human and personal foibles, because the grandson was such an honorable and decent person. Stunningly, there was an expression of a wish that he had been more gracious and understanding in life, like Issel was, and had been able to have a more centered life around his family and wife, as did Issel. He particularly said, "I should have been more concerned about people, like Issel is." He acknowledged some misgivings about "...running off all those guys [former players] at the University....", and wanted me to know that he was confident that Issel would play ten more years and eventually be inducted into the Naismith Hall of Fame (he did and was). But he was still Adolph Rupp, saying, "Issel tells me you're an honest shyster, Miller — now listen here damnit, you do right by him, do you hear me?" I would have, anyway — but I never forgot Rupp's icy stare that night when he challenged me — it was an Adolph Rupp demand, like he had made of hundreds of his players over his coaching career.

In spite of remembering Louie Dampier as a "...kid who simply wouldn't run fast enough in practice....", Rupp was convinced that he was the best shooting guard he had ever coached—"...give him a tenth of a second and he'd get that thing off and make damn near all of 'em." The thought of Dampier brought him to reminiscing about Rupp's Runts. A shroud of sadness engulfed him as he recalled the loss to Texas Western. He loved that team, saying, "You know what, Miller, they were damn near perfect—best passing outfit I ever had. Hell, they could have beaten that Syracuse team today by 25." Then—a pause and an incredible admission—he should have recruited blacks as soon as UofL and Western did, observing that "the University would have won two or three more NCAAs in the 1960s if I had." There was distinct aggravation with himself that he hadn't demanded more help from Kentucky Governors Combs and Breathitt between 1959-1967 to help him recruit African-American Kentucky high school players. "Would the Runts have beaten Texas Western with Unseld?" I asked. "Hell,

Haskins' boys wouldn't have come within 20 points of us."

He said, "What other players are you representing, Miller?" I said that we were working with Alfred 'Butch' Beard, who was having a great season at point guard with the Golden State Warriors [they would eventually win the NBA championship later that year]. Pausing, he gave me that piercing stare and admitted thinking more than once that with Butch Beard as a point guard, Kentucky would have won the NCAA in Issel, Pratt and Casey's junior year (1968-1969)—"Issel could have taken Alcindor (Kareem Abdul-Jabbar) out of the pivot and shot over him, and UCLA didn't have anybody who could deal with Beard, Pratt, [Larry] Steele and Casey." What's your all-time UofK team? "Don't know—too many good ones, can't name five, but Issel, Beard, Hagan and Ramsey have to be on it."

Did you ever have to go to the bathroom—but just couldn't take the chance of interrupting something really special? A conversation such as this had to turn to the greatest player he ever saw. It did. I remember the answer like it was yesterday—"It's hands-down—nobody could ever do what that Erving kid does—absolutely nobody." There was a long reflection about Dr. J.'s performance against the Colonels at Memorial Coliseum in the fourth quarter of the ABA playoffs the previous year. Rebounding from the defensive board, dribbling down the court and taking it to the basket for a slam dunk, then stealing the in-bounds pass and dunking all over again—and the Dr. J. Special—driving the baseline, past the goal and scoring with a swooping dunk hook shot, holding the ball in one hand. "Ten years from now all the kids will be trying to play like Erving," he said. They were. I've thought more than once since, what a shame it was that Coach Rupp never saw Michael Jordan.

What's the future of the college and pro game? Rupp expressed his belief that eventually the talent level of the college game would decline, because sophomores and juniors would be leaving for the big money in the pros. Now, it's even freshmen and high school players. Rupp observed, "[Julius] Erving [who had left the University of Massachusetts as a junior] is just the start of this thing." He predicted the NBA would merge with the ABA in a year or two and the NBA would double in size to include smaller cities, like Louisville. Then he waxed on about Louisville. "The big shots over there ought to go and get that city into the NBA. It would help that young Crum recruit, it would help Coach Hall and it would help the city and Kentucky grow faster. The best basketball, on all levels, needs to be in The Commonwealth." Then, an Adolph Rupp challenge: "Miller, you're one of those big shots over there in Louisville, why don't you get that done?"

By now it was past 10 PM Pacific Standard time [or 1 AM in Lexington]. It was time to go. It was one of those times in life when you didn't want something to end, but in fairness, it had to. Coach Rupp's feet were hurting and it had been a long day for him. As we left for the hotel, I asked the Coach if he had any regrets. "It was a 'Glory Road'—[pause]—I've denied it before, but I'd change a few things if I could do it all over again."

It was a short drive to the hotel. Coach Rupp was tired—enroute not much was said. As we turned the corner onto the Bay Drive to the hotel—one last question: "Coach, can I ever mention our conversation to anyone?" He looked at me and said, "Hell, no. Even if you did, no one would believe I ever admitted any of that stuff, anyway!" I laughed and said, "You're probably right, Coach, but I'll make you a promise—I'll never say a word to anyone about it, unless there's a reason that you would approve of." There was a long silence—Coach Rupp was thinking. Then as we pulled up to the hotel and the doorman opened the door, the grand old man looked at me and said, "Shyster, you've got a deal on that." We shook hands, he left the car and I took it to the parking lot. That was the last time I ever spoke to Coach Adolph Rupp.

Within 27 months the grand old man was dead.[237]

Why do I write about this now? Because that evening it became clear that Adolph Frederick Rupp had given much thought to The Glory Road and had realized (like most of us do at one point or another) he could have done better—if he had understood the concept of change, hadn't been so fearful of the unknown, and hadn't had such disdain for "big cities." It was equally clear that Coach Rupp foresaw the growing predominance and economic importance of the professional game in the future. Above all, it was manifest that he felt that the Commonwealth should be home to the very best at every level of the sport.

As he looked down upon us when Louisville lost the Kentucky Colonels a few years later, and as he watched what I'm getting ready to tell you about—Louisville's NBA Millennium effort—I believe Coach Rupp would have approved this revelation of our conversation that night at Mister A's.

And I also genuinely believe he would have been ashamed with those you're about to read about, who stood in Louisville's way, wouldn't accept the challenge of change and exhibited the fear of the unknown, all of which prevented "the religion" from reaching its ultimate height in, as he lovingly called, "the Commonwealth."

When the right time comes, I'll tell my little T-Man grandson about Coach Rupp. He'll learn about his success and his failure. Most importantly, Tristan will learn that all people—even great men—win and lose things in life, but it takes a very special man to accept and admit his life's mistakes, even if it's only with one person at a quiet dinner in San Diego, California.

Last, I'll make sure that Tristan will learn and realize that Coach Adolph Frederick Rupp, was a great man—and had once again had become a hero of mine—in the end.

There is no steady unretracing progress in this life; we do not advance through fixed gradations, and at the last one pause — through infancy's unconscious spell, boyhood's thoughtless faith, adolescence's doubt, then skepticism, then disbelief — resting at last in manhood's pondering repose of IF....

But once gone through, we trace the round again; and are infants, boys and men, and IFs eternally. Where lies the final harbor, whence we unmoor no more?

Herman Melville, in *Moby Dick*

PART TWO
Louisville's Four NBA Odysseys

Only those who risk going too far can possibly find
out how far one can.

T.S. Eliot

CHAPTER SIX

The First of Louisville's Four NBA Odysseys—Saving the Kentucky Colonels

The Athenians' victory over the Persian navy of Xerxes began the gloried Golden Age of the Greek civilization. By the mid-1970s the ABA, like the Athenians of yore, had accomplished a similar victory with its ascendancy to equality with the NBA. The ABA's untimely demise began the first of Louisville's four NBA odysseys—Saving the Kentucky Colonels.

The NBA Six-Pack

John Y. Brown, Jr.'s purchase of the Buffalo Braves from Paul Snyder shifted Louisville's opportunity for an NBA franchise from a merger with the NBA to an existing NBA team's transfer to Louisville. The Braves were highly competitive in the NBA; their star players, Bob McAdoo and Randy Smith, had been league All-Stars. Hearing the groundswell from thousands of saddened Colonels fans, Brown asked me, in my capacity as an elected public official, to help him find a "place" for Louisville amid this travesty. Together, we agreed on a game plan. I had four primary assignments:

1. Continue the Kentucky Colonels spirit in Louisville, by sustaining the Colonels Booster's Club; and

2. Promote a series of pre-season and regular season NBA games in Louisville; and

3. Meet with NBA owners, obtaining their prior approval to transfer the Braves to Louisville; and

4. Find 20 Louisville investors, each willing to commit a $100,000 investment for a total 49% interest in the Braves.

The Chicken Man

If there ever was a 20th century Kentuckian who appeared to understand change and who didn't fear the unknown it was John Y. Brown, Jr. He was the son of a highly successful criminal trial lawyer, John Y. Brown, who had defended Bill Spivey in the New York City point-spread scandals, had been a nationally-known Chautauqua circuit speaker in the 1920s, a friend and classmate of Uncle Ed Diddle at Centre College, and a long-time Kentucky politico who lost numerous political wars with A.B. "Happy" Chandler. Father John Y., while an eloquent loser in the political arena, was dynamic and demanding of his son, from whom much was expected and success was required as an essential life's ingredient.

In 1961, having graduated from UK law school and following a brief stint at the Ft. Knox Army base, John Y., Jr. and his father formed a law partnership, jokingly referred to by the father as "John Y. Brown, Jr. & Father." But the practice of law proved too dull and tedious for the peripatetic Brown, Jr. Upon marrying Ellie Durall, a vivacious western Kentucky coal miner's daughter and school teacher, Brown, Jr. was poised to begin his own career in Kentucky's explosive political thicket. As are most plans of mice and men, his embryonic political life was interrupted by a fateful meeting with one of his father's east Kentucky mountain friends — Colonel Harland Sanders of Corbin.

Sanders, a near comic caricature with white hair and goatee and daily dressed in a white suit with black string tie, owned a restaurant in Corbin whose featured cuisine was fried chicken. His recipe involved eleven secret herbs and spices embedded into the chicken by a pressure cooker. The result was fried chicken that remained moist throughout, and could be prepared on short order.

Despite the fare's uniqueness, Sanders Cafe had become a casualty of the federal interstate highway program — as Corbin's new interstate bypassed it. The cafe was sold to pay the quickly-growing debt. But the Sanders persona also included vestiges of P.T. Barnum—he was an inveterate promoter. He refused to give up and accept defeat. Despite his age (late 60s), the never-say-die Sanders began franchising his restaurant concept. By 1963 he had sold over five hundred franchises nationwide. But it was completely unorganized and had grown far beyond the Colonel's ability to manage and control. He needed organizational help and investors.

Understanding the concept of change, with absolutely no apparent fear of the unknown, John Y. and Tennessee businessman Jack Massey cobbled together $1,800,000 (Brown's portion being primarily borrowed) and purchased the Colonel Harland Sanders restaurants together with his secret recipe, thereby founding what was to become, in short order, the second largest fast food franchise in the world—Kentucky Fried Chicken.

Within several years the tireless Brown and his young business cohorts had nearly doubled the number of franchises. It was done at a time when there were no computerized cash registers, able to instantly track sales. During the early growth, the original franchise contracts were written on paper placemats and the backs of matchbook covers. Within another two years Kentucky Fried Chicken went public for $15 a share—which within a year had quadrupled and split. John Y. Brown, Jr., dozens of his friends, and dozens more franchisees from burgs the size of east and west Peoria to metropolises the size of Los Angeles, had become multi-millionaires— virtually overnight.

There had never been an American businessman who, single-handedly, had created so many millionaires in such a short period of time. They were a ready-made base of average men and women who had become community leaders throughout the nation—something that didn't go unnoticed by the national Democratic party. All in all, it was a phenomenal American business success story that even confounded Harvard School of Business professors. Once while Brown conducted a Harvard business school seminar, a professor opined, saying, "We don't understand what you're doing or how you're doing it, but we suggest you keep doing whatever it is."

Some five years later, ostensibly tiring from the 24/7 travel demand, John Y. merged Kentucky Fried Chicken with Heublein, Inc. in a $300+ million stock swap (which would approximate a $3 billion transaction in 2004 dollars). By his late-30s, John Y. Brown Jr. had become a national business celebrity. But he couldn't relax or rest; action had become too much a part of his life. There had to be another mountain to climb, as he would frequently reflect.

His 1973 re-purchase of the Kentucky Colonels was coupled with a multitude of other business ventures as he looked for that next mountain and an enlarged public involvement. He and an associate, Larry Townsend, produced a celebrity-laden national TV telethon, whose purpose was to extricate the national Democratic party from near bankruptcy after the McGovern presidential debacle of 1972.

Another venture particularly expanded his celebrity beyond the business world and into the middle of the nation's fast lane. He purchased a hot dog franchise, Lum's, from Miami-based Stuart and Cliff Perlman. While he liked them, Brown's interest wasn't particularly in hot dogs. Lum's and the Perlmans also owned the new and glitzy Caesar's Palace in Las Vegas, which had become the nation's leading celebrity showcase. Then there was the purchase of a posh tennis and yacht club resort on Ft. Lauderdale's intercostal waterway—Le Club Internationale. Like a beehive, it swarmed with celebrities from Mickey Mantle to crooner Andy Williams, to Hollywood actor Warren Beatty and sometimes served as a practice facility for a local teen-aged tennis sensation, Chris Evert.

John Y. was the king bee at Le Club. Brown's life had become bigger than life. He was operating on all cylinders. There were few who could match his electric lifestyle—but the fast-lane didn't interest Ellie Brown. They soon divorced.

Like most enormously successful people, Brown's life was a dichotomy of inspiration and foibles. He enjoyed and reveled in gambling — both in business and pleasure. Despite the personal imperfections (who some would call peccadillos), in the early and mid-1970s John Y. Brown, Jr. remained the single most capable and available Kentuckian to lead the state's challenge of change at a pace faster than the state's competitors.

There was his professed belief in Ralph Waldo Emerson's advice that a successful person never fears to "reach beyond his grasp," coupled with an expressed desire to see his native Kentucky become a world-wide household name, known for something beyond fried chicken, whiskey, tobacco, fast horses and the Hatfields and McCoys.

John Y. Brown, Jr. was a most valuable team leader, someone upon whom Kentucky could depend—or, at least, so I thought.

And away we go....

The monumental effort began. Volunteers from the Colonels Booster's Club abounded. Enthusiastic women and men came forward. Maxine Lutz and Judy Gaw helped run the twelve-hour-a-day operation. They were joined in decision-making by Bob Tiell, Dick Hayes and a host of others. Dedication was contagious. Membership quickly grew to nearly 1,000 — all amateurs in the sports industry, who devoted countless day and night hours to make it work. Al Schneider, the Louisville hotel magnate, donated the use of the old Kentucky Colonel offices in the Executive Inn hotel, adjacent to the Freedom Hall complex. Six games were scheduled.[238] It was called the NBA Six-Pack. The aged financial records (recently found) reflect a net-profit on gate receipts for the first five games totaling $79,368.83.[239] The Six-Pac was to conclude with an NBA regular season game in mid-January, 1978, with Ted Turner's Atlanta Hawks playing the Artis Gilmore-led Chicago Bulls. Arrangements were made for NBA owners to come to Louisville and join Commissioner Larry O'Brien in the festivities. Prior to the game, Kentucky Governor Julian Carroll was to host a cocktail buffet party for the fans and NBA dignitaries. All but four NBA owners committed. Two days prior to the game, Judy Gaw reported that the Freedom Hall seating chart indicated seat sales and commitments for over 13,000 fans. Then disaster occurred.

The next day, Kentucky became Alaska. An unprecedented blizzard hit Louisville and the entire midwest. Governor Carroll was required to close the state's highways, including the expressways surrounding Freedom Hall. In one-half day, twenty-four inches of ice and snow landed, with temperatures and wind chill dropping to fifteen below zero. Thirty-five minutes before the game Ted Turner arrived on the last plane before the Louisville airport was closed. The roads were so impassable that it took twenty minutes to transport Turner one mile from the airport to Freedom Hall. Despite the weather calamity, nearly 4,000 fans showed up. Even though the NBA owners party was canceled, the fans were joyous as the game drew near.

Ted Turner was (politely) in a state of rather significant inebriation, further enabled during his hazardous plane flight. He would have been a rather difficult passenger for a stewardess to turn down. He insisted he be left at the front door of Freedom Hall, and I parked the car. When I entered the arena, Turner was nowhere to be found. Then, all of a sudden, I saw him standing next to a young Andy Frain woman beside the Hawks bench. As quickly as possible I got to him. There he was, in an old, time-worn fedora and a too-long, old overcoat, with a tub of beer in each hand and a hot dog in the overcoat's lapel pocket with mustard running down the coat.

As I reached him he was indignantly slurring the words, "I'll have you know, young lady, I own one of these damn teams." Turner insisted on being allowed to sit on the Hawks bench (later getting in much trouble with baseball commissioner Bowie Kuhn over his same insistence about the Atlanta Braves). But, how could you resist? The Atlanta Hawks players were in stitches, as their homeless-looking owner sat down in the middle of the bench.

Freedom Hall's now-deceased and long-beloved melodious announcer, John Tong, introduced the players and then, spotting "the Mouth of the South" (as he was known at the time) on the Hawks bench, recognized him to the fans—whereupon Ted Turner went to center court, grabbed the microphone from Tong and offered a salute to the 4,000 fans in a noticeably-slurred but precious form, saying: "A salute to all of you. This is the greatest exhibition of courage, dedication and grit I've ever seen—Now, I'm goin' to drink this beer and eat this damn hot dog." The Freedom Hall fans erupted with the loudest standing ovation I've ever heard from 4,000 people.

Despite this unexpected weather adversity, we had succeeded in preserving the enthusiasm for and the integrity of the Colonels memory. Years later, when I once asked him if he remembered that evening, Ted Turner laughed raucously, admitting he did (somehow).

Most Louisville blizzards melt quickly, as did this one. After it did, Governor Carroll, Kentucky's economic development cabinet secretary, Terry McBrayer, and I met in New York with NBA Commissioner O'Brien and the league's outside legal counsel, a young David Stern. It was a productive meeting that concluded with O'Brien's support for the transfer of the Buffalo Braves to Louisville. Of particular note was O'Brien's press statement—"Not having the NBA in Kentucky was like having a fine dinner without wine; it doesn't make any sense." Couldn't have been stated better. Now, the next step—the approval of the transfer of the Braves to Louisville by the NBA franchise owners.

The "red-eye" flights

In the spring of 1978, with considerable trepidation bolstered by the gusto of a hound dog, the road show began. On day one, the score was 4-0. The four former ABA teams were a lock.[240] Then to the *verboten* NBA. Where do you start? Sage advice was offered by the Spurs' Angelo Drossos and Denver's Carl Scheer—"Go west young man"—I did, going as far west as possible.

In the Seattle offices of the SuperSonics on West Harrison Street, Sam Schulman (Sonics) and Larry Weinberg (TrailBlazers) were convinced in one meeting. Then to San Francisco, where Franklin Mieuli (Golden State Warriors) committed.[241] A quick red-eye flight to Los Angeles, found Jack Kent Cook (Lakers)[242] and L.A.-resident, Richard Block, (Phoenix Suns) agreeing to support the transfer of the Braves to Louisville.[243] The Drossos advice had been sound. The western swing was unanimous. The score was 9-0. The midwest was next.

At an afternoon meeting in the University Club in Houston's Galleria on Post Oak Road, Ray Patterson of the Rockets signed on and agreed to help with the midwest effort. It began with Joe Axelson of the Kansas City Kings, who knew the Louisville basketball market from his job with the Cincinnati Kings before the team's transfer to Kansas City. Axelson was on board. Then Sam Battistone of the New Orleans Jazz casually (and unconvincingly) committed.[244] The effort turned north to the Chicago Bulls.

It had been presumed that Bulls owners, Arthur and Bill Wirtz, would oppose the transfer of the Braves to Louisville, because the word on the NBA street was they had diametrically opposed the Colonels joining the NBA since they craved Artis Gilmore for their Chicago Bulls and knew they'd get him if they caused the ABA's demise. Wrong.[245] They were 100% supportive and even helped to line up Bill Davidson (Detroit Pistons) and James Fitzgerald (Milwaukee Bucks). The Cleveland Cavaliers' Nick Mileti required a day-long walk-through of his new coliseum in Richfield, Ohio that had been ribbon-cut by Frank Sinatra.[246] Batting 100%, we moved east.

Ted Turner at the Atlanta Hawks was still in the bag since his trip to Louisville[247], then with some help Abe Pollin (Washington Bullets) orally agreed via the phone.[248] Kentucky Derby connoisseur and New York sports impresario, Sonny Werblin, was enlisted to assist in convincing Mike Burke (N.Y. Knicks), which in turn brought us Gene Dixon of the 76ers (with the added encouragement of his general manager, Pat Williams). In the end, only Irv Levin, owner of the Boston Celtics, opposed the transfer of the Braves to Louisville. Later, there would prove to be a method in Levin's madness.

It had been a whirlwind trip and the stage was set. The approvals were obtained, albeit oral. It was hoped that "gentlemen's handshakes" among honorable men would be honored when the critical time came. There was no way to guarantee this.

Three of John Y's requirements had been met, and only one remained —the agreement of 20 Louisvillians to invest $100,000 each in return for a 49% interest in the Braves. Morning, noon and night that effort proceeded. Al Schneider and former Colonels part-owner Wendell Cherry were among the initial commitments. Ellie Brown (by then divorced from John Y.), and his father, John Y. Brown, Sr., Frank L Jones, Jr., Jack Gruneisen, auto dealer Ed Coyle, coal entrepreneur Martin Twist, restaurateur Ed Hasenour, C.P.A. Louie Roth and developer Frank Metz, along with famed local criminal lawyer, Frank Haddad, continued with commitments. We eventually reached sixteen in number (including several Lexington investors located by Brown). We were four short, but others were willing to put together four groups of $100,000 each: John Hubbuch, restaurteur Fred Kunz, then-Alderman Jerry Abramson, and John Anson. Brown refused the groups—it had to be twenty "singletons" as he called them. But the nation's economy was in the beginning stages of what some have called "the Jimmy Carter malaise." No old-line wealth in Louisville was interested. The cupboard was bare—no more were to be found.

The fateful time when John Y. would announce his intentions had arrived —the NBA annual meeting on Tuesday, June 13, 1978 at San Diego's Hotel del Coronado. The "Del", as it is known, is a magnificent national historic landmark, built in 1888 on 26 acres of San Diego coastline which during the 1930s through the 1950s served as the playground of the rich and famous —The Duke and Duchess of Windsor, Charles Lindbergh, Frank Sinatra and Marilyn Monroe, among countless others. Quite a place. Amid this art deco splendor, Brown had to be convinced to transfer the Braves to Louisville, even though we only had 16 investors at $100,000 each.

John Y.'s general manager in Buffalo, Norm Sonju, was a well-respected sports executive whose opinion was valued within NBA circles. He believed a move to Louisville was improvident. In April, 1978, he had written an extensive report for Brown comparing the cities of Buffalo, Dallas, Louisville, Minneapolis, Miami and Toronto. Devoting only four pages to Louisville,[249] it didn't take a rocket scientist to realize that he preferred Dallas (and all the others except Buffalo) over Louisville. The Sonju Report wasn't shared with anyone at the time. It was deemed then (and now, upon its re-examination) as a puff piece, whereby a wily executive disguises facts and reality in order to convince an owner of something that would benefit himself. It was particularly worthless, because Buffalo and Louisville were the only cities in the competition that actually had recent experience in major league professional basketball. It was inexplicable, at the time, as to why cities with no relevant track record could be compared to Louisville. The proof of the pudding of this mystery was clearly evidenced sometime later. He became the first general manager of the Dallas NBA team. Things were tense at The Del.

William F. "Billy" Reed, a nationally-respected and award-winning sports columnist with *The Courier-Journal* and Dick Fenlon, lead sports columnist for the evening paper, *The Louisville Times*, agreed to remove their reporter's hats and join me in San Diego as public-spirited citizens, to encourage a favorable decision from Brown. John Y. was always sensitive to favorable publicity and it was felt that their presence would be a real plus. Together we flew to San Diego, arriving on June 13th at 5:04 PM PDT. In an effort to pull out all the stops, on the evening of our arrival in San Diego Reed and I had dinner with Indiana coach Bobby Knight at a seafood restaurant called The Chart House across the road from The Del. If the opportunity presented itself, Knight agreed to encourage Brown's decision for Louisville.

Wednesday, June 14th, was consumed by conferencing with Brown and others who could influence him. The day began at a breakfast meeting with Carl Scheer of the Denver Nuggets. In preparation for the NBA meetings, I had spoken with Dan Issel about whether he would agree to be traded to a Buffalo Braves franchise *if* it was moved to Louisville. He was willing to consider the move. That morning an intense discussion was undertaken with Scheer about Issel's availability, *if* Brown would agree to transfer the Braves to Louisville. Scheer didn't commit. But he was willing to negotiate an Issel trade with Brown if the franchise transfer to Louisville became a reality. This was a huge step forward. Scheer wanted Louisville in the NBA and was fully aware of Issel's importance to the Louisville market if the transfer occurred—a positive way to start the day.

Lunch was shared with John Y. and Angelo Drossos of the San Antonio Spurs. Drossos strongly encouraged Brown's decision for the Louisville transfer, and further assured him the votes were there. Brown left to join an attractive woman who had accompanied him to San Diego—never knew her by any name other than Rocky. A series of afternoon meetings in the halls, at the swimming pool and all over the place occurred with Lakers assistant coach Stan Albeck, Nuggets coach Larry Brown, Stan Kasden, general manager of the Atlanta Hawks and a host of others.

Meanwhile, Reed and Fenlon pursued other angles and contacts. Late in the afternoon we met for an hour to compare notes. The columnists reported good news. During Brown's absence on Wednesday afternoon, he had promised not to make any decision outside our presence. But that decision-time was nearing.

Wednesday night, June 14 at 8:30 PM—the corner booth at the Del Coronado's famed B&S Bar was to be "the location." The columnists and I were fully rehearsed. I even carried one extra poker hand in my pocket to be played, if necessary. For several hours a well-oiled Shakespearean play was produced. Devil's advocacy was met with facts. The importance of the decision to Louisville's future was repeatedly stressed. Brown smoked his god-awful, smelly cigarillos. Numerous pit-stops to the lower level bathroom were required. It was relentless. Reed and Fenlon were particularly effective. It was a true 100% effort. A hearing-enabled fly on the bar room wall would have been proud. But Brown remained steadfast. A deal was a deal—it was essential in his mind that there be 20 local investors.

The time had arrived for the hidden poker hand — the final rabbit out of the hat. Humana's CEO, Wendell Cherry, and Louisville hotelier, Al Schneider, were willing to make up the $400,000 difference. This commitment, previously unknown to Brown, had been re-confirmed by my phone call earlier in the day. It was a stunner. At midnight we broke off. John Y. went to his room to think—with Rocky. The columnists and I wondered how much "thinking" was going to occur. We agreed with Brown to reconvene in the Crown Room for breakfast the next morning. Resplendent with its 30-foot high wooden ceilings and unique crown-shaped chandeliers, designed by Wizard of Oz author, Frank Baum, the Crown Room was a fitting place to learn the fate of the entire effort.

The columnists and I arrived in the Crown Room at 8:00 AM, the appointed time. We waited and waited—no Brown. So we enjoyed the largest breakfast buffet known to man. It was 9:00 AM before Brown showed up— still far too early for this notorious late riser. He was disheveled, appearing to have not slept more than a catnap. Brown carried his notes and information from the previous evening's work in a crumpled brown grocery sack (he admitted finding it at a 7-11 somewhere around the Del Coronado). With fingers crossed Reed, Fenlon and I awaited his words.

The answer was, "No." There were two reasons—lack of 20 investors and the Sonju Report. It was all over.

After some desperate pleading, Brown backed down and agreed to come back to Louisville to see if, with his help, we could round up four more $100,000 investors. We worked out of his office at Lum's headquarters on Linn Station Road for a week or so. It was virtually another telethon. Each morning Colonels booster, Dick Hayes, would put together the day's itinerary of phone calls and beginning every afternoon John and I would call potential investors. The calls would break for the dinner hour and resume into the early evening. Then we'd break and make up a list for the next day. It was relentless and the calling went beyond Louisville—out into Kentucky.

Having made an impassioned argument that the Sonju Report was prejudiced, Brown relented, providing me with the detailed financial information on the Braves and the Colonels. This information was particularly revealing and supported my prior argument that the Sonju report was skewed. From an attendance standpoint, the Colonels had exceeded the Braves:

AVERAGE REGULAR SEASON HOME GAME ATTENDANCE[250]

REGULAR SEASON	BRAVES	COLONELS
72-73	210,374 - 5,131 per game	298,746 - 7,113 per game
73-74	333,808 - 7,999 per game	344,442 - 8,201 per game
74-75	383,894 - 9,093 per game	366,534 - 8,727 per game
75-76	338,268 - 7,972 per game	291,270 - 6,935 per game
	1,266,344 7,549 per game	1,300,992 7,744 per game

Indeed, the Colonels attendance dropoff in 1975-76 was disturbing. However, who's fault was that? In the ongoing discussions with Brown, I refused to allow the Colonels fans to be assessed any responsibility for his decision to sell Issel prior to that season. It didn't require a Ph.D. to understand the sale of the Colonels most significant player had dramatic impact on the attendance in the Colonel's final season. John Y. reluctantly accepted the argument.

From an examination of the Braves and Colonels balance sheets, it was apparent that the Colonels were, at least, equally as productive as the Braves.[288] In 1976, the ABA Colonels possessed $502,899 more assets than the NBA Braves ($1,849,191 vs. $1,346,292). While the Colonels had a half million more in current liabilities, that included a $1,219,125 note to its general partner (John Y and Ellie Brown). The Colonels had no long term debt vs. the Braves $2,546,039 and only had deferred compensation liability of $357,472 vs. the Braves $1,866,163. Additionally, when John Y's sale of the Colonels in 1976 was factored into the equation, it was apparent that the Colonels asset/liability deficit of $648,443 and the Partners capital deficit of $1,138,145 (totalling $1,786,588) was fully recovered from Brown's net sale proceeds from the Kentucky Colonels of $3 million vs. his $1.5 million purchase price of the Braves.

Any comparison between the 1976-76 Statements of Operation[289] of the ABA Colonels and the NBA Braves was difficult because of certain variances caused by the operation of the franchises in two separate leagues coupled with the fact that the Braves were a corporation and the Colonels, a limited partnership. However, when the Braves NBA television revenue was added to the Colonels figures and the Colonels lease cancellation expense was deducted and when the NBA league assessments were added to the Colonels bottom line net loss, the net/net loss of the Colonels was $1,172,331 vs. the Braves' $1,317,699).

Finally, the inescapable fact was that the sale/trade of Dan Issel had resulted in an enormous detriment to the Colonels financials. Even deducting from the Colonels receipts the proceeds from Issel's sale, when re-computing what the Colonels would have received in revenue from gate receipts and other sources, the sale/trade clearly cost the Colonels' last year in excess of $1 million, which would have caused their last Statement of Operations to be nearly positive.

At my request, these comparisons had been examined by accountants and were found reasonable. The financial position taken with Brown was believed to be a sound. However sound, the argument proved futile. John Y. had made his decision. There were no additional investors to be found. It was a simple as that. Brown was not going to transfer the Braves to Louisville and would proceed with other arrangements.

After the exhausting year-long odyssey, I was worn to a frazzle. All we needed was $400,000—and the Speed Museum had just purchased a

Rembrandt painting for $1.5 million. Unfortunately, there had to be a press conference about it all. I should have taken a day or two off to freshen up —but I didn't. The obligatory press conference took place in my office on the 27th floor of Citizens Plaza.

It was explosive. I said some things I have regretted ever since — like, how many hot dogs and programs would be sold "watching that Rembrandt," or how many tour busses from Leitchfield would come to town to see it— and if there were any, would they spend the night and come back the next day for another viewing? With tongue in cheek, I questioned why anyone would come to Louisville to watch one Rembrandt, when they could travel to The Louvre in Paris or The Hermitage in Leningrad and see dozens of them. Would the Louisville Orchestra play the Star-Spangled Banner each time it was unveiled? Or would the Louisville Ballet perform Swan Lake at halftime? Or, if the Rembrandt made the playoffs — who would it play?

It was front page. A blast to end all blasts. There was a lot of mail about it. The editor of *The Courier-Journal* opined that I was a classic boob. Former Colonels owner and art patron, Wendell Cherry, thought it was hilarious. Wendell was a great guy. A day or two later, he escorted me to the museum, then provided me a tour along with a detailed explanation as to the Rembrandt's significance. My enlightenment was followed by drinks and a big steak dinner at the Top of the Towers restaurant atop the First National Tower. Those of the Louisville arts community who are still with us have remembered that performance until this day. However funny it might have been, it was stupid on my part. There was no reason why a Rembrandt and the Colonels couldn't have found a home together—as they do in many NBA cities.

This is a short rendition of an extraordinarily eventful year of effort. It doesn't even remotely do justice to the work and dedication of literally hundreds of volunteers and thousands of Colonels fans, who believed, hoped, worked and prayed for success. There's simply no way to describe in words the dedication of so many, and it's unfair to create a list. But, for sure, Maxine Lutz, Judy Gaw, Bob Tiell and Dick Hayes would be at the top of the first page of a multi-page list of from-the-heart givers. In the throes of Louisville's normally stifling summer heat, Colonels fans were on the literal edge of their seats, awaiting Brown's decision. Everything possible had been done to accomplish the goal of the NBA in Louisville.

It had been a gargantuan effort. It was a young person's time — a time of near greatness, a time of hope and a time of dreams—all of which, together, proved not quite enough.

There's a never-ending question. In the decades since, it's been asked of me by hundreds of people. Did John Y. let Louisville and Kentucky down by refusing to transfer the Buffalo Braves to Louisville? Is it his fault? Is it fair to criticize him for his refusal to relent? It's easy to say yes. But the fair answer is, probably no. To be sure, he provided total and complete cooperation and his full attention for months on end (something non-existent from local political leaders two decades later). For weeks, I daily witnessed the genuine agony of his decision-making. The lights in Lum's Louisville headquarters were ablaze well into each night. Papers, records, statistics and used styrofoam coffee cups decorated the place, as Brown wrestled with an intense internal conflict between several major tenants that had provided guidance for his business career. One of them was his friend Kenny Rogers' admonition of song—"You've got to know when to hold 'em and know when to fold 'em." The other grew from his business experience—"There's no good decisions in life, just decisions that you make good by hard work." Like many things in life, there was no clear answer. Lee Iacocca once said, "If you wait until you're 100% sure of a decision, by the time you're 95% sure, the opportunity will be gone."

It was John Y. Brown, Jr.'s decision. It was his team, his investment, his life and his money. It was also his opportunity to put his adopted city into the world's urban economic hub. He genuinely felt that multiple ownership was required for the Colonels to succeed in the Louisville of the 1970s. John believed that a major league team in a mid-sized city needed to be a 'community' thing, shared by a group of people and not given to the community by one person. This multiple-ownership model had proven successful in San Antonio, Denver and Indianapolis.

However, years later, Brown's decision seems disheartening and sad. History hasn't treated Brown's decision very well. Twenty-seven years after the demise of the ABA (in 2003), *Forbes Magazine* valued the four former ABA franchises that entered the NBA that evening in 1976 as being worth nearly one billion dollars.[253] More significant, when the value of the franchises in all of the former ABA cities is computed in addition to the value of the four former ABA franchises, the total worth of NBA franchises in all former ABA cities is $2.65 billion.[254] A rough calculation of the economic dollar impact since 1976 on the four ABA cities merging with the NBA is even more astounding. Calculating the 27-year average dollar spent and generated by each team at an average of $150 million per year (over the entire 27 year period), the (reasonably conservative) conclusion is reached that the market areas of Denver, Indianapolis, New Jersey and San Antonio have recognized $15.8 billion in revenue as a result of the NBA franchises in their cities — not even considering the multiple dollar impact of that revenue coursing through the economy of those cities.

Within a few months, southern Californian Irv Levin would trade Boston Celtics ownership to John Y. Brown, Jr. in return for Brown's Buffalo Braves and Levin would move the Braves to San Diego. There they became the San Diego Clippers. In 1982 the team was purchased by Los Angeles real estate mogul Donald Sterling and moved north, becoming the Los Angeles Clippers. In all the years since, the Clippers have been one of, if not, the most miserable and hapless NBA franchises. One can easily argue that had the Braves-Clippers moved to Louisville instead, the next two decades would have been vastly different for this franchise.

But they didn't.

Having acquired the Boston Celtics in the trade with Levin, Brown immediately brought in furniture magnate and investment tycoon, Harry Mangurian, from Fort Lauderdale as a minority owner. The trades of Celtics players abounded under Brown's ownership, and Beantown erupted. During this time I had several conversations with Boston's guru of pro-athlete representation, Bob Wolff. He was astounded with Brown's verve for wheeling-and-dealing, not understanding the rhyme or reason for much of what he did.

Within a year Brown would sell his majority ownership in the Celtics to Mangurian, who would proceed to sign Larry Bird—and the rest became the "new" history of the fabled Celtics.

Brown would later be introduced by Howard Cosell to the former Miss America and NFL sportscaster, Phyllis George, with whom he would enjoy a flamboyant and whirlwind courtship and shortly marry in a ceremony presided over by Norman Vincent Peale at New York's St. Patrick's Cathedral. The wedding was an extravaganza of the first magnitude, complete with the A-list of luminaries of the day such as Walter Cronkite, Milton Berle and Bert Parks, with Andy Williams crooning "Just the Way You Are." Within another half year, the political career that had been interrupted a decade and a half prior by his meeting with Colonel Harland Sanders was resumed. Entering the Democratic primary for Kentucky Governor, amidst a five-way flotilla of politically-tarnished Democratic politicians, he and Phyllis enthralled Kentucky's voters with a never-to-be-equalled, bust-out, furious political campaign. Brown's stunning primary victory was matched by an equally dramatic general election win over a former Republican governor, Louie B. Nunn, as John Y. Brown, Jr. and his superstar wife became the fifty-fifth governor of Kentucky and the state's First Lady.

Typical of his life and his career, John Y. Brown, Jr. never missed a beat. For the next four years, together with a highly-talented gubernatorial Cabinet that would have been fully capable of managing the affairs of the nation, Brown provided, probably, the best and most positive governorship (somewhat beset by the vestiges of Jimmy Carter's deflated economy and 20% interest rates) Kentucky had ever been offered, which proved one of Brown's two mottos—"There's no good decisions, just decisions that you make good by hard work."

Following the Bay of Pigs disaster, President John F. Kennedy is said to have remarked that victory finds a hundred fathers, but defeat is an orphan.

On that fateful June morning in the Del Coronado's resplendent Crown Room and the last midnight meeting in the Lums Louisville headquarters, President Kennedy's observation was exactly what we were feeling.

Had John Y. Brown, Jr. been willing to accept the Schneider/Cherry offer at the Del Coronado, Louisville would have been in the NBA with an immediately competitive team.

Had John Y. Brown, Jr. been able to believe that dedication and hard work by the many former Colonels fans would have made successful his decision to transfer the Braves to Louisville, in 1978 Louisville would have joined the group of cities that were soon to become the central hub of the world's economy—cities that by the year 2000 were the collective owners of a combined $4.232.83 trillion in gross product.

Had John Y. Brown, Jr. been willing to believe just a little more in Louisville's ability to manifest its destiny, Louisville would be a vastly different city today, with a far greater vision of itself and a far larger international purpose and position.

But he didn't, mostly because Louisville wouldn't accept his "challenge" to reach for greatness. Hard to blame him.

John Y. had followed the Kenny Rogers thought; he "folded 'em" instead of playing them. In the process, Louisville lost—and was orphaned for the first time in its NBA odyssey. Louisville had flirted with the NBA and remained standing on the doorstep—Waiting for Godot.

CHAPTER SEVEN

A Short Comedic Sojourn With Crazy Ted

In the 1970-71 season, the Cleveland Cavaliers became an NBA expansion team (along with the Portland Trail Blazers and the Buffalo Braves). By and large during the ABA's existence, the Cavaliers were a motley crew. Finally, during the summer of 1979, their owner, Nick Mileti, had enough and sold the Cavaliers to a Cleveland advertising executive, Ted Stepien. Thus began a three year reign of chaos and disarray in Cleveland-town.

Stepien would have fit right in as an ABA team owner when it was the seal's league. If it was zany, Crazy Ted had either done it or thought about doing it. Needing a new mascot for the Cavaliers, he hired "the Amazing Boot", whose multi-faceted talents included stuffing all sorts of objects into his mouth—from raw eggs to fire to donuts. The Boot was nearly as hideous as he was ridiculous. Even worse were the Cavalier cheerleaders, lovingly-called the Teddi Bears (for Ted, of course), whose game wardrobe totalled little more than twice the cloth of three sequined pasties. Very classy! Then there was the team's fight song—believe it or not—it was a polka. Crazy Ted didn't just do crazy things, sometime he said them.

In his opening press conference following his purchase of the team, Stepien was reported to have made an off-handed comment—something to the effect that the only thing wrong with the NBA was that it had too many Jewish owners. How about that for a brilliant remark? To be sure, the remark got ol' Ted a lot of attention.

No one knew what would happen next with Ted Stepien or what he would say or do. He was a walking-around disaster.

The former Cavalier owner, Mileti, had been very proud of Cleveland's new suburban Richfield Coliseum, which had been opened in 1976. That pride was justifiable. It was one of the first arenas to have suites, and they were remarkable. I remember one that had been decorated for a bank. The door of the suite resembled an old safe from the Wells Fargo days with the "big wheel" as the door opener of a silver metal door. Seating over 22,000, the glitzy Richfield Coliseum was something. NBA officials liked it, too, and had granted the All-Star Game to Cleveland for 1981.

But as the time for the All-Star game neared, things were a bit askew in Cleveland. NBA Commissioner Larry O'Brien had become increasingly exasperated with Ted Stepien and his antics. Under strict instructions from O'Brien, Stepien's only permitted involvement with the All-Star Game was to host a luncheon. Even that wasn't enough to tame Ted. The features of the luncheon were The Amazing Boot, who performed all his pyrotechnic stunts for the assembled luncheon guests, and the pastied Teddi Bears, who managed to visit nearly every table. The wives of the owners and players really thought this was *cute*.

In his three year ownership stint, Stepien went through six head coaches and thirty-nine trades. Several of these trades were with the Cavalier's rival —the Detroit Pistons—which, along with the Piston's hiring of the Stepien-fired Cavalier coach, Bill Fitch, helped form the foundation for the Pistons' eventual back-to-back championships in 1988-89 and 1989-90. Finally, Commissioner O'Brien had to act, prohibiting Stepien from arranging any further trades.

The 1981-82 Cavalier season was an unmitigated disaster, winning 15 games and losing 67—the worst record for an NBA team in a decade. The 1982-83 season looked no better, except for the unbelievable scoring-machine, World B. Free, at guard.

In early December, 1982, Stepien called me. He knew his gig was up in Cleveland. Stepien wanted out, and was inquiring as to whether there might be any interest in owing the Cleveland Cavaliers among the Louisville businessmen who were willing to invest in the Buffalo Braves. Details were discussed about what Stepien wanted. Interestingly, it was within the parameters of the money previously promised by the Louisville businessmen to acquire the Braves. Louisville might even have been able to do the deal with no money and just an assumption of the liabilities. The concept was intriguing—an NBA team for no up-front money.

I took an early morning flight to Cleveland for a one-day meeting with Stepien and his general manager, Bill Messick. The morning began in Stepien's office, which was awash with pictures of the Teddi Bears and Teddy. After the usual obligatory niceties, we adjourned for lunch to his club in the Statler Office Tower on Euclid Avenue. You guessed right—it was called Stepien's Competitors Club. Getting down to serious business, it was agreed that Louisville would have a maximum of twenty days to make a formal offer of purchase for the Cavaliers. With that handshake agreement Stepien further agreed to provide me a copy of the Cavalier's financial books, records and the contractual commitments. He returned to his office to get the documents and I left to get a hotel reservation. We agreed to have dinner that evening when I would receive the documents and we would further discuss the deal.

Stepien made the dinner arrangements for 7:00 PM at his favorite Cleveland restaurant, Au Pere Jacques. Considering Stepien's plight and that of the Cavaliers, the street name of the restaurant's location was certainly appropos—Chagrin Boulevard. At the dinner, I was provided with a foot-thick set of financials. I left Cleveland on the first flight out the next morning at 6:30 AM with Stepien's documents in tow and a (real small) glimmer of hope.

The next day the documents were examined. I was surprised. Despite the dishevelment of the franchise and the pitiful attendance, the liabilities weren't particularly onerous. Mileti had been a pretty good businessman and, apparently, Stepien hadn't had enough time to really ruin the franchise yet.

A few calls were made to some Louisville businessmen. There wasn't much interest. However, hotelier Al Schneider did express an interest in going to the next level of negotiations, if I decided that it was a good idea. Noted criminal attorney Frank Haddad was interested, if his business associate, Bill Mulloy was. Unfortunately (or fortunately) Mulloy was out of town.

Realizing there might be some limited level of interest, a call was made to Commissioner O'Brien. It only took one call to him to know that a hands-off approach would be a good decision. Louisville's opportunity with Stepien was immediately rejected and his documents were returned.

Thus ended Louisville's three-day sojourn with Crazy Ted.

Eventually, Stepien's interest turned to Toronto, Canada. Word had it that he almost sold the team to several Toronto businessmen. The word also had it that the team would have been called the Toronto Towers (because of the height of the players). Several months later, in May, 1983, the soon-to-be new NBA Commissioner, David Stern, helped locate several really "good guys" on the west coast—George and Gordon Gund. They purchased the hapless Stepien-owned Cavaliers, returned to their hometown, and the City of Cleveland said a collective, "Thank God."

Man is the only animal that laughs and weeps, for he's the only animal that is struck by the difference between the way things are and what they ought to be!

—Mark Lane, attributed to William Hazlett

CHAPTER EIGHT

Remember My Friends —
It All Began With a Mouse

The two decades following Louisville's loss of the Kentucky Colonels were the NBA's literal Coming of Age. The quadrupling of its box office and television revenue during the 1980s, energized by a popularity explosion starring Magic Johnson, Larry Bird and Michael Jordan, was stupifying. The league's remarkable talent, coupled with Commissioner David Stern's promotional genius, had facilitated the successful entrenchment into the NBA of the former mid-sized ABA cities Indianapolis, San Antonio, Denver, Charlotte and Salt Lake City. With the early 1990 internationalization of the sport following the nation's 1992 Olympic Dream Team and its telecast to 212 nations, the NBA had arguably experienced the swiftest revenue growth and market penetration of any professional entertainment business ever.

Decades of reflection and what if's

During those two decades, despite the NBA's phenomenal growth, any notion among Louisville's political and intellectual leadership about seeking a franchise in the league was primarily non-existent. Long ago, Louisville had morphed into Kentucky and the state's aversion to change and fear of the unknown—a morphing so complete that its long established inferiority complex had rendered the city incapable of perceiving itself as "major league."

Wittingly or unwittingly, as the case may be, Louisville's elected political leaders remained primarily occupied with providing routine governmental services. Missing during that two decade period of time was a local political leader whose ethos challenged Louisville's inherent complacency and inner-contentment or expressed the urgency of the city reaching beyond its grasp to excel in the world's competitive economic environment. A vision of the city's economic place in the 21st century was non-existent. Generally the local political leadership did what it did best—cheerleading. Much political spin was generated about how good everything was but, conveniently, never would a realistic economic analysis surface that compared Louisville's economic progress with its competing cities. The politicians didn't want anyone knowing the real truth.

However, somewhere along the line, after passing up the opportunity of an international airport in suburban Shelby County in the early 1970s, the city succeeded in attracting the national UPS hub. But since there was no vacant farmland around its 40-year-old, inner-city airport, to pull it off required the huge expense of uprooting thousands of people from their homes, dozens upon dozens of businesses and entire neighborhoods. A decade later the displacement remained incomplete. Some would observe this was typical of the foresight, vision and follow-through generally afforded by Louisville's political leadership over the years.

For one brief and electric moment in the entire 20th century Louisville did assert itself within the rurally-dominated state, and was surprisingly successful. It was a time that pre-dated Rupp's ascendency to hero-worship, as it began six days before Pearl Harbor and ended in December, 1945. It was the administration of Louisville's greatest mayor—Wilson W. Wyatt. A month after his inauguration. as the city's youngest mayor at the age of 35, the energetic Wyatt hit the state legislature with a whirlwind series of actions he had designated during his campaign as a twelve-point program to re-invigorate Louisville. Gaining the support of the Kentucky Municipal League, an urban caucus was formed in the state legislature for the first time since the 1848 Constitutional Convention.

In the first two months of 1942, legislation was passed: (i) requiring the state to fund the maintenance of city streets that connected to state highways, (ii) requiring the return of millions of dollars of sheriff's and clerk's fees to the urban county, (iii) authorizing the merger of the city and county Boards of Health, (iv) authorizing the creation of a joint city/county planning and zoning commission and (v) creating the Louisville Area Development Association (known thereafter as LADA), which became the precursor to the city's riverfront development corporation decades later. Of even greater impact was the first redistricting of the legislature since the 1891 Constitution (even though it was required every ten years), which increased Louisville's representation by 33%. All in all, eight of the twelve points were passed—and done so unanimously.[255] The quid pro quo was the urban block's support for legislation authorizing additional funding for rural school systems.

Wyatt's vision of the future didn't stop there. Several years later in 1944, when the Public Utility Holding Company Act required Standard Gas & Electric to divest itself of the Louisville Gas & Electric Company, Wyatt (along with the Republican-controlled Board of Aldermen) agreed to sell $85 million in 2% 20-year city bonds to purchase LG&E. The model was the city's very successful acquisition in 1856 and ninety year operation of the Louisville Water Company. It nearly happened, but was felled by a spider bite-induced death of Judge Arthur E. Hopkins, the Republican chairman of the Aldermen. The Republican successor of Judge Hopkins agreed with the Kentucky interests of New York Governor Thomas E. Dewey (who was running for President) and, led by multi-millionaire Jouett Ross Todd, reversed their position and defeated the bond issue. Had the acquisition passed, by 1964 Louisville would have owned, outright, a billion dollar utility, the cash dividends from which would have virtually paid for the entire city's operation. Fifty-five years later, LG&E (by then merged with Kentucky Utilities) was sold to English and German interests for an estimated value of $4+ billion.[256]

Does anyone wonder, at this point in Louisville's life, what $4 billion from such a sale of the city-owned LG&E would mean to the future of the community?

In the post-WWII era, the visionary Wyatt left Louisville to join Harry Truman's administration as the National Housing Administrator, after which he returned to private life to create what became the largest Kentucky law firm until the mid-1990s while enhancing his national political clout as a close confidant of and national campaign manager for Adlai E. Stevenson's two unsuccessful campaigns for the presidency.[257] Wyatt's progressive impact upon Louisville and its acceptance by the rural state legislature dwindled with his absence. It was briefly re-born by iconoclast Mayor Charles Farnsley, after which the city lapsed into another 50 years of what *Harper's Magazine* had ignobly referred to in 1937 as "...a museum piece...." and "...the city of let well enough alone."[258]

By the Millennium, as it was a half-century earlier in 1950, Kentucky was still one of the most rural states in the nation, continuing to rank next to last in its percentage of residents with a high school degree. If one deleted Louisville residents from Kentucky's calculation, it would be last, by a substantial margin. But it didn't have to be this way and it wasn't this way elsewhere.

During the 20th century many other states with historically-based rural economies, such as Texas, Virginia, Louisiana, Alabama, Indiana, Tennessee, South Carolina, Georgia and North Carolina had succeeded in escaping Kentucky's continuing predicament and became urbanized. The big cities of those states had economically prospered far more than had Louisville. They had done so through the realization and acceptance of their larger importance to the success of the state itself. While Kentucky's politicians frequently talked about the importance of Louisville's economic ascendancy (particularly in a state-wide political campaign), other states not only talked, but also accepted the brutal fact, enabling the success of their big cities.

But in Kentucky there was a continuance into the 21st century of Rupp's "big city" warfare. From my seat in Louisville I could still see it clearly. So while the thought occurred to me periodically that it might be interesting to challenge Louisville again, reality dictated otherwise. Life was pleasant, the law practice was inspiring, there were dozens of good books to read, golf to play, English Staffordshire pottery to collect, travel to enjoy, a wife to love, and children and step-children to nurture.

However, to be sure, Louisville (like most other mid-sized American cities) was giving some general appearance of change. The unanswered question was: Was it a change by osmosis or one of a spirit that was alive and restless? For the NBA odyssey to be re-invigorated in Louisville, there was only one way it could ever happen. Without aggressive and visionary local political leadership, it had to begin as had Walt Disney's dream—with a mouse, quietly entering the community through a hole in the wall at midnight, disturbing no one until it was prepared to be noticed—and then only by surprise—and hopefully the mouse would accepted it as a "nice" little mouse that won't upset too many things or the community's pre-ordained and stagnated agenda of inch-by-inch economic progress.

As the reader will see, that mouse quietly began to creep in through that hole, and would soon become a mouse that roared throughout the land — frightening a small but vocal group of self-styled Louisville leaders, who had prospered by limiting their competition by successfully using the city's reluctance to change.

The peripatetic City Alderman, Dan Johnson

The south-central area of Louisville has historically been an area of stately trees, middle-class homes and blue-collar Americans—the type of people who fought our nation's wars, sang the Star Spangled Banner with relish and made our country great. Two major changes have recently occurred there—the constant roar of jet planes from Louisville's international airport servicing the new UPS international cargo hub, and an influx of immigrant populations. This amalgam of old-line traditional Americans with Vietnamese, Koreans, Iranians and Mexicans has turned this proud enclave into one of the most complex and diverse political areas of Louisville. In the late 1990s its aldermanic representative was a UofL graduate with a B.A. in political science policy. While a political pro from the old school of pothole and drainage concerns, he was equally cognizant of the growing international nature of his constituency. Alderman Dan Johnson was his name and peripatetic action was his game.

A visit to Angelo Drossos' San Antonio, Texas in the mid-1990s had astounded Johnson. What he saw was a lively and vibrant center city teeming with pedistrians, day and night, that he felt was the direct result of the Alamodome's construction. In early 1997, saying to himself, "If they can do it, why can't Louisville?"[259] Johnson buttonholed aldermanic president Steve Magre about the construction of "...the biggest arena in America, period."[260]

Magre represented a similar socio-economic area, known as Schnitzelburg, primarily comprised of second and third generation German immigrants and predominantly Roman Catholic Democratic party regulars. Schnitzelburg was 87% white with 65% traditional Democratic voting trends. A long-time administrator for Louisville's Roman Catholic Archdiocese, Magre was an equally adroit old-line politician, who had exhibited periodic leadership in his position as president of the Board of Aldermen. Another alderman, Greg Handy, representing an area similar to that of Johnson and Magre, also became intrigued by the concept of

Louisville's aldermen taking a leadership role in the development of a downtown arena.

In the spring of 1997, Magre, Johnson and Handy were joined by four African-American aldermen—Denise Bentley, Lawrence Montgomery (a former basketball star for Evansville University), Cherie Bryant-Hamilton and George Unseld (Wes Unseld's older brother) as the Board hired The Gateway Group of Cleveland, to study of the issue of building "...the biggest arena in America."

The aldermen's financial analyst, John P. Nelson, had prepared a well-hidden but interesting financial report on February 27, 1997. He compared Louisville with thirty-six (36) metropolitan areas that possessed major league professional sports franchises to determine the comparative index of payroll growth in Louisville vs. those cities between the years 1985-1996. Nelson determined:

Thirty-Six (36) professional sports cities	26.77% increase
Louisville SMSA	27.59%
United States	21.77%

Nelson also compared Louisville with thirteen (13) Metropolitan Statistical Areas in states bordering Kentucky from 1985 to the 1996. This was a grouping of cities that compete with Louisville for economic opportunity, businesses and financial gain. In the analysis, Nelson's objective was to measure the relative increase in economic activity of Louisville versus the economic growth rate of these competing cities. From this study, Nelson concluded that "...Louisville generated a slightly higher growth in economic activity than the average of the thirteen (13) competitive cities from 1985-1996." Louisville had grown by 27.59%, while the average growth for the competing cities was 27.04%. The following are the graphic results contained in the Nelson Report, with the cities having the NBA, NFL or major league baseball being italicized and bolded:

City	1985	1990	1996		Percent Change
Louisville	83.46	96.09	106.49	27.59	10.82
Chicago	*89.43*	*102.63*	*106.25*	*18.81*	*3.53*
Cleveland	*84.60*	*101.38*	*105.49*	*24.69*	*4.05*
Cincinnati	*83.62*	*99.59*	*105.61*	*26.30*	*6.04*
Columbus	84.37	96.89	108.61	28.73	12.10
Dayton	94.39	102.19	103.94	10.12	1.71
Ft. Wayne	68.55	98.72	106.34	55.13	7.72
Indianapolis	*81.76*	*97.98*	*105.85*	*29.46*	*8.03*
Kansas City	*87.78*	*96.68*	*109.44*	*24.68*	*13.02*
Memphis	*78.73*	*97.50*	*108.15*	*37.37*	*10.92*
Nashville	*81.18*	*92.73*	*111.89*	*37.83*	*20.66*
Norfolk	85.08	99.54	102.86	20.90	3.34
Richmond	85.48	100.32	106.34	24.40	6.00
St. Louis	*92.15*	*100.80*	*104.23*	*13.11*	*3.40*

More significant was Nelson's conclusion, from this graph, that the percentage growth in economic activity in Louisville was quite dramatic from 1990-1996 in comparison with competing cities in the surrounding states. The average of competing areas growth between 1990-1996 was only 7.47%, while Louisville had grown by 10.82% from 1990-1996.

Several months later, utilizing Nelson's work, Gateway produced a Market Feasibility Study for a new arena in downtown Louisville (The Gateway Report). This Report opined that such an arena should be used by UofL's men's/women's basketball teams and would be usable for arena football, professional hockey and other premier events; and concluded that a downtown arena would have a positive economic effect with the city government, alone, being capable of financing $90 million of the bonded construction cost without fear of risking financial crisis or impairing its financial integrity.

Seeking a wider community involvement, the aldermen formed a 100-person citizens task force (Committee on Sports Strategy), which met, conferred and issued a report on September 30, 1997, recommending that: "Professional sports franchises should be pursued as should major amateur tournaments and championship events."[261]

It was a grandiose idea with a very short lifespan. Within several months and without any public notice, the University of Louisville took away whatever sea legs did exist by signing a new 25-year lease with Freedom Hall (which meant that the aging facility would be 66 years old at the end of the lease). The project withered. Some aldermen were to believe that the university had deliberately undercut their initiative. (As the reader will see, this wouldn't be the only time that UofL's athletic program would adversely impact an effort to reinvigorate downtown Louisville.) Others believed that they were at fault, themselves, for not pursuing the arena concept more directly with and through the Governor's office. The idea that had germinated within Louisville's legislative branch of government, with extremely positive citizen input, fell asleep for another year and a half.

In early 1999, Street & Smith's *Sports Business Journal* carried an article observing that Louisville was one of America's largest metropolitan areas without major league professional team sports.

Re-enthused by this article, on April 2, 1999, Alderman Johnson inquired about my interest in receiving a city contract that would authorize my pursuit of an NBA team as the prime tenant in a new downtown arena. Having never met Johnson, there was a general awareness of his perseverance and determination, but before accepting such a commission, it was deemed advisable to examine Louisville's position vis-a-vis the NBA marketplace. Of particular importance was an analysis of the NBA's success quotient in the other mid-sized American cities. What was their track record and what differences existed between Louisville and those cities? Louisville didn't need to be embarrassed, all over again, in a nationally-based effort to procure another major league professional athletic franchise. The previous failure in 1977-78 with the effort to transfer the John Y. Brown-owned Buffalo Braves to Louisville was painful to those involved and seriously damaged the city's reputation in the eyes of the national sporting public and entertainment industry. A three-week analysis revealed a litany of interesting facts.

First, while Louisville was not viewed nationally as a sports-minded city, its metropolitan area was, in fact, the largest American metropolitan market area (other than Las Vegas) without a major league professional sports team. Its 1996 primary/secondary/tertiary population component of its SMSA was comparable with the average SMSA of all the mid-sized NBA cities. Also noteworthy was the fact that Louisville's SMSA fully supported the only major league athletic entertainment that existed in Louisville (Churchill Downs and the UofL's basketball program) despite a national trend of declining attendance in thoroughbred racing and reduced television viewership and revenue streams for collegiate basketball. Additionally, it was significant that Louisville's SMSA had provided record-breaking support for the PGA golf championship at Valhalla and the Breeder's Cup races — all being facts that gave credence to Louisville's SMSA being capable of supporting major league professional sports, and particularly an NBA franchise.

Of even larger interest was the appearance of a striking difference in the business environment of Louisville. The old-line whiskey and tobacco industries had clearly given way to a swiftly burgeoning and new service-based economy, which had, in turn, created significant new wealth. Louisville appeared to have changed since the days of the effort to transfer the Buffalo Braves in 1977-78.

Despite these particularly pungent statistics there were still several major hurdles ahead:

(i) Louisville's view of itself as a college town, incapable of supporting major league professional team sports; and

(ii) Louisville's innate inferiority complex and fear of the unknown and its aversion to change; and

(iii) While an NBA team could temporarily play in Freedom Hall, the major portion of any package to lure an existing NBA franchise was the absolute necessity that Louisville (either alone or in conjunction with other governmental entities) agree to build and finance a new state-of-the-art downtown arena.

To be sure, each of these hurdles would require significant local business leadership dedicated to demanding that Louisville begin thinking differently about itself. The re-ordering of this mirrored-view of itself also required inspired executive political leadership from the city to activate and sustain the raising of the expectations and aspirations of Louisvillians toward becoming an economically-competitive major-league city. Based upon this three-week analysis, Alderman Johnson was advised such a commission would be accepted.

Thus, the process began with a few believers, who together wouldn't have filled a '56 Chevy. It was a quiet beginning, with little fanfare—as it needed to be. The mouse had to creep into the house.

It was a beginning that, by necessity, included numerous telephone conversations with various NBA-involved and affiliated individuals. This contact was essential in order to properly initiate the process—the fishing-line needed to be quietly put in the water. The NBA, while an international business, is still a rather small fraternity, whose decision-makers, in the span of a twenty-four hour period, had the full capability of internal contact. This communication bridge needed to be crossed. It was.

The general consensus of those intra-NBA calls was just as it was in the late 1970s: "We don't understand why Louisville's not already in the NBA."

The first big eye-opener

It was a lovely spring evening in 1999. Brad and Carla Sue Broecker were hosting a party at their splendid home in eastern Louisville. The occasion was the dedication of a gallery addition, whose primary purpose was to display Brad's extensive English Moorcroft pottery collection. The Broeckers had been friends since high school and Brad had been a fraternity brother at Vanderbilt. His business career had been nothing short of meterioric. Having created the Broadway Series that brought Broadway shows to Louisville, over time he had expanded it to a multitude of other mid-sized American cities. The Broadway Series was now a part of SFX Entertainment, the media/entertainment division of the massive conglomerate, Clear Channel Communications. This success had propelled Brad to the position as the unquestioned leader, trail blazer and visionary of the entertainment business in Louisville. Carla Sue was deeply involved in charitable work and a widely-read social columnist for *The Voice-Tribune*, a weekly newspaper with upper-income circulation. They were (and are) dear friends. From this party forward, Carla Sue and Brad Broecker were to play a vitally important and dramatically positive role in the soon-to-unfold Louisville NBA odyssey.

That evening presented an opportunity to talk with Don Parkinson, the senior vice-president of Tricon Global Restaurants, an international fast-food conglomerate, headquartered in Louisville and comprised of Kentucky Fried Chicken, Pizza Hut and Taco Bell, which had been spun-off several years prior by Pepsico. Being aware of the media reports about my impending study of Louisville's NBA prospects, Don expressed interest in the effort. He was asked — If a team could be convinced to transfer to Louisville, was there any interest at Tricon in considering acquisition of naming rights for a new downtown arena? Parkinson's response was a surprise.

The cocktails were put aside and a half hour room-corner discussion ensued. Tricon would be very interested should it come to fruition and Parkinson requested continuing private updates on the progress. My initial examination of the Louisville market vis-a-vis other mid-sized NBA markets indicated that for Louisville to have a ghost of a chance to obtain such a transfer, it needed to have the whole package tied together—including a novel and financially-significant arena naming rights deal. There was no other company headquartered in Kentucky that could make such a commitment, because the whiskey and tobacco industries weren't permitted to advertise in athletic venues. It was agreed that Tricon's name would never be mentioned without its formal corporate approval.

As the reader will see, this evening proved to be of signal importance to the odyssey—from the beginning to its end.

Meeting with Chema

Cleveland's Mallorca Restaurant was the site, on May 13, 1999, of an electric meeting with Thomas Chema, the author of the aldermen's Gateway Report. Chema, well-connected and extremely knowledgeable, with a B.A. degree from Notre Dame and a law degree from Harvard, had played a leading role in the redevelopment and rejuvenation of downtown Cleveland, headlined by the construction of Jacobs Field for the Cleveland Indians and Gund Arena for the Cleveland Cavaliers. Of even greater significance was the fact that he had recently participated in the assembling of several potential ownership groups for two different NBA franchises, one of which was the Toronto Raptors (which would eventually play an interesting role in the Louisville odyssey). From this work Chema knew these businessmen were familiar with Louisville as a potential NBA city and they would be interested in having serious meetings with the city's community and political leaders.

This dinner meeting concluded with a definitive ninety-day plan of action to put Louisville in a position as the logical city for the transfer of an NBA franchise. The plan was to conclude by a meeting with David Stern, prior to the annual September NBA league meeting in Vancouver, B.C. (My Daytimer calendar noted: "Good Meeting/we have a long way to go.") While we did have a long way to go, within one month of my Aldermanic commission, we were on our way.

By mid-June, 1999, a Chema-led meeting with potential NBA-ownership investors from Texas was being scheduled. Jerry West, the longtime general manager of the Los Angeles Lakers, had worked closely with these Texans and was interested in concluding his career closer to his West Virginia birthplace. They had previously committed to him that if they obtained ownership of an NBA franchise, he would be offered the job as general manager. West would be a natural in Louisville. Chema agreed, as did his Texas investors. Discussions about the Chema developments were held with Aldermen Magre and Johnson, because their active participation in the Chema/Texas investors meeting would be essential. Denis Fleming, legal counsel for Governor Paul Patton, was advised of the progress, and the Governor's availability to attend the meeting was obtained.

In two months the quiet progress had been remarkable. Then Louisville's small-town-itis rolled through the door and into the living room, like a gigantic white Trojan horse.

On the afternoon of July 8, 1999, a phone call was received from Doug Proffitt of the Louisville ABC affiliate, WHAS-TV. Proffitt intended to carry a story on the evening's news about the "secrecy" of the NBA effort. He was in possession of the game plan/timetable letter that I had sent to Chema containing references to the Texas businessmen and their commitment to Jerry West. I was astounded. This was terrible — Jerry West was still an employee of the Lakers, as its general manager. If the story was published, Chema and the Texas businessmen could be subjected to a contractual interference lawsuit by the Lakers. A letter was immediately prepared and faxed to Proffitt requesting that his station temporarily refrain from airing the story. The reasons for the request were explained. Proffitt ran the story anyway.

Shortly thereafter, an examination into the letter's leak proved that a copy of it had been given to Proffitt by Alderman Johnson's secretary, who was disaffected and whose employment had been then-recently terminated. Astoundingly, the "leaker" may have been my former client Greg Page's fiancee! With this breach of confidence, all efforts to create the meeting with Chema and his Texas investors were dropped. Fingers were crossed, as it was hoped that David Stern would not learn of this Gomer Pyle-like series of events. It was exceedingly important at this larval stage that Louisville not appear bush-league in Stern's eyes. Later, it was realized that he had never learned about it. Thank God.

Mayor Dave

The Mayor of Louisville at the time was David Armstrong. With degrees from Murray State University and the University of Louisville Law School in 1969, he had been appointed to a minor judicial post by then-County Judge Todd Hollenbach. In 1969, along with Hollenbach, who was only

30, I had been elected as the Jefferson County Attorney at the age of 29. The first four-year term with Hollenbach had been a dynamic and action-oriented experience. A number of innovative ideas had been proposed and actuated, including the construction of a new courthouse and jail to replace turn-of-the-century structures. However, we had also experienced several well-publicized major policy differences over plans Hollenbach favored, but were deemed legally or fiscally imprudent by our office. It was widely believed that Hollenbach, being upset with our non-support of these programs, had encouraged Armstrong to run against me in the 1973 Democratic primary for Jefferson County Attorney. True or not, it made little difference. Armstrong was soundly defeated.

For some unknown reason, it has always seemed since then that Armstrong has been obsessed with that loss and has never gotten over it. Despite my support for him in various other political races, we had never been close either personally or politically. His subsequent political career had taken him from the position as Commonwealth Attorney in 1975 to Attorney General in 1983. Upon being defeated for the Democratic Lieutenant Governor's nomination in 1987, he returned to Louisville to try the practice of law. Unsuccessful in that effort, in 1989 he sought and won the position as Jefferson County Judge-Executive, was re-elected in 1993, and in 1999 became Louisville's Mayor.

Knowing the eventual importance NBA officials would place in the Mayor's support, and knowing that Armstrong, as a life-long politician, had no business experience nor any remote understanding of the financial aspects of an NBA franchise, it was decided to advise him, privately, about the opportunity. After the Chema meeting in Cleveland, several direct attempts were initiated to facilitate such a private meeting. There was never a response to the inquiries. Surely, I thought, there must be some way to create a meeting.

Louisville attorney Bob Benson was a longtime Armstrong confidant. He was a former state representative and active with UofL's athletic program. His small firm had received hundreds of thousands of dollars in legal contracts from Armstrong to do something (about which no one knew much) and it was widely rumored that they had a regular Wednesday bridge game at Audobon Country Club. In an effort to be inventive, on July 22, 1999, I met with Benson. Louisville's opportunity to attract the transfer of an NBA franchise was outlined in detail and he was encouraged to assist in obtaining the Mayor's interest. A potted plant on a window sill might have been more responsive.

This glazed-over reception prompted phone calls with nearly a dozen prominent Louisville business persons in late July, 1999. It was learned that generally Armstrong did not accept phone calls or meet with anyone, unless he pursued the meeting himself. He was described by one longtime, but by then disaffected, supporter as a growingly peculiar lone wolf, traveling on his own ego trip "...in a very light truck!" This absence of communication skill was confirmed by several aldermen, who had experienced significant frustration with his unwillingness to meet and confer. To make matters worse was the bizarre communication process among the city's elected political leadership, by which Armstrong spoke to the aldermen through the press, and vice versa. With the differences between the executive and legislative branches being publically displayed, the result was an impossibility for compromise, because someone was, by necessity, always the public loser. This revelation was enormously disconcerting. It all seemed like a lot of child's play that would be very difficult to explain or justify to a major businessman seeking a new home for a multi-hundred million dollar business.

Upon reflection, it was determined to forget the NBA in Louisville project, finish the report to the aldermen, and proceed with more important things like family and the law firm's work and growth. Life is too short to be thrown into such an unsatisfactory and foolish public environment.

Time to fold 'em

A final report was issued to the Board of Aldermen on August 3, 1999, entitled "Louisville in the National Basketball Association."

It concluded that Louisville and its SMSA was a reasonably viable NBA market and the city government could conservatively afford to construct a downtown arena/venue without endangering its financial credit. But the challenge was unmistakable as I wrote:

"The elected political leadership of Louisville must decide whether or not it is interested in pursuing a franchise in the NBA. It is not a unique decision for a city's elected political leadership—the same decision has been made in Atlanta (in the early 1960s with the transfer of the Milwaukee Braves to Atlanta), in Indianapolis (with the transfer of the Baltimore Colts to Indianapolis), in Nashville (with the transfer of the Houston Oilers to Nashville) and in a number of other cities.

"If those leaders decide that it is not in Louisville's interest to pursue the transfer of a franchise in the NBA, then this entire matter should be put to bed—because Louisville does not deserve nor does it need another failure in the sports-entertainment market of the United States.

"That decision must be made based upon 'reasons', not 'excuses' because this examination of Louisville as an NBA market does not afford an 'excuse' for the decision to not undertake the effort.

"Louisville, while a legitimate NBA market, must be willing to exercise the requisite political leadership...."

What had begun in May, 1999 as a very hopeful opening scenario for a major business opportunity had crashed within a month, by press leaks from a malcontented clerical person and the unwillingness of its Mayor to meet and confer. It had been exciting, the opportunity was real—but the necessary and required political leadership was non-existent.

Post bow-out

Mid-summer is a slow news time in Louisville, so virtually any new story gets unexpectedly sizeable coverage. The Report to the Aldermen received considerable news coverage, not so much for its content as for the summer doldrums. Slow news time included Tony Cruise's popular two-hour nightly radio sports call-in show. On August 4, 1999, Cruise extended an invitation. He was a young and energetic sports radio personality who wasn't afraid of controversy. The topic of the evening was to be the NBA Report and dinner was offered at Hoops on Westport Road, the site of the show. My wife, Norma, and daughter, Alexis, who was completing her Ph.D. in criminal justice, joined the occasion. The ribs were fine, but within minutes there was a realization of a classic sandbagging. Cruise was totally against the concept of the NBA in Louisville. The evening was a struggle, but to Cruise's (and my) surprise there were more calls than expected and nearly half were favorable.

To Cruise's credit, over the course of the next several years he was to throw off the shackles of Louisville's self-doubt and become a positive force. As time progressed he began to see the reality and logic of Louisville's NBA opportunity. Cruise reordered his thought process to one of positivism — and rejected the mediocrity of the past, refusing to be overwhelmed by the mystery of change or a fear of the unknown. Instead, he was willing to endorse a determination for change through concerted action. Much of the eventual success in developing the concept within Louisville's minds-eye would be due to the opportunity for extensive public discourse provided by Tony Cruise and his radio sports talk show.

The remainder of August, 1999 in Louisville was a sad time—the local hero and icon, Pee Wee Reese, had passed. The 'Little Colonel' of Brooklyn Dodger fame had been the closest friend of Jackie Robinson and had played a major role in the integration of major league baseball. As it should have, Louisville's wake for Pee Wee suspended any thought of the future in the local sports pages, and for nearly a month Louisvillians looked back in time to honor Pee Wee and what he stood for. Pee Wee Reese—a great American, Kentuckian and Louisvillian, deserved every honor bestowed upon him during his lifetime and upon his passing. He was among the true gentlemen I've ever met.

As time would go by, I would find myself repeatedly wishing that the 'Little Colonel' were still with us to offer a few cogent thoughts to reluctant Louisvillians, who were fearful of the big leagues and the challenges of the future. For sure, Pee Wee Reese was one Louisvillian who understood change in society and the importance of taking a leadership position amidst the wave of change—he was certainly not afraid of change in the big leagues.

Meanwhile, Mayor Dave remained mute. As the summer rolled into the fall of 1999, Norma and I were invited to a cocktail-dinner party at Dr. and Mrs. John Holtman's home on September 5, 1999. Among those present was another of the mayor's confidants, Dave Snowden. As the owner of a local talent agency, Snowden's primary markets were regional Holiday Inn bars and state fairs, including Kentucky's. Snowden maintained a personal relationship with the general manager of Freedom Hall and had been appointed by Mayor Dave to the presidency of the local convention bureau. When Snowden was buttonholed about the importance of his help in reaching out to the mayor about the NBA opportunity, he responded that it would be difficult for him to arrange such a meeting, because Armstrong wasn't returning his phone calls, either. A peculiar response, because only fifteen minutes prior, Snowden was waxing eloquent in describing a private meeting he and his wife had just had with Armstrong.

Later in the evening Snowden sought me out with a staccato-like barrage of questions. If the NBA was pulled off, what would happen to the rest of the entertainment industry in Louisville? What would happen to Freedom

Hall? What would happen to UofL's athletic program? Far too many questions for a cocktail party conversation, but, since the questions presumed 'problems' rather than 'opportunities,' they clearly established Snowden's team membership. Snowden's approach was to be the first step down a long and tortuous path of negativism that the NBA project would tread over the next two and a half years. There would be others, many others. However, once a match is lit around a stack of dry kindling, a conflagration often results. The match had been lit.

The Fall of 1999

On September 24, 1999, the national sports scene was intrigued by an announcement from the NBA annual meeting in Vancouver, B.C. Bill and Nancy Laurie (the daughter/heir of Sam Walton [Walmart]), who owned the Savis Center in St. Louis and the St. Louis Blues NHL team, had purchased the Vancouver Grizzlies from John McCaw of Orca Bay for $200 million. This news further ignited the local kindling. Questions began coming, phone calls increased. Were we in touch with Laurie? Would Laurie move the team to Louisville?

Laurie had not been contacted, but had the time now come to make the call? One of the oldest adages of decision-making is—if you don't know how your effort will be received, you should wait a day in favor of further contemplation. By waiting a day, we later learned that Louisville had preserved its credibility within the NBA inner circle. Instead of calling Laurie, phone calls were made to certain individuals who attended the Vancouver NBA meetings. It was learned that the Laurie purchase had not been pre-cleared with the NBA Commissioner's office. NBA officialdom had been taken by surprise. Under the league's constitution, such a purchase and sale requires the approval of the league's Board of Governors. To obtain this approval, all the bases needed to be touched. This had been learned way back in 1977-78, when we were endeavoring to accomplish the transfer of the NBA Buffalo Braves to Louisville. The NBA constitution had been violated by Laurie and McCaw. It didn't make any difference that among the violators were billionaires and an heir of Sam Walton.

Ever the astute diplomat, NBA Commissioner David Stern allowed several months to elapse before aborting the sale and locating Chicago businessman Michael Heisley to purchase the Vancouver team with a commitment to do everything he could to maintain the team in Vancouver.

Heisley was a billionaire corporate turn-around artist, who owned forty-four businesses, a number of which were in Canada. Unknown to anyone at the time, within sixteen months Heisley would play a major role in Louisville's NBA odyssey.

Later in November, 1999 a phone call was made to Laurie. He was contrite over the Vancouver events. It was a pleasant call. While we would never meet Laurie, he, like Heisley, would play an interesting role in Louisville's NBA odyssey as it unfolded. However as the reader will learn, Laurie and his lawyer would be far from contrite when they reappeared in late March, 2001.

By Mid-October, 1999, as the kindling smoldered, there remained a continuing void of local political leadership. Mayor Armstrong's interest was absent, causing the aldermen to feel stymied and unsure of the proper course to take.

On September 27, 1999, Aldermen Johnson and Magre called a meeting of the Citizens Task Force. The electricity was surprising—full of vibrancy and the verve of unleashed activism. The intensity of the Task Force members' beliefs had not been previously appreciated. Many spoke up. Many were young people who addressed their long-term stake in Louisville's future. The young people to a one insisted that, with their lives and their children's lives ahead of them, they wanted to see Louisville take dramatic steps to get on the cutting edge as we moved into the 21st century. The fervor was exhilarating. Another speaker was particularly significant. Former Alderman Stanley Benovitz, an elderly local lawyer prominent in Louisville's Jewish community, eloquently pleaded for the aldermen's leadership on the downtown arena project.

The odyssey had begun with a mouse, whose adherents could be contained in a '56 Chevy. But now it was clearly observable that the local kindling was smoldering with increased intensity. The extent of the public's and young persons' desire to see real leadership in Louisville was apparent. They were not just asking for change, they were demanding it.

Darrell Griffith is the "Louisville Legend" who, as the chief surgeon of the Doctors of Dunk, had led UofL to its first NCAA championship in March, 1980. Thereafter, Griff had become an NBA All-Star with the Utah Jazz, playing his entire career in Salt Lake City. He had seen, first-hand, how a mid-sized American city could embrace an NBA team and succeed.

Having been born and raised in Louisville, he knew it would work in Louisville. Griff called, we met—and he asked to be in the front line of the effort. It was easy to see that he was a believer, an advocate and another young person who wasn't willing to sit on his butt and let Louisville's opportunity wither away. He wanted Louisville's political leadership to take action. Griff's determination and forthrightness were remarkable—he was a champion, who understood change and wasn't fearful of the unknown. There were few mid-sized American cities who had the luxury of a person of his talent, persuasiveness and persona. Griff was an important piece of the puzzle—a leader who understood the NBA industry and who knew Louisville was capable of being more than a college town. People would listen to Griff. He could assure them that the Utah Jazz had not damaged college basketball in Utah. That day in September was another signal event as the odyssey began to develop a new set of wings.

October, 1999 had been a typical fall month in Louisville. The court trial calendars were in full swing, which included a week-long trial for our law firm. In the midst of trial preparation, a phone call was received from Aldermanic President Magre and Alderman Dan Johnson. The aldermen had determined to act, despite the Mayor's inertia, by approving a personal services contract authorizing the pursuit of the transfer of an NBA team to Louisville. Various professional and family responsibilities had caused a several week sojourn from the process, and the call was a surprise. Doubts still existed about the undertaking because, except for the Aldermen, the public political leadership that was required had not appeared.

During the odyssey certain days brought unusually vibrant expectations. October 20, 1999, was such a day and evening. Members of our law firm had arranged for a meeting with a young persons' group at the downtown public library. The evening arrived with little promise but swiftly turned. Here was another group of young people, probably thirty-five in number, who were demanding that Louisville step up to the plate and change. It was a wide-ranging discussion that eventually centered around the importance of Louisville's NBA opportunity. Earlier in the day Doug Cobb, a dynamic, young and successful Louisville businessman, who had just completed a term as the executive director of Greater Louisville, Inc., visited our offices to inquire about the effort and to express the encouragement of the business community.

That evening Norma and I agreed. If the Aldermen would provide our law firm with a contract authorizing the opportunity to pursue the objective without political interference, we would jointly pursue the task. Were times changing in Louisville? Was the old yoke of Ruppian aversion to change and a fear of the unknown gone? I wasn't sure, but now we were really going to find out.

CHAPTER NINE

The Rockets Rocket into Louisville

It was a rainy Tuesday night, October 26, 1999. Our trial team was in the office preparing for the second day of a week-long trial when word was received that the Alderman had approved a $50,000 contract authorizing our law firm to accomplish the transfer of an NBA team to Louisville. While we were excited about the challenge, it would have to await the trial's conclusion.

A few days later a newspaper headline would dramatically tilt the pinball machine:

> "Rockets Rejected - Denied New Arena
> Rockets May Be Lured Away"
> *Houston Chronicle*, Wednesday, November 3, 1999

The Houston Fiasco

When completed in the early 1960s, Houston's Astrodome was considered the eighth Wonder of the World—a structural and engineering phenomenon seating over 65,000 spectators under one roof. For several decades it was the site of numerous national and international events, the home of Houston's major league baseball team and its NFL franchise, the Houston Oilers. But by the late 1980s it had become worn out and outmoded. In 1987, after giving serious consideration to the transfer of his Oilers to Jacksonville, Bud Adams persuaded the Republican Harris County

Commissioners to fund improvements in the aging structure.

A few years later, still dissatisfied with the deficient Astrodome, Adams encouraged the city's Democratic politicians to support the construction of a new Astrodome in downtown Houston. The facility would house the Oilers, the Houston Livestock Show and Rodeo and the Houston Rockets NBA team. But Les Alexander, owner of the Rockets, hadn't been consulted about Adams' plans and wasn't interested in a new arena unless his franchise controlled the basketball-related revenue streams and the basketball season dates.

For nearly a decade, talk of stadiums had joined politics and religion as subjects guaranteed to stir discussion. The debate grew as the Oilers won-loss record plummeted. From a Texas-competitive standpoint, a lousy team didn't deserve a new stadium and the Oilers had become atrocious. It had all begun several years earlier, when they lost a playoff game after leading 35-3 shortly after halftime. As the Oilers disintegrated, its fan base dwindled. Eventually, Houston and Adams had had enough of each other. He and his Oilers left for more placid pastures in Nashville.

Unwilling to accept even partial responsibility for the Oiler divorce, many Houstonians inexplicably shifted the blame for the loss to Alexander and his Rockets. This surreal position was taken despite the fact that the University of Houston's greatest basketball graduate, Hakeem Olajuwon, had captained the Houston Rockets to two NBA world championships. Even more perplexing for Alexander was that his women's team, The Comets, was the preeminent WNBA team, winning four WNBA world championships in the decade of the '90s.

In addition to being unappreciated and blamed for the Oilers' departure, the Rockets had serious financial problems. As a sublessee in the aging Compaq Center, their revenue stream was constricted. The prime lease was held by a minor league hockey team (Aeros) owned by Chuck Watson, the CEO of energy conglomerate, Dynegy. In Alexander's mind, it was unreasonable and bordered on being ridiculous that his NBA world champions would be subject to a sublease controlled by a minor league hockey team. Determined to change this absurdity, Alexander sued Watson to free his Rockets from the sublease. Alexander would soon learn that realism doesn't often prevail in Texas when it is pitted against good old boys with energy and oil patch connections.

Richard Rainwater, a Fort Worth billionaire who had backed and bankrolled George W. Bush's ownership of the Texas Rangers, also owned Houston's Greenway Plaza that provided air-conditioning and parking for the Compaq Center. In the Rockets litigation against Watson, the Texas state court ruled that Rainwater's company was a third-party beneficiary of the sublease between Watson and the Rockets and, as such, possessed the legal right to prevent the Rockets from vacating the sublease until its term was concluded in November, 2003. Inexplicably, Alexander didn't appeal the ruling. It was a final order. He had tried the Texas legal system and failed. The Rockets were stuck for six more years under the sublease.

Refusing to be cowed by Watson and his minor league hockey team, Alexander undertook a Texas-style business move. After post-litigation efforts to negotiate a more favorable lease with Watson failed, secret negotiations began to purchase the Edmonton Oilers, a National Hockey League team. It was Alexander's ploy to annihilate Watson's minor league hockey market by moving the Edmonton Oilers to Houston. The negotiations leaked— becoming another subject of public discourse in Houston. The ploy had backfired.

By this point the Admirals of Houston's sports boats were all pointed in different directions, as were the sports fans in Houston. Drayton McLane's baseball Astros cut a deal with Ken Lay of Enron to finance a new indoor baseball field. Houston billionaire Bob McNair was seeking an NFL expansion franchise to replace the Oilers which, due to the Astrodome's inadequacies, would also require a new stadium. There didn't seem to be enough room for Alexander's Rockets. Besides, who cared? Alexander wasn't from 'round there. Short of stature, born and raised in the Bronx, Jewish, with a funny accent, and worst of all he didn't look good in a Stetson and cowboy boots.

By 1999, the back-street business brawl had festered into a Texas-sized political war between officials of Republican Harris County and Democratic Houston, with Houston's major businessmen and women all taking sides — mostly against Alexander. It was bitter, like an episode of *Dallas* or *Falcon Crest*. Alexander wouldn't relent.

His next move was undertaken vis-a-vis his Democratic political clout. With support from the Democratic city officials, a referendum for a new Rockets arena was placed on the ballot in November 1999. Following this decade-long bitterness, distrust, and J.R. Ewingism, Houstonians went to the polls on Tuesday, November 2, 1999. In typically grandiose Houston fashion, voters approved over a half billion dollars in bonds for community improvements.[262] Yet, $80 million in hotel/rental-car taxes that would have funded the Rockets new arena (virtually none of which would be paid by Houstonians) was given the heave-ho by 54-46% and over 100,000 votes. Alexander's nemesis Watson, the minor league hockey team owner, funded the opposition. Primarily absent from referendum involvement were Astros owner, Drayton McLane, Bob McNair, owner of the new NFL franchise, the Houston Texans and Enron's Ken Lay. Their silence was deafening but fully understood by Houstonians. It meant they were against Alexander and his Rockets.

In a New York City teleconference on the Monday prior to the Houston referendum, NBA Commissioner David Stern discussed the potential movement of certain NBA franchises, including the Houston Rockets. He mentioned Memphis, New Orleans, Nashville and Louisville as interesting potential sites for transferring franchises. Following the failed referendum, without waiting a day, New Orleans Mayor Mark Morial and Louisiana Governor Mike Foster issued press releases affirmatively stating their intent to purloin the Rockets to New Orleans. Despite Stern's pre-referendum observation and Houston's ballot box rejection of the Rockets, the abrupt and overt action of Louisiana's politicos wasn't acceptable within the NBA. It endangered the league's image of stability. The Louisiana Bayou Boys were scolded about it, in due course, but as the odyssey proceeded, this powerful Louisiana executive political leadership eventually would adversely impact Louisville.

Les Alexander and his wife were proud and good people. They had given their all to Houston. They had tried to fit in, but their immense efforts had been rejected. The day following the referendum, the Alexanders left Houston for their Boca Raton, Florida, home. Rockets General Manager George Postolos, his wife Nicole, and their children left for Disney World and Houston festered as the Alexanders stewed — literally and figuratively a thousand miles apart.

The first call and the first action

On the evening of November 3, 1999 at about 6:00 PM, a phone call was received from Liz Mullen, of Street & Smith's *Sports Business Journal*. She was interested in discussing Louisville's pursuit of an NBA team, with particular emphasis about our intentions as a result of the Houston referendum. Nothing was confirmed other than Louisville's determination to achieve the transfer of an NBA team — from anywhere. The intrigue had begun.

Since no one had gone home yet that evening, an immediate meeting of our legal beagles was convened. While there had been a general awareness of the Houston referendum, we had not realized the massive extent of the business, political and social disaffection. It had been presumed that the Rockets franchise was not a realistic potential transferee, due to Houston's market size and the importance of its oil and space industries to the nation's economy. But now reflection was required. In 1999, the NFL wasn't extant in Los Angeles, the second largest city in the nation, and the Oilers had left Houston to prosper in the mid-sized city of Nashville. So maybe, in reality, Houston's position was vulnerable.

Whatever the opportunity was it had to be pursued and that pursuit had to start, immediately. Action options were discussed, thoughts flowed freely and decisions were reached as to the most advisable approach. The primary thesis by which we would be guided was the old adage, "You only get one chance to make a first impression." Through the office's internet and people-tracer systems, the Alexander's residence address in Boca Raton was located. The November 4, 1999 Fed-Ex letter to Alexander began:

Re: Houston Rockets (transferrable to Louisville)
Dear Mr. Alexander:

"I know you must be distraught as a result of the recent election results in Houston. However, as I'm sure you appreciate, oftentimes (in life as in sport) a loss can be a gain, if viewed in the macrocosm."

The letter invited him to consider Louisville, making a particular point of setting it apart from the improvident New Orleans/Louisiana public exposition of the day prior. He was assured of our ability to conduct private negotiations[263] and invited to speak with Commissioner Stern as to my credibility. Another letter was sent, via Fed-Ex, to Stern containing a copy of Alexander's letter and re-advising him of Louisville's determination. We crossed our fingers, said a quiet prayer and went home for the day.

Like the Athenians of yore, Louisville had put its toe in the water. Instead of a drawn bath, that water was soon to resemble the depth and expanse of the Pacific Ocean. In store was a turbulent ride across that ocean.

A day had gone by with nary a word. On Friday, November 5, 1999, Norma and I attended the Deaf Oral School's Antique Show at Louisville Gardens, an event we've enjoyed for years. We ran into old friends Don and Libby Parkinson. Our paths hadn't crossed since the spring of 1999 party at the Broecker's home. Don was now retiring as senior vice president of Tricon Global Restaurants. Also at the event were Jennifer and Jonathan Blum, another senior vice president at Tricon. After performing the introductions, Don inquired as to the status of the NBA effort. He was advised of the failed Houston referendum and the previous day's efforts to contact the Rockets owner. He and Jonathan affirmed their collective interest in Tricon's involvement with an NBA franchise move to Louisville. There was an extended discussion about whether a team's name could be changed to the Kentucky Colonels as a tie-in with KFC. Jonathan asked to be kept apprised about the developments. Business cards were exchanged. The importance of confidentiality was reiterated, because Tricon had not run the concept up the corporate flag pole, but both felt confident it would be favorably received under proper circumstances and providing there was a legitimate opportunity.

A marvelous week of excitement and opportunity had ended with the biggest possible interest level the effort could have obtained at such an early time — the interested ear of major executives for a multi-billion dollar international corporation, based in Louisville. It was hard to sleep that weekend—so much had happened so quickly. It was only the beginning. Before it all ended, there would be dozens of sleepless and anxious nights.

Rockets approach the launch pad

The following Monday, November 8, 1999, at 5:30 PM, the call came, from Mike Goldberg of the prestigious Houston law firm of Baker & Botts. As Alexander's and the Rockets' private legal counsel, Goldberg explained that his client had received the letter and spoken with Commissioner Stern, who suggested he make contact through legal counsel to initiate discussions about Louisville's interest level and availability.

The discussion was direct, frank and to the point. His client was considerably disheartened with Houston, its bickering, its climate (both temperature and emotional) and its multiple (savory and unsavory) vicissitudes; and had been encouraged by Stern to examine the franchise's transfer options fully and completely. Alexander's discussion with Stern allowed him to believe that we knew what we were doing in Louisville (which was good), and, as a result, he was undertaking an analysis of Louisville as a potential NBA market. Goldberg said his client wanted me to know that any decision to go forward with discussions would depend on whether the economic analysis of Louisville was positive and whether Louisville was prepared to build a downtown arena, with a minimum of political dissention. If that proved to be the case and if the Rockets decided to move from Houston, Goldberg promised that his client would give Louisville full consideration. We left the phone call agreeing that both sides had a lot to do. Another message was loud and clear: the only people (other than Commissioner Stern) who could be informed of the call were the Governor, the Mayor and the president of the Board of Aldermen, and each of them had to understand and agree to confidentiality at this point in the effort.

The moment was exhilarating. There were high-fives all around the office. Within only six days, Louisville had positioned itself as a potential alternative for the Houston Rockets franchise transfer. But the excitement was only momentary. The real work was now to begin and there was one rather large problem—the confidentiality restriction would make the initial stages of the effort extremely difficult. Somehow, with no public vetting, we were going to have to find a way to convince the many people who needed to know that the opportunity was real. Without public disclosure, the business community (and the public at large) would most likely think I was crazy, just leading everyone on and smoking something in my briar pipe. But another adage was also applicable—"Where there's a will, there's a way." So the process to find the way began.

Phone calls were initiated to old Vanderbilt classmates in Nashville, who were active in that city's public affairs. It was essential to understand, from the inside, the real story about how mid-sized Nashville purloined the Oilers from Houston. Office personnel were asked to find out everything that was available to know about Les Alexander and his wife, Nanci. The staff located names of several Louisvillians with winter residences near Alexander in Boca Raton, thinking that, at some point, they might be able to be ambassadors for Louisville. One of them was the "Golden Boy," the famed Notre Dame and Green Bay Packer star, Paul Hornung. He was a friend—the contact could be quickly made.

Many things were quickly learned about the Alexanders. For years they had been among the largest private charitable patrons in Houston. Millions of dollars had been donated to various Houston charities, from the orchestra to the world-famous M. D. Anderson Cancer Clinic. Their interest in the arts and other charitable causes was a match made in heaven for Louisville's charitable endeavors. That would be a real selling point for a certain segment of Louisville's doubting Thomases. The Rockets Clutch City Foundation had been organized for the purpose of connecting the team's management and players with Houston's service and charitable programs and had donated more than $5 million to local charities. Alexander's fortune had been made as a securities broker/trader in New York and later they had moved to southern California. It was also learned that Nanci Alexander was a dedicated member of PETA. Once she had been held to some ridicule in the Houston media over her refusal to permit helium balloons at Rocket games for fear that they might get into the outside air and endanger birds. Of equal interest was Les Alexander's passion for thoroughbred horse racing. It would be intriguing to know them and see how they shared life with these seemingly conflicting interests. An interesting couple that piqued one's curiosity. It was an exciting beginning.

Tora–Tora–Tora

The NBA odyssey would eventually resemble a Coney Island roller-coaster ride, fully capable of reaching lofty zeniths and lowly nadirs in the course of a single day—sometimes even a single hour. The strain of this dichotomy would become enormous. Surprise was to be the hallmark. But there was never a bigger one than the one that occurred on November 12, 1999—from only eighty miles distance.

For years William F. "Billy" Reed had been a personal and professional friend. During his tenure as lead sports columnist for *The Courier-Journal*, he had been enabled to obtain many unique stories about our law firm's professional athletic clients. There were up-close-and-personal articles about the Colonels ABA championship year that no reporter could have obtained without an inside opportunity. He was given exclusive scoops on John Y. Brown's sale of Dan Issel to the Baltimore Claws and Issel's eventual transfer to the Denver Nuggets. There was intimate day-to-day involvement with the effort to lure the Buffalo Braves. Repeatedly, Reed had authored articles encouraging the Braves transfer to Louisville. He had been present at Del

Coronado NBA meetings, personally participating in the effort to convince John Y. Brown to effectuate the transfer. Reed had believed, with all his heart, that Louisville should be in the NBA. Of the many other opportunities for access to our clients certain ones stand out as special and unusual.

He met privately with Cincinnati Bengal quarterback Ken Anderson at the 1982 Super Bowl in Detroit when the Bengals faced Joe Montana and the 49ers in what was to become one of the most famous and the most widely-watched Super Bowls in history. Reed had been intimately involved in the early development of Greg Page's heavyweight boxing career capped by one-on-one access to Page and Don King following the 1981 Kentucky Derby, when Page agreed to King's promotion contract. Reed was present in Las Vegas when Page lost his eventual championship fight with Tim Witherspoon, getting exclusive interviews with everyone. This rendition only touches the surface of the opportunities that were provided to Billy Reed to enhance his reporting career. Then there was the personal friendship.

Representing his legal interests upon his employment termination from *The Courier-Journal* following the newspaper's purchase by Gannett, we negotiated a contract for him with Host Communications, enabling his matriculation into the private sector at a dollar value far in excess of his *Courier-Journal* salary. Timely that contract was — facilitating his life's dream to provide for his daughters' collegiate education. Thereafter, he had returned to *Sports Illustrated*; and, having lost that employment, in the fall of 1999 became a bi-weekly columnist for the *Lexington Herald-Leader*. Norma and I had become concerned about Billy. He seemed to have great difficulty keeping a job—and he was getting older, like all of us. We had discussed those concerns with him.

Billy Reed was often called "Brother Bill" by me. We had shared life's experiences and family concerns, crying on each others shoulders when things went wrong and celebrating together when they went right. Other than myself, Norma and our children, Brother Bill was among the happiest celebrants at our wedding on Valentine's Day, 1983. He was one of the guys who would orate at my funeral or vice versa, whichever came first. I considered Brother Bill a real friend. Boy, was I wrong.

Without calling for an interview or an inquiry of any kind, from his perch at the *Lexington Herald-Leader* Brother Bill chirped an unimaginable broadside at me, my professional integrity as a lawyer, the Louisville Board of Aldermen and the whole concept of the NBA in Louisville, concluding:

"So it's a disastrous idea that deserves a quick death. But politicians being what they are, you can bet Miller will tell the Aldermen what they want to hear, and that they'll use that to keep this boondoggle alive. Shame on them. For the 50cent cost of this newspaper, they're getting better advice than what they'll get from Miller for $50,000."

An unannounced, surprising and confusing bolt out of the blue, written by a skilled writer, who fully understood the subtleties of wordsmithing. Such wording was, unmistakably, a deliberate attempt to impeach the effort, and my personal and professional credibility. Why would Brother Bill shoot at his thirty-year friend's integrity from the hip? Why wouldn't he even show the common courtesy to call before he took the shot? Norma was equally astonished.

For some inexplicable reason, our friendship had become expendable cannon-fodder for Brother Bill. A discussion with the editor of the *Herald-Leader* revealed this wasn't the first time Brother Bill had undertaken an unannounced sniper shot at someone without any forewarning or an interview. The *Herald-Leader's* editors were gracious with apologies. They were accepted and the opportunity for a response was provided. It was availed.

Reed's malcontented diatribe was to continue. Throughout the early stages of the NBA effort in Louisville, the shrillness of Reed's writing grew, becoming even more bizarre after his employment was terminated with the *Herald-Leader*. Shortly thereafter Reed, once one of America's premier sports columnists, had found his career relegated to writing once a week for UofL's weekly sports paper for season ticket holders. Several sports journalists, knowledgeable of my long-term friendship with Brother Bill, called to ask, "What's wrong with Billy?" There was no discernable answer to the question —at the time. Later, we would learn of Demon Rum's "demonry."

Reed had allowed some form of hidden animus to guide his poisoned pen, destroying our friendship in the process. His ill-tempered and vitriolic columns and his inconceivable appearance before the Muhammad Ali Museum Board of Directors (subsequently discussed) reflected far more than a disagreement. It had become his cause celebre. He had to defeat the effort BAMA (by any means available), whatever the cost. It was sad to see a friendship like ours self-destruct. An apology, repeatedly requested, was never forthcoming.

A call to the Golden Boy was also non-productive. Paul Hornung's gut-instinct caused him to believe Louisville wasn't economically capable of maintaining an NBA franchise. He genuinely felt he was right. Following a lengthy discussion, Hornung agreed he would be a good citizen and keep his opinions to himself, until the issue could be further developed. As opposed to Reed's approach, Paul promised to speak favorably about Louisville, if he ran into the Alexanders during the winter months in Boca Raton.

Paul was (and is) a class act. He proved that a gladiator, who has life experiences in the arena of competition and endeavor, generally is a more broad-minded and grounded individual than a pundit, whose life's experience has consisted of little more than sitting in the stands and watching, having never fought the good fight on the arena floor.

Thanksgiving turkey was good

On Monday November 15, 1999, David Stern called to discuss the Reed column. Remembering that we were friends, he didn't understand Reed's off-the-wall position. His call, prompted by Reed's single column in a college-town newspaper, verified what was already known — as the Disney refrain goes, "It's A Small World After All." This reality was something we would remember everyday thereafter throughout the odyssey.

Stern encouraged our continuing efforts, expressing his appreciation for the confidential nature of the process to date. Encouraging my contact at any time deemed necessary, he offered the offices of the NBA for research or any questions, as long as we honored the confidentiality of the negotiations with Les Alexander. Finally, he inquired as to whether any arrangements or discussions about naming rights had been conducted with major companies. He was told that discussions had been undertaken but there was no present authority to disclose the corporate name to him, but he would be very happy when he could be told about the particular company's interest level. His response: "Bruce, I'd like to be that happy sooner than later." Knowing Stern's dry wit and unique way of delivering a message, his riposte was a clear signal—Tricon's permission to divulge its identity to Stern had to be obtained—very quickly. Now, things were really popping.

On a bi-weekly basis the developments in Louisville and Houston were being relayed back and forth with Alexander's lawyer, Mike Goldberg. In late November it was suggested he, Rockets COO George Postolos, and Alexander consider a confidential visit to Louisville to meet with various business leaders and the Governor of Kentucky. There was no immediate response.

During Thanksgiving Week, contact was made with representatives of or persons knowledgeable about the status of other NBA franchises, including the Los Angeles Clippers, the Charlotte Hornets, the Golden State Warriors, the Vancouver Grizzlies and the Orlando Magic. The fish-net needed to be spread wider. It was inadvisable to direct our sole attention toward the Rockets. Such a strategy would put them in the driver's seat in the event of any subsequent negotiations. It was apparent that certain franchises were in various stages of considering the concept of relocation. Some had considered it. Some hadn't, but figured they might in the future. Some were unsure but doubted they would undertake the effort. Whatever the response, there was, indeed, a glade full of un-picked fruit trees.

From the outside looking in, this thing really seemed to have some real legs.

Since my father's suicide on November 30, 1965, that day had always been my most difficult day of the year—day for reflection and remembrance of childhood and young adult dreams, along with the inspiration and encouragement he had bequeathed me—all cut too short by his unanticipated death.

Dad had a pretty rough childhood. His father, Fountain, was a race track enthusiast with unusual mathematical skills. He enjoyed employment with tracks around the country as an odds-maker, before totalizator boards were common. One evening as a child, I witnessed Fountain correctly adding a ten column set of ten deep figures—backwards in fifteen seconds. Early in Dad's life, Fountain's affinity for the track had resulted in a significant loss of family money. Despite being the salutatorian of Louisville's Manual High School in 1923, Dad wasn't permitted to accept a scholarship to the Wharton School of Finance at the University of Pennsylvania. Instead, to help support his family, he accepted a job as a teller at the old Louisville Trust Company while attending the Jefferson School of Law at night. When the bank closed in the Depression, he moved across the street to a teller's position with the old Fidelity & Columbia Bank, that eventually became Citizens Fidelity, that eventually became PNC Bank. Eventually Dad rose to the position as vice president in charge of the bank's trust company. He met mother at Citizens Fidelity. She worked there, too.

Dad was a hale fellow well met with what, as a child, seemed like a million friends. The respect for him appeared boundless. The bank and the "customers of the bank" (as he called them) were his life outside our home. But at home Dad was a tough cookie—a Bobby Knight. The toughest guy I ever knew. There was no spin-zone in the Miller household—unless it was your head for not paying attention. The stories about J.R. Miller are legendary, as are the one-liners, like: "Use your head for something other than a hat rack!" or "Are you a man or a mouse?"

"How could this powerful and grand exemplar of life itself take his own?" was the politely unasked question on everyone's mind at the funeral. Reality found his trick knee buckling, which caused a fall outside the bank where his head impacted the street curb. It was a severe blow—resulting in tintinnitus (ringing in the ears)—that was uncontrollable. For three months he barely slept. The doctors tried everything. Finally, the Mayo Clinic in Rochester, Minnesota agreed to intercede. Unbecomingly, Dad declined the opportunity. Should have been a signal. But we didn't see it. Shortly thereafter, the toughest guy I'd ever known and probably will ever know, put an electric meat carver to his throat and ended his life.

The impact of this life that had ended was immense, and never better exemplified than on December 3, 1965. So many people came to pay their final respects that the funeral director decided (with my permission) to delay for a day the final services. With flowers filling the entire first floor of Pearson's Funeral Home, Clyde Pearson told me it was the second largest funeral he had ever serviced. As the entourage left for Dad's last ride to Cave Hill Cemetery, I'll never forget how frigid it was. But, when it was all over, I remember that I wasn't cold at all. Actually, I was profusely perspiring. As I looked around at Dad's honorers that day, it dawned upon me just how big the shoes were that I had to fill. He was a hero to a lot of people—including me. Nary a week has gone by since, when I haven't re-realized the enormity of those shoes.

So, November 30 was rough—always the toughest day of the year for me. A day that annually ended on a sad but reflective bummer, which the up-coming Christmas and the sheer joy of life the yuletide season embodies, was zealously dedicated to overcoming.

On the morning of November 30, 1999, the decision was made to take the chance at making something different of that day. Jonathan Blum had been kept current on the fast-moving events, but had not been told about the Rockets interest level nor had he been apprised of the latest phone conversation with Stern. With fingers crossed and with a hope to change that year's November 30th and a silent prayer, a phone call was made. Blum was told that Tricon's permission was now needed so the NBA Commissioner and the lawyer for an unnamed NBA team could be apprised of Tricon's interest in naming rights. He wanted to know if this was serious, to which I responded, "as serious as a heart attack." Blum promised to conduct internal discussions with the CEO at Tricon and he would be back with the answer before mid-December.

Mistletoe and the Millennium

Christmas of 1999 and the upcoming New Year's Millennium celebration was a positive and joyous time. Blum and Tricon's CEO, David Novak, had decided they were willing to meet with any team owner who wanted to come to Louisville on a confidential basis; but until a meeting was actually agreed upon, Tricon's name could only be referenced as "a New York Stock Exchange Company." Blum's, Novak's and the governor's meeting schedules were reserved between January 4-12 and 15-24, 2000.

A cursory report was given to the aldermen on December 16 without revealing the identity of the six teams contacted and only referring to "a New York Stock Exchange Company." The news and sports reporters' curiosity and antennae were gradually becoming more alert. The required confidences of the Rockets and Tricon, along with Stern's level of interest, had been maintained. Nothing would happen to defeat that confidentiality during the December holiday season, but it was easily recognizable that the confidentiality problem would escalate if our progress continued through the Millennium.

With the arrival of the Year 2000, an enormous question was unanswered. Was this to be Louisville's time? No one knew, but a-hell-of-a-lot still had to be done.

The Phone Call

The 21st century began much as the old century ended—with the telephone.

On Thursday, January 6, 2000, the call came from George Postolos and Mike Goldberg, arranged several days prior to the Millennium. Prefacing the call, on January 5, 2000 limited permission had been obtained from

Blum to reveal the name of Kentucky Fried Chicken as the potential naming-rights entity for the Louisville arena. As noon approached things grew tense around the law firm, magnified by my morning's visit to the dentist.

People like Postolos and Goldberg place a high value on time, as do most successful people. The actual time of the call's arrival was at 12:01. Only a minute late. It lasted for several hours. The purpose of the call was quickly made clear—a decision had been made, but there were two major 'ifs.'

If Louisville could deliver a publicly-financed arena with revenue streams going to the Rockets, with limited public dissension and with reasonable and energetic majority support of Louisville's political and business leadership; and if there was no way to orchestrate a successful arena referendum in Houston in the fall of 2000, then Louisville would be the Rockets first transfer option.

Alexander's preliminary research had satisfied him about Louisville's potential as an NBA market. Unbelievable—we had won! Or had we? The two 'ifs' were significant and further compounded by a set of perplexing exigencies resembling the snakes on Medusa's Head or the Kremlin's bizarre but beautiful Palace of Facets.

The Rockets sublease expired in November, 2003. Barring an economic gate receipt disaster in Houston, the Rockets would not break their sublease lease with the Compaq Center. Realistically and legally, it was impossible for Louisville to make the required arrangements for a public bond issue to construct a $220 million arena without revealing the governmental commitment and guarantee as to the prime tenant. But if the Rockets allowed it to be disclosed they were transferring to Louisville, attendance would inescapably plummet in Houston.

Quite a conundrum.

To be sure, the time lapse provided adequate time for Louisville to plan and construct the downtown arena, estimated to take between 24 and 30 months. If necessary and if approved by the NBA, the Rockets could actually play in Freedom Hall temporarily. Therefore, the time-frame of the action became as critical as the decision-making process itself. The league constitution contained a transfer application deadline of March 1 for the succeeding season. Needless to say, there was no way that such an application could be prepared and filed in the two months between January and March 1, 2000. Therefore, we were looking at March 1, 2001, as the earliest possibile time for a Rockets application to transfer. Consequently, Louisville had fourteen months to pull it all together.

It was clearly the well-expressed hope of Postolos that a second Houston referendum would occur in November, 2000 and the entire Rockets' management intended to dedicate all the time and effort humanly possible to accomplish that. It was much easier for the Rockets if a settlement could be reached and the peace-pipe smoked in Houston. However, it was equally clear that their hopes were not high. Alexander hadn't been back to Houston in the two months since the November 1999 referendum rejection. If a second referendum couldn't or didn't happen in Houston or if it did and failed again, Louisville would be Alexander's first transfer option—provided Louisville could deliver. A remarkable bit of news.

When the Tricon interest was mentioned to Postolos, there was a pause in the conversation. He was intrigued with the concept of Kentucky Fried Chicken as the naming-rights partner, and even more interested in the teams' name change to the Kentucky Colonels. Postolos had grown up in San Antonio amid family connections to the ABA's San Antonio Spurs. His father, Luke Postolos, was the best friend of Spurs majority owner Angelo Drossos. While attending Harvard Law School, where he graduated magna cum laude, George Postolos had worked in the Spurs sales office in the summers, and upon his father's death, Drossos had virtually become his surrogate father. ABA ties, among old ABA-folk, run very deep. Postolos knew the Kentucky Colonels were the class of the ABA. This was distinctly in Louisville's favor.

However, Postolos was also a brilliant tactician not to be swayed by emotion or fond memories. He had much at stake. Upon graduation from Harvard Law School, he accepted a job with the prestigious New York Law firm of Wachtell, Lipton, Rosen & Katz, with close NBA ties, and was soon selected by Stern as special assistant to the Commissioner. Either at Stern's suggestion or Alexander's request and Stern's approval, Postolos had been sent home to Texas in October 1998 to lead the Rockets final foray with Houstonians. It would be his assignment to make a silk purse out of a sow's ear for the Houston Rockets in Houston or negotiate the team's transfer elsewhere. The eventual decision would be Alexander's, but the day-to-day work was a Postolos responsibility. Alexander was to take a step back from the ferocity of the process, hoping the distance between Boca Raton and Houston would aid in calming the Houston waters. Our research proved this set of assumptions to be correct. It was incumbent that they be accepted as reality. Postolos was a bright as they come, a star on the rise who was a likely successor to Stern as NBA commissioner. The stakes were high, very high, but Louisville was in the game.

Postolos made it clear we needed to begin the enormous process of "...getting our ducks in a proper row...." As my notes reflect, he precisely stated, "...talk was cheap and action was required, because...action is what really counts, not talk." A half-billion dollar decision was in the process of being made by the Rockets owner, Les Alexander. An equally important decision would have to be made by Louisville, its officials and citizens.

Complicating that process toward decision was the inescapable fact that none of this could be made public in Louisville. We did agree that the story would eventually leak. Both the Rockets and Louisville had to be prepared for that occasion and the longer such a leak could be avoided, the better. One promise was made to Postolos—that leak would not occur from Louisville. As time would prove, it wouldn't.

The phone call was over. Pages of notes had been made and my head was spinning with exhaustion. But being tired had to wait. Upon reflection, fighting exhaustion at this point may have been a major mistake. It might have been wiser to relaxe and give some quiet thought to the dynamics of the call. Later it would be realized that the actual Rockets spokesman and final decision recommender was really Postolos. Since November, the phone and correspondence contact had been and would continue to be with Goldberg, but over time it would gradually become apparent that on the occasions when Postolos was directly involved Goldberg had little to say. That should have been a key as to who was the closest confidant of Alexander, but on January 6, 2000, it wasn't.

Instead of reflection, immediate calls were made to the governor's office, Blum and Magre. All were pleased with the progress but concerned about the extent of the work that was now required. Magre felt that, even though the Rockets' name couldn't be mentioned, there was still a need to immediately meet with Aldermen Johnson and George Unseld. Somewhat reluctantly, I agreed because the NBA is a small fraternity. There was concern on my part that Unseld would hear a rumor from his brother, Wes, who was in management with the Washington Wizards. The meeting was held the next day at our law offices. There was no mention of a specific team or the specific naming-rights company. It was simply reported that there was a particular team and a major corporation with whom we were beginning negotiations.

Mayor Dave's AWOL

The time had come to renew efforts to meet the Mayor. Lo and behold, after eight months a meeting was scheduled for Thursday, January 20, 2000. To accomplish it required his scheduler being told the top corporate officials of "a New York Stock Exchange Company" wanted to meet him about the transfer of an NBA team to Louisville. Sometimes it's amazing what a half-truth can achieve—it was true that such businessmen wanted to meet the Mayor, but they were already in town!

Blum and my law firm members could be completely trusted to hold the negotiation's confidence. Considerable experience with economic development at the state level for a dozen years allowed for a full comfort level about the governor's understanding of the importance of confidentiality. But now we were moving to another area—city government—which would quickly double the number of those knowledgeable, and quadruple the leak potential. Could we trust the mayor to maintain the confidentiality? How about the people he used to make decisions? Blum was concerned.

It being important to obtain a general overview of municipal bonding, a quick meeting was calendared with Spencer Harper. He was one of Kentucky's most knowledgeable public bonding lawyers and one of the most gracious and dignified lawyers I have ever known. During his outstanding legal career, Harper had authored many of Kentucky's public bonding statutes. His free, with no commitment, up-to-date tax-exempt bonding seminar clearly reflected that the city could issue bonds to construct a downtown arena, contract with an NBA team to use the facility, and the NBA team could receive the revenue from a naming-rights deal. Furthermore, it was apparent that if the arrangement were properly drawn, it should not adversely impact the city's financial condition.

On Wednesday, at working lunch with Blum, we agreed upon a parallel process, namely the public piece and the private piece. The private piece would be carried forth with a full court press and not revealed, publicly. Blum asked me to provide him information and details by January 31st on every arena naming-rights deal. He also agreed to participate in a meeting with the governor and to initiate internal action within Tricon. Lastly, plans were made for the next day's meeting with the Mayor. Most of the discussion centered around our mutual concerns about leakage of confidential information. Despite the concerns, it was mutually agreed the risk had to be taken—he was the mayor.

On Thursday morning, January 20, the Mayor canceled the long-sought meeting. For two months we had been working on the private part of the process. It had reached the point where the negotiation of a possible deal with the Houston Rockets was in the offing. But the Mayor was too busy to meet with the top officials of "a New York Stock Exchange Company." Blum was flabbergasted. I was, too. Our astonishment, like the song refrain, had only just begun.

Upon learning that the mayoral meeting had been aborted, the governor canceled our planned meeting in favor of a business trip to Europe. In the course of the phone call with the governor's chief of staff and general counsel, the contents and significance of the January 6 call were reiterated. Both indicated the Governor was prepared to "carry the ball across the goal line," but he needed to see local political initiative. The expression was, "He's the governor of all of Kentucky, not just Louisville, so Louisville's political leadership needs to step forth—if they do, he'll be there to make it happen." That expression of the governor's willingness to be involved would remain constant throughout the process over the next several years, as the opportunities would increase and the local political leadership would repeatedly stumble and trip over itself.

As January drew to a conclusion, the first call from a Houston reporter came—from Mark Berman, Fox News. Berman would, over the next several months, become the most persistent Houston reporter. He pried, tried and cajoled, and over the course of time would genuinely share his off-the-record belief about the strong possibility that Louisville was going to take the Rockets from Houston. But in the beginning the response was the agreed-upon refrain: "We will neither confirm nor deny that we are in discussions with the Houston Rockets." It was reiterated several times in the call. Now, with the national news media and other NBA-related calls coming more frequently, the intensity was developing.

The Millennium's first month had been a solid and reasonably encouraging start. Phone calls were useful for a lot of talk, but little real action. But action of significant magnitude was just around the corner.

The Louisville/Rockets story breaks

February is always a particularly gruesome month in Louisville. The charms and joy of the December holiday season have worn off and the New Year's festivities are long past, yet there remains several months of limited sun and bleak skies before spring breaks, roses bloom and the awe-inspiring Kentucky Derby arrives.

February began by joining the Broeckers on our annual London antiquing trip. It was a nice respite complete with some successful scavangering. Upon our return, there was a phone message from Mike Goldberg, requesting an immediate call. The Daytimer noted, "I'm apprehensive. Don't have a good feeling about it, but don't know why." There was no action to report to Goldberg.

Goldberg's call was returned immediately at 10:00 AM (9:00 AM Houston time), February 8, 2000. My apprehension was misplaced. The Rockets' battles in Houston were continuing and remained inflamed. Alexander had still not been back to Houston since the November referendum. Goldberg and Postolos would begin what was described as a road show within eight to ten weeks, and Alexander had made some decisions. It was unrealistic to expect that only Louisville would be considered, so I wasn't particularly surprised to learn of a road show involving several unnamed cities. Goldberg said it was essential that Louisville's position be placed, at least generically, in talking points memo form, within a month. The dynamics had changed. I agreed to increase the intensity of Louisville's efforts.

Was this a bum's rush? Why had this transpired all of a sudden? It would take only a few hours to learn the answer.

The long-awaited meeting with the Mayor was scheduled that afternoon with Aldermen Magre and Johnson, Armstrong and his staff assistants Bruce Traughber, Steve Tetter and Jane Driskell. Although I didn't know Traughber very well, he seemed to be an intelligent and deliberate sort of individual. Driskell had worked in the state Justice Cabinet when my wife served as Cabinet Secretary, and she found her to be a pleasant, skilled and dedicated person. They both were known to be very loyal people. Feeling that both would eventually play large roles in the NBA odyssey, it was important to convince them about the urgency of events and to initiate their learning process.

During the meeting Armstrong didn't say much—just listened and nodded. He looked terrible, having been recently diagnosed with myasthenia gravis, a rare neuromuscular disorder. His mind seemed to wander and his eyes looked cloudy and distant. In an effort to get his attention, I revealed that the Houston Rockets management and ownership had been in discussion with me since early November and were very interested in Louisville as a potential transfer city. The news evoked little response.

Surprised by his lethargic response, a specific question was mandated: "Do you want me to stop this, right now? If you do, I can, but I can't wait much longer, because it's going to be too late." Armstrong's answer was short, but direct, "No, go ahead." I re-asked, "Are you sure?" and his answer was, "Yes, and you should work with Bruce and Jane." Thinking I might need to contact him on short notice, I requested his cell phone number, promising to use it only in an emergency requiring immediate contact. The number provided was the Mayor's office phone number, found in the phone book. In an atmosphere such as this, there was no way I could reveal Tricon's name. Not a very good start with Armstrong. It was perplexing.

My wife, Norma, is perhaps the most perceptive person I have ever known. Wanting her thoughts about the Mayor's peculiar attitude, that evening we went to Big Spring Country Club for an early dinner. Upon our return home there were phone voice mails requesting callbacks from sports reporters in Seattle, Los Angeles, Houston, Miami, New York, Chicago and some other NBA cities. What in the hell was going on? Clearly, the home phone couldn't be used to find out, because a busy signal would indicate to other callers that we were home. Ergo, the cellphone. The home phone continued ringing. Norma joked, "This is like election central." It was. Mike Goldberg was reached at his Houston residence and an astounding message was received. The Louisville-Houston story had broken late that afternoon in Houston, presumably from a distraught front office employee who was afraid the team would leave and she would lose her job. Goldberg remembered my promise and my wager—the story wouldn't break in Louisville. It hadn't. But now, in one evening, it was a breaking national sports story. The next morning could be a disaster, unless somehow we could devise a way to gain control over the course of events.

The first of many all-night stands began. With the aid of my Apple laptop, a press release was written and re-written throughout the night. At daybreak it was faxed to Goldberg in Houston and Stern in New York, with the accompanying note that it would be publicly released at 1:00 PM EST, unless I was otherwise advised. Stern's secretary called indicating he was in Oakland for the NBA All-Star Game that weekend. She agreed to forward the fax to him ASAP. By 10:30 AM Goldberg had called with his approval of the statement. Stern called at noon (9:00 AM in Oakland). Expressing his appreciation for Louisville's continuing confidentiality commitment, understanding that we had to move forward and indicating some exasperation with the developments in Houston, Stern wished everyone well with one admonition, "Bruce, be careful and use your head on this." I had my instructions, permission and a reasonably serious admonition.

At 1:00 PM on February 9, 2000, the first of many Louisville NBA press conferences was held. It was an anxious gathering. Louisville wasn't used to this. Nor was I used to giving press conferences by reading prepared texts. The office staff had prepared the room and were anxiously standing around its edges. Aldermen Magre and Johnson joined Darrell Griffith to offer remarks. The reporters were primarily non-sports reporters, who were in some measure perplexed about the significance of the moment. Like most minor-league sports cities, Louisville's sports reporters generally didn't come to work until mid-to-late afternoon. In fairness, most quickly realized this was a real news story with major ramifications. They tried hard.

With a deep breath and the ritual touching of a medal my father won in a 1923 oratorical contest at Louisville's Manual High, I began. I refused to name the Houston Rockets as the NBA team, but everyone knew; it was all over the media in Houston. Magre spoke briefly and Alderman Johnson's happiness was abounding as he could see his dream coming true. Griffith was eloquent about Louisville and the opportunity. I answered no questions. The only non-scripted comment made was that this would require a "monumental effort." Did that ever prove to be accurate!

Walt Disney's mouse had sneaked into the house, as Louisville had been caught by complete surprise. The surprise was as big for us as it was for everyone else. The only seemingly negative initial comment came from UofL coach Denny Crum. That, like so many things to come, was confusing. In 1977 he supported the Buffalo Braves transfer to Louisville. But now Crum's Cardinals were having a terrible year and he was in the beginning stages of a battle for his job with the university's new athletic director, Tom Jurich.

While there had been little initial negativism, sure as the night follows the day, it was coming. The questions were two—when and from whom? Meanwhile, the phone rang off the hook. John Y. Brown, Jr., was ready to help, but he didn't understand why he hadn't been informed of what we were doing. Was this to be the problem? Even though they couldn't be told, did others think they should have been in-the-know'?

The next evening, February 10, 2000, was encouraging, yet eventually to become utterly confounding. UofL had soundly beaten Syracuse at Freedom Hall. It was an extremely important victory for Denny Crum, one that was vitally necessary to quiet the increasing question of whether his coaching intensity was declining as his age advanced. At halftime, I sought out UofL athletic director Tom Jurich. Having only met him once at a welcoming party upon his arrival in Louisville, I felt it was important speak with him face-to-face. Following initial pleasantries, he pointedly stated that Denny Crum did not speak for the University's athletic department. He did, and he was in favor of the NBA effort for Louisville, believing that the NBA would be a significant recruiting tool for the University's athletic programs. It was all up-front and straight-forward. Jurich was clearly expressing, at least initially, positive encouragement. I assured him that no deal of any kind would ever be reached with any NBA team without the University's full opportunity to negotiate their joint participation in a new arena. He was appreciative about that commitment. We warmly shook hands and agreed to meet. It was a happy moment. The University and its athletic director might be in our corner. When I returned to our seats and told Norma, she smiled from ear to ear. In time this event would prove to be symbolic of Calvin Coolidge's remark (cleaved from Ralph Waldo Emerson) in the Dakotas Black Hills: "A foolish consistency is the hobgoblin of little minds."

Hectic times require reflection (often the sooner the better). The week of the Louisville/Houston story was no different. The evening of Sunday February 13, 2000, was availed for some quiet time. Who would the naysayers be? When and how will they organize? Aversion to change and fear of the unknown were too ingrained in Louisville for the opportunity to be passed. The naysayers' eventual appearance was inescapable. I concluded it would be indirect, at this point, it being far too early for a frontal assault

Within a week the retired UofL basketball coach, Peck Hickman, died. Now, all the founders of the Kentucky religion were gone — only their memories were left. Peck's and Pee Wee Reese's acceptance of change and refusal to fear the unknown were going to be needed in the NBA odyssey, and they would be sorely missed. It wouldn't be long before we needed both of them and their can-do attitude to counter Louisville's aversion to change. Seems the good ones leave us too soon.

The next morning Harold Workman, like John Y. Brown, Jr., called to express his disturbance about not being consulted. As the longtime manager of Freedom Hall, Workman believed he had a proprietary interest in Louisville's sports and entertainment scene. An immediate meeting to assuage him was arranged at his Freedom Hall offices. Negative impulses radiated. His body language was terrible. Workman's dreary eyes and his darkened face were reminiscent of the Baltimore Claws owner, David Cohan. He couldn't have slept much all weekend and he wasn't a happy camper. Realizing Freedom Hall couldn't compete with a dazzling new downtown arena, the concern was clearly his personal loss of control over local entertainment offerings. All manner of assuaging was endeavored, to little avail. You could write it down: Harold Workman was a Ruppian and nothing would change him. He was going to be opposed to whatever we did, regardless of its significance, period. Time would reflect the considerable extent to which he would go to stymie change.

Soon a call was received from Workman's major talent finder, Dave Snowden. Now, instead of being unable to create a meeting with Armstrong, his approach was from another angle. As a friend, Snowden felt I should know that his connections with the Las Vegas entertainment industry were convinced the Rockets were moving to Las Vegas. Louisville didn't have a chance and I was wasting my time. As expected, it didn't take long for the anti-rumor mill to get organized. While still indirect and *sub rosa*, the storm was coming. An investigation of Las Vegas' potential involvement was required.

To be sure, on any given weekend enough money fell off the Vegas tables to make the annual bond payment on a glitzy new arena. But, Commissioner Stern's anti-gambling position had been staked out as early as 1992, when he testified before Congress encouraging the passage of The Professional and Amateur Sports Protection Act. Its adoption outlawed a state government's legalization of gambling on sports (grandfathering-in Nevada). Stern had been praised for his testimony, and, in the fall of 1999, he publically commented that the league would have considerable difficulty approving Las Vegas as a franchise site, unless it ceased accepting wagers on NBA games. With the total of such wagers approaching nearly a half billion dollars annually in the Vegas economy, there was no realistic way NBA gambling could be taken off the board. While Las Vegas Mayor Oscar Goodman was known to be very sports-minded, it was also generally known that prior to the Vegas cleanup his early criminal defense legal career included the representation of several of the city's most notorious gangsters. Despite all this, Snowden's rumor still couldn't be discounted, so the watch was on. Las Vegas would be added to the agenda of the next meeting with Commissioner Stern.

Corporate interest level continued as old friend, Louisville Gas & Electric's President, Vic Staffieri, committed active but non-specific participation, provided the NBA became a reality in Louisville. On February 17, 2000, Tricon recommitted to negotiate with the Rockets whenever they came to Louisville and to invite the Alexanders as its Derby guests. Tricon was now moving closer to public involvement. But the most important event of the week was to occur on Friday afternoon and Saturday evening, February 19, 2000.

Louisville Pursuit Team organized

For several months Jonathan Blum and I operated as an unofficial Pursuit Team. It was publically unknown, which it had to be at that stage. While Blum and Tricon's participation were vital, more players were needed—at least two more, for sure.

I didn't know Todd Blue. He had requested a meeting to discuss the NBA. There had been a lot of such calls. The Blue meeting figured to be just another hour spent talking, which was directly adverse to the Postolos admonishment, "Don't waste your time talking." Easy for him to say. But when there's a need to energize a city, talking has to be undertaken.

From my office conference table, Blue could be seen coming down the hall. He was young, well-dressed, alert and with vigor in his step. Confidently thrusting out his hand to offer hand-shake congratulations on the effort, Blue directly stated he wanted to do whatever was necessary to pull off the NBA. When asked to describe himself, Blue quickly proved to be one of the persons we needed to find. At 30 years of age, he was wealthy, well-spoken, well-connected and well-educated with an international business degree from prestigious George Washington University. Following his graduation he had lived in Chicago as a metals trader for a scrap iron and steel company. Upon his return to Louisville in 1995, he joined with his brother, Jonathan, in the management of his father's company, Louisville Scrap Metal. The company had been sold in 1998. Blue was active in the community serving on several charitable boards, but had considered leaving Louisville for greener pastures. In his judgment, Louisville was too far behind the times and seemed to be regressing more every year. The city presented limited future opportunities for him and his family. He felt this may be the last chance for Louisville to grab the brass ring and move to challenge Nashville, Indianapolis and other competing cities. Blue had heard all the Louisville Spin, been invited to join Leadership Louisville, attended east-end cocktail parties and had basically given up on local politicians.

In David Stern's mind, the Louisville NBA odyssey required a capable, attractive and effective spokesman for and organizer of the young people and mid-sized businesses of Louisville. The future had to be touched, motivated and inspired to action. Over the next several years, Todd Blue would become an integral, vibrant and dedicated member of the Louisville Pursuit Team. His positive and youthful approach, good humor and determination would prove to be critical at numerous times throughout the odyssey. While we hadn't met formally as the Pursuit Team and wouldn't receive that moniker for a while, the third cog of that team was now in place.

Often, in human endeavors, important events occur in unusual settings. One of those occasions was a wedding reception that Saturday evening at Big Spring Country Club. Fred Goldberg, a highly-respected older lawyer who had developed one of Louisville's significant mid-sized law firms, cornered me for a routine cocktail party conversation about the latest books we'd read. Soon we were joined by Ed Glasscock. The conversation turned (as most did at this time) to the NBA in Louisville. Glasscock expressed considerable interest and listened intently as the details (that could be) were revealed. Later in the evening, Fred privately expressed how essential it was to involve Glasscock in the effort, observing, "Nothing can ever get done around here without Ed's involvement." I had always respected Fred's insight and, upon reflection, he was clearly right.

Glasscock, a UK law graduate from Leitchfield, was a highly intelligent, action-oriented, invigorating person with a sound legal mind and considerable political acumen. Over the years he had led the amalgamation of several major local law firms into the largest firm between Chicago and Atlanta with over four hundred fifty attorneys. Frost Brown Todd possessed the unique skills that would be required to negotiate bond deals and multi-hundred million dollar financing arrangements. As its managing partner, Ed was cool, collected and an adept conciliator, skilled at bringing people and ideas together. As the President of Greater Louisville, Inc., he offered an entré into Louisville's business elite, which eventually had to be involved in the process.

On Monday, February 21, 2000, I phoned Glasscock and asked for his leadership, personal involvement, assistance and that of his firm in Louisville's NBA odyssey. He enthusiastically agreed.

The formation of the Louisville Pursuit Team was complete. Jonathan Blum would create the Tricon/naming-rights piece with the resources of Kentucky's largest home-based and multi-national corporation. Todd Blue would organize the mid-sized businesses and the region's young people. Ed Glasscock would help coordinate the political/local major business effort and make available the immense legal resources of Frost Brown Todd. We would meet and confer, plan and direct, act and react and together — and make it happen. Drawing blood wasn't required to create the requisite unity of purpose, it was inherent within each person. All wanted to see Louisville move to the next level and become a relevant city in the world's 21st century. Without any of these individuals and their dedication, the entire process would have never gotten past first base. With them, we were in business and had a realistic chance.

The Pursuit Team would operate as a counterweight against the soon-to-arrive invasion of negativity and fear of the unknown. Over the next several years much would be asked of the Team, but individually and collectively they would prove up to the task. To be sure, there were to be tense times among us and several events would bring considerable disagreement (to be fully-discussed later), but the bond was sound. No city endeavoring to attract an NBA franchise had what we had; I was satisfied about that. Within a week, David Stern would agree.

The last week of February, 2000, was encouraging. Major action began to replace talk. Jurich agreed to meet on March 1 and NBA Commissioner David Stern confirmed a meeting in New York for Monday, February 28.

On Wednesday February 23, Greg Stumbo, Majority Leader of Kentucky's House of Representatives, carried forward his commitment by announcing his support for a new downtown arena. Glasscock's leadership and encouragement caused Greater Louisville, Inc.'s retention of the Dallas Division of PricewaterhouseCoopers to undertake an immediate economic study of the Louisville market's ability to support an NBA franchise.

The week ended by a Saturday breakfast with state representative Larry Clark. He was the Jefferson County delegation chairman, with considerable clout in the Capitol's legislative halls. I had known Clark for years and always admired his tenacity. His legislative career had begun in the mid-1970s with my and County Judge Hollenbach's support. For years he had effectively represented the interests of the middle-class area of south-central Jefferson County. As a straight-speaking solid individual, his word had always been his bond — the kind of guy I liked and respected. Bob Evan's breakfast food was excellent, as was Clark's interest. Fully aware of the importance to Indianapolis of the Indiana Pacers and Conseco Arena, he was convinced Louisville had to do the same thing. His complete support was promised and deeply appreciated. The Daytimer note says: "Good and satisfactory supportive meeting." Within several months Clark's clear and precise 100% commitment on that Saturday morning in late February would, like Jurich's, become utterly confounding.

The Big Apple and The Commish

A Sunday afternoon flight from Louisville to New York generally finds a half-full plane. February 27, 2000, was no different. Norma and I were both excited and anxious. In less than eighteen hours we were going to meet with David Stern. A lot of hopes and dreams were on the table. The first (and only) mistake of the trip was our hotel reservation — The Marriott Marquis Hotel on Times Square. It was awful. Terrible service, worse room and a boisterous convention. I couldn't sleep, not just because of the noise, but also the importance of the next day.

Stern, one year my junior, was the son of a Chelsea, New York delicatessen owner. His driven work ethic had been learned behind the counter of Stern's Deli. As a kid and a Knicks fan, he unspectacularly shot a few hoops in the local Chelsea park. After obtaining a B.A. degree in political science from Rutgers, he graduated in 1966 from Columbia School of Law. Solid work habits, intellect and legal acumen led to a position with the major New

York City law firm, Proskauer Rose, which represented the NBA. Quickly, Stern gravitated to that opportunity, becoming the NBA's outside legal counsel — where we first met during the Buffalo Braves transfer-to-Louisville effort. Both young lawyers then, we were handling some exciting business. I liked Stern and the feeling was mutual, as a valued friendship had been maintained for nearly twenty-five years.

In 1980 he was named the league's Executive Vice President and later was chosen to succeed Larry O'Brien as Commissioner; it was 1984, the year Michael Jordan joined the Chicago Bulls. The Commissionership was awarded to him primarily as a result of a remarkable agreement he struck in 1983 with Larry Fleisher, the NBA Players Association counsel. It was revolutionary: a collective-bargaining agreement that provided for inter-league revenue sharing of the national television contract and a cap on players salaries.

As Commissioner, Stern immediately began to make a difference on other fronts. The league was in deep financial trouble with the NBA Finals being shown on tape-delay. Seventeen of the twenty-three teams were losing money with league-wide average attendance at 11,141 per game. Within a few years six teams from mid-sized cities were added. They flourished with revenue sharing from the national television contract. Stern marketed Jordan, Larry Bird and Magic Johnson — internationally. Soon the international television rights rivaled the American rights in dollar value. With the international offices of the league opening in nearly a dozen countries, the NBA Properties revenue stream doubled every year for a decade. In 1990, the Associated Press honored him as the Sports Executive of the Decade, and by 2000 the value of an NBA franchise had increased by a multiple of seven with attendance averaging nearly 17,000 per game per franchise. Under his leadership, the NBA had literally become The World's Game.

David Stern is a wonderfully personal individual and an exquisite dresser, who calls 'em as he sees 'em. There's little spin zone around Stern. He can be as tough as he needs to be. Few words are minced and he possesses a compelling dry wit. Surprisingly, he hordes little memorabilia, preferring to savor the moment. His world is the exciting present and the future, not what happened yesterday. Jealously guarding his personal privacy, he adores his family and multiple board memberships, such as Rutgers and Gallaudet Universities, the Thurgood Marshall Scholarship Fund and New York City's Beth Israel Medical Center.

Truly, one of the most remarkable persons I've ever known.

Ten AM on Monday, February 28, 2000, was the appointed time. We walked to the Olympic Tower on Fifth Avenue, elevatored to the 15th floor, entered the NBA offices and were quickly escorted to Stern's private conference room. Along the wall in the hall were action shots of old ABA players Dr. J., Artis Gilmore and Dan Issel. They'd been there a long time. I always felt it was neat that the old ABA had such a prominent spot in the halls of the NBA executive offices. David and Deputy Commissioner, Russell Granik, entered the conference room from David's office. Stern was his usual disarming self — his first words, "Why Norma, you look better than ever!" Some guys could say something like that and those in the room would think it was so much B.S. But with David, it was different. It wasn't B.S. It was a genuine and nice thing to say (plus, he was right!). Warm handshakes were exchanged and some great memories of our earlier days in the ABA/NBA merger were shared. The most critical meeting yet had begun. This was now action (not talk).

Louisville's plans and efforts were thoroughly outlined. The presentation had been rehearsed until it was memorized. No stone was left unturned. It took an hour to complete. A position paper had been prepared, which described Louisville's and Kentucky's players — who they were and what part each would play in the on-going effort. Stern and Granik were advised about Greater Louisville, Inc.'s retention of PricewaterhouseCoopers. Stern had been waiting since late November to learn the identity of Louisville's naming-rights company. Prior to leaving for New York, Blum had provided permission to reveal Tricon's name and interest level to Stern. As Tricon's name was revealed, Stern's eyebrows rose over his glasses. He was intrigued with the concept of Tricon Global Restaurants and Kentucky Fried Chicken's interest in naming-rights in an association with a Louisville NBA team. A master marketer, Stern viewed Tricon's involvement as a marketing genius stroke. In the international world of the NBA, money and clout spoke loudly and there were few companies in the world with a larger global marketing footprint than Tricon's 32,500 Pizza Hut, Taco Bell and KFC stores. A pleased Stern agreed to honor Tricon's confidence.

It was now clear—the NBA Commissioner realized we were serious in Louisville. The presentation was complete. It was David's turn. Fingers (and even toes) were crossed.

Stern was impressed and particularly pleased with Tricon's potential involvement and Greater Louisville Inc.'s selection of the Dallas division of PricewaterhouseCoopers. He believed it to be among the preeminent sports economic analysts in the country. Then began the facts from the NBA side of the equation.

It was 50/50 whether the Rockets would move from Houston. No matter what we did, Louisville could not force the decision. It had to happen based upon events as they developed in Houston. We were advised to spend our time getting our Louisville ducks in a row. We shouldn't be distracted about what was or wasn't happening in Houston or anywhere else, for that matter. We should not over-promise Louisville or over-negotiate with the Rockets.

It was readily apparent Stern was very fond of Les Alexander and was saddened about the treatment he was receiving in Houston, both personally and business-wise. Stern had been deeply impressed with Alexander's leadership and business acumen in the recent NBA labor negotiations in which he had proven to be an incisive, sound and thoughtful gut instinct-type decision-maker. Stern attributed it to his business background as a securities trader, which required immediate, crisp and decisive thinking.

From the Commissioner's mouth came the answer on Las Vegas (and David Snowden's Vegas rumor)—Las Vegas, Nevada would not receive an NBA franchise "...as long as I'm breathing and Commissioner of the NBA." He was fully cognizant of diametrically opposed to the risks involved in the close-proximity of a gambling mecca and major league sports.

He deemed it absolutely essential that we get the mid-sized businesses in Louisville organized immediately. The big boys, like Ford, make local participation decisions of this magnitude in a Detroit committee room. But mid-sized business decisions are made at a desk in Louisville, by one or two community-minded businessmen and women. We needed to have those entities fully and completely organized. He was confident this was the major secret of the NBA's success story in America's mid-sized cities.

The main point was then made (as recorded word-for-word in my Daytimer): "I don't know if Louisville wants to be a major league sports city, but if it does and if it is prepared to do what it has to do to become one, then it'll get one of these teams. I don't know which one. It might be the Rockets and it might not. It might be the Hornets and it might not. But it will get one, if it is prepared to do what is necessary."

A furtive glance at the wall clock said it was 12:15 PM. We'd met for over two hours. It didn't seem near that long. No one was anxious to break the meeting apart. David couldn't have been more charming, forthright or encouraging. His charming dry wit was ever-present. As we moved to the conference room door, he pulled me aside and said with a wink, "Bruce, do me a favor. As you go through the process, try to act like you're not from Kentucky." Dry wit is best met with equally dry wit. I said, "Does that mean I have to wear shoes?" With laughter, Stern said, "So long, my friend —stay in close touch."

Norma was excited about the positive vibes. As the elevator door closed, she said, "It's like old times." And it was. She (and I) were convinced we were going to pull it off.

We went across the street and north up Fifth Avenue a block to the NBA Store and got a bunch of NBA stuff for our little buddy, Tristan. The thought occurred—someday soon there will be a shelf of items in this store with the Kentucky Colonels logo. What an achievement it had been years ago for Indianapolis, San Antonio and Denver—now it was Louisville's turn. Tristan got a Reggie Miller Pacers shirt and an NBA logo-festooned bedsheet and Norma bought a Rockets denim shirt. My purchases were a pair of cufflinks and bag tags for the Rockets, the Charlotte Hornets, the Vancouver Grizzlies and the Orlando Magic—a purchase that would eventually prove to be somewhat prescient.

As the month of February, 2000, drew to a close the Daytimer notation read: "Absolutely best month I've had in years." Indeed, it was.

First half of March/action and reaction

Seems the NBA odyssey in Louisville was destined to always battle a backward disconnect. March, 2000 was no different. It came in like a docile lamb and went out like a raging, full-maned lion—all beginning with two long-sought meetings on March 1.

In the mid-1990s there were numerous problems with UofL's athletic program, including a less than satisfactory graduation rate and Title IX compliance. Tom Jurich was hired away from Colorado State University in October of 1997 to correct these problems and reinvigorate the program. As athletic director, Jurich hit the ground running with a high-energy approach to the challenges. Immediately, the football team achieved success from a prior 1-10 season to a 7-4 record with the new coach he recruited, John L. Smith.

The March 1, 2000 Jurich meeting was positive from its beginning to end. It was clearly stated and understood by Jurich that formal discussions with the Rockets were to begin in March and the University's desired joint-participation arrangement was an important facet of those discussions. In an effort to make sure the University's position was protected in the negotiations, it was requested and Jurich promptly agreed to submit a detailed proposal outlining a joint-participation arrangement desired by the UofL to be included, in full, with the talking points memorandum given to the Rockets management. I encouraged Jurich to be inventive about a possible joint relationship between UofL and the Rockets. It was particularly noted that in our upcoming meeting we would require that UofL be given a full opportunity to negotiate the joint-participation arrangement, privately and face-to-face, with the Rockets negotiating team. Jurich was warm, outgoing, positive and receptive to the opportunity. He committed to get me a draft of UofL's talking points proposal within a week.

There was only one problem: Jurich's agreed-upon and promised joint-participation proposal would never arrive—ever—throughout the entire odyssey for the next two years.

In the afternoon of March 1, 2000, Tricon officials, Blum and Chuck Rawley, President of KFC and I finally met with Mayor Armstrong. Again accompanying the mayor were Traughber and Driskell. Blum expressed Tricon's desire to receive first right of refusal on the arena's naming rights, which was accepted by Armstrong without discussion. Not a bad beginning. No dollar figures were discussed, but Blum promised that the amount of their financial commitment would not embarrass anyone.

I advised the Mayor that Stern was highly complimentary of Louisville's initial efforts and strongly recommended the formal organization of the city's mid-sized businesses. The importance of confidentiality was stressed, with which the Mayor agreed. He promised to conduct prompt discussions with the editor of *The Courier-Journal* and the County Judge. According to him, he and the County Judge had weekly private lunch meetings, which would offer a perfect occasion to discuss the opportunity. As in my prior February meeting, Armstrong's eyes still appeared glassy and his mind seemed to periodically wander. It was a pleasant meeting, but devoid of any real connect or bridge between Armstrong and anyone else in the room.

After the meeting, as we walked on Sixth Street, Blum stopped and asked if I thought Armstrong was feeling ill or "out-of-it." My response: "Who knows? No one ever sees him much except from a distance or on TV." It was mutually agreed that while the Mayor's interest wasn't particularly impressive, it was, at least, a start—and we'd go forward from there.

The second day of March brought a confounding telephone call from Traughber. Apparently, the Mayor was displeased because he hadn't been included in my meeting with Stern. I explained that Stern and I had been friends for twenty-five years and that relationship was the primary precipitator of the meeting. Further, at this juncture, Stern wasn't interested in being involved in the politics of Louisville's decision-making. The political part would come later after the business aspects of the transaction were further delineated. I asked Traughber to encourage the Mayor's understanding that it would be inappropriate for Stern to meet with Louisville political figures at this point in the discussions, because it might appear presumptive on his part and viewed as if he was interfering with the Houston franchise's business. It was explained that, in Stern's view, the first decision was required from the Rocket's ownership. After that, the league's attention would be directed to the political exigencies of potential transfer sites.

Even with this explanation, which I felt should be reasonably understood by the Mayor, Traughber wasn't sure he would be satisfied. I volunteered to discuss all this with the Mayor and Traughber assured me he would relay my words, immediately. This whole thing with the Mayor was getting increasingly perplexing. It was only the beginning.

The implementation of Stern's major suggestion was now imperative. The mid-sized businesses had to be organized. On the evening of March 2, the first meeting was convened at Big Spring Country Club. A detailed presentation of the effort and a synopsis of the Stern meeting were presented to forty-four business men and women. David Snowden was present. Without reference to his indirect Las Vegas rumor, it was directly answered by the observation that Stern had specifically confirmed Vegas was not and would not be a contender. The meeting was a rousing success. The mid-sized business community organized that evening, selecting Todd Blue as its Chairman and Bob Clarkson as Treasurer. The dedication of their involvement would repeatedly represent a major factor in Louisville's near success, and become one of the many things about which Louisville should, forever, be proud.

A pseudo Machiavellian interlude

The third day of March began with yet another confounding telephone call about the Mayor, this time from Magre, who reported that in a morning meeting the Mayor had expressed his opposition to the formation of the Gateway Group. It was now inescapably apparent that a surreptitious disruption of the effort by the Mayor had begun. An age-old Machiavellian principle finds that to kill an idea, you first try to destroy it non-obviously. It's a classic stratagem — weaken the legs and the table falls. Without much question, objecting to the organization of the mid-sized businesses was a leg-shot, because their organization had been deemed absolutely critical in Stern's eyes, and Armstrong had been told this by me several days prior. There were to be more leg-shots. We wouldn't have to wait more than several weeks for the next one.

The mid-sized businesses were organized, despite the Mayor's opinion. A month prior, I had specifically provided the Mayor the option to conclude the NBA effort and he explicitly responded that I should go forward. That was where we were going: to march forward in March.

Marching forward in March

On Monday, March 6 Goldberg confirmed the talking points memo meeting date in Houston for March 15, 2000. We had nine days to draft the memo. Things were beginning to click.

For several months I had calendared the evening of March 7, 2000. The Denver Nuggets were in Indianapolis to play the Pacers, Iit would be my first opportunity to see Dan Issel face-to-face since the odyssey began. Issel enjoyed the confidence of certain decision-makers in the NBA and I couldn't wait to see him. Norma, Brevin, Carter and my best friend, the little two year-old T-Man, joined on the trip to Indy. The game was fun and the T-Man loved the Pacers mascot, Boomer. But little T-Man didn't quite understand the NBA-thing; he was cheering, "Go-Cards." The post-game discussion with Issel was revealing. The word on the NBA street was that Alexander was extremely interested in Louisville.

While in Indianapolis, Blum called on my cell phone. Tricon had entered into a retainer agreement with Dean Bonham of Denver to represent its interests in the naming-rights negotiations. Bonham was a nationally-recognized sports industry negotiation expert, who had been intimately involved with the arrival of major league baseball in Denver. His retention was a clear indication that Tricon had moved their involvement to the next level. Another positive signal.

Securing the governor's direct involvement was now absolutely essential. It began in his office on Thursday, March 9. Along with Governor Paul Patton, the full-team of gubernatorial advisors was present: Chief of Staff Andrew "Skipper" Martin, General Counsel Denis Fleming, Deputy Cabinet Secretary Jack Conway, Cabinet Secretary Crit Luallen, and Economic Cabinet Secretary Gene Strong. Expressing excitement about the opportunity, the governor committed his leadership and willingness to provide the normal economic and tax incentives, such as tourism tax credits, offered to any major corporate transfer to Kentucky. A bill was discussed that was quietly winding its way through the General Assembly. It would permit the Governor, by his simple signature, to return all state taxes from a project approved by the Governor to the local governing body to assist the local government in funding the development—in this instance to fund an arena bond issue. But it wouldn't become law until July 1, 2000 and that might be too late for the Rockets to utilize in their decision-making. When advised that a talking-points memorandum for a Rockets management meeting was needed within the week, his staff was directed to get involved. The governor's final statement was most important: "Bruce, Louisville needs to be in the major leagues. Let's get it done." I couldn't ask for a better first meeting.

That evening Blum called to express his growing concern about the Mayor's interest to lead the NBA initiative. Earlier in the day he had learned that the Mayor had not delivered on his promise to speak with the editor of *The Courier-Journal*. Blum simply couldn't understand why the Mayor would commit to do something like that, and then not do it. While he was pleased with my report of the governor's meeting, Blum was intent—KFC must see evidence of local governmental leadership, because it cannot be in a position of being the fall guy if it fails. For Blum, the key to the governmental involvement was a bond commitment from the city.

Over the weekend of March 11-12, came the next bump in the road. It was learned that Steve Higdon of Greater Louisville, Inc. thought the process should be slowed down until the report was received from PricewaterhouseCoopers. While Higdon was a forward-thinking leader who was intrigued about the NBA opportunity, there was an understandable concern that the report might not be favorable. In such an event GLI would be too far out front. The report wouldn't arrive for several weeks. But we couldn't wait two weeks. Every single day mattered. The Rockets wanted a generic commitment in mid-March. The NBA in Louisville concept was now being pushed and pulled in every direction. Pursuit Team Member Ed Glasscock promised that he would help Higdon and GLI appreciate the importance of moving forward, without delay. He did. But an even bigger problem was to erupt on Sunday, March 12.

The Mayor had fired the Police Chief! It was a confounding situation replete with the lack of inter-personal communication skills, which inevitably exacerbates racial conflict. It was one of those "he said, she said" things. The general public, African-American leaders and the police were up in arms, and the story wasn't local. For some inexplicable reason, Armstrong had given an interview to *The New York Times* and Rev. Jesse Jackson had responded with threats of demonstrations and marches.

With its concentration of African-American officials and players, the NBA is one of the classic examples of successful racial integration in America. At this most critical moment, three days before the talking-points meeting in Houston, when it was essential for Louisville to reflect racial harmony, it was nationally exhibiting itself as a southern dinosaur—a city where the state legislature hadn't approved the 13th and 15th constitutional Amendments until 1976. This impression was further verified by several calls received from friends around the country. Great timing!

The day before the Houston visit on March 14 with the leadership of Greg Stumbo and the chairman of Louisville's state legislative delegation, Larry Clark, a House Resolution was passed 84-14, encouraging the Governor's issuance of tax incentives to lure the Rockets to Louisville. The State Legislature had acted, and the governor's office was pleased with their initiative, resulting in his message to me: "...full speed ahead."

Houston meeting — The Ides of March

For the preservation of maximum confidentiality, absolutely no one, including law office personnel and lawyers, were aware of our trip to Houston. Cell phones were turned off. Were a problem to develop requiring urgent attention, my secretary, Dorothy, was told there was a memo as to our location in my desk. At the moment it seemed the secrecy may have been overplayed a bit, but it was to be a stroke of good luck, as the day and next days events transpired.

The afternoon Continental direct flight to Houston was taken. Norma and I were aboard. Like in New York City on the evening prior to our meeting with David Stern, the Houston evening of March 14, 2000, was a non-sleeper. Too much adrenalin was flowing. Thoughts of the presentation stirred as answers to obvious and non-obvious questions exploded in my mind along with the worry over covering for Louisville's recent national image problem with the Mayor and the police. Norma finally got to sleep. I didn't.

The term the Ides of March had its derivation in 44 B.C. when Julius Caesar was assassinated by Brutus and others. It had arrived, again, on March 15, 2000, for the 2044th time. The destination, One Shell Plaza, 49th floor. Baker & Botts was (and is) one of the nation's pre-eminent law firms with 684 lawyers and a prestigious list of clients from the oil patch and beyond. One of its partners was James Baker, who had served Presidents Reagan and Bush as Secretary of the Treasury and State. Pretty impressive.

We were ushered to Goldberg's corner office at 9:00 AM. Over the course of the previous several months I had learned a lot about Goldberg. Born in Houston, he had graduated magna cum laude with a Phi Beta Kappa key from Rice University and received his law degree with honors from the University of Texas. His wife, Carol, was born and raised in Memphis and was degreed. As a board-certified trial attorney, he was the Ford Motor Company's chief trial attorney in the American southwest. Goldberg was quick, intelligent, alert, and didn't occupy a corner office on the 49th floor in one of America's largest law firms because he was on scholarship. He was there because he had earned it. His closeness to the Rockets was exhibited throughout his office by many framed pictures of his family and children with various of the team's players. This guy, like so many we would run across on the odyssey, was no slouch. With Goldberg was the Rockets decision-maker, George Postolos.

The full presentation was delivered, including an informal talking points memorandum that had been carefully but hurriedly prepared over the previous several days in conjunction with the governor's office. It was discussed paragraph-by-paragraph. The message was the same as in the January 6 phone call: if Louisville would agree to build a downtown state-of-the-art arena and permit the Rockets primary control of revenue streams it generates, Louisville was the logical transfer city, unless Houston could provide the political guarantee of a favorable referendum result in November,

2000. Alexander's desire to be appreciated was stressed, as was his continuing doubt that a positive political climate could be achieved in Houston. I told Postolos that if Alexander had provided Louisville two NBA and four WNBA championships, we would be naming a street for him rather than kicking him out of town. He agreed, but reminded me of his admonition in our January phone call, that action, not talk, was the prerequisite.

Interestingly, Postolos then initiated a collateral discussion, beginning with the question: other than a fried chicken salesman, what is a Kentucky Colonel? I had been alerted to this question in a prior phone call with Goldberg and was prepared. The Kentucky Colonels history was explored dating back from the long-riflemen at the Battle of New Orleans to its present charitable endeavors. The exclusive conferral of its membership by the governor intrigued Postolos, noting the similarity with baseball's Texas Rangers. The multitude of promotional tools the Kentucky Colonels offered fascinated Postolos. The meeting moved to a working lunch in a private room at The Plaza Club on the top floor.

The view was breathtaking. As the vast expanse of the fourth largest market area in America was taken in, the wonder was inescapable—why would all these people allow the world champion Houston Rockets to leave? I asked that question of Postolos. Looking directly into my eyes and with an apparent pang of sadness in his voice, his answer was philosophically direct: "Texas is a state whose heritage loves the raw physical power that football exemplifies. Unlike Louisville, there's no understanding of basketball's graceful artistry. It's as simple as that, Bruce." The depth of this observation's finality was pungent, leaving great hope for our effort.

Thankfully, the day had brought only passing mention of the Mayor's firing of the Police Chief and the demonstrations in Louisville. I had decided if it was mentioned, there could be no spinning; there were too many resources available enabling them to find the facts. My only comment was that there had been a misinterpretation between the Mayor and his Police Chief, which now appeared to be under control. Particular note was made about Louisville's outstanding record in race relations, of which they were aware. Most of the discussion over lunch dealt with UofL. Postolos was very interested in reaching a workable "win-win" arrangement between the Rockets and the University. He felt there were many things that the Rockets had to offer UofL, and Rockets owner, Les Alexander, was desirous of speaking directly with Dr. John Shumaker, president of the university.

As we left for the airport, Postolos pointedly stated — if Louisville can deliver the informal talking points proposal, then it's Louisville vs. Houston, with no other realistic competitors. In our assessment of the day's meeting, Norma felt it had been a roaring success. I agreed. But the positive vibes from the Houston meeting were to be short-lived.

"There's a Brutus among us!"

In our absence, Mike Kitchen was the ranking member of our law firm. I had full confidence in his judgment. The events of the next day would prove correct my opinion of his coolness under fire.

Upon our return to Louisville, the home phone carried a foreboding voicemail message from Kitchen. That morning Blum had faxed a letter addressed to me and the Mayor, expressing extreme dissatisfaction with the circulation of Tricon's name as "the New York Stock Exchange Company." The letter demanded governmental leadership and expressly withdrew Tricon's commitments if that governmental leadership wasn't forthcoming or if the faxed letter became public knowledge. Kitchen was alarmed. During the day the press had called the office about Blum's letter, prompting Kitchen to hide it under his deskpad. His message assured me that no one in our law firm, other than he, had seen it. As a result, Kitchen was insistent—the press leak must have come from the Mayor's office. It was too late to call Kitchen, as he had a household full of young children.

The next day, Blum refused to talk or meet. A lengthy letter was prepared and hand-delivered to him explaining that we weren't in Louisville when his letter was faxed and that Kitchen had protected its confidentiality until our return. Without Tricon's commitment, Louisville had no realistic opportunity with the Rockets or any other NBA transfer candidate. Had three months work evaporated? The next day, Friday, found Blum still unwilling to meet. That evening the fishnet would be re-spread across the water.

Periodically, Norma and I had private dinners with Senator Mitch McConnell and his wife, Elaine Chao. My relationship with him was unusual. We had been heated antagonists in the late 1970s when he served as County Judge and I as County Attorney. Gradually over the years we had grown to like and appreciate each other. By the late 1990s these unscheduled dinners had become something that was mutually enjoyed and anticipated.

That Friday evening we met for dinner at Le Relais, a quiet upscale restaurant in Louisville's old Bowman Field airport terminal building. It had always been the dinner location, due to its proximity with our home and the McConnell's Louisville residence. The conversation quickly turned to the NBA effort. McConnell wanted to know the full story. Everything, including the Houston meeting, was explained to him, except the potential involvement of Tricon. Correctly sensing a major opportunity for Louisville, the Senator was desirous of participating and volunteered to speak with James Baker about Louisville's NBA effort. With full realization of his nationwide connections, it was suggested the real key to success was a naming-rights sponsor. If he could assist in obtaining UPS's commitment, it might be the final piece of the puzzle. He committed to go to work on it, immediately. Without mentioning Tricon or the problems with them, maybe we had a shot with UPS as a replacement.

On the Tricon front, a mind-numbing event was about to happen.

Noon on Saturday, March 18 brought a call to our home from Blum. He began with an Ides of March reference: "We have a Brutus among us."

Blum had pieced together the mystery of his letter's leak. He believed my and Mike Kitchen's explanation that I was in Houston. He did not believe the Mayor's—which was that Blum's fax had been sent to the general city government fax machine, which enabled its leakage by the Aldermen. Blum's secretary had been former Mayor Abramson's secretary and positively knew the fax number she used went directly into the Mayor's private suite at City Hall. Blum was convinced that the Mayor had leaked his letter, believing that he could blame its leakage on the Aldermen, so that Tricon would pull out, signaling the death of the NBA effort in Louisville.

Blum apologized for questioning my integrity. The apology was unnecessary, but accepted. Honest brokering was essential. I told Blum that since Tricon was going sideways, on the previous evening Senator McConnell's efforts had been sought to seek a naming-rights commitment from UPS. Blum was magnanimous and understood. To be sure, this wouldn't be the last or only problem with Blum and Tricon. But their involvement would continue to make the odyssey sensible and realistic within NBA officialdom. By the next Tuesday, Blum indicated that "KFC was still interested, but it must have answers to the questions in his letter"—which were that the local government had to take some initiative. There was no disagreement on this point. Without any discussion of the potential Tricon pull-out, Magre was advised it appeared that the Board of Aldermen was going to have to take the lead. Magre agreed, but wanted one last face-to-face meeting with Armstrong.

Magre's Wednesday, March 22 meeting with Mayor Dave was unsatisfactory. He sought the Mayor's leadership on the NBA initiative, but it wasn't forthcoming. Now, the Mayor was considering the NBA effort to be an aldermanic initiative. Magre suggested that the County Judge's direct involvement might be helpful. A meeting with her was arranged for the next day.

County Judge Rebecca Jackson was a Republican political novice, who in the early 1990s had entered a race against a long-time Democratic County Clerk. With the support of the newspaper, she had won. In Kentucky, the County Clerk is one of those functionary government positions that doesn't require any particular skill in public leadership. Basically, the office would function with or without a County Clerk. Lawyers would file their deeds and mortgages, pay the filing fee, which would be deposited in a bank, the documents would be placed of record and returned to the filer. The custodians would clean up the offices in the evening and it would open the next morning with the same things being done all over again. Now, as County Judge, she had exhibited caution and hadn't appeared to be possessive of very inventive or imaginative skills. Still, she seemed to be alert and well-intentioned with an ever-present and hopeful eye toward her political future beyond the clerkship.

The discussion began with the County Judge indicating she had heard nothing from the Mayor about the NBA opportunity. Norma's mouth fell agape. Profuse apologies were made as I told her of the Mayor's commitment on March 1 to advise her in their weekly meetings. Jackson laughed saying, "Weekly meetings are a figment of his [the Mayor's] imagination. They do not occur." We had less than an hour to correct the Mayor's incredible falsehood. Woman-to-woman, Norma went to work. It was an arduous task. In the end, the County Judge indicated that the county was left with a $280 million bonded indebtedness resulting from Armstrong's tenure as County Judge. Consequently, she didn't see how county government could significantly participate in an arena bonding proposal.

March was, indeed, going out like a lion, but there was still hope that

McConnell might be able to attract UPS to line up with Tricon, and if he could, then maybe he could help with his fellow Republican in the County Judge chair. Friday afternoon March 24, the Senator called to report that the top officials of UPS in Atlanta had been contacted, were considering the opportunity and would be calling me on Monday. On Monday, March 27, Tom Weidemeyer of UPS's Atlanta office phoned. The call was pleasant, but UPS was not interested in naming-rights. They would, however, be interested in participating otherwise.

By now the internal rumor mill of City Hall was in high gear. The Mayor was moving at full speed to blame me and the Aldermen for what he had anticipated to be Tricon's impending pullout. The Board of Aldermen was upset. The Mayor's message was simple—the NBA was dead and it was my fault. He had pulled it off without firing a shot, publicly. Word of the death knell was circulating everywhere in City Hall.

Daytimer notes: "The whole thing is crashing internally." After all the work and effort, I refused to let this happen. The strategy had to change. Attention needed to be directed, outwardly.

Correspondence was sent to the Rockets advising that our planning was moving swiftly on a parallel public and private business path and insisting on a confirmed date for meetings in Louisville. For the first time, truthfulness had taken a back seat with the Rockets' negotiators. There was no choice. Had they known the full extent of the internal political disruption in Louisville, they (and any sensible businessman seeking a corporate relocation) would have politely declined further discussions.

Something also had to be done to turn the Mayor around, so a lengthy letter explaining the full extent of the opportunity and requesting a face-to-face private meeting with him as soon as possible was drafted and hand-delivered to the Mayor.

March ended on an uptick with a breakfast meeting at The Jefferson Club with GLI's Steve Higdon and our firm's Mike Kitchen. As I entered the breakfast room, Higdon was literally beaming from ear to ear. The reason was that the PricewaterhouseCoopers Report was to be released on April 15 and the preliminary draft was very favorable. On that basis, Higdon promised that GLI and the local business community would take a pedal-to-the-metal initiative and the Mayor's support would have to follow. This was great news for the initiative. I can't remember when a simple scrambled egg breakfast tasted better.

March, 2000 had been a disaster. The Mayor's surreptitious conduct had nearly succeeded in aborting the entire effort. The law firm's $50,000 contract with the Aldermen had been exhausted, with way too much time spent dealing with or about the Mayor's personal peculiarities and recalcitrance. But quitting at this point would be publicly irresponsible. Practically speaking, there could be no renewal of the contract, because that would present the Mayor with yet another opportunity to kill the effort. So my time—all of it—was now uncompensated. It would remain that way for the entirety of the NBA odyssey for another twenty-one months, totalling nearly 2,500 hours of uncompensated time and over $30,000 in expenses.

First half of April, 2000/Dinner with "the Shu"

It was April Fools Day and the Mayor responded to my letter. The response was self-laudatory, surveying his extensive efforts and self-professed skill over the years in attracting business to the community. He didn't understand. While it was a business, an NBA franchise was also an entertainment vehicle, with unusual and tangential revenue streams. A reply was required. In it I pleaded, repeatedly, for a one-on-one meeting so he could be informed and we could work together. Such a one-on-one meeting, without staff assistants, would never, ever occur.

Dan and Sug Schusterman are dear friends of ours. Dan, a charming raconteur, was then recently retired from Brown-Forman as vice president of national/international sales and Sug is a most gracious and delightful woman. They are both involved with many community-wide charities and frequently hosted private dinner get-togethers at their home. Fully understanding the economic engine an NBA team would provide for Louisville, they were constantly asking how they could help with the effort. At my suggestion earlier in the winter, the Schustermans had promised to create an environment for a private discussion about the NBA with the President of the University of Louisville.

On April 1, the Schustermans hosted such a dinner. It was an exquisite evening. Lucy Shumaker was absolutely charming, vibrant, outgoing and an inviting conversationalist, while her husband seemed more reserved, initially. John Shumaker was a Greek scholar with a Ph.D degree from the University of Pennsylvania. In 1995 had accepted the presidency of UofL following a tenure as President of Central Connecticut State University.

Upon his arrival in Louisville, this Greek scholar was confronted with, among other things, the jock-mentality of collegiate athletics. Other than his early professorial career at Ohio State, there was no other such situation in his higher education experience.[264] Being adaptable, Shumaker quickly gained the required appreciation for the importance of collegiate athletics in the minds of Kentuckians. As he warmed over the evening and became more expressive, Shumaker admitted an amazement about lack of a pressing concern among Kentuckians about the quality of collegiate education versus the supreme importance of collegiate athletics.

Shumaker had worked closely with the governor in achieving state legislative passage of an important program called "Bucks For Brains." The result had been UofL's receipt from the state of nearly a hundred million dollars to be privately matched for the purposes of luring nationally-renowned professors and researchers. Shumaker's initial years at UofL had been a success, with an easy matriculation into Louisville.

However, as time and events would dictate, Shumaker was far from what he appeared to be. Irrespective of the Shumakers eventual collective implosion (discussed more fully later), the Schustermans' dinner that evening was a signal success. Dr. Shumaker had listened intently, asked questions and expressed considerable interest in and desire for the University's participation at the appropriate point in any negotiations. I assured him, as I had Jurich, that no negotiations would occur without a prior commitment from an NBA owner of the willingness to forthrightly discuss a financial working relationship with the University for the joint use of a new arena. Shumaker was promised a full opportunity to privately meet with the owner of any NBA team and was particularly interested in opening discussions with the Rockets owner. He quickly seemed to comprehend and appreciate the economic importance of Louisville's joinder with the twenty-eight cities in the NBA, as well as the international impact the NBA would create for Louisville and the enormous benefits to be derived by the University's greater exposure to the world.

While there was no agreement or commitment from Shumaker that evening, the dinner was deemed to be very productive. Mutual cooperation was pledged and accepted across the table. An ardent handshake concluded the evening. If it had existed, it certainly appeared the fear of the unknown had been dispelled. The Daytimer note reads: "Best conversational dinner we've gone to in years."

The next several days produced a continuing uptick — Mike Goldberg confirmed the weekend of May 12-13 for the Rockets visit to Louisville, and in a lengthy Houston radio interview Postolos admitted no significant progress with the Houston Sports Authority.

As mid-April arrived the worm continued to turn. Tricon's consultant, Dean Bonham, believed it was 60/40 that the Rockets would remain in Houston, but Louisville remained behind Baltimore in the third position. Blum felt this was positive. Actually it was more than positive, because I knew Baltimore would never be accepted as a transfer city. The Washington Wizards majority owner, Ted Leonsis, and Abe Pollin, the long-time but now only part-owner (but still a quiet, major force within the NBA inner circle), would not permit competition in Baltimore, thirty miles from Washington, D.C.

PricewaterhouseCoopers Report

For nearly a month the NBA odyssey had gone sideways in Louisville. It was exceedingly fortunate we had been able to keep quiet the political confusion with the Mayor. From the outside-looking-in, it appeared that Louisville was the major contender for the Houston Rockets. But something had to occur within Louisville to invigorate the process. That event happened.

Wednesday April 19 was a beautiful spring day in Louisville. The powers-that-be were cobbled together in the main conference room of LG&E Energy. Present were most of the Aldermen, the Mayor, the County Judge, governor's representatives, interested business men and women and the press. All were assembled to witness the public revealing of the PricewaterhouseCoopers Report. The computerized Powerpoint presentation was professional and complete. Just as Stern had said in late February, these guys knew what they were doing.

The basic question was answered—yes, the NBA could succeed in Louisville. The underlying question that could not be answered by the Report remained: Was Louisville willing to do what was required to become a professional major league city? That was Stern's pungent question in February and my continuing concern.

The answer required a self-analysis of Louisville by Louisvillians, most particularly its political leadership. It required positive thought. It required confidence. It required the city's determination to move to the next level. It required an eradication of the long-established and ingrained fear of change.

What would be the response? To be sure, leadership was required. The kind of leadership Pee Wee Reese had exhibited when he put his arm around Jackie Robinson on that fabled day at Crosley Field, when the boo-birds had collected to express their collective disdain of Robinson; the kind of leadership and forward thinking that was ingrained within the gentle giants, Uncle Ed Diddle and Peck Hickman, as they led the great change to include African-Americans in major collegiate basketball. Was there any political leadership in Louisville capable of such a feat? That was the question. The answer was too frightening to contemplate, but there's eternal hope.

Now, the Mayor had no choice. The long-awaited Report had taken away his backoff room. He had to publicly become favorable and he did. But, now the question would become Postolos's original issue back in that early January phone call—actions, not talk, speak the loudest. The Mayor could talk, but talk doesn't walk—action does.

Ramifications from the PricewaterhouseCoopers Report reverberated both near and far and throughout NBA officialdom. The echo was heard in Charlotte, North Carolina, where the Hornets were experiencing continued and increasing pain of a deteriorating governmental relationship. There were phone calls from various Hornets-affiliated and interested persons. Was Louisville interested in the Hornets? Evan Weiner, a widely-read internet sports columnist, wrote that the Charlotte franchise was on the auction-block for transfer and Louisville was an interesting possibility. There was a surprising call from an Orlando Magic official: Was Louisville interested in negotiating with the Magic? Everyone in the industry knew that PricewaterhouseCoopers' Dallas division was highly credible. Their favorable Report was of enormous significance.

Todd Blue's Gateway Group of mid-sized businesses was now operating in fourth gear to organize a cocktail dinner party in honor of the Rockets negotiating team. Bobby Clarkson had taken charge. A 5 foot, 6 inch whirling dervish of a man, Clarkson had grown up in modest blue collar Louisville, and with determination and a solid work ethic had created one of the largest and most successful insurance agencies in the region. Clarkson the salesman was determined to succeed; everyone knew that he would put on a great spread. I never had to give it a second thought.

With the General Assembly *sine die*, the Governor's office was now more focused. He had assigned Deputy Cabinet Secretary, Jack Conway, as his day-to-day point-person for the effort. Conway was a very personable and incisive young thinker. Having received his B.A. degree in Public Policy Studies at Duke and his law degree with honors from George Washington University, he had quickly become a valuable contributor to the governor's initiatives. A better selection couldn't have been made. Conway was alert, vigorous and actively concerned about the future of his hometown. He wasn't afraid of change and had a mind-set attuned to the challenges and opportunities of the future. With Conway's addition the base and breadth of Louisville's effort had solidified even further.

Within a day or so, something of even deeper importance occurred. The message had now hit Houston broadside.

On Wednesday, April 26 *The Houston Chronicle* reported that the contenders for the Rockets transfer were down to two cities — Louisville or Las Vegas. Louisville's efforts were fully explored in the article, but not much was said of Vegas. Didn't make any difference. Stern's position on Vegas was already ascertained. Rockets fans had organized a Save Our Rockets website, and its first page bore a large picture of Rockets All-Star center, Hakeem Olajuwon, upon whom was super-imposed a Kentucky Colonels uniform! They were worried—really worried—in Houston.

Daytimer noted: "Right now I'm enthused, if we can just get DLA off his ass."

With the positive impact of The PricewaterhouseCoopers Report, the public vetting of the NBA in Louisville had begun. It caught the anti's off guard. When the report turned out positive, they were stunned. The anti's ability to organize was further complicated because Louisville was in the middle of the Kentucky Derby festivities—the one time a year when Louisville shines on a national pedestal. Historically, Louisvillians of every bent and stripe go overboard to impress their Derby guests. The visitors had to leave the city thinking Louisville was heaven on earth; no divisiveness or anything that would damage that image could be undertaken.

In a Pursuit Team meeting, I predicted the positive vibes would last all the way through the Rockets visit on the weekend following the Derby. So, the strategy was developed by the Pursuit Team: we would have one month (from April 15 to May 15) to effectively inform and gel public opinion. The naysayers couldn't and wouldn't even begin to touch it until after May 15th, when the Rockets left. Then we'd all be in it together, all by ourselves

—and the naysayers would unite. The prediction was to prove accurate, ironically, to the very day.

May, 2000

The NBA odyssey in Louisville was still subject to a backward disconnect. As with March, which came in like a lamb and went out like a lion, May would come in with May flowers and end with April showers.

On Wednesday, May 3, Ed Glasscock hosted a meeting of Greater Louisville, Inc. and the Gateway Group. It was the last available day to plan the Rocket's visit before the Derby time crunch. Details of the Rockets visit were discussed and assignments were passed out. It was reported that the Mayor and the County Judge had still not met to discuss the NBA effort. While the governor was prepared to make his presentation to the Rockets, he still was insisting on local political leadership and initiative from the Mayor and the County Judge. We would be ready. Or would we? Somehow, during the week after the Derby we were going to have to come up with a financing plan—not definitive—but based upon some form of reality in order to provide sufficient sustenance to a continued interest level from the Rockets.

Fusiachi Pegasus won the 2000 Kentucky Derby in the sixth fastest time ever. All were happy and proud. Louisville had pulled off another Derby. Now, attention turned to the Rockets management visit. While Glasscock and his law firm were diligently working with the Governor's Office to put together a tentative financial plan, Tuesday, May 9 would become a significant day in the odyssey. Previous discussions with local Merrill Lynch representative, Jeffrey Sexton, had produced a seemingly high level of interest within Merrill's national offices. That day, Chris Melvin, the managing director of Merrill Lynch's International Sports Finance Group, headquartered in the North Tower of the World Trade Center, came to Louisville. This meeting was world-class in its importance.

As one of the world's major players in athletic venue financing, Melvin had supervised Merrill Lynch's worldwide involvement as lead or co-lead manager for billions of dollars of arena/stadium construction and sports financing. The list was literally staggering.[265] For nearly two hours I was given the inside information on all the Houston players, with particular emphasis on the internal dissention and the personality/capability makeup of the Houston Sports Authority members. Louisville now had a real strategic advantage. Now we knew, from the inside, the nature and extent of Houston's problems, and I felt that we could easily deal with it if we could just get the Louisville act together.

Of primary importance was information that, because of its commitments for Enron Field and the new NFL franchise stadium, the maximum that the Houston Sports Authority could afford in bonds for a Rockets arena was $82 million. It was also clear that $82 million wouldn't get the job done for the Rockets; considerably more public or private financing was required. The Rockets visit was now three days away, and Melvin's information was of staggering significance. Despite its size and wealth Houston was being stretched beyond its bond financing capabilities. It was abundantly clear — financially, Louisville was in the driver's seat, but it had to be willing to deliver with action.

My return to the office was met with a shock. Steve Higdon reported that the Mayor was threatening not to attend the Gateway Group dinner on Saturday evening, because his name didn't properly appear on the invitation! How is it humanly possible to go from the Melvin meeting and its importance to such malarkey in the course of only fifteen minutes? The bewildering mayoral performance (or lack thereof) continued.

The next day, Wednesday, May 10, began with Traughber calling to say the Mayor had now become convinced the Rockets were using us, and the PricewaterhouseCoopers Report wasn't accurate, because Louisville's business community couldn't afford the season tickets. Upon questioning, Traughber admitted this latest news was based upon no empirical data. GLI representatives spent the rest of the day encouraging a positive attitude from the Mayor. The inescapable fear was growing: our local politicians were on the verge of making fools of themselves on the national stage.

Meanwhile, Bobby Clarkson reported 123 acceptances for the Saturday evening dinner. The volume of acceptances had necessitated the dinner's move from Vincenzo's to the top floor of the Humana Building. Clarkson had delivered, just as we knew he would.

It was now Friday May 12. No one knew what the Mayor or County Judge would say at the next day's meeting with Rockets management. At 1:00 on Friday, a press conference was conducted to advise the local media of the weekend's events. They were led to believe the Postoloses and the Goldbergs were arriving on the 10:00 PM Continental flight from Houston.

We had other plans. Our Houston guests were brought to Louisville on a Tricon private jet. Upon landing, they were whisked to the Seelbach Hotel. I would later apologize to the Louisville media for misleading them about the flight arrangements.

Rockets arrive in Louisville

It was one of those beautiful late spring days, and Louisville was on the national sports map for the second weekend in a row. With the work of the mid-sized businesses and Bob Clarkson, it was perfectly orchestrated. Nicole Postolos and Carol Goldberg were escorted by Todd Blue's family to Saturday morning services at Adath Jeshurun Temple. It had been learned several weeks prior that if the Rockets moved to Louisville, the Alexanders and Goldbergs would attend Adath Jeshurun. Apparently, the rabbi was a former Houstonian. The wives were introduced to the congregation and had a private visit with the rabbi.

Meanwhile, Postolos and Goldberg were given a walking tour of the Water Company arena site and downtown Louisville. When one walks to the edge of the Belvedere next to the George Rogers Clark statue and gazes across the near mile-wide Ohio River, then turns around and looks back at the Louisville skyline, it brings up goose-bumps. It really is some skyline, and that's exactly what George Postolos said. Our guests were driven to Tricon's headquarters, a new/old Georgian mansion. The meeting began promptly at noon in Tricon's Board of Directors room.

Following a table featuring the full gamut of Tricon specialties (Kentucky Fried Chicken, Taco Bell and Pizza Hut pizzas), Governor Paul Patton offered an effective and positive presentation, assuring his full support and intention to actively negotiate the Rockets transfer to a successful conclusion. The available business tax incentives, including tourism tax credits and the new tax increment financing statute were noted. Patton was in his element. As a successful businessman, he understood a business person's thought process. He delivered. What followed was, literally, a staggering embarrassment.

Glancing at the Mayor, the County Judge said, "Girls first!" She proceeded with a Chamber of Commerce-type rendition of the community's attributes that might have won third place in the girl's state high school speech contest. Her assurances about Louisville's excellent public school and park system had the resonance of a passage from Rebecca of Sunnybrook Farm. We'd have been better off just passing out a brochure. This was followed by the homily, "This whole thing is kinda-like a mating process — it takes a while." A "mating process" — why, that's just what the Rockets management needed to hear when they were in the midst of making a $500 million corporate relocation decision. Sadly, there wasn't a hook to get her offstage.

Now it was the mayor's turn. There was a near-audible sound of fingers crossing. He began by touting his business initiatives, such as securing UPS for Louisville (which was actually accomplished by others). It seemed like he was running for re-election, but our visitors couldn't vote in Kentucky. Surely, it would get better. Surely, he would look at and speak directly to our guests, instead of gazing at the various corners of the room. But it didn't happen. Not a word about what he would do to lead the effort. No mention of a bond issue. No vision, no leadership to carry the ball across the goal line—absolutely nothing. The Governor politely listened and periodically looked at his shoes. The eyes of Goldberg and Postolos appeared to glaze over. Then Mayor Dave joined the others and sat. The room was in a collective state of utter disbelief. Norma looked at me with a blank stare as did Glasscock and Blum. The quiet of the moment was overwhelming. No one said a word. The next words could have well been those of Rodney Dangerfield in Caddyshack: "Who stepped on the duck?" It was, literally, awful.

Following the debacle, Blum, Novak and Tricon consultant Bonham spent an hour in Novak's private office with our guests. Afterward, Postolos appeared re-enthused. Hopefully, Tricon's talent had made up for the Mayor's and County Judge's performances. On our way to Churchill Downs for a few races, Postolos waxed eloquent about the Governor and his presentation. Then he remarked, "...seems like a lot of cities have a mayor like that." Then, "Just what is it that the County Judge does?" He was reminded of our March 15 meeting in Houston when it had been noted that mayors come and go, but things like Tricon are permanent. Postolos said, "I know. I guess we can all thank God for that." It was apparent that the Gateway Group mid-sized business party that evening was swiftly moving to the status of a make-or-break event. Everything would depend on Bobby Clarkson and the city's mid-sized businesses.

And did Clarkson ever deliver! A soirée to end all soirées. Dozens and dozens of businessmen and women visited individually and in small groups with Postolos and Goldberg. Norma and Carla Sue Broecker took charge, making sure Nicole Postolos and Carol Goldberg met all the women in the room. Senator Mitch McConnell and Elaine Chao were enchanting tablemates for our guests. Conversation flowed freely and alertly. There can not be enough good things said about the determination and quality of Louisville's business community effort that night. It was purely and simply remarkable. Unaware of the disaster that had earlier befallen the effort and unbeknownst that the chips were really on the table, the mid-sized business community of Louisville hit a Hank Aaron-style grand-slam home run. Standing ovations, pleas for and encouragement of the move to Louisville, commitments for suites and season tickets and advertising — everything one could possibly hope would happen, did. As emcee of the event, I made sure that Postolos and Goldberg were given the microphone after they and their wives were each presented with Kentucky Colonelcies. Both were genuinely exuberant in their praise of Louisville and the evening's festivities. We had swept them off their feet. Louisville's mid-sized businesses had done themselves proud. It was wonderful and I couldn't wait to tell Stern.

As we walked back to the Seelbach Hotel that star-bedazzled Louisville night, Postolos quietly said to me, "Bruce, I don't know about your Mayor, but I can tell you this, I'd give anything to have that same excitement in the Houston business community. You've completely convinced me of the Louisville business community."

The next morning our guests were taken to the Tricon hangar for their flight back to Houston. It was Mother's Day. Everyone, including Postolos and Goldberg, had plans for the day in honor of our women. As Postolos boarded the Tricon jet, feeling an analogy was in order, I inquired, "George, on this Mother's Day, can I report a conception?" Postolos cleverly responded, "I don't know, but with that business community support, for sure, a birth in Louisville won't take nine months." Didn't quite know how to read this but, to be sure, his and Stern's primary concern about the interest and capability of Louisville's business community was alleviated completely.

When something is finished in our lives, like a child or grandchild's pre-kindergarten years during which is required constant nurturing, loving, caring, worrying, dreaming and praying, there's a tendency to be proud of the effort, experience some regret it's over and tear up when considering what the future will bring. As the Tricon jet rose from the ground and disappeared into the Mother's Day morning sky over Louisville, a tear rolled down my cheek. While there was a twinge of pride and relief because our business community's performance had been sterling, the anxiety over what lay ahead politically was overwhelming.

As events were to unfold, after all the dedication and determined effort of so many good and decent people and the success of the endeavor to that moment, the result would soon prove tragic.

That morning would be the last time we would ever see George Postolos or Mike Goldberg.

Louisville stumbles as the Ruppians take the court

A month of positives that started with the Report of PricewaterhouseCoopers had ended with the visit of Postolos and Goldberg. Now Louisville was on its own. The ultimate questions would now be answered. Could it take charge of its future and avoid its inferiority complex, fear of the unknown and aversion to change? What would happen when the Ruppians took the court? As predicted in mid-April, the negatives wouldn't wait a single day.

The confounding routine of politicos speaking to each other through dueling press conferences began immediately with County Judge Jackson initiating the process. She announced the county couldn't participate in the arena's bonding, a fact already fully understood and accepted by Postolos. Seizing the moment, within an hour the Mayor was publicly responding that the city couldn't do it alone. All this was accomplished by noon on Monday, with full knowledge that the governor supported the effort but expected local political leadership. Instead of exploring ways of working together, within three hours of the first business day following the Rockets departure, the Ship of Fools with its two captains, Armstrong and Jackson, was sailing into the sunset.

With the failure of executive local political leadership, the ball had been lateraled to the Aldermen. Would the Board of Aldermen take the lead and send the message that was needed by introducing an arena bond ordinance? At the Humana dinner, in the presence of aldermanic president Magre and several mid-sized business leaders, Postolos had discussed his desire for an Aldermanic initiative such as the introduction, for a first reading, of a bond issue ordinance. It was clearly understood Postolos would consider such a move to be a significant signal from Louisville. The mid-sized business leaders had taken Magre aside and encouraged his leadership initiative. At his request, a draft ordinance had been prepared by our law firm, but the statutes required a public hearing, which was creating some Aldermanic reluctance. One Alderman, Bill Allison, felt that instead of an arena we needed to consider more funding for soup kitchens. Now, that's one of those statements you have to run through your mind a time or two. What did soup kitchens have to do with this?

The local state legislative delegation began to weigh in. Their leader, Larry Clark, had assured me in March of his support for a new downtown arena and the effort to lure an NBA team to Louisville. Now, for some reason, he had done a complete one-eighty. Rumors were afloat as to a quid pro quo that could explain his reversal. Some guessed that he had been provided better seating at UofL games. Others suggested a previously unadmitted friend or family member had been admitted to UofL. A few felt he might be upset over not being sufficiently included in the planning process. No one seemed to understand why he had changed position after leading the passage of the state House Resolution encouraging economic incentives for the project. To compound matters, Clark wouldn't speak with anyone. By mid-week, after our visitors had gone, the Ruppians had hit their stride.

In spite of the negatives, a positive but preliminary report was received from Glasscock's law firm. The city's bonding could be done for less than $12 million a year in principal/interest payments. With the state's tourism tax credits and a rental agreement from the Rockets of $4-to-5 million annually, the city's maximum exposure was between $2 and 4 million, and we hadn't even begun negotiating. As a result, Magre assured the Pursuit Team that he was now ready to submit the ordinance for at least a $175 million dollar bond issue, just as he had promised Postolos. It was getting intense. Louisville's delivery was required. There was still a sense that local momentum was fading, because the Aldermen weren't acting decisively. On May 30, again under pressure, Magre advised the Pursuit Team he would initiate the ordinance in five days. This was reported to Goldberg.

The next day, May 31, the Houston Sports Authority announced its willingness to issue $175 million in bonds with $8.5 million in annual rent paid by the Rockets and all revenue streams flowing to them. It was just like Chris Melvin had said; the Houston Sports Authority couldn't afford it. The phone lines were afire. Talk wouldn't work now, action was required. The ball was in Louisville's court, and it had to act and do so promptly.

June, 2000

June began with my e-mail to the Mayor, pleading for his leadership and action. There had been more than a dozen such e-mails before, and there never was a response. There would be none this time, either. A June 1 headline in *The Courier-Journal* caught everyone's attention: "Houston Offers Plan To Keep NBA Team." The deal was just as reported in the *Houston Chronicle* the previous day. Billy Burge, the Sports Authority's Chairman was quoted: "If Houston cannot successfully pass this referendum, then they will be moving to another city." Magre observed that the Houston plan "...gives us a basis to develop our proposal. It has been made very clear what Houston is willing to provide. Now the onus is on Louisville."

The clock was ticking for Magre to initiate aldermanic action. The State's CFO, Jim Ramsey, convened meetings with the city CFO Driskell and county CFO Stenberg. The results didn't appear positive. The State was prepared, but there was continuing local reluctance.

On Tuesday, June 6, Mike Goldberg notified me that soon Alexander was going to make some decisions about whether to agree for a second referendum or give up on Houston. If Louisville was interested, it needed to be prepared to act. Stern's advice in February was recalled: Alexander is a thoughtful by quick decision-maker. Little sleep, constant phoning and meetings occupied nearly the full 24 hours of each day. A vacillating editorial in *The Courier-Journal* wasn't helpful. Mixed messages from Louisville were radiating everywhere. Stern called with a question: It's getting close to decision time—what's going on in Louisville? What's happened? No adequate answer could be given.

Deadline or no deadline?

Eight days had now passed since Magre had committed to introduce a bond ordinance in five days.

On Thursday, June 8, Goldberg called at mid-morning. Magre's commitment for a bond ordinance first reading must be fulfilled no later than June 16. Goldberg was going to Tokyo between June 16-20, and was then to be hospitalized for an operation after which he and Alexander were going to decide whether the Rockets would pursue a second referendum in Houston or look elsewhere. Then Goldberg specifically said that evening he was going to "...another state to meet with its Governor....without an affirmative act from Louisville, the Rockets would consider reopening discussions with St. Louis, New Orleans and Baltimore. Louisville must be prepared to make at least a non-binding commitment to serve as a 'stated intent' by no later than Tuesday, June 13 that was acted upon by June 16."

What had happened? Where did these other cities come from? For three months Louisville had been the only transfer contender. Where was Postolos in all this? However, there wasn't time to contemplate Goldberg's authority or the seeming absence of Postolos from the putative decision. An immediate conference call was convened with the Pursuit Team. It was collectively determined that *Courier-Journal* reporter Chris Poynter had to be told, in order to advise the public of the challenge being presented to Louisville's politicians. Blum and Glasscock arranged for a 5:00 PM meeting with the newspaper's Editorial Board. Urgency for action was made clear and was recognized by *The Courier-Journal* editors. It was the lead story under the masthead of its Friday, June 9 edition. Even though it was known for several months that the county was financially strapped and couldn't participate in the bonding, County Judge Jackson was quoted in the article as saying that "maybe it is time for us to look at the Houston Rockets and say, thank you for allowing us to be a player, and if we can't meet your timeline, then maybe you do need to look elsewhere."

In the news story Magre directly disagreed with Jackson stating: "For me at least, it's not that big a surprise. This thing needs to move forward for them and it needs to move forward if it's going to be the Rockets for us as well."

Yet, while Magre was professing to understand the urgency, there was still no bond ordinance before the aldermen. *The Courier-Journal* is on the internet, fully available for Houston's perusal. The story generated a series of calls back and forth with Goldberg, who was angry with me that I had publically divulged his ultimatum and that the three other cities were mentioned. A very heated argument ensued in which I said, "What's wrong with telling the public the truth? Everything that was said was exactly as you said it. I have contemporaneous notes reflecting it. How were we expected to get action, without informing the public and the local leadership about the time table you established?"

As everyone involved knew, Goldberg had been asking for a non-binding commitment for several months. Now we were taking action to obtain one. "Where was Postolos?" was demanded by me of Goldberg. He's not available, was the reply. Meanwhile, the anti-forces in the local state legislative delegation had rallied. According to them, Louisville simply wasn't going to have a gun put to its head. Everything had deteriorated. The house of cards had fallen apart.

That evening Norma and I agreed Louisville was making a fool of itself. With no executive political leadership, the Rockets transfer to Louisville would never happen. That evening I called Postolos at home to discuss the strange developments. He was gracious, vaguely alluding to internal problems in Houston, expressing he was in a bind and asking for my understanding. It was hard to give. Seems like everyone was in a bind. More thought and reflection allowed the realization to fully germinate that there was, indeed, an internal power struggle on the Rockets management team. Norma had sensed it when they and their wives were in Louisville. A woman's intuition is virtually infallible. Further reflection enabled our recall of Stern's February advice to pay no attention to what's going on in Houston, get your own ducks in a row in Louisville.

Years later Kenny Rogers' advice was again cogent: "You have to know when to hold 'em and know when to fold 'em." It was time to fold 'em.

In a protracted phone call, Blum was advised of my withdrawal from active participation and the same message was left with Blue and Glasscock. Blum and Blue insisted that I rethink the decision. Feeling their request was entitled to consideration, I changed my mind and decided to give the Aldermen one more opportunity to assume political leadership. On Sunday, June 11 Aldermanic president Magre and Alderman Johnson were informed that unless the Board of Aldermen publicly reconstituted my authority by an immediate vote of confidence along with a first reading of the bond ordinance we had prepared, I was withdrawing. Magre promised that if the Mayor didn't act the Board of Aldermen would. On Monday, June 12 the Mayor, sensing impending Board of Aldermen action, advised Johnson that he was putting a package together. Johnson and Magre agreed to wait for the Mayor's action.

For some reason or another, it always seemed that few in Louisville's political realm realized *The Courier-Journal* was daily available, worldwide, on the internet. Everything reported in it was read, instantly, in Houston. As a result, Louisville's implosion had became publicly known in Houston. On Tuesday, June 13 *The Houston Chronicle* reported in major headlines about the failure in Louisville. The headline read: "Louisville's Efforts To Draw Rockets Foundering." The article quoted from the County Judge's letter to the Mayor in which she wrote, "Please do not issue any statements of commitment or send a memorandum of understanding at this time on behalf of the County." The next day *The Courier-Journal* headline read, "State, County May Not Fund Arena." This prompted seven members of the Board of Aldermen to sign a letter to the mayor, encouraging his action and their support. One vote had been lost, which meant there weren't enough votes to override a mayoral veto. The vote lost was that of Alderman Melton. He had originally signed the letter, but later visibly scratched out his signature. What a debacle!

Feeling it was essential to discuss the situation with Commissioner Stern, the call was placed that afternoon. The entire course of events of the previous week was explained with Stern suggesting to ignore the internal problems in Houston. He reiterated his comments about a Houston referendum that were carried in *The Houston Chronicle*, to wit, that if "...they [Houston] do [put a second referendum on the ballot] and it's approved, we'll be there. If not, we won't be there." Stern encouraged me not to give up, that it might be advisable to call Postolos again, and concluded by reminding me of his admonition from the February meeting that there were other franchises— other fish in the pond. Taking Stern's advice, a call was made to Postolos that evening. Saying that Nicole was so upset she had written a letter to Norma apologizing for everything, George asked a favor, to which I agreed: Goldberg would be excluded from further discussions about the Rockets transfer to Louisville.

Thursday, June 15, brought a call from Steve Higdon indicating that GLI was exasperated with Armstrong and that he and Glasscock were going to take over and make a Louisville presentation to Postolos themselves. Daytimer noted: "I appreciate it, but I'm out for the time being." At this point, I had given up the ghost.

Louisville's opportunity with the Rockets was dead. State CFO Jim Ramsey had decided that the state's involvement was not possible, because a new arena downtown would be in competition with Freedom Hall, which would prevent state tourism tax credits. Since the tax increment financing statute that contained no similar anti-competitive provision wouldn't be operative until July 1, no state commitment could be made until then— which was too late. Ramsey's position was a polite way of delivering the failed local political leadership message from the governor.

In the hope of reinvigorating the process, the business community launched its final effort consisting of bumper stickers along with print and radio/television advertising. The June 18 *The Courier-Journal* headline read, "Executives Launch Push For Arena." Mike Seale, the local president of defense contractor United Defense, observed: "This is not just about the NBA or pro basketball. This is about helping build a more vibrant city." As a Republican, Seale was determined to re-orient the County Judge's vacillation. Emergency meetings with the County Judge were held, to no avail.

There's a strange anatomical reaction that sometimes occurs following a death. It's known as the death rattle. The Houston Rockets segment of Louisville's NBA odyssey experienced one. On June 21, 2000 UofL's athletic director Tom Jurich announced that UofL and Freedom Hall were exploring the possibility of building a new arena on the state fairgrounds property. An obsequious quote was attributed to Jurich: "Obviously, we don't want to get in anybody's way downtown." University President Shumaker was also quoted, saying the discussions were in the brainstorming stage; "We're revising the physical master plan of the campus and we have to begin to speculate four or five or ten years out what the future of our facilities in athletics are going to be, and I think that it emerged as a possibility for discussion."

The Courier Journal's lead editorial entitled, "As usual, Louisville flaunts instead of resolves its divisions," couldn't have been more prescient. There was little question among those involved that the University in concert with Freedom Hall officials had chosen a most unusual time to announce nothing other than a Shumaker brainstorm and a speculation "...four or five or ten years out...." This timing of what was otherwise a non-announcement destroyed any hope of an effective bargaining position for Louisville with the Houston Rockets.[266]

Mayor Dave "acts"

After months of inaction and no discussion with anyone on the Pursuit Team, on Wednesday, June 28, at a 5:00 PM press conference, Mayor Dave publicly announced that a Louisville proposal had been faxed to the Rockets. A $220 million Louisville arena would be built, with Alexander being personally required to pay Louisville an up-front and one-time payment of $42.7 million, with Tricon's naming-rights money going to the city to help retire the bonds and with the state legislature being required to approve a ticket tax to supplement the annual bond payment.

A picture in the Webster's Dictionary next to its definition of "preposterous" might have included a copy of this letter. Since the state legislature was not to meet until January, 2001, Alexander couldn't even begin to consider an offer contingent upon a state legislative vote six months later, when he had to make a decision within one month. In addition to the banality of the offer itself, if Mayor Dave had actually tried to find a worse time to present it, he couldn't have. His fax hit the wires on the evening of the NBA draft, and Les Alexander was in Houston working with his staff to decide who the Rockets would draft. But it was even worse than that.

The Mayor's offer, addressed to Postolos, had spelled Postolos' name wrong not once but—can you believe it—three times. POSTULOUS. All I could think of was Stern's February witticism: "Bruce, while you all go about this, try to act like you're not from Kentucky."

The June 30 headline in *The Houston Chronicle* read: "Louisville stumbles in pursuit of Rockets." The article began: "If attracting the Houston Rockets is a race, Louisville's a scratch. That City's effort to lure the Rockets, already sputtering in the six weeks since team officials visited there, has taken an almost comedic turn. The latest twist is a letter this week from Louisville Mayor David Armstrong to Rockets officials Michael Goldberg and George Postulous (sic). The twist is that 'Postulous' is known to family, friends, business associates and the media as George Postolos, the Rockets Chief Operating Officer."

The *Chronicle* article further explored the absurdity of Armstrong's presentation and concluded: "The Rockets and Louisville have been negotiating since at least December, and a Louisville attorney hired to attract the NBA said in February he had made 'substantial progress' in discussions with a team, which other sources confirmed was the Rockets. In May, Rockets officials visited Louisville. They have since become increasingly perplexed with that city's efforts."

Louisville appeared to the nation's sports industry like the gang who couldn't shoot straight. It was awful. Mayor Dave had made a mockery of a half-year's effort by dozens and dozens of dedicated private citizens. The next day he left town for a multi-week vacation, somewhere. On Friday afternoon, July 7, with the mayor on vacation, his CFO, Jane Driskell, called to say the mayor had asked her to inquire as to my ideas about "what to do now." My response was rather short. She was told: "For starters, tell him to spell people's names correctly, then remind him I've known him for 30 years. If he wants to call me, I'll speak to him one-on-one. Otherwise, I'm not interested in passing messages via messengers."

At this point, nothing could be done to put Humpty Dumpty together again. The charade was as sad as it was absurd. The call from Mayor Dave never came.

One last phone call, then "the end"

On July 25 a call came from a person who must remain confidential. The advice was plain and simple: "Take out the provision requiring 2001 state legislative action, negotiate down and spread out the $42.5 up-front payment required from Alexander and agree that the naming rights go to the Rockets, and Louisville might be back in the ball game." The response was: "We can't allow the mayor to make a fool of Louisville, again. We have to step aside from the process for the time being."

On Friday, August 4, the Houston Sports Authority and the Rockets signed a Memorandum of Understanding. The Houston and Harris County legislative bodies would vote to put the referendum on the ballot in November, 2000.

Indeed, the Rockets had rocketed into Louisville challenging the city with its first opportunity in 23 years to become a major league sports city. It had emerged in the winter of 1999 from the dedication of a few people, who could have fit into the proverbial telephone booth. At the beginning, because of the inability to reveal Tricon Global Restaurants' serious naming-rights interest and that the Houston Rockets were the suitor/suitee, many Louisvillians believed that the NBA in Louisville was little more than a hoax.

From this rather ignominious beginning, the concept of the NBA in Louisville had burgeoned in a half-year by virtue of the encouragement from NBA Commissioner David Stern, the increasing interest and growing support received from Tricon Global Restaurants, a developing consensus of the under-45 crowd, the dogged leadership of the Pursuit Team, the dedication of Todd Blue's mid-sized business Gateway Group, the eternal hope of Alderman Dan Johnson, the splendid advocacy of Steve Higdon and Greater Louisville, Inc., and the reality of the PricewaterhouseCoopers Report. What six months prior had been unthinkable by many Louisvillians had actually happened — a crisp reality, repeatedly blazoned across *Courier-Journal* headlines and eventually among most Louisvillians that the Houston Rockets were seriously considering a transfer to Louisville, Kentucky.

Despite the enormous efforts of numerous publicly-spirited leaders and despite the hundreds of phone calls from just plain folks encouraging the continued work, the Houston Rockets portion of the odyssey was to eventually fail in the mid-summer of 2000 due to a total abject failure in local executive political leadership that was, literally, staggering in its depth of incompetence. To be sure, the Ruppians and their aversion to change and fear of the unknown had played a role in that failure, but their role was of minor significance, easily overcome by solid dynamic executive political leadership, the likes of which were required if Louisville were to join the other 28 cities comprising the world's economic hub.

The beginning chapter of the odyssey's Millennium trip had been an unmitigated debacle. But there was hope that, like Churchill's tome about World War I, there would be a Beginning, an End of the Beginning, a Beginning of the End, and an End. If that was to be the case, had Louisville survived the "Beginning"? If, so, only barely. Without much doubt, the Beginning hadn't caused the surfacing of any Normandy-like political leadership heroics about which Louisville could be proud. But, for sure, the Beginning had accomplished several significant things. Even though it had seriously stumbled, for nearly five of the first six months Louisville had effectively competed, even to the point of becoming the nationally-recognized logical transfer candidate for the Rockets, and NBA officialdom, including the NBA Commissioner, had recognized that Louisville's business community made it a viable NBA city.

We must always change, renew and rejuvenate ourselves otherwise we harden.

Goethe

CHAPTER TEN

The First Sting by the Hornets

As July, 2000, came to an end spirits were pretty low. The next several days were spent with Norma, our children and step-children and my best buddy, Tristan. He was only two and a half and didn't understand the depth of the loss. He was still OK as long as "Barney" was on. Good ol' Tristan — win or lose, we were still best pals.

Carolina comes a-callin'

In my last phone call with David Stern it had been made clear that if Louisville ever got involved again, it could do so only by direct person-to-person negotiations with the NBA owner. We could never again get caught up in a franchise's internal power struggle. While direct, my position was carefully tempered, because it had been Stern's request that the Rockets discussions be undertaken with Postolos and Goldberg. While it was important to remain cognizant of Stern's authority, it was also important for him to understand that Louisville had to look out for its own interests. Stern was, as always, gracious in understanding the predicament, regretted the misfortune that had befallen us, but politely recalled the woeful lack of Louisville's executive governmental leadership. It was a friendly, frank and direct discussion that concluded with his thought-provoking question: Is the business leadership in Louisville strong enough and sufficiently well-organized to take the quiet lead in creating a plan of action and financing structure for the arena's construction and then quietly endeavor to convince the reluctant local politicians?

A portion of my credibility with him had been gained by avoiding "Chamber of Commerce BS." His question offered a marvelous entré to step over that line and sing My Old Kentucky Home. Often, discretion is the better part of valor. I side-stepped the opportunity. I wasn't sure, but agreed to consider the concept.

The first few days of August were spent with the celebration of my daughter Alexis's wedding. I was really proud of her. In May, she had earned her Ph.D. in criminal justice and was soon to begin her collegiate teaching in Louisiana. It was one of those marvelous times when a parent realizes that all the work, love, thought, concern and caring for all those years — all the wonderful moments and difficult times of a child's growth and development — had congealed into a marvelously talented young woman. My youngest daughter, Sarah, an accomplished artist and an award-winning art teacher in Louisville's public school system, was the beautiful and radiant Maid of Honor. She was really proud and happy for her sister. The joy was further enhanced because my son, Jamie, was in town for the wedding. He was the head golf professional at a course in Pinehurst, North Carolina. We played a round of golf at Big Spring. I hadn't touched a club in months, but still shot an 85. Jamie beat me by fourteen shots. I still remembered the first time he beat me years ago — it was a squeeker on the 18th hole. Now it wasn't even a contest. We met twice on each hole, at the tee and on the green. As Bobby Jones once said of Jack Nicklaus, and Nicklaus later said of Tiger Woods, "...he plays a game with which I am not familiar."

What a weekend. There's nothing like the love of family and children to clear your head of the trauma and disappointment of life itself. Shortly, Alexander Graham Bell's invention interrupted all that.

August 8, 2000, a typical August day in Louisville — stifling hot. To their credit, the mid-sized business group was still trying. Republican businessman Mike Seale refused to believe he couldn't change the Republican County Judge's thought process. Republicans believe they have some sort of innate understanding of business and business opportunities, so Seale had arranged a meeting with County Judge Jackson for 1:00 PM. He, along with Bobby Clarkson, Todd Blue, and Jim Patterson, Jr., had choreographed the meeting for several days. I wasn't interested, but they insisted I attend. Reluctantly, I agreed. By noon, I had finished the morning's mail and returned some phone calls when the receptionist intercommed me. A guy called Ray Wooldridge was on the phone. I thought for a moment—who the hell is Ray Wooldridge?

Then I remembered. He was the co-owner of the Charlotte Hornets. I paused for a moment, sat down, collected my thoughts and picked up the phone.

The discussion began with the usual pleasantries. He was calling from Spain. Earlier in the day, Stern had suggested he consider initiating private discussions about Louisville's potential as an alternative home for the Hornets. Wooldridge understood that Louisville had been devoid of local executive political leadership during the Rockets negotiations. That didn't matter to him (which was good!). He was inquisitive about the Louisville business community's interest in an NBA franchise. Charlotte's business community had gone south on the Hornets. Further evidence that the remarkable effort of Louisville's mid-sized business community in pursuing the Houston Rockets had made a distinct impression within the NBA.

It was obvious that Wooldridge had spoken with Stern, because he knew we would insist on direct ownership contact in any negotiations. He wanted to know how quickly a preliminary meeting could be conducted with his lawyer and financial advisor, before he personally came to town. I told him that we would meet with his lawyer, only if he made an absolute commitment to meet in Louisville within a month of the lawyer's meeting. Wooldridge quickly agreed, committing that his lawyer would be calling later in the afternoon, to make the travel and time arrangements. We exchanged office, cell and home phone numbers and the call was over.

Following the useless but obligatory meeting with the county judge, I placed a call to Stern. He was on vacation. Fully cognizant of Stern's intense work schedule, it was inappropriate to intrude on his August vacation. So for awhile we would be on our own.

At mid-afternoon a call was received from Wooldridge's Atlanta lawyer, Craig Wagner. He was pleasant, all business and directly responsive to his client's instructions. A request was made for a copy of the package that Norma and I had delivered to Stern in February, including the report I had prepared for the Board of Aldermen in August 1999 and the PricewaterhouseCoopers Report. The conversation moved to the Louisville business community's support of the NBA. I was reluctant to say much. Because of the Mayor's confused approach with the Rockets, I was unsure about the business community's interest level for a new effort. Additionally, the Pursuit Team wasn't aware of any direct Hornets interest, nor was I sure of my continued interest level. The saddle sores still hurt. Apologizing for not being very communicative I explained, it was "a little too soon." Wagner understood but wanted me to also understand his client desired to expedite the Louisville discussions. With his direct insistence getting my attention, I agreed to meet in our offices on August 21 with him and Wooldridge's financial advisor, Dan Barrett from Manhattan Beach, California. The meeting would be a confidential working session, followed by his return to Louisville with Wooldridge in mid-September.

At 8:00 that evening as I tried to digest the events of the day, Wooldridge called from Spain to make sure Wagner had spoken with me. It was 2:00 in the morning in Spain and he had been unable to reach Wagner to confirm that contact had been made. I found this interesting. There could be little question about the timely urgency of Wooldridge's interest. The rest of the evening was spent trying to determine the answer to several questions—Do we start all over again? If so, where do we start and how do we start?

Two things were apparent. The initial background research on Alexander and the Rockets had proven invaluable. Therefore, it was essential to do another in-depth analysis of what was going on in Charlotte. Secondly, under no circumstances could we involve the local politicians at this point, except for Alderman Johnson, who could help by maintaining his finger on the political pulse. Stern's rhetorical question had to be the template. If we were going to get back in the water, the Louisville business community needed to be fully and completely organized and prepared to take a private leadership role. Experts on major-league professional team economics and arena financing needed to be involved in the creation of an arena financing plan. Then, once a bond financing plan was created, the politicians would have something to work with that had "legs" based upon expert input. It would have to be a private effort first, then a public one, as opposed to a parallel effort, as with the Rockets.

The Daytimer note was precise: "We're going to do it differently this time."

Charlotte's tarred heels

The next morning our paralegal, Brevin Gaw (Tristan's dad), began gathering the *Charlotte Observer* articles about the Hornets and their ownership. It was completed by mid-afternoon. The articles were nearly three inches thick. Brevin said, "This is really sad."

As a child, the Hornets original sole owner, George Shinn, had grown up in abject poverty around Kannapolis, N.C. So destitute was Shinn's family that as a child, after his father died of a stroke, he witnessed the sheriff's sale of his family's home and gas station. Not a particularly accomplished student, Shinn was last in his high school class. Undeterred by his lackluster academic performance, he worked his way through a local business school—eventually buying the school—then other schools. After creating a chain of business schools, he created another chain—car dealerships—all of which within fifteen years had made him a multi-millionaire. Before it all started, in 1972 he married Carolyn. Together, they raised two sons and a daughter. It was a wonderful family and a genuine American success story.

By late 1986, having enjoyed immense private business success and a long line of bank credit, Shinn's restless driving personality led him to actively seek a larger public involvement. With unrequited swagger, he cobbled up Charlotte Mayor, Harvey Gaant, went to New York with a retinue of Charlotte police bodyguards, rented a limousine, drove to the NBA headquarters on Fifth Avenue next to St. Patrick's Cathedral and announced to David Stern that he and the Mayor were "...here to get an NBA team for Charlotte." Shinn's élan was engaging and Stern remembered it, describing the event to Norma and me in our February 28th meeting. Before long Shinn had succeeded in convincing Stern to support the award of an NBA expansion franchise to Charlotte. The victory occurred on April Fool's Day, 1987. Charlotte, North Carolina (which had been half the size of Louisville in 1950 and during the ABA days could only support a regional franchise), had hit the big leagues and George Shinn was driving the Cadillac Eldorado as an NBA owner. There was a week-long celebration including a downtown parade with a reported 100,000 people wildly cheering his and Charlotte's bravado and success.

As always, success beget more success in George Shinn's life. For years thereafter the Charlotte Hornets led the NBA in attendance and, as late as 1995, Shinn had sold the staggering number of 21,000 season tickets. The Hornets success had enabled the once-destitute son of a gas station owner to become a Charlotte patron. There were donations of hundreds of thousands of dollars to the Charlotte Symphony and millions of dollars for men's homeless shelters. This largesse was matched by even more donations to and the raising of more millions for the Mecklenburg County park system, facilitating the purchase of several thousand acres of land, nearly doubling Charlotte's public park system. Shinn had become a remarkable public citizen.

The 5-foot, 6-inch dynamo had written five books; three were entitled *The American Dream Still Works*, *Leadership Development* and *You Gotta Believe*. All of them had come true for Shinn. The best-sellers gave full credit for his success to an unwavering belief in God. Billy Graham-worshiping and God-fearing Charlotte loved George Shinn. There were frequent appearances on Pat Robertson's "700 Club" and Shinn was often mentioned as a potential gubernatorial candidate. Some even postulated he would succeed North Carolina octogenarian, Jesse Helms, upon his retirement from the U.S. Senate. There were multiple honoraria, the most noteworthy being the National Horatio Alger Award. It was a beautiful life. However, as the song goes, "Into A Good Life Some Rain Must Fall." But for Shinn, instead of some rain, a raging thunderstorm blew up.

The previously infallible George Shinn began to make mistakes. In a headstrong move he traded away Hornets All-Star center, Alonzo Mourning, because his salary expectations were too rich. Then, in an effort to quiet the fans' discontent, he signed another player for more money than Mourning had sought. That player didn't pan out. Others were traded over monetary disputes. Soon the moniker of cheapskate became attached to Shinn in the growingly-harsh Charlotte press. Undeterred, he fired head coach Dick Harter for non-performance, but unbeknownst to Shinn the timing was terrible — the day Harter's father died of cancer. Then, Shinn terminated Hornets general manager Carl Scheer, who was beloved in North Carolina as the father of the old ABA Carolina Cougars. The front office and management turnstile continued to spin, as Shinn fired Hall of Fame coach Dave Cowens over another salary dispute. All this occurred during the 1995 addition to the Charlotte sports scene of the NFL Charlotte Panthers. An instant success, the Panthers enjoyed NFL Playoff and Super Bowl contention from the beginning. The Hornets were no longer a major league monopoly in Charlotte. What had been one of the most successful NBA franchises was degenerating into a swirling public relations eddy. The worst was yet to come.

On the morning of September 5, 1997, Shinn offered a ride to a woman he met while visiting a drug rehabilitation center. From that point forward, whomever's rendition of the "he said, she said" diatribe you believed made little difference. Either story was catastrophic. The sordid soap-operatic sexual encounter eventually culminated in an eleven-day, nationally-televised Court-TV civil trial for money damages against Shinn. Among the plaintiff's witnesses were several Hornets cheerleaders, who testified that Shinn had sexually harassed them as well. For Charlotte press time, Shinn's tawdry escapade rivaled President Clinton's with Monica Lewinsky. Clinton and Shinn were synonymous in the eyes of Charlotteans — they were charlatans.

Eventually, Shinn won the battle. The jury refused to believe the cheerleaders or the plaintiff, awarding them no money damages. But Shinn had lost the war. His wife of 25 years divorced him, his property was divided up with Shinn keeping ownership of the financially-strapped Hornets with the secure investments becoming Carolyn's. The Charlotte wrath for Shinn would get even worse.

Reeling from the financial pressure of his diminished wealth, a year later Shinn considered a partial sale of the Hornets. The negotiations were highly-publicized, raising hopes for a new beginning among Hornets fans. Eventually the purchase offer was rejected. It had been made by North Carolina penultimate hero, Michael Jordan. The deal-breaker was publicly-discussed. Jordan wanted control over the Hornets player-personnel decisions. George Shinn refused.

Shinn had turned his back on his wife, his community, and now, Michael Jordan. Being utterly unwelcome in Charlotte, the one-time Charlotte business tycoon and patron moved out of town to Juniper, Florida. A persona non grata in deeply religious and devout Charlotte. From Mt. Everest to the bottom of the ocean in a half-dozen years. Unbelievable.

Enter Ray Wooldridge, another self-made multi-millionaire. Wooldridge, the son of hard-scrabble Memphis parents who operated a small neighborhood grocery store, learned the importance of a solid work ethic at an early point in his life. Odd non-descript jobs and the preparation of tax returns enabled him to work his way through Mississippi State University. In 1965, with an accounting degree in hand, he married his high school sweetheart and was ready for the big world outside Starkville, Mississippi.

Wooldridge's early business career was one of nomadic mobility with employment in Memphis, New Orleans, Boston, Jersey City, Philadelphia,

New York City, Tampa and finally Atlanta. While employed by Hertz in Atlanta, he had been assigned the task of selling used U-Haul-It trailers whose leases had expired. There was little interest in them as used trailers, but a surprising amount of curiosity in their alternative use as portable offices. Used U-Haul-It trailers began selling like hotcakes. Wooldridge succeeded and learned.

In 1982, he formed his own company that leased used trailers for offices and school classrooms. Quickly the business concept expanded to the construction and sale of pre-fabricated factory-built modular units. New markets were discovered, even expanding to hospitals and prisons. Within fifteen years Wooldridge's company, Space Master International, was a nationwide chain of offices in 26 cities and annual sales approaching 30,000 units. It had become the third largest modular unit sales and leasing company in America. Late in 1998, Wooldridge sold his business to its major competitor, Williams Scotsman, for what was variously reported after capital gains taxes to be a net of between $274 and 375 million.

A divorced multi-millionaire with five children for whom he was custodially responsible, Wooldridge set out to do three things: (i) to continue devoting full attention to the lives of his children and his mother, (ii) to enjoy the perks of his new-found wealth and (iii) to acquire an ownership interest in an NBA team. His intrigue with the NBA came from his years as an Atlanta Hawks fan. He had owned a suite at the old Omni and followed the team while developing a close personal friendship with Hawks coach, Mike Fratello.

Wooldridge's new wealth thrilled him. Like Shinn, there was a justifiable pride in his business accomplishments. Wooldridge's was another real-life Horatio Alger story. He owned a ritzy winter home on tony Fisher Island in Miami's Biscayne Bay, a jet plane, a yacht and a Rolls-Royce. Personal enjoyment was gleaned from scuba diving, snow skiing and the maintenance of a high skill level at casino blackjack, frequently practiced at the Atlantis in Nassau. Then there was his residence in Atlanta called "the Castle" by his neighbors. It was reported the Castle contained a fresco in which Wooldridge appeared as an orating Roman senator and prominently included his five children and mother. The Castle was renowned in Atlanta for its festive yuletide lighting exhibition and the annual and gargantuan Christmas party, hosted by Wooldridge, for Atlanta's underprivileged children. Reportedly, these holiday festivities were spurred by the rather sparse Christmases he experienced during his childhood in Memphis. All this largesse allowed one to think Wooldridge was a loud and bodacious person. This was absolutely incorrect.

In reality, Wooldridge was a very cautious, quiet, private and sensitive person. He worshiped his mother, phoning her on a daily basis, often in the middle of business meetings (a fact witnessed on two separate occasions during my meetings with Wooldridge). It was little known or reported that Wooldridge dearly loved, cared for and was deeply concerned about his five children, one of whom was autistic—facts that were all well hidden by the largesse surrounding him.

Lastly, Wooldridge's biggest non-family hero was none other than Louisville's own Muhammad Ali. Early in his business career, he had met Ali. He later confided in me that this meeting was one of the highlights of his non-family, non-business life. In little more than a year, Wooldridge's love of and respect for Ali would play a pivotal role in the final Hornets portion of the Louisville NBA odyssey.

Shortly after the sale of Space Master International, Wooldridge considered purchasing the Sacramento Kings, but became uninterested. Sacramento, California was too far away from his mother and children. After Shinn's negotiations with Michael Jordan had failed, in November 1998 Wooldridge requested an opportunity to meet with Shinn. Within seven months, in July, 1999, Wooldridge purchased a 35% interest in the Hornets from Shinn for $56 million, with a two-year option to purchase majority control. The purchase agreement provided for evenly split decision making on all matters except for certain exclusive responsibilities — Shinn for player personnel decisions and Wooldridge was to accomplish Charlotte's commitment for a new arena or negotiate the Hornets transfer to another city, if that became necessary during the process.[267]

Wooldridge began negotiating for a new downtown arena with the Charlotte City Council. By early 2000, things weren't going well. The Charlotte mayor told him the most the city would fund in a bond issue was $60 million. Undeterred, Wooldridge proposed an arena with the city funding it entirely—all $220 million. It was a terrible start. He was negotiating like a businessman does every day, but the venomous hangover from George Shinn's mistakes was overwhelming. There was no negotiating in Charlotte with or about the Hornets.

Worse, Wooldridge had violated what had become known as the

Charlotte Way of doing things. As a very private person, whose personality was only offered to his closest friends, family and children, Wooldridge didn't cotton to Charlotte's gentile networking. For years in Charlotte, most public decisions had been facilitated by a small group of prominent businessmen—major officials of Duke Power, First Union Bank, Wachovia Bank and the Bank of America. These decisions had showered much success upon Charlotte. As a result, these power-brokers believed they had made Charlotte into a new Atlanta. Thereafter, whatever was going to happen in Charlotte had to come through them. Wooldridge thought that being a part-owner of the Hornets would provide him automatic entré into this Charlotte establishment. He was ostracized, as the connection with the city's power-elite hadn't occurred. It was in meltdown.

The genuine and real Ray Wooldridge would be witnessed by me, repeatedly, over the next year, but never more telling than in a very private but compelling conversation at David Novak's Christmas party on December 1, 2001. As will be subsequently discussed, it was our final effort to encourage him to transfer his team to Louisville. Wooldridge told my wife, Norma, that he never understood how he could write a check for $56 million and be criticized in the press conference on the very day in which the purchase was announced. Wooldridge was a complex individual, as were most enormously successful people, who yearned for appreciation and to be invited to participate in a city somewhere with his Hornets.

It should have been a relatively easy assignment.

Clearly, the sexual allegations about Shinn, together with Wooldridge's nouveau riche approach to life, would be easy targets for Louisville's Ruppians, once they got in gear. Certain Louisvillians like those in Charlotte, who fashioned themselves as power-brokers, had always found it convenient to look down their noses at outsiders who threatened their Louisville hegemony. The Hornets ownership would provide them with plenty of stones to throw. It made little difference that certain of these resident and non-resident Louisville power brokers lived in their own well-decorated glass houses. Conveniently, those glass houses had no mirrors in which to examine their own peccadillos.

Without a doubt, if the Hornets ever developed into another NBA opportunity for Louisville, it would be a consummate test of the aversion to change of Louisville's naysayers.

Louisville Pursuit Team reorganizes

Based upon this examination, it was clear that if Louisville was to successfully purloin the Hornets, it would be essential to create a plan that excised Shinn from controlling ownership. This was a new wrinkle. Local ownership had never been an issue with the Rockets, because Alexander was their sole owner and intended to remain so. The Hornets were different. There was already multiple ownership.

Clearly, the Pursuit Team needed involvement, but the August doldrums were upon us. Blum was with his family on vacation in Martha's Vineyard. Due to his position as the incoming President of GLI, Inc., together with his responsibilities for the November metro government referendum, Ed Glasscock was other-directed and unavailable. Todd Blue was.

We had an in-depth discussion about the Hornets opportunity and the importance of creating a financial arrangement to acquire Shinn's interest or reduce it to a significant minority position. Our research about Shinn's financial crunch and cash-draining divorce was thoroughly discussed. There was an additional concern. If the team were to transfer to Louisville, under its present ownership arrangement, Wooldridge's exclusive authority over the team's location would be concluded. But Shinn would still have exclusive control over player personnel decisions. Even though the Hornets had succeeded in "Kentucky-izing" the team with former UK stars Mashburn and Magloire, someone other than Shinn needed to be responsible for such decisions. The importance of this had been learned decades ago, because the Kentucky Colonels had to have a distinct Kentucky flavor and the person responsible for it had to understand the religion in Kentucky. Therefore, for a variety of reasons, Shinn was the more expendable of the two owners.

Blue was encouraged to consider organizing a group of investors. He seized upon the concept with relish, viewing it as the opportunity of his lifetime for the city. His approach was reminiscent of the three decades-old enthusiasm of the ABA Kentucky Colonels five young owners. Pretty exciting stuff. Maybe my original thought that there really was a whole new generation of young, dynamic, local business leadership was true.

Meanwhile, "back at the ranch," Aldermanic President Magre was trying to figure out how to reinvigorate the Rockets' interest. An unfortunate realization had finally dawned on him. At the critical time he had fumbled the football by failing to timely introduce the bond ordinance he promised to Postolos and the mid-sized business community. Magre's idea of reinvigoration was a meeting with the Mayor. I wasn't interested unless Mayor Dave was willing to invest himself, personally, in the effort. But, in the hope he might finally be willing to work together, I agreed to attend the meeting.

After some opening remarks from Alderman Johnson, Magre took the initiative, expressing that the Board of Aldermen desired to work in concert with the Mayor on a continuing NBA effort. He politely scolded the Mayor: "If we could be working together the Rockets might still be a live possibility," suggesting the best way to accomplish this was for the Board of Aldermen and the Mayor to jointly hire me as a consultant with authority to bring a deal to the Mayor and Aldermen for their collective consideration.

Armstrong declined, simply saying No! while assuring Magre the Rockets were still interested in Louisville and that he continued to speak frequently with Postolos. In view of the Mayor's refusal to create a cooperative working relationship, there was no mention of the Hornets. But if there was, in fact, ongoing conversation between Armstrong and Postolos, it would be a bad idea for us to initiate discussions with the Hornets. The NBA world was too small. The right hand had to know what the left hand was doing. This had to be checked out.

That evening my call to Postolos was informative. There had been only one phone call between Postolos and Armstrong in a month and a half, the purpose of which was to acknowledge and reject Armstrong's ill-timed and mal-informed offer of late June. The Rockets fully intended to place the arena on a November referendum in Houston. Postolos believed that there was finally a modicum of peace between Alexander and the Houston big-hats. They were even anteing up money for television ads. Being his usual gracious self, George fondly remembered his weekend in Louisville and the wonderful Humana dinner. He let me know that his and Nicole's Kentucky Colonelcies, presented during the Humana dinner, were prominently hanging in their den. We agreed to get together immediately if the referendum failed and concluded the call.

The Mayor's assertion of frequent contact with Postolos was, at worst, a lie and, at least, another brain implosion. In either event, it was far from the first of such occurrences. The Daytimer noted: "All B.S. Simply doesn't want to work with anyone—Can't even tell the truth—Bunker Mentality."

The next morning Glasscock was brought into the loop about the

Hornets opportunity and the latest exemple of the Mayor's perfidy. Glasscock suggested the Governor needed to be told of the new possibilities and encouraged to take a proactive role in view of the Mayor's duplicity. He volunteered to undertake the task. Upon learning of the developments, Blum was still revolted over the Mayor's lack of leadership and very skeptical. He agreed with the concepts that any further effort had to be undertaken with the ownership of a team, not the lawyers or management personnel and it had to be done privately, without the involvement of the local politicians, at least until a bond financing deal was relatively in stone. Within several days, Glasscock reported the Governor was prepared to move forward with any private initiative that might be undertaken.

The Pursuit Team was now in the loop and in agreement with the concept of taking our time and not precipitously jumping back into the water. It was also agreed if the Houston referendum failed, I would immediately contact Stern and get authority for person-to-person discussions with Rockets owner Les Alexander. Also, it was noted, if the Houston referendum failed and the Hornets were still discombobulated in Charlotte, there would be two separate ownership entities with whom to negotiate, an attractive set of circumstances.

The bottom line: we'll take our time, yet act in earnest.

Within a week or so, the Blue family indicated their willingness to negotiate the purchase of all or part of Shinn's interest in the Hornets and to offer their land next to Louisville's new minor-league baseball field as an additional carrot. Todd Blue felt that a real estate development consisting of the arena and a residential/office building complex across Main Street, in which the Hornets ownership (including Shinn) could participate, was an attractive method to provide Shinn with an investment opportunity in a much larger development to facilitate the purchase of Shinn's Hornets interest.

Novel thinking. This idea was particularly attractive because with the Blue property in the negotiating equation, there would two arena sites available in downtown Louisville, which increased the potential negotiating positions with the Hornets ownership. Of larger importance was that Blue and his family were totally supportive of the NBA effort, even if the Hornets ownership preferred the Water Company site on Third and Liberty Streets. They would not continge their participation on the use of their property, it would just be a larger financial involvement if their property were involved. Blue was encouraged to be prepared for discussions about his family's proposal when Wooldridge came to Louisville in September.

The value of our research had again been productive. In April, hoping to further encourage a positive response from the Charlotte City Council, Wooldridge had tossed around the idea of developing the property adjacent to a proposed new arena in Charlotte, with a 400-room hotel, an office tower and condos that would cost an additional $200 million. He even began negotiating for options on 10 acres of land through his bank, First Union Bank.

Now it seemed that we were beginning to get our ducks in a row. Louisville was always in a unique negotiating position with the intangible value of the religion of basketball. No other city could offer that. But now we were ginning up something equally important that might be attractive to NBA businessmen. A real "big city" financial arrangement comprised of several potential downtown arena sites, with several potential financial arrangements coupled with a naming rights commitment from a major international company. With this addition into the negotiating equation, Louisville was a realistic competitor with any other city, both tangibly and intangibly. The buffet table offer would enable Louisville to negotiate from a much stronger position.

Ray and The Wagman come to town

On Monday August 28, 2000, The Wagman and Dan Barrett arrived in Louisville on a Delta flight from Atlanta. It took a while to learn of Les Wagner's moniker—The Wagman. Its origin was never learned, nor was it important to know.

A Boston native, The Wagman graduated magna cum laude in 1973 from Tufts University and received Order of the Coif honors upon his 1976 graduation from the prestigious University of Virginia School of Law, where he also served on its distinguished law review. His law firm, Wagner Johnston & Rosenthal, was a mid-sized firm of eleven lawyers specializing in a business and commercial law practice and enjoying an attractive and significant clientele. The pre-check on The Wagman gave evidence that he was a skilled lawyer with a substantial law practice headquartered on Peachtree Road in Atlanta's ritzy and upscale Buckhead. No chopped liver was The Wagman.

They were in the office by 9:00 AM. For the next and uninterrupted six hours, the agenda was thoroughly discussed. Lunch was ordered in to conserve time. No Chamber of Commerce-type chatter about the quality of Louisville's school and park systems, or whether the Hornets and Louisville would make a "good marriage!" The subjects of conversation were the known facts, issues to be resolved and questions to be answered. Both seemed pleased with the meeting product. They were driven to the Water Company site that had been shown the Rockets for an on-the-ground walk-around. Then to Freedom Hall for an exterior drive-through of the facility, whereupon they were deposited at the airport. Wagner shook my hand saying, "Ray is going to be very pleased about all this." Within two days he was calling to request further information in preparation for Wooldridge's upcoming visit.

The Pursuit Team was given a full report. My Daytimer noted: "Blum pleased w/Hornets progress." At 2:00 PM on the afternoon of Friday, September 8, The Wagman called. He and Wooldridge would be in Louisville on Tuesday evening, September 12 and all day on Wednesday. Old friend, Tom O'Hearn (manager of the Galt House), agreed to take care of our guests. Suites were reserved at the Galt House. Wooldridge requested that discussions begin on Tuesday evening at a private dinner with Blum and me. Knowing Wooldridge was a gourmand, it was suggested to Blum that the trendy Bardstown Road restaurant, Lilly's, be reserved. Blum made the dinner arrangements, to begin at 7:30 PM. Everything was arranged and set and another one of those silent prayers was delivered. Over the next two days, that prayer was to be answered in aces and spades.

The Wagman and Ray were picked up at the Galt House and immediately expressed appreciation for the reservation. Their rooms were splendid, complete with fresh vased flowers and large baskets of fresh fruit. O'Hearn had done good. We arrived at Lilly's promptly at 7:30. Blum was already there.

The next five hours easily qualify as one of the most dynamic and effective meetings I've ever participated in, anywhere, anytime. Jonathan Blum was purely and simply outstanding. There was symmetry in the conversation and direct eye contact across the table all night. The conversation flowed like we had known each other for years. There was a quiet genuineness and pleasantness about it all coupled with an intensity level that was unmistakable. If there was ever a question about Tricon's interest level, there was no doubt that night. It was easy to see why Blum was the Senior Vice-President in charge of Tricon's world-wide public relations. His approach was perfect — "We don't care what team it is, we intend to get one in Louisville, and if turns out to be yours, that's fine."

Wooldridge was particularly pleased with the thoroughness of the PricewaterhouseCoopers Report. He felt that attention needed to be given to developing an arena financing plan. I agreed. During the Rockets effort we hadn't completed that work and there was a new wrinkle in the statutes. Kentucky's legislature had passed a new tax-increment financing statute, empowering the Governor to authorize the return of tax revenue generated from a project back to the City to assist in bond retirement. Nothing was needed other than the governor's signature. The Wagman's ears perked up. Wooldridge quickly turned the conversation to the governor, inquiring about his interest level. It was assured, provided we could reach a proper and fair business arrangement.

Wooldridge suggested it would be helpful to have a "scrubber," whom he defined as a well-respected businessman who could opine about the quality of the bonding and financial plans when they were completed. Blum and I agreed to find such a person. Then we really got down to business. A sheet was torn from Lilly's menu and used by The Wagman to pen a series of deadlines for the Louisville effort. Letter of Interest by December 1, 2000; Letter of Intent by December 31, 2000; Memorandum of Understanding between Louisville and the Hornets on February 28, 2001; Charlotte files intent to transfer on March 1, 2001; Charlotte cancels its lease on April 1, 2001; Construction begins on Louisville arena on June 1, 2001. As the evening continued, it was learned that Blum and Ray enjoyed the same wine, Opus One — and Lilly's had it. We closed the place up after midnight and I returned The Wagman and Ray to the Galt House.

The next morning at 8:04 AM, the following e-mail was sent to Jonathan:

Jonathan:

First, a thank you for picking up the tab last night. Secondly, in my wildest dreams I don't believe that I could have hoped to have experienced a more productive dinner meeting than we participated in last night. Specifically, your presentation of KFC's interest and (more importantly) its determination to make this happen was powerful and certainly struck a chord w/ Wooldridge. When I arrived in the office this morning, there was a voice mail from Craig Wagner (2:15 AM). He thanked me profusely for putting the dinner together, expressed that he and Ray had just concluded a near two (2) hour meeting regarding the entire situation, with particular reference to Louisville. Wagner expressed how impressed Wooldridge was with your presentation and how determined Ray was to "move the ball down the field with Louisville." He reiterated Ray's statement that it's 90/10 that the Hornets will leave Charlotte; and that Ray doesn't believe that there's much of anything that Charlotte could do, at this point, to alter the odds. Neither Ray nor Craig see any reason to meet with me this morning at 9:00, in view of the breadth of our discussions last night. They will be here for the 10:30 mtg w/ Magre, the lunch w/Blue and the afternoon mtg w/Clarkson. I'll report to you on today's events. Thanks again for everything.

—Bruce Miller

P.S. Why don't you consider running for Mayor!!!

Magre's morning meeting with Wooldridge reflected a general reluctance on his part to take the lead in the local government political process. He did offer that nine of twelve aldermen were willing to sign off on a reasonable deal. Wooldridge's suggestions to Magre were sound. The major point was simple. He would like the discussions to be below the radar screen for the time being, while the business community endeavored to fashion a realistic arena financing proposal. Thereafter, Wooldridge felt the Governor should become involved, and only after the bases were covered with him would there be aldermanic and mayoral involvement. Magre quickly agreed, seemingly relieved the responsibility arrow was pointing elsewhere.

The Vincenzo's lunch meeting with Todd Blue rivaled the previous evening at Lilly's. After Blue outlined the general picture of his family's interest in partial local ownership of the Hornets in conjunction with the use of their land as an arena site, Wooldridge showed interest and wanted to see the property. The previous night, on the way to Lilly's, I had taken him to the Water Company site. He wasn't impressed. Having spent several million dollars designing an arena for Charlotte, Wooldridge felt his design would be lost in the confines of the center city, much as the Omni's design had been lost due to the surrounding high-rise structures in Atlanta. He believed a $200+ million arena needed to be part of an open space as a landmark and surrounded by trees, statuary, water fountains and other inviting amenities as a part of the arena.

After lunch, Blue took Wooldridge to the roof of the Cobalt Building.

Wooldridge was stunned. The view of the Ohio River from the restaurant designed in his new arena would be exceptional. He even had a name for it — The River Club. The adjacent structures across Main Street were easily transformed into office, retail and residential space. It had the possibilities of a major real estate development, exactly like he had proposed for Charlotte. Wooldridge was enthralled and felt that Shinn would see real value to the site. Daytimer references him saying, "This is absolutely perfect." Wooldridge told Blue: "This is where we want it. Forget the other site. Together, we'll make this development the official Gateway to the South." After leaving the Blue site we drove to Freedom Hall. Arrangements had been made with Harold Workman for a quick walk-through. As old as it is, when empty, the immensity of Freedom Hall is still quite impressive. On the way back to the office, Ray observed: "It's better than Charlotte Coliseum."

Back at the office, the meeting with Bobby Clarkson couldn't have gone better. After explaining the PGA Tournament's successful promotion at Valhalla several weeks prior, on behalf of the mid-sized businesses Clarkson committed their full participation in a season ticket campaign and positively expressed his belief that the Hornets would be an immediate financial success in Louisville.

The silent prayer of nearly two days ago had been answered. Louisville's business community had done it again. Even if you tried to view the presentations of Blum, Blue and Clarkson as an uninterested observer, there was still no question about the quality of the effort. Louisville was in the hunt. At the airport, Ray expressed his appreciation for the time and said he'd be back in touch with us shortly.

Jonathan Blum was not aware of the Blue family interest in ownership participation. Nor was Blue aware of the enormously effective presentation that Blum had made during the Lilly's dinner. Within two days the Pursuit Team met, which provided the opportunity for them to explain to each other their meetings with Wooldridge. Everyone was pleased and hope was springing eternal.

Something else had happened on September 15. *The Houston Chronicle* reported a major development. The headline read: "Aeros Owner Reverses Stand, Supports Arena Deal." Les Alexander's longtime nemesis, Chuck Watson, who had been the key financier of the previous year's successful anti-arena campaign, had done a one-eighty and announced his strong support of the upcoming referendum. All just as Postolos had said, several weeks before, would happen. For all practical purposes, Watson's support was the final piece of the Rockets puzzle — the referendum would pass. Our attention needed to be concentrated on a one-team negotiating position — the Houston Rockets were out. Another bolt from the blue struck.

Dateline/Memphis, Tennessee

Jonathan Blum had been informed by Tricon's consultant of an increasingly credible rumor that Wooldridge was secretly working with Memphis as a potential transfer site. He was concerned because Wooldridge was born and raised in Memphis and Federal Express had a sizeable presence there and in professional sports, generally. These rumors of other cities were always occurring, but this one might have some legs.

For decades Memphis had sought to be a major league professional sports city, and repeatedly failed. The possible entry of Memphis was a little disconcerting. An all-out information gathering effort would begin.

After several weeks of phone conversations and every discreet inquiry that could possibly be made with several well-placed friends dating to my undergraduate and law school days at Vanderbilt, not a trace of evidence of a Memphis-involvement was found. There was total and complete silence in Memphis. Within five months, this silence would become deafening.

September: Quiet in Louisville, Chinese torture in Charlotte

The mid-sized business group's membership was expanded in numbers and scope. A web-site was created along with a bumper sticker campaign. Each morning the first order of business was an examination of the *Charlotte Observer*'s web-site. Every article involving the Hornets was immediately e-mailed to the Pursuit Team. Of particular interest was a September 14 article reporting Wooldridge's refusal to meet with the Charlotte mayor and the city council's arena committee. Charlotte politicians had been demanding proof of Wooldridge's assertion that the Hornets were losing over $1 million a month. Wooldridge had agreed to provide it, but not publicly. A perfectly reasonable position by Wooldridge, but Charlotte politicians sought a public answer — they wanted scalps. The impasse was growing. It was to get worse.

In an effort to satiate and quiet Charlotte's politicos, Wooldridge publicly acknowledged that the Hornets season-ticket sales for the upcoming season would drop from 20,000 to a level around 12,000. The significance of this was missed; it represented far more than a Hornets financial debacle. An escape clause in the Hornets Charlotte Coliseum lease, permited the team to terminate its lease if a minimum of 15,750 season tickets were not sold. That escape clause could save the Hornets $20 million in lease termination penalties should the team move at the end of the upcoming season. This information was verified in a discussion with an NBA official. An extremely important piece of information. More was coming.

In a long phone call late on Friday afternoon, September 22, The Wagman was less than optimistic about Hornets longevity in Charlotte, because the politicians were now accusing Wooldridge of insincerity. Neither he nor Wagner had attended the first negotiating session, because they had just realized that the general manager and the negotiator for the Charlotte Coliseum was Denny Crum's son!

Walt Disney's "It's a small world" refrain had hit the Hornets in the face. In view of the obvious Louisville connection, Wooldridge sensed that a news story about the Hornets transferring to Louisville was in the offing. Assurances were given that the story wouldn't originate in Louisville. But, within a day the on-again/off-again talks in Charlotte, were on-again. Then they were off-again.

A week later on September 29, another thirty-minute call from The Wagman revealed that no progress had been made in Charlotte during the previous week. If by October 3 they were no further along, Wooldridge had ordered the formulation of a bullet point list of things that needed to be done to facilitate the move to Louisville. The Wagman asked for my cooperation, it was promised, but I insisted on a person-to-person assurance from Wooldridge. Within an hour, Wooldridge called and the assurance was given. The Pursuit Team was immediately informed and collectively felt the news was positive.

The next morning's *Charlotte Observer* revealed even more problems for the Hornets. As arena negotiators rolled up their sleeves and began to negotiate, the Charlotte business community announced it would play no substantive role until the team owners and the city politicians agreed on a plan and publicly shook hands. The bankers were sitting on their hands.

Despite the Chinese torture being applied to Wooldridge in Charlotte, very little was happening in Louisville. The Pursuit Team had agreed with Wooldridge upon a course of action, a private initiative to create a financing plan that, when completed, would be given to the politicians. It seemed to make sense, fitting nicely with the timetable that had been established by The Wagman at Lilly's. Except for Todd Blue, the requisite intensity within the Pursuit Team had evaporated. Blum's interest level, once so high at the Lilly's dinner only a few weeks prior, had understandingly taken a back seat to pressing business concerns at Tricon. Glasscock remained enmeshed with Louisville's metro referendum.

If Louisville was going to pull this off, there had to be an intensity level — a "fire in the belly." Two weeks had been lost.

It's October, when the leaves turn and fall

You only turn 60 once (if you're lucky). That was happening to me on October 7, 2000. Norma and I decided to celebrate the big day in North Carolina. We hadn't seen my son's new home or the golf course where he was working as its pro. The passage into old age was celebrated in Pinehurst. The golf was fun. Jamie was happy and it was great seeing him. It all made made turning 60 not too bad — but strange things were happening down the road in Charlotte.

The rumor mill had exploded. Wooldridge was looking at other cities. While we denied any Louisville meetings, the Hornets-logoed plane had been seen in the St. Louis Airport. The Hornets responded that someone had leased the Hornets plane and flown it to St. Louis on non-related Hornets business. Wooldridge publicly denied ever discussing the transfer of the Hornets to any other city. Neither our denial nor his were true, and I didn't believe the St. Louis/Hornets plane explanation, either. I was sure that they had flown to St. Louis and met with either Bill Laurie (who had tried to purchase the Vancouver Grizzlies and move them to St. Louis) or his lawyer. I later learned from credible sources that this was true.

The time was swiftly coming when the Pursuit Team was going to have to get on the stick and put The Wagman on the spot about our seriousness. This was all relayed to the Pursuit Team. There's an old adage—sometimes you have to hit the bull between the eyes with a sledge hammer to get its attention. The sledge hammer worked.

The Pursuit Team met on October 10 for the first time in nearly a month. The participants were Blum, Glasscock, Blue, Mike Harreld, CEO of PNC Bank, and me. Harreld had committed to fulfill Wooldridge's request to be a "scrubber." I was pleased with Harreld's willingness to participate. He, undoubtedly, would make a significant and valuable contribution as we moved forward, because his influence extended far beyond Louisville as he had been heavily involved with the improvement efforts directed toward higher education at the state level. He was a solid addition. Harreld also pledged to get the PNC Capital Markets Group in Pittsburgh involved in the preparation of an arena bond financing plan.

I was also delighted that Glasscock's attention had returned. While the merger referendum was vital, the NBA odyssey was becoming demanding and his acumen was sorely needed. I had always viewed Ed's participation at the highest level was imperative. He and his firm had much to offer and that talent level was absolutely essential if we were to carry the ball across the goal line. Everyone re-pledged 100% dedication to the effort and it was genuinely felt that the opportunity was, now, real.

Scarborough Sports Marketing Report

Louisville always seemed to luck out at critical times. It happened again. Scarborough Sports Marketing, a division of Scarborough Research, is a partnership of the Arbitron Company and VNU Marketing Information, that produces market research. Its work is considered to be the bible of American sports marketing. On a twice-yearly basis its market reports are prepared for and delivered to a broad list of clients that comprise major media advertisers, major sports leagues, broadcasting companies and advertising agencies. From February, 1999 to March, 2000 it had been compiling data sets to measure market consumer and lifestyle information. That research had included interviews with over 180,000 adults in the 64 largest metropolitan areas of America. The analysis included an assessment of fan avidness for particular professional sports. On October 23, 2000, the results of their year-long study were announced in New York City. They were stunning.

The cities with the highest concentration of avid NBA fans were: San Antonio (28%), Indianapolis (24%) and Salt Lake City (20%). Then the shock wave hit — Louisville ranked in a tie with Phoenix for 6th place at 15%! Even more amazing was Lexington (Ky.) with a 12% level, which tied it for 15th place including existing NBA cities of Orlando and New York. Of even greater interest was that Louisville was ahead of Memphis (with a 14% NBA fan avidity) and Charlotte (11%) and New Orleans (9%).

Now, in addition to the PricewaterhouseCoopers Report, the Scarbough Report offered independent proof that the NBA would succeed in Louisville.

Its fan avidness for the NBA exceeded all competing cities for a franchise transfer as well as 23 of the 29 cities that already had an NBA franchise. When Louisville's 15% fan avidity was coupled with Lexington's 12%, a reasonable argument could be made that the total of 27% reflected that the Louisville 'market area' (including Lexington) was the second best market in America — in terms of NBA fan interest.

Utterly astounding. As with the PricewaterhouseCoopers Report, it was literally a lightning bolt that went across the bow of the national professional sports and entertainment industry. Louisville was for real. What would the Ruppians do now? They had no empiric evidence to support their aversion to change.

The Louisville strategy changes

A month and a half had elapsed since the Pursuit Team had agreed to assume the task of formulating an arena financing plan, which, when completed, would be turned over to the politicians. But absolutely nothing had happened. Tricon and Blum continued to be otherwise-directed and Glasscock was deeply immersed in the metro referendum. While Todd Blue and the Gateway Group were uplifted with the Scarborough Study, being happy wasn't getting the job done.

Three trial briefcases of books, records, documents and notes were spread out over our dining room table. The evening was spent reviewing previous efforts of various cities to acquire major league professional teams. The conclusions were inescapable. Our plan of action was incorrect. There had never been a situation where a city's business community had undertaken an exclusive leadership role in the acquisition of a professional major league franchise. In every instance, there had been leadership of some kind or another from elected officials, particularly when a governmental entity was expected to provide the financing vehicle to with which to fund the construction of the arena/stadium. However, within three months we would be confronted with the first example of a totally private, "below-the-radar-screen" effort. It would be a complete surprise.

The evening's thought and review was convincing: no NBA franchise would seriously consider Louisville without a governmental entity being willing to invest political clout into the process. While the process involved business concepts, by its very nature the process was, inescapably, political, requiring governmental participation and commitment of a significant nature.

The plan had to be changed. A local political entity had to get involved. The County Judge and Mayor were hopeless, leaving only the Board of Aldermen. They were going to have to publicly reinvigorate the effort by re-installing me as the negotiator with the sole and exclusive responsibility to express the city's position, negotiate with the putative franchise on behalf of the city and to bring the private business community and the other political entities together for the purposes of the presentation of a proposal to any NBA team. If the Aldermen were unwilling to do this, then we wouldn't have a chance to make a credible presentation to any NBA franchise. If the Board of Aldermen would, then we might be able to rejuvenate the effort back to where it was with the Rockets. The Pursuit Team was advised by e-mail of the changed strategy. In the hope of invigorating the Board of Aldermen, a copy of the Pursuit Team e-mail was sent to aldermanic president Magre requesting an immediate meeting.

Todd Blue was particularly determined in thinking that someone, whether it was Tricon or the Board of Aldermen, absolutely had to publicly step up to the plate. Another scheduled Pursuit Team meeting had been canceled by Blum and Glasscock, prompting an e-mail to the Pursuit Team concluded with: "In spite of the inability to meet, I hope that each of you will have a chance to peruse my faxed letter of this morning. If we're going to try to do this we've got "miles to go before we sleep.""

Finally, on October 30, the Pursuit Team met at Tricon's headquarters. At Blue's insistence, Blum agreed to go public with Tricon's naming rights commitment, *if* the Board of Alderman agreed to formally reconstitute my authority to obtain an NBA team transfer commitment to Louisville. Blum insisted that the aldermanic action must be an ordinance, in addition to a contract, because an ordinance was a law and provided enforceable authority for me to bring a deal to the city for its consideration.

Magre was advised via e-mail of the "New York Stock Exchange Company's" position. An ordinance had to be introduced before November 14. Meanwhile, the Houston referendum was about to occur. On November 4 *The Houston Chronicle* reported the pro-arena PAC called "Let's Build It Together" had raised and spent more than $2.3 million.[268] Postolos had accomplished his goal. The Houston big hats were supporting his owner, Les Alexander. Despite Louisville's loss, I was happy for George and Nicole —they were really nice people.

Out of curiosity, the night before the referendum, I called Postolos. He was anxious. In spite of the money spent, there were nearly 100,000 more absentee ballots than in the 1996 presidential election. Neither Postolos nor anyone else knew where these extra votes were going to fall. An argument could be made either way. I advised the Pursuit Team to Stay Tuned!

The next day was a big day in both Houston and Louisville. On November 7, the Houston referendum passed, resoundingly, as did Louisville's merger with Jefferson County. While the merger wouldn't be official until January, 2003, when it was official Metro Louisville would be the 16th largest city in America governed by one governmental entity.

Wooldridge and the Governor weigh in

Wooldridge had always been interested in Louisville's merger referendum, viewing its passage as evidence of the city's desire to send a message it wanted to be big-time. On Wednesday morning, November 8, The Wagman called to ask if the metro referendum had passed. He was pleased. It hadn't gone unnoticed to him that the Houston referendum also passed — as he said, "Looks like it's down to the Hornets, now." He was right. I told The Wagman that we were going to change the game plan and get the Board of Aldermen to take a leadership position. Wagner needed to report this to Wooldridge.

Within a few hours, Wooldridge called. He was as delighted about the successful merger vote as any Louisvillian I knew. It was a clear expression of Louisville's determination to move forward and had significantly set itself apart from Charlotte. The reasons for the change of our game plan were fully discussed. Wooldridge understood, particularly in view of the now-invigorated political climate in Metro Louisville. IF the Aldermen were willing to undertake the political leadership role and IF Tricon goes public, as committed, Wooldridge agreed to cancel his plans and spend an entire week in Louisville working with us, the aldermen, the governor and the business community. Absolutely no progress had been made in Charlotte. The call concluded with Wooldridge's observation, "The Kentucky Colonels...sounds pretty good to me."

The Pursuit Team and Magre were immediately advised of this development and of another interesting nugget. The latest issue of *Sports Business Journal* reported that the Hornets had lost a mid-six figure major advertiser—Lowe's. It had been a sponsor since the team's inception in 1988.

Often the NBA odyssey was a ride of fits and jerks. November 8, 2000, was *not* another one of those days. After learning of Wooldridge's pleasure over Louisville's metro election results, Governor Patton said he was willing to use the new tax increment financing statute along with tourism tax credits to assist in funding a new arena downtown. Patton's commitment came during a meeting arranged by Louisville Aldermen Magre and Johnson. The meeting was a frank discussion lasting from 6:15 to 7:45 PM in Magre's office. Patton qualified his statement by expressing some concern about the competition issue between a new arena and Freedom Hall, but felt that could be resolved by his office and local politica! leadership. He also mentioned receiving some vibes about UofL's continuing desire to build its own arena next to Freedom Hall. Obviously, two arenas couldn't be built and the taxable revenue stream from an NBA team far exceeded those of the UofL's men's basketball team. Some kind of accommodation with the University was going to be necessary. I assured him that both Jurich and UofL's president had been and would be included in the discussions, when it got to that point. He also thought it was important to get the support of Larry Clark and David Karem (the titular leaders of the Jefferson County legislative delegation).

The Tricon/Aldermanic roller-coaster ride

There was never a dull moment in this odyssey. We seemed to always be getting somewhere, yet nowhere. Just as everything began to fall into place, another 1950s-type jitterbug dance started, this time at Tricon.

Acting on advice from its consultant, Blum had decided that Tricon couldn't honor its previous commitment to go public, even if the aldermen passed an ordinance giving me the sole authority to negotiate. Tricon was off the roller-coaster. The aldermen also began looking for the side-car. Magre's committed super-majority of nine had dropped to seven. There was concern over the payment for my services. Norma was furious, feeling that everyone involved was candy-assed and we needed to forget it. While she was right about the candied nature of their derrieres—the question was, do we quit because of it?

Following another near all-night stand, I backed down further. Alderman Johnson was advised that our law firm would be willing to forego the receipt of any fees or payments from the city until a deal was cut, that was approved by the aldermen and the NBA, and the bonds were sold to finance the construction of an arena. Under this scenario, our fees would come from the bond sale proceeds. From a financial standpoint, this was extremely dangerous for my law firm, but I was willing to make the commitment to move the ball down the field. I so advised the Gateway Group, Blum at Tricon and others who were involved in this process.

Lastly, Alderman Johnson was told that if the Alderman didn't formally approve my and our law firm's authorization as the city's exclusive negotiating authority at the next meeting, I would be required to notify the NBA team and the NBA offices that Louisville was formally withdrawing from the process. I simply was not going to leave the Hornets and the NBA holding the bag awaiting evidence of Louisville's governmental intestinal fortitude. The Hornets and the NBA had a huge decision to make, and that had to be respected. It was a strong message; the Aldermen had to stand tall or we had to fold the Louisville tent.

On the evening of November 14, 2000, the Board of Aldermen passed the resolution, by voice vote, with one dissenting ballot. The Wagman and Wooldridge were notified of the action in a joint conference call, and they were pleased. We were in business again. David Stern had been kept continually apprised about Louisville's odyssey. The next morning, November 15, he expressed delight that the aldermen had stood tall.

Despite its passage, Norma wasn't very pleased. She felt that our law firm shouldn't be expected to give our time away. Community responsibility was one thing, but weren't we carrying it a little too far and depending too much on a bunch of people who were afraid of their shadows? As time and events would unfold, she would be right.

With the Aldermen stepping forward and accepting responsibility, the public was entitled to know about the game plan. At a press conference I announced that an NBA owner had been in Louisville, there had been on-going discussions with him since September, there was an agreed upon time-table for action and an experienced group of out-of-town financial experts had been lined up and were "putting together the whole package, including financing—what the team would have to do and what would have to occur locally."[269] This was accurate, as the PNC Capital Markets Group had been working with the Hornets financial advisers for a month in the development of an arena funding bond mechanism, but that was all that could be said at that point.

Another all-night stand was undertaken. Now, with the necessary authority being granted, the prior plan had to be reconfigured. Private letters and calls were made to everyone who had or could conceivably play a role in the process. One contact was particularly essential. The quickest way to reach the UofL President was via e-mail, because he was out of town but assiduously checked his e-mails. It was sent at 6:54 PM on November 15.[270]

To reinvigorate and recharge the Pursuit Team, e-mails were sent, suggesting a meeting to: (i) to develop our November/December strategy; (ii) to have a frank discussion regarding our respective beliefs as to the proper process and the tactical order of its occurrence; and finally (iii) to consider other local leaders who should be involved in the process. I frankly said we need to enlarge the table to make sure that we have a broad-based, diverse and dedicated presence of the community at the table. The e-mail concluded: "Gentlemen: we have an enormous task in front of us—a task which will require the very best we (individually and collectively have to offer) and if the time-frame designed on Lilly's menu when Jonathan Blum, Wagner, Wooldridge and I met is operable, then we only have 1,104 hours between today and December 31st, when a Letter of Intent is required. I don't think that there's any recipient of this e-mail who's not up to the challenge."

Letter of Interest to Wooldridge
The Pursuit Team had twelve days to get its act together. The Letter of Interest, agreed to at the September Lilly's meeting, was due on December 1. On Saturday November 18, from 8:30 AM to noon, Blum, Blue and Glasscock, joined by his bond specialist Bill Skees, met in our offices with Mike Kitchen and me. A to-do list of responsibility division was agreed upon.

Blum would immediately initiate the approval mechanism of Tricon's franchisees. Without revealing what was entailed, it was described as a complicated process that would take some time, but in view of the progress that was being made it had to start. Blue would deliver to The Wagman information on the Blue site including topography, hydrology, environmental, borings and continue the expansion of the Gateway Group's activities and presence. Glasscock and Skees committed to work with the PNC Capital Markets Group on a daily basis to assure that there would be a working draft of a financing plan utilizing the tax increment financing statute available by mid-December. My job was to have another discussion with the UofL president, continue discussions with the NBA, Wooldridge and The Wagman and work with the Governor's office in the completion of the language for the Letter of Interest. A definitive set of goals.

The week of November 20 was highlighted by two important commitments. Former three-term Mayor Jerry Abramson, now a partner in Glasscock's law firm, was the most popular local political figure in several generations. On Wednesday, November 22, he was provided a frank and up-to-date status report on the NBA project. During the phone conversation Abramson committed support, provided the new metro government would be financially protected in the deal. As the odds-on favorite to be the first Metro Mayor of Louisville, his blessing was important. His only opposition was Armstrong, and it was concluded that absolutely no one thought Armstrong had any chance to defeat Abramson. As a result of his support, I agreed to tape his television show, "News 'n Views" on November 27, for showing Sunday, December 3.

Generally once or so a month Norma and I are privileged to enjoy dinner with old friends Carla Sue and Brad Broecker and Carole and Jerry DeWeese. On Saturday evening, November 25, we convened at J. Timothy's. As the dinner conversation gravitated to the NBA, Brad committed to do anything asked of him to bring the NBA to Louisville. I had known Brad felt this way, but the direct commitment, at this point, was significant. He believed an arena in downtown Louisville would represent an enormous enhancement for downtown entertainment, including his Broadway Series. His reasoning was unique in the Louisville thought process — several million new people coming downtown every year to events was not competition for downtown arts. It represented an encouragement for people to "get off their duffs," get out of the house and come downtown and do something. Refreshing. He also gave me some interesting food for thought. If the city and one of these teams wanted to have the arena operated by an entertainment company, he was sure that SFX Entertainment, which owned his Broadway Series, would be willing to do it "in a New York minute." This was big.

Multiple drafts of the Letter of Interest were created and reviewed by the Governor's Office, Blue (with some revisions), Blum (who was in Wisconsin on business), Aldermanic President Magre, and Glasscock. The Letter of Interest was qualified by three requirements: (i) a letter signed by

Wooldridge and Shinn certifying Wooldridge's authority to negotiate; (ii) a mutually-signed and confidential negotiating agreement between Wooldridge and me on behalf of the city; and (iii) a copy of Charlotte's final offer, which had been rejected by Wooldridge and the final demand of the Hornets. The Letter of Interest required a two-day confidential meeting in Louisville during December and provided a substantive list of criteria for those discussions. It was sent, via Federal Express to The Wagman on Monday, November 27.

It was a busy next weekend. While watching the televised drama certifying George Bush's victory in Florida over Gore by 537 votes and Gore's announcement that he would contest the election, the draft of a personal seat license agreement was prepared for consideration and use by the Gateway Group. A draft naming rights agreement was prepared for Tricon and sent to Blum and Tricon's consultant. The seat license agreement was distributed to the Gateway Group at its meeting on Tuesday, November 28. At the same time The Wagman called, formally accepting the Letter of Interest and requesting it be e-mailed to Wooldridge and sent it to Stern. That was immediately done. There were encouraging comments from The Wagman: "You all have made more progress in two months in Louisville than Charlotte has in a year," and "There's nothing like the Gateway Group in Charlotte," and "Looks like the train's leaving the station in Charlotte."

Amid this progress, Billy Reed still clutched his poisoned pen. Now, Aldermen Magre and Johnson and I were joined in his latest article entitled, "The Three Stooges." It was to continue, get far worse and more embarrassing (for Reed).

November 30, 2000 provided more positive news. The Charlotte politicians had publicly announced their own plan for the Hornets providing for a new Hornets arena that would require state legislative action, including the expansion of hotel/motel taxes and its permission to conduct a referendum in Charlotte. But Wooldridge was agitated. The Hornets ownership must file a transfer application with the NBA by March 1, for the subsequent year, and there was little hope the state legislature would cooperate. More difficult for Wooldridge was that a Charlotte referendum in May or November, 2001, meant that he was stuck for another year in Charlotte losing $1 million or so a month, or another $15 million.

Wooldridge wanted to speed up the Louisville discussions. He had selected the Blue property as the site for the arena and wanted that decision used in our preparation of the arena financing plan.

December, 2000 meetings—Do we or don't we meet?

On Friday, December 1, Norma and I had our routine weekly joy of an evening with our little T-Man. Since it was only five days before his third birthday, a Toys-R-Us walk-through was in order! During an examination of Wrestlemania guys, the cell phone rang and thus, in the aisles of Toys-R-Us, began a long call from The Wagman.

Wooldridge had decided that the Charlotte requirement for a referendum was a deal-breaker. Since 2001 was election year for the city council, the arena and the Hornets would invariably become a political football, which Wooldridge wouldn't permit. But there was a problem with Louisville, too. Wooldridge couldn't enter into an exclusive negotiating agreement, as had been required in the Letter of Interest. He wouldn't answer the question why, but the reason was inescapable: there was another city being considered. The retort had to be strong. It was, via an e-mail, on Saturday morning December 2. I required a formal (if not public) expression from Wooldridge of his interest in transferring to Louisville, if a satisfactory arrangement could be negotiated.

Near-daily calls were now shared with The Wagman, beginning the next day Sunday, December 3. A two-day meeting in Louisville was requested, despite Wooldridge's unwillingness to sign an exclusive negotiating agreement. We were at an impasse. But Martin Hanby of PNC Capital Markets Group in Pittsburgh was reporting considerable progress in developing an arena financing plan with the Hornets. For several weeks, they had spoken daily and e-mailed financial information and data back-and-forth. Hanby felt that face-to-face discussions were important and would be valuable.

Another option was provided to The Wagman on Monday December 4. "If Wooldridge can't or won't sign an exclusive negotiating agreement with us, then would he agree make a public announcement that the Hornets would file an Intent to Transfer somewhere on March 1, 2001?" Wagner agreed that Wooldridge would consider that option and call on Wednesday with his answer.

On Wednesday, December 6, Wooldridge asked, "If I announce by mid-January that the Hornets intended to file an application to transfer on March

1, 2001, will you agree to meet with The Wagman and Barrett on December 12-13, in Louisville?" He, specifically wanted discussions with Blue about his site, with the Gateway Group about its willingness and ability to sell season tickets, and a financial discussion with the PNC Capital Markets gurus. A response was promised by noon on Friday, December 8.

An immediate conference call with the Pursuit Team brought major disagreement between Jonathan Blum and Todd Blue. Blum had been convinced by Tricon's consultant and was adamant that Wooldridge was using us. Blum was advised not to meet with Wooldridge again until there was some kind of overt pubic demonstration or statement by Wooldridge that the Hornets were leaving Charlotte. Such an action by Wooldridge was imperative in order for Blum to successfully complete his discussions with the franchisees. Blue felt that we had to meet face-to-face with them, that we could not let the opportunity wither away. That evening I made a decision. We would meet on December 12 and 13 with The Wagman and the Hornets finance guru. Everyone (except Blum and Tricon) agreed.

On Friday, December 8, The Wagman was told of our agreement to meet on the two days Wooldridge requested. He was pleased. Within an hour Wooldridge called, personally, expressing his appreciation for our cooperation. He was particularly magnanimous about Tricon's unwillingness to meet saying, "There's plenty of time to deal with them. The thing that's important now is a development of a collaborative dialogue with everybody else." I thanked Ray for his forthright approach. Needless to say, Tricon's position, however justified by them, wasn't very helpful at that particular moment.

It was a wild weekend. Between the U.S. Supreme Court's enjoining the Florida recount of the Bush/Gore election pending oral argument on Monday and e-mail preparatory work with Martin Hanby of PNC's Capital Markets Group, there was little time to spare. Monday, December 11 was occupied by conference calls between Glasscock's bond guru, Bill Skees, and the PNC Capital Markets Group. They were ready. The bond financing plan made sense and looked terrific.

The Oakroom at Louisville's Seelbach Hotel is traditional yet exotic. Al Capone is reputed to have regularly dined and played poker there in a corner room. Tuesday evening, December 12, The Wagman, Barrett, Todd Blue and I dined there. While the pleasantries were enjoyable, there was an intensity to the occasion, pretty much all business and Wagner had the agenda.

The Blue property was still the cat's meow. Our tactic with an all-encompassing real estate deal, to reduce or remove Shinn's ownership interest, had been well received. It was clearly stated that the real estate deal was just as important as the team and the arena. Regarding the arena, itself, the Hornets desired to operate it, with the quid pro quo that they would cover any loss on operations, thereby eliminating the city's downside operation risk. The Hornets were insistent that UofL play in the new arena. The Wagman delivered Wooldridge's message: tell Shumaker, as quickly as possible, that Wooldridge wanted a private meeting with him by mid-January. Toward the end of the dinner, I had one question. What is the "other city"? The Wagman was honest. Not denying there was one, he said he couldn't tell me the name. Within thirty hours, we would find out which one it was.

Wednesday morning Dec 13, PNC "scrubbers" from Pittsburgh, Bill Skees (of Glasscock's law firm), Todd Blue, Mike Kitchen and I met with The Wagman and Barrett regarding the bond financing numbers. The Hornets contingent was pleased with the progress and many thoughts were exchanged. There would be continuing contact between Barrett and the scrubbers as the numbers were further developed. Wednesday afternoon, the Gateway Group representatives, Bob Clarkson, Mike Seale and Jim Patterson II, met our guests along with Darrell Griffith. It couldn't have gone better. The Wagman was particularly impressed (as had been the Rockets management) that within two weeks back in May, the Gateway Group had obtained commitments for 32 suites (willing to pay $80,000 annually), without even utilizing GLI's membership list. The names on that list were discussed in depth. Griffith was eloquent.

Late Wednesday, after the Gateway Group and Griffith left, Wagner, Barrett, Blue and I had a concluding meeting during which a number of continuing to-do's were discussed. Everyone agreed that the meetings were enormously productive. By this time snow was falling in a blinding rage. Blue quickly left for home. With the temperatures dropping precipitously, there was a problem; the Wagman and Barrett had already checked out of the Seelbach and their Delta return flight to Atlanta had been canceled. New Seelbach rooms were arranged. Now, it was 7:00 PM. The Wagman and Barrett requested a private office to have a discussion and a portable computer printer. Mike Kitchen made a portable printer available, instructing Barrett as to its operation. They wanted to work, and Kitchen and I needed to get home before the roads became impassable. Instructions were provided as to how to lock the office when they left.

The next morning, unknown to our guests, one of our secretaries discovered from our computerized faxing system that a fax had been prepared on Barrett's laptop, printed off Kitchen's portable printer and sent to George Shinn. The other city was disclosed in the fax. It was Memphis!

So now we knew the city we were competing with.

Memphis, Tennessee, next to the Big Muddy

For thirty years, Memphis civic leaders sought the city's entry into the NFL. They would lose twice in the 1970s, to Tampa and Seattle. After the demise of its ABA teams (Memphis Pros, Memphis TAMs and Memphis Sounds) Elvis' hometown's dreams continued and were given added life via 'King Cotton' and the founder/owner of Dunavant Enterprises. From a small business founded in 1960 on Front Street by his father, by the early 1980s William B. Dunavant, Jr. had created one of the largest privately-owned cotton merchandising companies in the world. In the early 1980s Dunavant joined with a large group of wealthy entrepreneurs to form the United States Football League (USFL). The ownership group was stellar, including Donald Trump (New Jersey Generals), Alfred Taubman (Michigan Panthers) and Kentuckian Donald Dizney (Orlando Renegades).[271]

After the USFL folded, Dunavant, still determined to put Memphis in the major leagues, began to consider purchasing the San Antonio Spurs in 1988. The price tag of $50 million was rejected. Dunavant continued his NFL pursuit in the early 1990s by assuming control of Memphis Pro Football, Inc. from FedEx chairman, Fred Smith. His early accomplishments were several, including a tentative lease on the Liberty Bowl, which put Memphis squarely in the middle of the competition for NFL expansion with Baltimore, Charlotte, Jacksonville and St. Louis. While Memphis was well-positioned, it lost. A new stadium, not the Liberty Bowl, was required by the NFL as expansion went to cities with new stadium commitments: Charlotte, Jacksonville, St. Louis, Baltimore (and later, Nashville). My Tennessee and Vanderbilt connections had assured me that the Dunavant syndicate was not involved. They would later prove to be correct.

There was another big hitter in Memphis: the Kemmons Wilson family.

Wilson had been at one-time a local home builder. His son, Spence, had been a classmate at Vanderbilt. One day at school, years ago, Spence had told me the story of how in 1951 his father, on a family auto trip to Washington, D.C., had problems finding a place to stay for the evening and returned to Memphis vowing to build a chain of motels. Wilson named the hotel Holiday Inn, because that was the name of a movie starring Bing Crosby, and it just seemed to fit. The rest was history. But the Wilson family interests weren't involved in Memphis' NBA chase.

With its construction of The Pyramid in 1991, discussions had ensued about any Memphis NBA potential, particularly in view of its breathtaking new arena. These discussions were fueled by Memphian Sidney Schlenker, who had sold his interest in the Denver Nuggets for $65 million. Schlenker's interest had been encouraged by the NBA's formation of an expansion committee in October, 1992 headed by Jerry Colangelo. This Schlenker-led Memphis boomlet disintegrated as the word leaked that Stern desired the NBA expansion to be in Canada — Toronto and Vancouver. Memphians were particularly aggravated by contemporaneous events in Nashville. Gaylord Entertainment (owner of Opryland in Nashville) had paid a non-refundable $100,000 application fee to seek an NBA franchise for Nashville. Nashville Mayor Bredesen rubbed Memphis's face in the dirt. He announced an arena plan to be funded by a 77-cent property tax hike and a tax increment financing district, originally approved by Tennessee's general assembly to aid the Memphis efforts to lure an NFL franchise. For Memphians, it was considered a highwayman's robbery. Nashville was using what Memphis considered to be its statute to gain an NBA franchise. With the subsequent award of the NBA expansion franchises to Canadian cities, Memphis's interest waned.

Upon losing the NFL Oilers' franchise to Nashville, in January, 1997, Memphis Mayor W.W. Herenton and Shelby County Mayor Jim Rout reformulated the Memphis & Shelby County Sports Authority, with the assignment to lower major league expectations and devote attention to smaller one-time events, very similar to what Louisville was to do several years later (after nearly one hundred U.S. cities had similarly acted). But the major leagues still intrigued Memphis. A year later, the Memphis Sports Authority retained Max Muhleman from Charlotte to examine the city's NBA potential. *The Commercial Appeal* reported Muhleman's advice on June 25, 1998: "There is potential. I hope that the authority will take a measured, realistic, but stick-to-it position and try to explore it further." He also gave the advice — plan to spend a million dollars to attract an NBA team.[272]

There was nothing else that could be learned about Memphis' NBA aspirations except one intriguing *Commercial Appeal* piece by its leading sports columnist, Geoff Caulkins. Word had circulated that Memphis might be considered as a potential site for the new NBA Developmental League, sort of a minor league to the NBA. On Sunday, April 23, 2000, four days after the announcement of Louisville's PricewaterhouseCoopers Report and three days prior to *The Houston Chronicle* article that narrowed the race for the Rockets down to Las Vegas and Louisville, Caulkins wrote: "Why would we want another rinky-dink franchise in Memphis? Why would we want to watch a collection of players who have to improve before they could suit up for the Dallas Mavericks? Why can't we realize that if something is going to work in this town, it has to be the real thing, not some lesser variation on the theme? ....The only NBA I want to see in The Pyramid is the actual one.... What we need is more vision, more excellence, more people willing to go out on more limbs in the pursuit of greatness in the community. It doesn't matter if its arts, sports, business, anything. It matters that it's quality. So dream big, shoot for the stars, try to do the impossible. Otherwise — and I ask this in the nicest way possible — why even bother? [273]

Could it be said any better?

The Big Muddy's Big Secret

Months later we would learn that on Friday, May 4, while Louisvillians and the world's sporting public were galloping to Churchill Downs to see the Kentucky Oaks and prepare for their mint-juleped Derby escapade the next day, the NBA Commissioner was in Memphis. It was an unpublicized meeting. Stern's purpose was an NBA advertising arrangement with FedEx. The meeting was with Mike Glen, FedEx's executive vice president of market development and corporate communications (Blum's counterpart official at FedEx). In trying to interest FedEx in the NBA, Stern spoke expansively of the league's global impact. Soon thereafter, FedEx's CFO, Alan Graf, in a conversation with Staley Cates, president of Southeastern Asset Management, Inc., explored the value of an NBA franchise in Memphis, and Graf opined that it would be extremely important and a recruiting tool for corporations. Thereafter, at Cates' request, FedEx's Graf and Glen arranged a meeting between Cates and Stern in June, 2000 at the NBA's New York offices.

At the very moment Louisville's executive political leadership of County Judge Jackson and Mayor Dave was falling down face-first with Louisville's Rockets opportunity, Memphian Cates was pitching Memphis to Stern. Then in August, while Wooldridge was initiating private discussions with the Louisville Pursuit Team, he had also begun similar discussions in Memphis with Staley Cates, his brother, Andy, Gayle Rose, and attorney Marty Regan.

Soon after in the fall of 2000, J.R. "Pitt" Hyde, founder and majority owner of AutoZone became involved with the effort, at about the same time the Louisville effort was going sideways on funding its effort and agonizing about my authority to negotiate. This was followed by a Memphis Pursuit Team trip to visit Wooldridge in Atlanta on October 16, a week before the Scarborough Sports Marketing Report was released, which found Louisville to be the sixth best NBA market in America. Memphis was below Louisville. Hyde had now funded the Memphis Pursuit Team, which was paying its lawyer and covering all expenses. Of course, Louisville couldn't afford such luxury! The Memphis Pursuit Team even retained Ellerbe-Becket, the famed arena design firm, to examine The Pyramid, which produced a big problem. Contrary to their hope, The Pyramid could not be a permanent NBA home. Even though it was built in 1991, in early December, 2000 Ellerbe-Becket advised them it would cost $192.2 million to retro-fit it.[274]

So while in September we had been clued into the possibility of a Memphis effort by Tricon's consultant, we didn't have any idea of the depth and extent of the its effort. It had been totally secret. But we still had a governor who was willing to utilize the tax-increment financing statute to build a new arena and an economic analysis supporting Louisville's market reality, we had beaten Memphis to David Stern's ear by nearly six months and we had Tricon — all of which still put Louisville ahead of Memphis.

But, unknown to us, we had been in serious competition with a then-secret competitor and, to be sure, the confusion of our public officials and the lack of ability hadn't been helpful.

Letter of Intent to Wooldridge

The Christmas holidays were spent with two goals in mind: completing the long-committed Letter of Intent to Wooldridge, and having a discussion with John Shumaker. The Letter of Intent was drafted and re-drafted, eventually obtaining the approval of the Pursuit Team and the Governor's staff. It was sent to The Wagman on December 29 via Federal Express.

Ed Glasscock and I operated on two separate fronts, I with Shumaker and he with Owsley Brown Frazier. Shumaker was his usual pleasant self in a December 21 phone call. He was brought current on all developments and told that early in the year 2001 we anticipated that the owner of a particular NBA team would seek to have a private discussion with him. Congratulating me on our progress, he suggested we get together at the UofL/Murray game that evening. Earlier in the day Glasscock met with Frazier, the most prominent UofL financier. Comparing notes at midday, Glasscock reported Frazier had an open mind about the NBA and was willing to negotiate with any NBA team we were pursuing. That evening Shumaker reaffirmed Frazier's position and his willingness to meet with an NBA owner.

So we ended the year 2000 in a positive mode, although unaware about the magnitude of Memphis' secret efforts and amazed with Charlotte's growing disdain of the Hornets and their ownership.

The Tar Heels decision hiatus

2001 began as 2000 had ended, with continuing confusion in Charlotte. The messages were so mixed that it was difficult to get one's arms around the course of events. Charlotte and Wooldridge differed as to who would receive the arena naming-rights money. Then, in separate announcements, Wooldridge offered his willingness to pay annual rent of between $3 and 6 million in a new arena and the City Manager was again proposing the new arena's packaging into a $287 million bond bundle that would include the Mint Museum, a science museum called Discovery Place, an African-American Cultural Center, an aquarium, an uptown park and other community amenities. Harmony for a day.

But then came what was to be the penultimate question: when would the Charlotte referendum occur? Wooldridge insisted on an early summer vote, but the City Council voted 8-2 to bundle the projects into a single referendum, making no decision about the referendum's timing. The business community interjected itself, as the chairman of the city's Economic Development Council insisted on the referendum occurring in September or November.

This confusion was further aggravated by holiday vacations of The Wagman and Wooldridge until January 8. On January 9, Wooldridge honored his mid-December commitment to me by announcing he had no choice but to file with the NBA the Hornets Intent to Transfer from Charlotte on March 1. This was appreciated, but they had been possessive of Louisville's Letter of Intent for over a week, with no response.

More secret (but very important) action in Memphis

The weekend of January 13 and 14 was spent with the T-Man, capped off with a visit to the annual model train show—a fascinating time for the little guy, to watch as the little HOs transverse incredibly realistic scenery and for a grey-haired granddad to watch the little guy watching a long-ago part of his history pass by.

The respite was nice, but the next day, Monday, January 15, something happened in Memphis that we would find out about later, which would eventually (many months later) have a devastating impact on Louisville's NBA odyssey.

On that day the Memphis Pursuit Team met with John Calipari, the new Memphis University basketball coach. Calipari had been an extremely successful college coach, failed in the NBA, and had come to Memphis to resurrect its collegiate program. He was a star and had captivated Memphians by successfully recruiting the nation's number one high school player, Dajuan Wagner. The meeting began anxiously — all involved knew that Calipari could kill the quietly germinating NBA in Memphis concept. They could picture him ranting and raving about the NBA, how terrible it was, what an awful basketball product it was and how it would financially damage the university's basketball program. They could even envision him demanding a public referendum and even challenging the community by threatening to leave the university if the NBA came to Memphis. In sum, they could picture Calipari letting his ego get in the way of Memphis's economic development. But that didn't happen. Calipari heard them out, their plans, desires and intentions to make it a "win-win" for the university and the city. Calipari's response was: "Their commitment to me at the time was, it would be a win-win, that they would make the university whole. If you're looking at the bigger picture, as long as we're made whole, as long as they're looking after our interests, it's just another thing that raises the image of the city."[275] Calipari looked at the big picture, set his ego aside, and gave the Memphis NBA effort his blessing. As the reader will see, sometime later Louisville would not be as fortunate to have a community-minded collegiate coach in its midst.

Running out of time

By virtue of our four-month's old, hand-written Lilly's menu commitment to Wooldridge, a Memorandum of Understanding was required to be signed by February 28. There were only five weeks left.

I was perfectly willing to battle Memphis head-on, but not Memphis *and* Charlotte.

The time had come to insist upon at least a privately-delivered business decision that the Hornets were irrevocably leaving Charlotte. That decision had to be made by the week of January 22, because a finalized agreement couldn't be cobbled together in four weeks. A business decision from Wooldridge was politely and firmly demanded. Mixed messages from Charlotte continued as the time drew to January 22. The City Council had even rejected Stern's request to come to Charlotte and meet.

For a week or so, I had become increasingly intrigued with events in Vancouver. The Grizzlies were terrible, attendance was in the cellar, and their owner, Mike Heisley, had been grumbling (to some extent publicly) about his predicament. With no Hornets business decision forthcoming, on January 23 I phoned Deputy Commissioner Russ Granik. He and Stern had read the Louisville Letter of Intent to the Hornets and were very pleased to know where we were in the process. He also acknowledged they were fully aware of the declining time that Louisville was presented with vis-a-vis decision-making in Charlotte. Lastly, and most importantly, neither he nor Stern had any problem if I determined to redirect Louisville's attention to the Vancouver Grizzlies. The next week was spent pondering how we should approach the Grizzlies and assimilating every bit of information we could find on Mike Heisley and his Vancouver Grizzlies.

An intriguing Canadian connection

John Bitove, Jr., is the son of a Canadian billionaire capitalist, John Bitove, Sr. He is known in Toronto as a young, perepetetic and reclusive Indiana University graduate from the early 1980s. On April 23, 1993, as the president of Bitove Investments, he formed Professional Basketball Franchise, Inc., and in partnership with Allan Slaght of Standard Broadcasting and the Bank of Nova Scotia's, Borden Osmak, made application for an NBA franchise in Toronto.

While Bitove's group was the underdog to the Palestra Group, comprised of Canadian road contractor Larry Tanenbaum, the Canadian Imperial Bank and Labatt Breweries (founders of the Toronto Blue Jays) and another group led by several rock concert promoters and featuring Magic Johnson — Bitove was ever-determined and far more clever. He had proposed a new downtown arena on a Toronto subway line; the others preferred less centrally-located sites. Within seven months Bitove's Group was awarded a franchise for $125 million, upon condition that they resolve the league's problem with Ontario's provincial gaming company that permitted wagering on NBA games and that they sell a minimum of 12,500 seat licenses for the new downtown arena.

By May 16, 1995, the NBA had assuaged the Ontario provincial government by agreeing to donate $1.5 million to medical research and $2 million in international television ads during NBA telecasts to promote Canadian tourism and Bitove had obtained 50% deposits on 15,300 seats for the new Air Canada Centre, to be constructed. Bitove was granted the Toronto Raptors franchise.

While Bitove no longer owned the Raptors, his involvement with the NBA was deeply significant. The Bitove family had long been a major owner/operator of fast food franchises in Canada, but by the mid 1990s had sold out their interests and moved to Ireland. More important though was that John Bitove, Jr., remained in Canada with his portion of the family's money, and on June 8, 1999, Bitove's company, SA Acquisitions, had purchased from Scott's Restaurants 345 Kentucky Fried Chicken stores in Canada — making Bitove the largest KFC franchise owner/operator in Canada.

I had known of Bitove's original acquisition of the Raptors franchise since it occurred and had discussed it and Bitove's then-impending acquisition of the 345 Canadian KFC franchises with Tom Chema in our Cleveland meeting. While I'm sure Jonathan Blum was aware of his franchise ownership, Bitove's interest in the NBA would never be mentioned between us because I always felt it was important for Blum to learn of Bitove's NBA interest on his own, although it would all play a large role in the next adventure of Louisville's NBA odyssey.

Saturday night, January 27, was another big family birthday celebration. This time it was Brevins (the T-man's dad). I asked the now three-year-old T-man, "What do you like better, a bees or bears?" Without waiting an instant he said, "Bears, Booce." Was that an omen? Time would tell.

He who hesitates is last.
Mae West

One person can make a difference, and everyone should try.
John F. Kennedy

CHAPTER ELEVEN

Grizzled By Graceland

Margaret Thatcher has written: "Lack of consensus is no reason for lack of leadership"—an interesting observation by a remarkably effective leader, which directly bears upon the course of events that found Louisville being "Grizzled by Graceland."

Your (international) Vancouver Grizzlies

An internationally-televised NBA was conceived in the late 1980s featuring the electric-stardom of Michael Jordan, Larry Bird and Magic Johnson. It was given birth when the 1992 U.S. Olympic Dream Team, starring the greatest NBA players, was witnessed by a hundred million world citizens. It began to flower in February, 1993, upon the realization by the NBA that its product was a hot property in Hong Kong and due to Hong Kong's impending takeover by China, thousands of wealthy Hong Kongers were relocating to the posh Vancouver British Columbia's upper-class suburb of Richmond.

While the NBA was exploring the idea of becoming an international league, Arthur Griffins was building a $163 million hockey arena in Vancouver for his NHL Canucks. The arena needed more tenants. Vancouver's growth possibilities and the NBA's internationalization were a match made in heaven. After a year of discussion, on April 27, 1994, Vancouver's Griffins was granted an NBA franchise for the 1995-96 season. Like Toronto, the Vancouver franchise award was with strings — Griffins had to also sell 12,500 season tickets by December 31, 1994. He did and thus jump-started the NBA's international expansion.

Soon realizing he couldn't afford the $150 million NBA expansion fee plus a $163 million arena, Griffins sold the Canucks, the Grizzlies and the new arena to Seattle billionaire businessman John E. McCaw. Within several years, due to an expensive divorce (rumored to cost him upwards of $500 million) and the declining Canadian dollar exchange (causing nearly a $50 million loss in four years), all three entities were placed for sale by McCaw. Following Stern's aborting of the Grizzlies sale to Bill Laurie, he prevailed upon Mike Heisley to purchase the team from McCaw. Jumping at the opportunity, Heisley wrote a $160 million (U.S.) check to McCaw. Uncharacteristically, prior to his acquisition, the adroit Chicago billionaire had undertaken little due diligence. The Grizzlies financial disaster multiplied.

Over the 5+ years of McCaw/Heisley ownership the Grizzlies lost more games, faster, than any team in NBA history; by early January, 2001, a mind-numbing 336 losses in 427 games. As inept as the Grizzlies were on the court, their bottom line was more deplorable. More than 65% of the Grizzlies' expenses (players' salaries and travel-related expenditures) were incurred in U.S. dollars, while their Vancouver revenue was received in Canadian dollars, which was only 66 cents for each U.S. dollar. Upon Heisley's acquisition, this woeful state of affairs was coupled with an unexpected recession in Vancouver's natural resource-based economy and McCaw's cancellation of the prior expense-sharing arrangement between the Canucks and the Grizzlies. In five years the Grizzlies season ticket base dropped from 12,500 to 4,800. By the 2000-01 playing season, there was only 60% suite occupancy, at a per-suite average of $45,000 Canadian (or $29,700 U.S.) with an average game gate of $300,000 Canadian (or $198,000 U.S.) per game, both of which were one-fifth of the NBA average. The local TV package was returning about $4 million Canadian (or $2,640,000 U.S.) or a fifth of the NBA average. On the court and in the bank, it was utterly hopeless in Vancouver.

First call/first meeting with Mike Heisley

With the voiced approval of Deputy Commissioner Granik and an intensive weeks study of the Grizzlies, at 10:00 on Monday morning, January 29, 2001, a call was placed to the Chicago offices of Grizzlies owner, Mike

Heisley. His executive secretary, Sue, received the call. First impressions are lasting and mean much — Sue was most cordial and gracious, offering that Heisley was in a plane returning to Chicago. Realizing my good fortune to speak with such a pleasant person, I availed the opportunity to describe my authority from the City of Louisville and need to arrange a meeting with her boss to discuss the Grizzlies transfer to Louisville. Sue responded, "I'm sure he'll be pleased to speak with you. He's to call from the plane shortly. I'll give him your message and see that he calls you before 7:00 this evening." Anyone who says a secretary isn't important simply doesn't know what he's talking about. Every successful person I've ever known has employed a highly competent and efficient secretary. Sue was one, for sure.

Ironically, within ten minutes of that call, Hornets financial analyst, Barrett, called with good news. He was fully satisfied with the bond financing figures he had received from the PNC Capital Markets Group and was going to report this to Wooldridge. At mid-afternoon, the Pursuit Team was advised about the effort to contact Heisley.

The pleasant Sue had her boss well trained. At 7:00 PM sharp Monday, January 29, the promised phone call was received. It was to last thirty minutes. Heisley was exceedingly quick on the uptake, reciting his absolute determination to move the Grizzlies out of Vancouver before the next season, because he projected a season loss approaching $40 million. He volunteered that, "David talked me into this, and while I'm pleased to be an NBA owner, I'm not going to lose that kind of money any longer."

Heisley liked the idea of Louisville's NBA market potential, but hadn't considered it as an alternative, since he understood from discussions with the NBA offices that the Hornets were moving to Louisville if "things didn't work out in Charlotte." I assured Heisley that we weren't shopping Louisville. It was explained that while we had negotiated with the Hornets owners for several months and were even to the point where arena bond financing figures were being developed by the NBA, the Hornets ownership and PNC Capital Markets Group, I couldn't get a definitive business decision out of Wooldridge and there was only thirty-one days before the March 1st transfer application deadline. Heisley understood, made a particular point of expressing his appreciation for my frankness and agreed to immediately obtain Stern's permission to talk with us. If it was obtained, he and his troops (as he called them) would come to Louisville before the week was over.

Assuming Stern's permission would be granted, Heisley set some precise negotiating parameters. For the Grizzlies transfer to Louisville, he'd require a real estate deal surrounding a new arena and an ownership participation by Louisvillians. He specifically stated there would be no transfer to "...any city that did not offer a minority ownership interest." There were two specific reasons for this: (i) local ownership was essential in a mid-sized city and (ii) his lawyers were requiring it for estate-planning purposes. He jokingly remarked, "When you meet me, you'll see why. I'm too fat." Without any details, I made sure he understood that both a real estate development opportunity and a minority investment were negotiable in Louisville.

After this rather abrupt dissertation about his requirements, he asked an interesting question: "Bruce, let me ask you something. I've got forty-four businesses and my family gains no enjoyment from them. I bought this franchise because I wanted to own one business that would be fun for my family, and it isn't fun in Vancouver. Are the Louisville guys that are interested in the NBA fun, family-type guys that enjoy life or are they jerks?" The response: "We have our share of the latter here, but they're not involved with me." Heisley retorted, "Good, then let's do some business."

Lastly, we agreed on a major point. Neither he nor I had the time to play negotiating games — honesty and forthrightness would be the hallmark of our discussions and our mutual commitment. There would be no surprises discovered from the nation's newspapers. He would tell us what he was doing, what other cities he was visiting and he would not shop our deal around. I told him I didn't want to know other city's offers and didn't want him to tell other cities of ours. His statement on this requirement was equally forthright, "If I was with you, I'd shake your hand on that."

Over the years I've found it difficult to assess people and their attitudes over the phone; I need to be with them in person. However, Heisley seemed a bit different. His straightforward honesty transported over a phone line, because it was his very essence as a person. Heisley seemed enthused, we exchanged all phone contact numbers and bade a short farewell. He would assiduously maintain this commitment throughout the next two months. On only one occasion, I didn't. There would come a time (discussed later) when I snooped, trying to surreptitiously find out another city's offer.

Within forty-five minutes, at 8:47 PM, Andy Dolich, Heisley's Vancouver business operations manager, called from a cell phone prior to a Grizzlies game in Vancouver. Heisley had spoken with Stern and he, Heisley and

Heisley's lawyer, Stan Meadows, were coming to Louisville on Friday, February 2. With those two calls began the most tumultuous two months of Louisville's thirty-year NBA odyssey.

Mike Heisley was by far the most engaging and personally charming owner we would meet on the NBA odyssey. As the son of a railroad worker, he had grown up in Virginia and worked his way through Georgetown University in Washington, D.C., graduating in 1960. His business career began with the computer division of RCA. In 1973, Heisley was hired away from RCA to turn around a conveyer manufacturer in Easton, Pa. Within a few years he succeeded, becoming its president. Leaving Easton he went to Chicago, bought Conco, Inc., sold off four divisions to pay the acquisition costs and the remaining debt of the company. So began Heico Acquisitions, Inc., which during the 1980s initiated a multitude of other acquisitions from Chapter 11 bankruptcy proceedings. By the mid-1990s Heico Acquisitions owned 44 corporations in the United States and Canada, whose primary business emphasis were telecommunications, steel-wire products and pre-fabricated buildings, resulting in Heisley's listing amongst Forbes Magazine's "400 Wealthiest Men in America."

The business side of Mike Heisley was far less than one-half of the man. He was real, genuine and dearly loved his wife, Agnes, and his four daughters, speaking of them constantly. Deeply immersed in his suburban hometown's life, he had been instrumental in the significant improvement of St. Charles, Illinois' public education system. A dynamo with a booming voice that enabled full control of his environment, Heisley relished each aspect of his life and seemed to put everything in its proper perspective. He was one of those guys who was the proverbial life of the party, fitting in anywhere, from the most elite country club to a corner bar in Schnitzelburg. Mike Heisley's personage seemed to combine the best attributes of Adolph Rupp's focused and single-mindedness to succeed with Uncle Ed Diddle's humanity and love of people. During the upcoming two months, he would run that entire gamut in Louisville with astounding aplomb. It was easy to see. If the Grizzlies transferred to Louisville, Mike Heisley's effervescent personality would instantly cause him to become a larger-than-life personage throughout the community.

The Pursuit Team was excited. Finally there was an owner who wanted to get down to brass tacks and make a business decision. Blum was in New Orleans, not to return until 7:30 on Friday night, too late to meet with Heisley. He requested a full report and authorized me to express Tricon's willingness to negotiate for team and arena naming rights. Glasscock, Blue, Higdon were all available.

Friday, February 2, began with a personal note to my Daytimer: "May be huge day. Be calm and collected." Promptly at 10:00 AM our guests arrived at the J. Bruce Miller Law Group. As I walked around the corner into the reception room to say hello there was this fire plug, who in a booming voice said, "Is this the Bruce Miller I made the deal with on the phone?" Responding yes, Heisley responded, "Well, I'm Mike Heisley. Let's shake hands and get started." What a great way to start!

Sitting around my office conference table and following expressions of appreciation for the quick opportunity to meet, Heisley abruptly stated he had four options: (i) stay in Vancouver and lose another $40 million, (ii) move to another city, but that city had too many roadblocks, (iii) sell the team or (iv) move to Louisville. If he came to Louisville the deal he required was simple: he valued his team at $250 million, and with its $80 million debt, the net value was $170 million, so there would need to be a real estate and financial deal approaching $85 million to get a 50/50 ownership division on the transfer of the Grizzlies to Louisville. Then Heisley said, "Bruce, you wanted to get to the basics quick—that's it."

I responded that we might be able to meet those requirements, but questioned his opinion of the team's value. "The Vancouver Grizzlies aren't worth $250 million." His response: "Bruce, the Grizzlies are like a Derby horse in Vancouver. Of little value there, but a horse like that in Kentucky where the Derby is, and called the Kentucky Colonels, is valuable because the people here value basketball." Indeed, an interesting assessment since he referenced the Kentucky Colonels. Did he already know of Tricon's interest? Time to test Heisley's forthrightness.

I asked what other city he had talked with and he quickly responded, Nashville, volunteering that in November six Nashville movers and shakers had invited him there and entertained him at a NHL Nashville Predators hockey game. He met a slew of country music stars and received the full Chamber of Commerce treatment. They had gone to Chicago in early January and tried to convince him that a renovation of Nashville's Gaylord Arena would permit the Grizzlies and the Predators to function alongside each other. But there was a big problem with Nashville. The hockey team had primacy on the arena revenue streams and dates and its major league arena football team (the Nashville Kats) had second dibs. So Nashville was not even a possible contender. Then he volunteered, "Bruce, there aren't many cities that are realistic and available. We're looking at Louisville. Then we're going to look at Las Vegas, Anaheim, Memphis, New Orleans and Long Island. That will be it. One of those cities is going to get the Vancouver Grizzlies. We will be in one of those places next season, period." A powerful incentive, to be sure.

Then the political question was necessary. Do you want to meet with any politicians? The answer (again proving his awareness of Louisville's prior experience) was, "Are the governor and the city council still on board?" Answer: "Yes!" "Is the Mayor still the problem he was during your Rockets effort?" Answer: "Yes!" Heisley observed, "I understand he's not too popular around here," and then inquired about the remaining length of the Mayor's term and whether he would have competition if he sought re-election. The answer was, "The Metro Mayor election is in November 2002, and the former three-term Mayor is the odds-on favorite." Question: "Where does he stand?" Answer: "He's in favor of the NBA being in Louisville, provided a fair deal can be struck." Heisley quickly responded, "I'll leave the governor and the city council up to you guys, then we'll worry about the Mayor later. I don't have the time to worry about him now." Pretty hard not to understand this point-blank statement.

The next question was, "Do you all have any food around here?" We left for lunch at Vincenzo's. On the way out, I introduced Norma to Heisley. He said, "How is it that such a beautiful and stately young woman would marry an old, grey-haired guy like Bruce?" He said that everyone in his family was "short and fat"—all about 5 foot 5 or so—including the guys who married his daughters. The last unmarried daughter had been recently given a little advice from Heisley: marry a taller guy, because every time there's a family picture the photographer has to kneel down to take the picture! Everyone (including Heisley) roared with laughter. The guy was a real trip.

Gabriele Vincenzo had been pre-contacted about serving our table himself. We were joined by Todd Blue, Ed Glasscock, and Steve Higdon. Heisley was still in rare form. Having ordered a Caesar salad, Gabrielle brought a huge offering. Looking at the salad and then up at Gabriele,

Heisley observed, "We have a problem: I order a Caesar salad and you bring me a Julius Caesar salad!" Another round of raucous laughter.

The straightforward approach like a Sherman tank, right down the middle-of-the-road, continued. Glasscock and Higdon were hit with the $85 million local investment requirement. To say the least, they were stunned. Following lunch, we left for the Blue site. Todd gave the presentation. Heisley thought it was a fabulous site for an arena, particularly with the river view and surrounding real estate development opportunities. Then Blue drove the entourage through Louisville's medical center on the way to Freedom Hall. Heisley noted, "This thing is as big as Houston's, there must be a lot of sick people around here."

Upon our arrival at Freedom Hall, Workman was typically distant. We were given a tour of the facility, the suites and the dressing rooms. Before leaving for the airport, Heisley pulled me aside in front of Freedom Hall, grabbed my elbow Lyndon Johnson-style and said, "Bruce, this is a wonderful opportunity for my team and your city. Stern tells me you all can get this done quickly and we need to move quickly. Meadows will be calling you tomorrow to flesh out the business deal. Louisville looks terrific."

It was an incredible day, absolutely straightforward, intense, to the point, and yet down-home, real and genuine. It was overtly obvious: Heisley was a direct decision-maker, fully capable of making a decision and not looking back. He embodied a combination of John Y. Brown's two competing life's principals that guided his Buffalo Braves/Colonels decision making: "You've got to know when to hold 'em and know when to fold 'em"—and "There are no good or bad decisions, just decisions that you make good by hard work." A lot different from our experience with the Hornets ownership.

On Saturday, Meadows called, just as Heisley said he would, simplifying the Grizzlies deal even more. Heisley didn't want to discuss the arena piece at this point—only the business deal. If and when the business deal was in place, we'd turn to the arena.

Meadows was as tough as the Rocket's Goldberg and as clever as the Hornet's Wagman. He had been a senior partner (along with 982 other lawyers) with Chicago's McDermott Will & Emery law firm that represented Heico Acquisitions. As Heisley had jokingly explained, because it was cheaper to hire him than to pay his legal fees, Meadows left to become Heisley's personal legal counsel. It was quickly clear — no Heisley-type fun with

Meadows, who quickly volunteered he was the tough guy and Heisley was the softie. So there would be no mistake, I told Meadows that both tasks for Louisville would be performed by me.

So, beginning with the tough guy stuff, a direct point was made — the Grizzlies $250 million franchise value was overstated for a Vancouver location, but might be accurate for a Louisville location. If Heisley was going to insist on an enhanced franchise value in Louisville, then Louisville had the right to insist on receiving credit for its contributions to that enhancement, namely the Tricon naming rights, the real estate deal around the arena, and the sport's heritage in Kentucky. Meadows agreed that if this was a counter-proposal, it wasn't necessarily off base.

Next a question and an observation. Question: "How long have you and Mike Heisley known David Stern?" Answer: "A few years." Observation: "I've known him since 1978 and I doubt that he will approve a transfer without an arena commitment in place." Meadows agreed that I was "...probably right, but, Heisley was going to have a long meeting about everything with Stern at the upcoming All-Star game." It was clear that Heisley's transfer thought process had not been sufficiently vetted with Stern. We parted with the understanding that he would deliver our counter-offer to Heisley.

There was restlessness in Charlotte. On Sunday afternoon, February 4, The Wagman called. Hearing that Heisley had been in Louisville, he was concerned and wanted to make sure I remembered that Wooldridge intended to file his application to transfer on March 1 and he had asked Stern for permission to file for two cities, Louisville and Memphis. It was obvious the Hornets were trying to protect themselves from Heisley's determination to transfer the Grizzlies. I reminded The Wagman that Louisville was running out of time waiting for a definitive business decision from Wooldridge and we couldn't wait any longer. It was clearly noted we much preferred the Hornets, because of their already-made UK player connection and because the Hornets would be much more quickly successful in Louisville than the Grizzlies. Wooldridge's willingness to dually-list Louisville with Memphis was appreciated, but Louisville had to protect its interests. We agreed to stay in touch.

Heisley gets the thumbs-up to move from Stern

February 5 is Norma's birthday. This year we celebrated at her daughter Mitch's home. While she had a terrible cold, nothing could dampen the festivities, and the happiest camper was the T-Man singing, "Happy Birthday Dear Barner—Happy Birthday to you." Norma's always been called Barner by the T-Man. As a tot, he couldn't say Grandma Norma—instead, out came 'Barner.' Now everyone, even including the T-Man's friends, call her Barner. About as precious as it gets.

Barner's birthday was also a bombshell day in the NBA odyssey. Sam Smith, then with the *Chicago Tribune*, was one of the nation's premier NBA scribes, renown for his ability to obtain inside scoops from the NBA. On that day he had written, "It's a done deal, there's already a pledge to move the Hornets to Louisville." Calls were coming from everywhere: local media representatives Bob Domine and Tony Cruise along with Bonnie Rosen of NBC 6 in Charlotte, Julie Tashi of WFNZ in Charlotte. There was deep concern that Smith's story would have an adverse impact on our efforts both with the Hornets and the Grizzlies. In order not to make a mistake at this juncture, after advising The Wagman, Heisley and the NBA offices of its contents, I distributed a generic press release nationally: "There have been various reports in the national press over the past several weeks concerning the upcoming March 1, 2001 deadline which the National Basketball Association recognizes for applications to transfer a franchise to another city for the next basketball season — in this instance, the 2001-02 season. I will neither confirm nor deny discussions with anyone or any team or any team owner; and assuming those conversations have taken place I will not discuss or characterize any of those discussions. It's reasonable to presume that these discussions would occur in the week prior to the NBA All-Star game, as that's when they began last year regarding the Houston Rockets. I will say that we have worked, continually, 'under the radar screen' for many months and I believe that Louisville has a reasonable opportunity to be considered in the front row for a transfer of any NBA franchise that will or may seek a transfer, if in fact any of them do seek to file for transfer on or before March 1, 2001. The next several weeks will be critical to that opportunity, and we shall continue our work and efforts as we move forward through February. During that time, whether or not I will have any public comment or statement will depend upon the circumstances, as they develop."

The chess-match was in high gear. Having engaged in a phone argument with Todd Blue about the dollar value of his family's land deal, on Thursday, February 8, Meadows rejected our counter-proposal. His rejection was rejected unless it was personally delivered to me by Heisley. I simply refused to, again, get into dealing with go-between lawyers. Within an hour Meadows was calling back to apologize and request that we all come to the All-Star game in Washington, D.C. to meet with Heisley and discuss the counter-proposal. This was viewed as yet another ploy to get us into a spot with the press and the Hornets. Meadows was told we would only come to D.C. with an invitation from David Stern. Meadows' foray was quickly cleared up.

On Friday, February 9, there was another frank conversation with Heisley. With full respect for Meadows and his abilities, Heisley was reminded that I intended to deal directly with him, because he was the owner. Heisley agreed and further concurred that he didn't want us at the All-Star game fearing the press frenzy would adversely affect his meeting with Stern, the purpose of which was to obtain transfer permission.

There was one request and two faithful promises from Heisley. The request: to get our business proposal together and make sure Tricon did, as well. The two promises: (i) we would talk on Monday morning prior to his meeting with Stern and he would come to Louisville on Friday, February 16, for private meetings with everyone involved in the business side of the deal. Then there was another request: Tell the Tricon guys to have some Kentucky Fried Chicken ready for lunch on Friday, because he loved it.

The Pursuit Team was advised and pleased. Now it was necessary to make sure that Aldermanic President Magre and Alderman Johnson were in the loop. A lengthy meeting was conducted with them and they were excited. To simplify things, they were given one major responsibility—to make sure that there are at least eight solid votes on the Board. It was clearly presented: "If you can do that, and we can put an acceptable business deal together, then we've got a real shot at pulling this off." They accepted their responsibility.

Since the next week was fully loaded with depositions, a day-long mediation and our seventeenth wedding anniversary, the only way to deal with Heisley's request for a business proposal was the cancellation of the depositions and another all-night stand. It was really cold in Louisville that Friday. After dinner, I returned to the office — for some unknown reason in a golf shirt and light sweat pants. The proposal would be drafted that evening and then vetted by the Pursuit Team and the governor's office. Progress was being made—when the building fire alarm went off. Would I honor it at 11:00 PM? Deciding discretion was important, I did, and nearly froze to death standing outside in zero temperatures waiting for the firemen to extinguish the garage fire. Some homeless person had set a fire in the Dumpster. I guess he was cold. My cell phone had been left in the office. Finally, the building's night watchman let me use the emergency phone — Barner picked me up at 2:00 AM and I thawed out by Sunday's All-Star game in front of the fireplace.

As promised, on Monday, February 12, 2001 at 8:45 AM Mike Heisley called. His meeting with Stern was to begin in fifteen minutes. Afterward at 11:00 AM Stern would announce that the Grizzlies had been given permission to transfer to another city and the announcement would be on a media teleconference call, with Stern accepting questions. Heisley suggested that a Louisville reporter be on the call. Chris Poynter was alerted. At the appointed time, the story was carried nationwide: "Vancouver Grizzlies given permission to transfer, by Stern."

The Pursuit Team was alerted—they had to be ready for Friday's meeting with Heisley. Preparations began. Architect Carlton Godsey was notified. At Alderman Johnson's request, Godsey had worked with Ellerbe-Becket in the development of an arena schematic and needed to be present on Friday, as was the PNC Capital Markets Group. Blum called from a Tricon plane that evening to assure me that Tricon would not embarrass anyone and that it would make a "balls-out" presentation to Heisley.

Heisley's second visit to Louisville

Wednesday, February 14, Valentine's Day, was our eighteenth wedding anniversary. We've shared the day with others in different ways. For many years we had a blow-out Valentine Party at our residence, but it had gotten out-of-control—no one could be taken off the list and others had to be added, because the uninvited, who expected an invitation, became aggravated. Answer to such a problem—end the big party. This year the celebration was to be a small surprise (for Norma) dinner party with the Broeckers, the Schustermans, the DeWeeses and local interior decorators Mark Eliason and Wayne Jenkins. Surprises abounded on several fronts.

Late that afternoon, two days after Stern's announcement, state senator

Tim Shaughnessey presented a bill in the General Assembly limiting and delaying the use of the new tax increment financing statute for a downtown arena. An employee of UofL's medical center, Shaughnessey was a nice young man who absolutely adored seeing his name in the paper. The amazing thing about politicians like Shaughnessey is they never seek knowledge before expressing an opinion. Someone once joked his most appreciated Christmas present was a scrapbook and a roll of Scotch Tape. There's always a few of those around in politics, who know they can get more ink by being against something than for it. Sometimes they realize that they're not accomplishing anything by being negative and sometimes they don't. Those realizing this are usually the ones who move to higher offices. Shaughnessey's bill was killed the next day by senior state senator David Karem. But he did succeed in getting his name in the city's newspaper, and every other city's newspaper that was seeking an NBA team. This wasn't particularly helpful. Instead of concentrating on Heisley's upcoming visit, the entire next day was spent putting out fires and assuring the Hornets ownership, the NBA offices and Mike Heisley that the Shaughnessey publicity stunt was dead-on-arrival. Unfortunately, his insatiable need for newspaper mention would continue throughout the Grizzlies effort — being less and less credible each time it belched forth and, most particularly, as the Governor became more publicly supportive.

As our guests arrived, our then-13 year-old dog, Teddy, was hit by a car. Like any old dog, Teddy was a family fixture. I didn't think he was going to make it. Jerry DeWeese and I took him to the vet. We had to leave him overnight. Upon our return at 9:00 PM after a pre-dinner wine, the steaks were grilled and we finally sat down for dinner at 10:00, only to be interrupted by a call from an Orlando Magic official wanting to discuss Louisville's interest in the Orlando Magic, if they, too, made application to transfer on March 1. Valentine's Day had been another roller-coaster ride.

With the Shaughnessey publicity belch successfully quieted, the entire day of February 15 was spent preparing for Heisley's Friday visit. The arena presentation by Godsey and Ellerbe-Becket was ready and Blue was prepared to make a comprehensive real estate development presentation. It was assumed that Tricon was preparing with its consultant. The evening was spent with our little buddy, the T-Man, who helped us get Teddy home from the vet, and fielding a phone call from an inquisitive Vancouver sports reporter.

Friday, February 16 arrived. It does every year, but this year the day was a little bigger than normal. Blue picked me up on the way to the airport to meet Heisley and Meadows. The billionaire and his lawyer arrived on an $89 Southwest flight from Chicago. As Heisley and I walked through the Louisville airport, out of curiosity the question was asked, "Why did you take a Southwest flight, instead of using a private jet?" The answer was typically Heisleian—"You can't talk to anybody on a private jet. I learned a lot about Louisville on that flight. Several guys thought the Grizzlies ought to move here—they sounded pretty convincing to me."

When we arrived at Tricon, architect Godsey, Blum and Tricon's CEO David Novak were already present. Godsey made a short presentation about his arena design and work with Ellerbe-Becket and Heisley was given the schematic design. He liked the design, expressed appreciation for Godsey's work. Then Heisley took charge as he always did, but there was a twist. After his meeting with Stern, it was readily apparent (as I had thought it would be) that the business side had to also include our arena financing plan. This was a significant advantage for Louisville, because no other city was as far along as we were in arena design and bond finance planning and it couldn't be done by any of those cities in the two weeks that were left before the transfer deadline on March 1. Quickly put on the table were Heisley's "drivers for decision"—a stadium deal with revenue streams and naming rights and a business relationship with Tricon. Local investors weren't mentioned, which surprised everyone. Blum offered Tricon's decision drivers as being the arena, team naming and logo rights. The morning hadn't accomplished much other than positioning, and the discussion of an ancillary business opportunity between Heisley and Tricon. The ever-inquisitive Heisley queried Novak about KFC's business in China, which was its fastest-growing market. It required nine months to build a KFC store in China and Heisley suggested that one of his companies could save Tricon considerable money and time by using its pre-fabricated buildings. He had met "all the Communists" (as he called them) and made the arrangements to do business in China. Novak immediately summoned KFC's international officers to the meeting. It was intriguing to listen to them discuss the business aspects of a deal in China.

Lunch time had arrived and just as Heisley requested, Tricon's entire menu was "Finger Lickin' Good." The afternoon session began with Heisley saying, "Time to get down to basketball business." The question to Blum and Novak: "OK, what's the dollar value of your naming rights?" Prefacing his answer by indicating that their consultant hadn't fully advised them yet, Blum put $40 million on the table for both the naming rights and the team name. Heisley's left eyebrow raised and he paused for a moment. Then after a few questions about how the governor's tax increment financing statute operated and graciously expressing his appreciation for the lunch and the time, Heisley asked to be taken to the airport. Todd Blue drove and I accompanied our guests. Heisley had expected much more from Tricon and it was obvious. On the way to the airport, I apologized for wasting his time. He was, as always, courteous, simply saying matter-of-factly that Tricon didn't understand the economics of the NBA and the value of an NBA team name. We shook hands and they entered the airport. It appeared we were through.

On the way home as I commiserated with Blue about the failed opportunity, Blum reached me by cell phone. Expressing his apology and disappointment with the meeting breakup, he requested Heisley's cell phone number. I said, "Jonathan, you promised me you wouldn't embarrass us and you did. I don't know what you can do to correct the situation, at this point." Blum responded, "I do, we're going to double our offer." Within fifteen minutes Jonathan called to report that Heisley was very thankful for the reconsideration. To check, I called Heisley myself. He reiterated his pleasure, saying, "I don't know what happened since we left, but for sure, now, Kentucky Fried Chicken's talking turkey."

It was a critical day in the odyssey. Blum had salvaged a swiftly-sinking ship. Throughout the entire process Heisley honored his commitment— he did not shop or reveal the Tricon offer. But it would be shopped and revealed later, by two local politicians.

The Grizzlies open contact with Memphis

On Saturday, the day after his Louisville visit, Heisley called from his Chicago home to express his appreciation for Louisville's interest. In keeping with his promise not to surprise us via newspaper articles, he told me that Meadows was going to Memphis on Monday while he went to St. Louis and then to New Orleans on Tuesday. I reminded Mike that I didn't want the Tricon offer shopped and he reminded me, "I promised you I wouldn't, and I keep my promises."

It would be much later and after the fact that we learned what happened in Meadows first Memphis meeting.[318] During the previous week, in a conversation with Grizzlies general manager, Dick Versace, Memphis sports agent Jimmy Sexton suggested that Heisley ought to consider Memphis. Sexton's suggestion was unknown to the totally separate Memphis Pursuit Team that had been quietly pursuing the Hornets. In preparation for Meadows' visit, telephones rang off the hook in Memphis that Sunday— resulting in the Sexton team of Grizzlies negotiators learning about the Memphis Pursuit Team's discussions with the Hornets. When Meadows arrived in Memphis for the Monday, February 19 meeting, he was told by Sexton that another Memphis group had been pursuing the Hornets. Meadows was later quoted as saying, "He told me that in the car. I think if he had told me that while I was still in the airport, I probably would have gotten on another plane."[276] Attending Sexton's meeting were the Memphis and Shelby County mayors and the Sports Authority chairman, Reggie Barnes. Meadows advised the group of the Grizzlies needs, those being arena revenues and a major corporate affiliation and that this all had to be done by March 1.[277] Not much to really worry about, at that point, even if we had known what had happened.

After his St. Louis and New Orleans trips, on Wednesday, February 21, Heisley divulged in a New Orleans press conference that he was considering four cities—New Orleans, St. Louis, Anaheim and Louisville, stating that "The biggest asset going for Kentucky is that it, probably along with Indiana, has the greatest concentration of basketball fans in the world."[278]

Only a week to go and Louisville was in the driver's seat.

A week left before the transfer deadline

It was time to act boldly. Fully cognizant of the dwindling time and Heisley's city tour (which had not yet included Memphis), at 9:00 AM on Thursday, February 22nd a letter was faxed to Heisley suggesting I was prepared to put a written proposal on the table.

Another positive forty-five minute conversation followed with Heisley revealing that his meeting in St. Louis had lasted about an hour with the quick conclusion that Laurie and St. Louis were "out"; and, while they put on a good show in New Orleans with good music and even better food, he was very doubtful about the Grizzlies ability to succeed in that marketplace, simply saying, "There's no Tricon there."[279] In a non-remarkable way he added, "There's something crazy going on in Memphis and I don't understand it. I haven't been down there, but Meadows says they're interested, so I'm going to try to find out about that. But I'm running out of time." He requested I send him the proposal and that Blum call him. Later, Blum reported that Heisley was very receptive to Louisville, thankful for Tricon's willingness to participate and appreciated the call.

We would later learn that at the very same moment of Heisley's call, Wooldridge was in Memphis meeting with its Pursuit Team and mayor. Showing a three-foot plastic model of his proposed Charlotte arena, Wooldridge was trying to determine if the Memphis mayor was really interested in the Hornets. The mayor, apparently, was caught off guard, saying they were interested, but it all depended on the Grizzlies, which surprised Wooldridge. Memphis had not been listed in the media as being considered by Heisley.[280]

Even if we had known this, it wouldn't have been of much concern, because Louisville had been in direct discussions with Wooldridge, his lawyer and financial analyst for months; and, since December we had known that Wooldridge was talking to Memphis. Had we known it, at the time, we would have laughed at Memphis, because their right hand didn't know what their left hand was doing. But we wouldn't have had the last laugh!

In preparation for drafting Heisley's proposal, February 23 was spent in Frankfort with Aldermanic President Magre, Louisville state representative Paul Bather, and the Speaker of the Kentucky House of Representatives, Jody Richards. The governor's office had prepped Richards and he was receptive, committing to throw the entire weight of his office behind the project. With Richards' and the governor's commitment coupled with Magre's continuing personal assurance of at least an eight vote majority on the Board of Aldermen, I returned to Louisville to prepare the written proposal. It was a forty-eight hour job resulting in a fifty page document. On Sunday February 25 it was FedExed to Heisley's office in Chicago. He was returning there on Monday afternoon from Anaheim.[281]

At that point, February 25, only four days remained before the transfer deadline. After a month of 25+ hours of in person and phone conversation with Heisley, my analysis had reached the conclusion that the only realistic contenders for the Grizzlies were Memphis, New Orleans and Louisville. So the fifty page proposal was designed to analytically compare these three cities with as many statistics and specifics from verifiable sources as could be found. Of particular (and surprising) note was that Louisville had 506 businesses with annual sales in excess of $10 million versus 485 in Memphis and 410 in New Orleans. It ended with a particular point:

Mike:

As you quietly sit in your chair or on your sofa late in the evening on February 28, 2001, in Chicago making this decision, if you remember anything about this paper, please remember that nothing, even remotely similar to all this, could ever occur in New Orleans or Memphis. To be sure, opening night in New Orleans or Memphis or Louisville will be balloons and seashells, complete with kleig lights celebrities, and politicians of all 'ilks', who will be basking in the glory of the 'new-found event.' However, inescapably, the initial lustre will fade. After the initial lustre is gone in New Orleans or Memphis, Mike Heisley's team will just be another team, another event, another 'thing to do' there—why?—because there's no 'heritage', there's no 'foundation', there's no 'underpinning', there's nothing there that's the equivalent to the importance of this 'kids game' in Kentucky.

But, in Kentucky, after the initial lustre is gone, it will still be basketball, the religion of Kentucky. I rest my case.

At 5:00 PM on Monday, February 26, Heisley called to thank me for Louisville's proposal. He was exhausted. In keeping with his original commitment to deal honestly, he noted that Anaheim's arena (The Pond) had no revenue streams available, all were committed to the Walt Disney company's Mighty Duck's NHL team. Plus, he believed that the Lakers would strenuously object to sharing the Los Angeles metro market with a third team (all of which were supported by various newspaper articles). Adjacent to DisneyWorld in Anaheim, was a recently opened amusement park called "The California Experience." Its logo featured a grizzly bear. Despite the symmetry of logos, Heisley had decided Anaheim was out, unless he could sell the Grizzlies to Disney. That wasn't likely since Disney's CEO, Michael Eisner, was trying to sell Disney's professional sports team interests. That left only Memphis, New Orleans and Louisville. My analysis had been on target—there was significant hope and yet a major concern.

On Wednesday, February 28, the day prior to the transfer deadline, Heisley was considering a trip to Louisville to meet with the Board of Aldermen and the governor for lease negotiations with Freedom Hall. Obviously, it would be to Louisville's distinct advantage if Heisley was here on the day prior to the transfer application deadline. I told him we'd "drop everything" if he came to town on Wednesday. The Pursuit Team, Tricon, the governor's office and Magre were asked to get ready for a meeting on Wednesday with Heisley. They did.

The concern was that Heisley had told Stern that he thought he needed more time to make a decision. I didn't believe the extra time was to Louisville's strategic advantage.

Mayor Dave's negatives and the transfer deadline day

A wag once observed that certain things are sure in life—death and taxes being among them. In Louisville's NBA odyssey several other things were also sure, one of which was a publicly negative action at virtually every critical moment from Mayor Dave Armstrong. Like the night follows the day it was guaranteed—and the opportunity wasn't missed at this critical juncture.

In another displaced press conference where he spoke to people through the press (instead of the phone) Mayor Dave said: "No one has talked to me about any of this." So, on the day before Heisley's ultimate decision, instead of concentrating on Heisley, my and Ed Glasscock's time was spent meeting with Armstrong and his staff. They were told Heisley didn't request a meeting with the Mayor, he was only interested in the governor's commitment and a business arrangement with Tricon, at this time. To allay his concerns about the state's participation, Armstrong was invited to call the Governor, right from the meeting, to discuss the level of the governor's interest. He refused, denying that he was aware of the governor's commitment to use tax increment financing for the arena bonding. However, I knew he was aware of it because the governor's office had told him several weeks prior. Aldermen Magre and Johnson were present and specifically confirmed eight votes on the Board to approve issuing bonds to construct the required arena. A request was made of Armstrong to issue a public statement encouraging Heisley to select Louisville. He refused.

That night Louisville lost, too. Heisley called our residence to let me know he wasn't coming to Louisville the next day. After polling the Board of Governors, Stern found them willing to grant Heisley an extension until Monday, March 26.

There was one nagging question that simply had to be asked: "Mike, if you had to make the decision tonight, what would it be?" "Bruce, without a doubt, my Grizzlies would be Kentucky Colonels. But I need more time to be absolutely sure."

So the ultimate question became: Could Louisville sustain its position with Heisley for an additional 26 days? I had serious questions whether we could. It was inevitable, there would be another round of Heisley's visits to the competing cities. What would happen in Charlotte? Would the previously silent Memphis erupt? There would be rumors of every kind, character and description. UofL would probably be looking for a new coach to replace Denny Crum. Who would it be and what would he have to say? Tricon had delivered, but would a major company from another city deliver? Blue's site and real estate development was acceptable, but would another city present a site and a development that was equal or superior? Louisville's Ruppian fear of the unknown had never generated to any observable level of significance, but now it would. The Mayor hadn't had a prominent podium providing the opportunity to embarrass himself, as he had done with the Rockets, but now he would. Would the governor be able to minimize another mayoral stunt? Would there be another round of Rebecca at Sunnybook Farm utterances from the County Judge? One could only think, wow, what a mess!

Up to this point, the Grizzlies effort had been unaffected by Louisville's peculiarities, but it wouldn't be anymore. The finish line had been moved two furlongs further away and there was concern that a lot of people (local and otherwise) would busily go about putting stumbling blocks between Louisville's opportunity and the finish line.

The first week of March — 26 days to D-Day

It was March 1, 2001. We had twenty-six days to sustain and protect Louisville's position with Heisley. An intense Pursuit Team meeting was held at Tricon, during which responsibilities were divided and accepted. Absolutely every angle was explored, from the Governor's continued support, to UofL's participation, to the sustenance of the Aldermanic votes, to the crystallization of the local investment package. The opposition cities were assessed. It was the best meeting the Pursuit Team had experienced. It ended by Blum confidently stating, "Guys, we're not in this to come in second. We're going to win." We parted company with the warmest of handshakes. It was a hell of a team. The action began.

That afternoon there was a long-expected announcement. Denny Crum had accepted an $8 million buy-out of his remaining contract as UofL's basketball coach and athletic director, Jurich, had a short list of replacement candidates. For several months a public war had been waged between Jurich and Crum supporters. Many felt that Crum deserved better than to be run out of town on a rail. Not only was he a Hall of Fame college coach, but for nearly thirty years Crum had contributed countless thousands of hours in charitable activity around Louisville. If you had a charity that needed a push, all you had to do was ask Denny Crum, he'd be there and fully participate. Despite his team's recent difficulties on the court, Denny Crum was deeply ensconced into Louisville's fabric — a real class act was Denny Crum.

The Wagman called—to make sure one point was fully understood—the Hornets still intended to list Louisville as a transfer city on March 26. There had been no progress in Charlotte. Again, we agreed to stay in touch. To complete the day, an intriguing call came from California. Dr. Daniel Rascher, with a Ph.D. in economics from Cal-Berkeley, was one of the nation's most noted sports market analysts. He was the founder of Sports Economics, Inc. that enjoyed a long and impressive clientele list including the NBA and a number of its teams. He wanted me to know that his in-depth economic analysis of 25 non-NBA cities as potential NBA markets had rendered Louisville far superior to Memphis or New Orleans. The only thing he couldn't assess was the political will and leadership of the three cities, which he specifically noted in the study. Dr. Rascher intended to share the information with the NBA. I wasn't particularly happy about the timing of his contribution, because while I knew nothing about the political leadership qualities of Memphis' or New Orleans' politicians, I knew of Louisville's lack thereof fairly well.

With 25 days remaining before the NBA filing deadline, my wife and I were honored by another not unexpected personal shot-from-the-hip from Brother Billy Reed. It was replete with more name-calling. Being unusually vituperative, an e-mail response followed.[282] The effort to calm Brother Bill's tirades would bear no fruit. They continued with increasing frequency and inanity.

My new best friend, The Wagman, called again at 4:45 PM on March 2 with more news. It now appeared that a June 5 non-binding referendum would occur in Charlotte. The City Council was to approve it by a 6-5 vote on Monday and then the state legislature had to act by April 5 to permit the June 5 referendum. It was reiterated (for the second time in a week) that the Hornets already had prepared their Letter of Intent to Transfer listing Louisville and Memphis and would file it on March 26.

There was other action on the potential private investment front. Old friend Larry Townsend agreed to contact Hollywood director Jerry Bruckheimer (who owned a several thousand acre get-away farm in central Kentucky). Others were contacting Hollywood actor Tom Cruise. Darrell Griffith was reaching out to Johnnie Cochran, and Todd Blue was actively exploring potential Grizzlies' participation with investors in the Minnesota Vikings and family friends in Chicago. Tricon was working with its consultant to further enhance its offer.

The first week of March had gone well in Louisville, but three more weeks remained.

The second week of March — 21 days to D-Day

For the very first time, Heisley had expressed concern about the Mayor's continued vacillating statements. In a 10:30 AM Tuesday March 6 phone call, he requested a meeting with the Mayor. The Pursuit Team conferred and reached an immediate consensus — no way was that going to happen. Blum had received approval from the KFC franchisees, who by their franchise agreement had a participatory right in advertising and promotion decision-making of this magnitude and he didn't want to see the Mayor "...screwing up everything all over again." During the call, the opinion changed.

We would agree to set up a mayoral meeting for Heisley, but would delay it so we could prep him and have a much larger group of meetings that might blunt any adverse reaction to the Mayor. Upon learning that we would create a comprehensive set of meetings with the governor, the mayor, and all other politicals, which would be embellished by Tricon's final and enhanced offer, Heisley was ecstatic. We agreed on the date, Thursday, March 15. The ploy worked. We now had a week to get all the Louisville boats pointed in the proper direction.

The date was even more prescient—a year prior Norma and I had delivered the well-received informal talking points memo to the Houston Rockets' management. Now, exactly a year later, we might finalize a deal. An immediate meeting was requested with the Mayor and it was arranged for 3:00 that afternoon.

The Mayor's meeting was attended by me, Blum, Blue, Glasscock, Bill Skees (Glasscock's bond specialist) and the Mayor. Blum was really strong — absolutely insisting the Mayor develop an enthusiastic attitude about this opportunity. Armstrong backed down upon the direct confrontation, saying he would support it if the Governor permitted the use of the tax increment financing district, but doubted that the Governor would do so, saying "...he has always required legislative approval for its usage." Skees looked at me and I at him. There the Mayor was, again, not telling the truth, this time in front of people who knew — the Governor had never used the tax increment financing statute. In reality, the Mayor's flawed observation didn't make any difference, because the Governor had already committed to utilize the TIF district as the arena funding vehicle, and it would be finalized the following day. When we parted, Blum looked at the Mayor—right in the eye—and said, "Mayor, we're counting on you to honor your commitment in this meeting." Within a week, Blum was to be utterly flabbergasted by Mayor Dave.

The next day, March 7 at 9:00 AM a full compliment of those involved was present in the Governor's office—the Governor; his chief-of-staff Skipper Martin; his CFO Jim Ramsey; his general counsel Dennis Fleming; the deputy chief-of-staff assigned to the NBA project, Jack Conway; Speaker of the House Jody Richards; Ed Glasscock; and Board of Aldermen President Steve Magre. Jonathan Blum and I drove to Frankfort together and joined them. It was a successful meeting. Later in the day the governor committed to draw the TIF district lines, after a tour of the proposed arena area. Blum and I returned to Louisville on top of the world.

Within an hour, Blum would be knocked off his pedestal. His consultant reported rumblings that Memphis and Shelby County, in conjunction with AutoZone and FedEx, had submitted a proposal to Heisley committing the construction of a new $250 million arena in downtown Memphis behind Beale Street. Despite my commitment to Heisley, I agreed to re-enlist my Vanderbilt snoops to seek intel on the alleged Memphis offer. Later in the day, Blum patched former Mayor Abramson into a phone call with me. Abramson reiterated his support of the NBA in Louisville. So we left the day on the uptick.

Old friends Brad and Carla Sue Broecker had always been supportive of the NBA odyssey, and at this critical juncture stood tall again. A late afternoon meeting in our office and an evening dinner at J. Harrod's included Brad and three SFX Entertainment executives from Dallas and New York. Brad had invited them to explore their interest level in negotiating an arena operating agreement with Heisley and the city, should it be determined that such an arrangement would be preferable. The message was loud and clear —due to its age and decrepit condition, Freedom Hall was retarding Louisville's entertainment offerings. They could list literally dozens of acts and entertainment groups who regularly declined to play in the aged Freedom Hall. SFX was perfectly willing to meet and confer about such an opportunity, if and when the proper time arrived. Another option had been created for Louisville's buffet-table offer to Heisley.

To quell the Ruppian aversion to change rumblings that were beginning to be heard, on Thursday, March 8, the Blue family's real estate development proposal was publicly revealed through *The Courier-Journal*.[283] He and his family were willing to give the city the Blue property (valued between $15-20 million) as the arena site, thereby saving the city a similar cost to acquire either his property or the Water Company site. Unreported was another Blue family initiative: an option on an additional tract of land in the general area. The land deal would now be a huge development, complete with retail shopping, dining, with moderate to upscale condominiums. The Blue family divulged arena plans that had been drawn by VOK Architects of Chicago, depicting a state-of-the-art arena on their property, directly adjacent to the recently constructed minor league baseball field. The value of this gift plus an additional cash infusion would be negotiated with Heisley into a Grizzlies minority ownership position. It was reported front-page, above the centerfold.

As the days counted down, Louisville was holding its own. I was proud of what we had accomplished, but a full understanding of Louisville's diabolical fear of the unknown meant it was far too early to celebrate.

By Friday, March 9, the governor was formulating his presentation to Heisley; the County Judge and the Mayor had committed to meet with Heisley; and the State/City/County CFOs had agreed in principle on a TIF financing plan for Heisley. The Gateway Group was preparing another Vincenzo's cocktail/dinner (like the Humana/Rockets spread) with the acceptances approaching one hundred and expected attendees to total one hundred fifty. All the boats seemed to be pointing in the proper direction

The UofL question was about to be dealt with.

In a morning meeting at Dr. Shumaker's private conference room with Todd Blue, Blum, Glasscock and UofL's board of trustees vice-chairman, Jessica Loving, Shumaker and Jurich had favorably viewed (but not committed to) the concept of a revenue split between the University and the Grizzlies for the use of a new arena. The general concept involved a joint marketing effort on suite sales between the Grizzlies and UofL for the 80 suites (instead of already sold 24 at Freedom Hall)—with the money being split on a pro-rata game basis between UofL and the Grizzlies. At an average suite price of $100,000 and with UofL playing 17 home games and the Grizzlies 42, this alone would mean an additional annual revenue stream to UofL approximating $2+ million and there were numerous other revenue streams available for negotiation. The percentages and details would be worked out in face-to-face negotiations between Heisley and Shumaker. The final cherry for UofL's banana split was Jurich's request; it was agreed the arena bond issue would contain $5 million to construct an on-campus basketball practice facility for UofL, to be accomplished by the Governor drawing the downtown TIF district south down I-65 until it got to the UofL campus, then into the campus to contain the area where the practice facility would be built. This was something Jurich particularly desired, or so he said.

It had been a hell of a week, capped by a very favorable editorial in Saturday's *Courier-Journal* and another vital opportunity provided by Carla Sue and Brad Broecker on Saturday evening, March 10. Old friends Jerry and Carol DeWeese were life-long friends of the President of the University of North Carolina at Charlotte, Dr. James Woodward and his wife, Martha, who were in Louisville for the Conference USA post-season basketball tournament. The Broeckers hosted a private dinner for them. Dr. Woodward was very knowledgeable about the Hornets situation in Charlotte. State senator Odom, who was UNCC's biggest political patron, was not going to permit tax increment financing to fund the Charlotte bond issue, and Charlotte had no back-up plan. He opined that the referendum would be held, funded primarily by the Hornets owners and it wouldn't pass. He was convinced that the Hornets were leaving Charlotte, unless there was new ownership, and the effort to find local investors in Charlotte had failed.[284]

The lead article in Sunday's *Courier-Journal* was headlined, "Plan for arena uses new tax law." It described in detail the uniqueness of Kentucky's tax increment financing statute, permitting the return of sales and use taxes to such a project. Other similar state statutes didn't provide for the use of such basic taxes. Ruppians remained quiet and befuddled as numerous unsolicited letters to the editor supporting the effort began to appear. The Pursuit Team's desire to inform the public about the bond and financial commitment was succeeding.

The third week of March — 14 days to D-Day

Monday, March 12, 2001, was one of the signal days in the entire odyssey. Positives abounded. The TIF financing plan was crystallized between the Governor's staff, PNC Capital Markets Group and Glasscock's law firm. In a morning conference call both former Mayor Abramson and I encouraged Magre to draft and give a first reading of an ordinance on a projected bond issue. Blum had succeeded in getting Senator McConnell to encourage the County Judge's full participation and support in the Heisley meeting. A late afternoon meeting with Bob Clarkson provided an update on the Gateway Group's Vincenzo dinner, which was now approaching 150 acceptances. At 5:30 PM, at Stern's request, Deputy Commissioner Granik called and was given a full status report on the upcoming plans for the Heisley meeting. Granik expressed great pleasure with Louisville's progress.

Late that afternoon, the governor, accompanied by Chief of Staff Skipper Martin and Deputy Jack Conway, surveyed by car the suggested TIF district downtown area around the Blue site that was preferred by Heisley. With full knowledge of Heisley's site preference, the mayor had spent the better part of the day trying to wangle an invitation into the governor's car. Mayor Dave wanted the TIF district to include the Louisville Water Company site, then directly north all the way to the Ohio River. If drawn in that configuration, the district would have included all the taxes gained by the state from the headquarters of the state's largest public utility, LG&E Energy Corporation. It always seemed Armstrong was paddling his boat in an opposite direction, no matter how much success and headway was being made. The governor rebuffed Armstrong's negative incursion, believing that the arena's success should stand on its own and not be supplemented by any pre-existing businesses, particularly the state's largest utility company. The decision was that it would be the Blue site, if that's what Heisley preferred. March 12 had been a fine day. There were two days left before Heisley arrived. But continued confusion was on the horizon.

"If some concessions were made for us, I think we would listen. I'm open to listening, and I'm for bringing an NBA team to town." So said Tom Jurich on March 12 as reported by *The CourierJournal*.[285] But three days prior to this statement there had been a several-hour listening opportunity, in which was offered to UofL the only thing requested by Jurich. The proposal had been well-received by both him and the university's president. What else, other than what was discussed, was needed? A telephone call to Glasscock or me would have helped more than a press statement. My only previous experience with a university president and an athletic director was as a student at Vanderbilt. There it would be inconceivable for the athletic director to ever attempt to control the university's decision-making in a matter requiring the school's participation in Nashville's economic development. Normally, the president of a university is responsible for determining the future course of a university, particularly as it relates to community matters. Surely that would be the case at UofL! (That would be true, provided the university president's attention is not diverted by misadventures such as a marital tryst).

The Machiavellian move

The morning of Tuesday, March 13, was fully occupied with the continuing effort to make sure that all bases were covered for Heisley's visit. In an early afternoon hour-long conference call with the Pursuit Team, Tricon's consultant had several suggestions: (i) have Magre attend the Heisley meeting and hand Heisley a letter of support from the nine aldermen and a copy of the bond ordinance to be initiated; (ii) make sure that Heisley understood Kentucky law required no referendum; (iii) make sure Heisley understood that there would be instant office space available to the Grizzlies the moment he made his decision, and (iv) under no circumstances, allow the mayor to have a private meeting with Heisley. Bonham observed that it was clear "...that the mayor was trying to sabotage the effort." Later in the mid-afternoon, Magre advised that his briefings with Aldermen Melton, Allgeier and Handy had gone well and he felt he regained his nine favorable votes.

If further proof of the Bonham-observed mayoral sabotage were needed (and it wasn't), it was to be provided several hours later.

Several days prior to March 13 the mayor had appointed a blue ribbon committee to examine the arena financing proposal.[286] That afternoon they had been summoned together at 5:00 PM in the Jefferson Club for their first meeting, to hear from the Pursuit Team and Glasscock's bond specialist, Bill Skees, about the financing plan and the extent of Tricon's participation, both of which had been explained in detail to the Mayor a week prior. The committee looked strangely uneasy as they collected to begin their assignment.

Glasscock and Skees began with a fully-detailed explanation of the bond financing plan including information that the annual principal/interest payment for at $220 million bond issue would be $11.3 million, based on the then-current interest rate. It was explained that: (i) the governor was agreeable with the Blue site around which the TIF district would be drawn, then it would be extended south along I-65 to the UofL campus to include a practice facility for UofL, as promised to Dr. Shumaker and Jurich; (ii) that the governor had agreed to annually return to the city the first $5 million that the TIF district earned in state taxes to be used by the city in retiring the bonds; (iii) that the Grizzlies might be willing to consider making an annual rent payment (but it had to be negotiated), (iv) that there were additional revenue streams PNC Capital Markets Group had delineated totalling approximately $3 million annually,[287] leaving the city's annual contribution to the bonds at $3.5 million at most. In other words, for a maximum of $3.5 million annually, the city could own a $220 million arena, and the $3.5 million capital contribution from the city represented about ten percent of the annual money available in the average city's budget for capital expenditures.

It was further noted that I was prepared to negotiate twenty days a year during which the city would have exclusive control of the arena for any purpose it desired, with the revenue stream from this usage designated as an additional method to retire the city's portion of its annual obligation.

Finally, I advised that Heisley was willing to sign a liquidated damages clause mandating his payment of the entire remaining bonded debt, if he moved the team elsewhere before the bonds were paid off.

No committee member said a word.

It was Jonathan Blum's turn. He advised the meeting that Tricon's financial commitment approached $100 million, which would be paid to Heisley to rename the team and to name the arena. This was the standard procedure in arena/stadia naming-rights contracts. The only thing that wasn't standard was the full dollar amount of Tricon's commitment. It was the sixth largest naming-rights commitment ever offered in America for an arena/

stadium and the largest such commitment by any mid-sized city.

Without giving an opportunity for the committee to ask questions, Mayor Dave leaped into the discussion. Before these 25 very ill-at-ease businessmen and women, he looked at Blum and with visible anger told him, point-blank, that Tricon's offer was unsatisfactory, observing, "If I had been negotiating it, I would have gotten more, because a company as big as Tricon could do better."

Everyone in the room was stunned over the indescribably rude remark. No one knew what to say or do. Glasscock was sitting on Blum's right and I on his left. Immediately after the mayor's remark, Blum began to rise from his chair. Both Glasscock and I pushed down on his legs to keep him seated. A few committee members, sensing the discourteousness of the statement, asked several questions in an obvious effort to cut the steel-like tenseness. After responding to the committee's questions, we thanked the members for their interest and attention and began easing our way out of the room.

As we left the building for the parking lot the normally placid Blum was livid, saying to me, "I may have to tell Novak tonight that we need to pull out of this. Our company doesn't need this and shouldn't be treated this way." Being aware of Blum's efforts and the pressures upon him to deliver for his company and the interests of KFC's franchisees (like Bitove in Canada), I felt sick for Jonathan. After he had the opportunity to drive awhile, I reached him on his cellphone and pleaded for his calmness and avoidance of any rash decisions, at least for the evening. Blum promised.

The next morning's *Courier-Journal* quoted Mayor Dave as concluding that the financing plan was too risky for the city.[288] Of course, every city that was vying for the Grizzlies knew of Mayor Dave's latest negativism, as did Heisley and the NBA offices. At 8:14 the next morning I sent the following e-mail to Armstrong:

David:

I've been down here since 4:00 AM trying to figure out WHY ON EARTH you were so rude to Jonathan at last night's meeting. All of the invitees (Glasscock, Blum, Blue, Skees and myself) were eager to give you and your group all the necessary information and had prepared for this meeting for the entire afternoon, yesterday. After all that, to say to Jonathan, in front of 30 people, that their offer was "short" and that if YOU had negotiated it you would have demanded a higher participation is utterly and completely incomprehensible. For your information, the Tricon offer (with the "add-ons" including advertising, etc.) is MORE $ than has EVER been put on the table for a mid-sized city major league participation. For your information, the NBA offices believe that this offer is of the "highest quality" and are "deeply impressed." Tricon has been advised in this by the TOP consultant in the country, and they have reached these numbers on their own. Brown Todd has been advised by one of the TOP financing teams in the country as well as a financial consultant for an NBA team. I have contributed volumes of information from the NBA to them. This is a plan that will accomplish the goal of bringing a major league franchise to Louisville. It will provide the University with a state-of-the-art arena. It will allow the University to pay for Pitino, without the necessity of raising additional cash. To say the least, I was utterly and completely flabbergasted with your remarks to Jonathan which served to demean HIM, the largest company headquartered in Kentucky, and the work of at least a dozen people from here AND around the country who have dedicated themselves for the last five (5) months to making this happen on a just and fair basis for all concerned. Lastly, if Jonathan wasn't such a decent and respectful person, he would have gotten up and walked out of that meeting. To be sure, he told us this when we left your meeting. I have nothing else to say other than I was totally embarrassed."

Two days later the only response I ever received from Armstrong to nearly thirty e-mails in three years was received. The following was his response, and my reply on Sunday March 18: "Armstrong, Dave" wrote:

"Sorry you are embarrassed. I'm confident that you're taking full advantage of the circumstances."

My reply: "I did 'take advantage of the circumstances' for the community as a whole, by successfully keeping Tricon in the game in spite of the circumstances you, unfortunately and unnecessarily, created. It would be more productive if you would accept the fact and understand that I'm (as well as a number of others are) trying to help you."

The governor had prepared and mailed a several-page letter to the state legislators explaining the importance of his commitment to Louisville and Kentucky. Meanwhile Mayor Dave sought more opportunities for negative input. The next day about an hour before he was to meet Heisley for the first time, he held another impromptu news conference on the City Hall steps in which he opined the financing plan wouldn't work, because it placed too much burden on the city.

Within an hour of the mayor's statement, Mike Heisley and Stan Meadows were met at the airport and driven to the Galt House, where old friend Tom O'Hearn had, again, rolled out the red carpet. Having freshened up, Heisley, Meadows, Norma and I walked the several blocks to Vincenzo's where the Gateway Group and Bobby Clarkson had arranged a duplicate of the Rockets' dinner.

One hundred-forty of Louisville's top business people, along with aldermen, state representatives and senators were present to meet Heisley. Many indicated their desire to participate, purchase season tickets and suites and place advertising. From the cocktail party we were ushered into the grand dining room for dinner. The governor sat next to Heisley. They quietly talked for over an hour, not even finishing their meal, when the speeches began.

Former UofL All-American Junior Bridgeman (who only a day prior had attended the mayor's blue-ribbon committee) extolled Louisville's basketball heritage and its NBA interest. The floor was given to Louisville Legend, Darrell Griffith, who enlivened the crowd with a hell-fire-and-brimstone oration premised with Louisville's need to obtain an NBA franchise. Gov. Patton presented Kentucky Colonelcies to Heisley and Meadows. At the head table, in addition to the governor, Heisley and Meadows, were Glasscock, Clarkson, Speaker of the House Jody Richards, me and the mayor. Glasscock and I periodically glanced at the mayor, who sat mute, never saying a word to Heisley and hardly speaking to anyone else.

With the dinner celebration's conclusion, Glasscock and I demanded a meeting in his law offices. The attendees were the governor, his Chief of Staff and General Counsel, the mayor, Traughber and Driskell from the City, Glasscock, Skees, Blum, Magre, Todd Blue, a few others and me. It began at 11:00 PM. As the participants collected around an enormous conference table in Frost Brown Todd, I had deliberately situated myself next to Mayor Dave, because I fully intended it to be a "come-to-Jesus" meeting in which Mayor Dave was directly confronted. I had put up with enough of Mayor Dave's duplicity. The stakes were too high for high-school antics and coy gamesmanship. For months the governor had been calling for local political leadership, and, tonight we were going to have it, one way or the other if we had to stay there all night. It had every likelihood to be an explosive meeting, to say the least.

Time elapsed with everyone being congenial and polite. No one seemed to want to get down to brass tacks. Glasscock and I hadn't insisted on the meeting to have a mutual admiration society conclave. Shortly after Glasscock called the meeting to order, I rose, looked down at Mayor Dave, pointed my index finger at him and accused him of knowingly and deliberately sabotaging the NBA effort, to which he offered a tentative denial. His equivocal reply was met with the litany of examples of his near year-long perfidy. Mayor Dave's voice quivered—he actually appeared he might cry. The governor was irate. He observed, "I sat next to a billionaire tonight, who wants to move his business to Louisville and you all can't get your act together." Glasscock performed at his best by calming the waters so that by 2:30 AM everyone, including Mayor Dave, had agreed to publicly support the plan that had been prepared and offer it to Heisley later that morning at Tricon. While Mayor Dave had requested a few changes so he could save face, there was no change in the plan.

The next morning I picked up Heisley 8:40 AM. The morning's *Courier-Journal* carried a front page story about Heisley's arrival and the Vincenzo party. The story under the headline expressed the mayor's objection to the plan that he had voiced on the City Hall steps the day prior. Heisley looked at me and laughed, saying, "What's wrong with this guy? Doesn't he know that the largest KFC franchisee in Canada used to own the Toronto NBA team?" I told Heisley that was not known by Armstrong and shouldn't be publicly mentioned, and assured him that after the previous evening's dinner, we had a long meeting with Mayor Dave and he was, now, in total support.

Everything was ready at Tricon's headquarters. As we drove up to their portico we were met with a pep band playing "We Will Rock You", homemade signs proclaiming "Louisville Wants Grizzlies," a six-foot chicken and a twenty-foot banner, "Grizzlies Say Yes to Louisville." It was an enthusiastic greeting by hundreds of Tricon employees. The occasion was immediately created affording Mayor Dave the opportunity to publicly-honor his demanded commitment of the previous evening. With Mayor Dave inescapably and publicly on-board, the private meeting, in which Louisville made its offer, began. The next morning, *The Courier-Journal* front-page article began: "It all came together in 24 hours. On Wednesday morning, Louisville Mayor Dave Armstrong rejected a financing plan for building a downtown NBA arena, calling it unworkable. At 11:00 AM yesterday, after hours of intense negotiations, he announced a financing deal had been struck."[289]

Heisley was quoted in the article: "I feel they've made a very attractive offer. I think (the arena) will be a great place for us and the University of Louisville and Rick Pitino." The vice chairman of UofL's board of trustees, Jessica Loving, endorsed the plan, stating, "From my perspective, I don't see any downside for the university. It's an opportunity to do something good for the state, the city and the university. It's a win-win situation for everybody involved." Heisley stated, "I think (the arena) will be a great place for us and the University of Louisville and Rick Pitino."[290]

Despite itself, it seemed Louisville had pulled it off. Heisley and Meadows left that Thursday afternoon satisfied and pleased with Louisville's proposal. Their destination was Memphis, Tennessee. They never returned to Louisville again. There was a reason.

While Heisley was in Memphis, on Friday night the athletic director of UofL did a one-eighty, completely distancing himself, publicly, from his prior favorable statements and the governor's and mayor's publicly-stated offer to Mike Heisley, saying that he had serious reservations about playing in a new downtown arena and further stating that the university had committed to nothing. The University's president, Shumaker, "couldn't be reached for comment," so it appeared that the athletic director was speaking for the University of Louisville and its mission to the entire community. Of course, the story was carried in the *Memphis Commercial-Appeal*—and everywhere else—and of course, the powers-that-be in Memphis and Mike Heisley knew that the University of Memphis and their new coach, John Calipari, were supportive of the NBA.

The fourth week of March — 7 days to D-Day

Feeling it important for community leaders to understand the nature and extent of Tricon's commitment, Jonathan Blum had generally revealed the nature and extent of Tricon's financial proposal to at least forty people over the previous several weeks. It was always on a need-to-know basis. The advisees had included the governor, the mayor and their immediate staffs, the mayor's select blue ribbon committee, the top officials of UofL, certain aldermen, members of both political parties, local business persons and the editorial board of *The Courier-Journal*. Every one of these leaders, even those opposed to the NBA, had been honorable and held the information in its proper confidence. Believing that his informational program should include the leaders of the local state legislative delegation, Glasscock arranged a meeting on Saturday morning, March 17, with the delegation chairman, Larry Clark, state representative Mary Lou Marzian and state senator David Karem. I had expressed reservations about such a meeting, because Larry Clark had completely flip-flopped during the Rockets effort and refused on repeated occasions to meet with me. He had even declined to meet with a life-long friend of his, who was active in the Gateway Group. All of this left me with a bad feeling about Clark. I wasn't sure about his character on the issue. Glasscock disagreed, feeling that they should know and could be swayed, particularly since the governor, the mayor and so many others were on board. The meeting was held that Saturday morning. I did not attend.

The following Monday morning, March 19, Clark and Marzian called a press conference, announcing to the world (and Memphis) that Tricon's commitment to the Grizzlies was $100 million for arena and team naming-rights.

The justification for the announcement was to inform the public that none of the Tricon $100 million was going to the arena's costs—it was all going to Heisley for the naming rights of the arena and the team. They thought the public needed to know this, despite the fact had been publicly stated on dozens of occasions and included in numerous *Courier-Journal* articles. What hadn't been publicly revealed was the dollar amount of Tricon's commitment.

There's no way to describe the adverse effect of this announcement revealing the dollar amount of Tricon's proposal other than to say at that critical moment it was the dumbest thing that anyone could have possibly done. In reality, it was beyond dumb—it was literally stupefying. It would be like Eisenhower calling a press conference the day before D-Day to tell the world (and the Axis powers) that the Allies were going to swarm Omaha and Utah Beaches the next day. Or a union leader calling a press conference and explaining what his union would demand at the next day's bargaining table. The major and most critical piece of Louisville's offer had been given away and publicized worldwide. Because of the largesse of Tricon's offer and the national presence of Kentucky Fried Chicken, the news went all over the country, being carried in every major newspaper from Vancouver, B.C. to New York, from Anaheim to Memphis to New Orleans. Someone even said it was covered in many European newspapers.

Now, Memphis or any other city knew exactly what they had to do to beat Louisville. Who in their right mind would do something so foolish? From Larry Clark's position as a local labor leader, it made absolutely no sense, because the local labor unions whose members would construct the arena were the immediate beneficiaries with hundreds of jobs resulting from the expenditure of $200 million.

My mind wandered back to Stern's jocular admonition: "Bruce, as you go through this, try to act like you're not from Kentucky." Stern's effort at comedy had now morphed into a tragedy. Kentucky had made a fool of itself, again. Shortly thereafter, from solid and credible sources I learned the real damage of their actions. Prior to the Clark/Marzian scrapbook collection entry, the FedEx offer to the Grizzlies had amounted to only between $40-50 million. Now, being knowledgeable of the financial extent of Tricon's offer, FedEx had time to equalize or approach Tricon's offer. And that's exactly what happened.

By mid-week following the Clark/Marzian debacle, after FedEx checked with its major institutional and significant block shareholders, they increased their offer to $92 million for naming rights. Now due to the breach of confidence, Memphis had a superior offer. Both cities could provide an arena with tax increment financing and a major corporate investor with reasonably similar dollar offers, but Memphis had a private minority investment approaching $100 million and Louisville didn't. Even if it had wanted to (and it didn't), there wasn't time for Tricon to enter a bidding war.

The final few days were spent with the Pursuit Team frenetically calling all over America looking for minority investment. It was an eighteen hour-a-day effort, with limited success. Blue succeeded in obtaining a $10-15 million oral commitment from family friends in Chicago, who had other financial interests in the Louisville area. There were other possibilities, but we couldn't find enough. Thursday, March 22 at midday, Blum decided to call Bill Laurie. Amazingly, Laurie had some interest resulting in a Pursuit Team conference call with him on Friday, March 23 at noon.

Attention was also focused on the Hornets; they were still intending to file application to transfer. On Friday, March 23, The Wagman remained confident Louisville would be included in Wooldridge's final decision to name two cities. It would be Louisville and Memphis. But the tenor of his voice was peculiar; something was going to happen on Saturday, which he couldn't discuss, but might have a major bearing on what would occur on March 26.

I went to bed Friday evening with a feeling of unease. The Ruppians, averse to change and fearful of the unknown, had made their play. It was a damaging play, to be sure. Inescapably, for some reason, I felt they weren't finished. I was right.

48 hours to D-Day, enter Rick Pitino

Saturday morning, March 24, Blum was informed by Wooldridge there was going to be a conclave between him, Heisley and Stern. Wooldridge had been non-specific, but allowed Blum to believe it would be a critical discussion. On Saturday evening, The Wagman delivered the news. Neither team could select two cities. They each had to pick one and Heisley had to make his selection first—by no later than 9:00 AM on Monday.

Two days before Heisley's decision, another sideswipe on Louisville's NBA odyssey occurred. The Saturday March 24 *Courier-Journal* carried a front page headline: "UofL may not be in NBA deal." Within the article was the first quote from UofL's new coach, Rick Pitino: "Our home is Freedom Hall...that's where all the All-Americans played and that's where we're going to play."

Glasscock and I both found it strange that a newly-employed coach would interject himself into the middle of a public policy matter. It was hard to believe that Pitino would be opposed to the NBA, because he would be objecting to the very dream of his players. The other side of the proposition was that Pitino didn't want any competition for the public's attention. Pitino didn't have much else to say—this time around. Of course, at that time we didn't know, but both Wooldridge and Heisley did. Memphis' collegiate coach, John Calipari, was fully-supportive of the NBA coming to Memphis. Pitino's statement of non-cooperation was carried nationwide, because the transfer of the Grizzlies and possibly the Hornets was a national story. Thankfully we had been given advance notice of the latest Jurich/Pitino announcement. Upon advising the governor of the predicament, we obtained the following statement from him, which was also included in the sub-headline: "The arena can move forward without a commitment from the

University."

The roller-coaster ride continued. Down, then up again. On March 24, 2001, the story about the largest KFC Canadian franchisee (345 stores) having previously owned the Toronto Raptors broke in the *Memphis Flyer* newspaper. My Vanderbilt snoops were all over it, calling me in the afternoon to let me know that the word was out, all over Memphis, that Louisville had won, because of the KFC international involvement.

24 hours to D-Day

With 24 hours to go, Sunday, March 25, was action-packed, beginning with a Blum brainstorm. He located a Kentucky Fried Chicken franchisee in the Dominican Republic and arranged to deliver several boxes of their very best to Heisley, who was holed-up in his estate there, with his wife and Meadows.

Then came competing newspaper stories. The Sunday edition of *The New York Times* was reporting that Memphis had won. Heisley assured, in a phone call, that this was erroneous—no decision had been made. We were pleased with the lead article in *The Memphis Commercial-Appeal* which opined that the Memphis financing plan wouldn't work. By midday on Sunday, Glasscock, Blum and I felt that if we could find more private investment we could still win, and were anxiously awaiting Laurie's return call to Blum with what had been promised to be a creative offer. *The Courier-Journal's* Chris Poynter called to reveal that a fellow *Commercial-Appeal* reporter had learned that Pitt Hyde was lowering his financial commitment, believing that one-half of the Grizzlies weren't worth $90 million.

By 4:00 PM in the afternoon on Sunday we had Laurie's offer. He'd purchase the Grizzlies for $225 million and bring it to Louisville, if there was 30% local investment. The hitch—his investment would be a loan at 7% interest to be repaid from the team's revenue stream. He wanted the right to operate the arena in Louisville and the right to receive Tricon's naming rights fees. This was utterly ridiculous, but we still had to negotiate with him.

That evening, between 8:00 and 9:00 PM, a fiery conference call with Laurie's attorney, Dick Thomas, and his COO (Brent Karafiuk) was conducted. On our end of the phone were Blum, Glasscock, Bruce Traughber, Todd Blue and me. Laurie's lawyer reiterated the offer. Upon being told it was unacceptable, he wouldn't budge. We were getting nowhere. After blathering around for about forty-five minutes, I told Thomas that his client's offer was ridiculous and absolutely the wrong way for his client to enter the Louisville market — with a $157 million loan, expecting repayment at 7% interest from the team's operation. Thomas challenged me that I was ungrateful, and the response was that these people on this end of the phone might be from Kentucky, but we weren't pulled to work on a horse-drawn pumpkin truck. And if that is your final offer, it's rejected, completely.

The call ended. There was no way that I or anyone else on the phone could support such a stupid proposal — it couldn't possibly be justified, publicly or otherwise. I remembered Heisley's description of his Laurie/Thomas meeting and was dissatisfied with myself that Heisley concluded his meeting in less time that we concluded our phone call. Laurie was out. Plus, even if we had agreed to the offer, I seriously doubted Heisley would have sold his franchise to Laurie anyway.

Twelve hours remained before Heisley made his decision. We had done all we could. We had fought the good fight. The decision was someone else's. Somehow, each of us needed a good night's sleep. I didn't get one, nor did anyone else.

D-Day: March 26, 2001

Each of us, whomever we are, have had and will have dramatic days in our lives. Each of us begin such a day in our own special way. Some of us pray, some of us hug our spouses, some of us gaze at pictures of our children or grandchildren, some of us go to our parents' gravesites for reflection and communion with our past, and some of us try to get a breakfast down even though we can't taste it. On March 26, 2001, I was no different, except I did them all.

The morning's headline in *The Courier-Journal* was accurate: "Louisville & Memphis make final pitches for NBA team." The story began, "Yesterday there was a blizzard of international phone calls between Heisley, his lawyer and officials in Louisville and Memphis." While correct, it was only half the story of the previous day.

It was a crisp and windy morning as I drove to the Tricon headquarters where the Pursuit Team was collecting. Everyone was to be either there or available, except Mayor Dave. He was out of the country on a junket to Israel, something that politicians seem to live for and can't be passed up. We all, including County Judge Jackson, collected in the executive suite while the press and hundreds of Tricon employees were in the main lobby awaiting the news, which would be delivered at 9:00 AM.

At 9:00 sharp Blum's phone rang. As we each rose and stood around Blum's desk, the message was quickly read on Blum's face—Heisley had chosen Memphis.

Each of us, whomever we are, also deal with the immediacy of a rejection in different ways. I remember sitting on Blum's couch, looking around the room and thinking how everyone was so obviously numb with exhaustion. In a few moments I got up and walked into the hall. Time for a little private time. My cell phone rang—Mike Heisley was calling.

I can count on one hand the number of times that I have been on a phone call with another grown man when both of us were in tears. The decision was "among the most difficult I had ever made," Mike began. He admitted to changing his mind four times on Sunday. Upon awakening that Monday morning he had determined to select Louisville, but changed his mind at the last minute. It boiled down to a money decision. If he had made the decision from his heart he would have chosen Louisville. His wife, Agnes, had suggested a rhetorical question: "Isn't one's heart more important than one's money?" His reference to Agnes brought Mike's virtual breakdown on the phone. I remember saying to him, "Mike, a man as good as you will be blessed whatever your decision, I just don't know what's going to happen here." He asked me to thank everyone in Louisville for their effort and their hospitality and expressed his sincere best wishes to me and Norma. I said, "Mike, will I hear from you again?" and he responded, "Yes," and I did.

It was now necessary to go to the lobby and tell the press and the hundreds assembled that Louisville had lost. We collectively agreed to do this with as much pride and determination as possible; easier said than done. We did the best we could. My Teddy Roosevelt quote that had been given to me by the late Wendell Cherry after the Buffalo Braves transfer loss, years ago, was about all I could handle without melting in front of the cameras. Teddy had said it all: Far better it is to dare mighty things to win glorious triumphs than to take rank with those spirits who neither enjoy much nor suffer much because they live in that grey twilight that knows neither victory nor defeat.

We reconvened in Blum's office and the decision was made—Blum would contact Wooldridge, immediately—the Hornets still had the option to select Louisville and it needed to be pursued. Upon being contacted about the revised plan, the governor agreed. After several calls between Blum and Wooldridge, I, again, went out to sit on the front steps of the building. Being completely exhausted, I needed to collect my thoughts. Plus, I had a strange sensation that something very peculiar was about to happen; things just weren't adding up.

At 4:00 PM, the Hornets selected Memphis, too! What in the hell was going on? In a less-than-pleasant phone call at 5:00 PM, I requested an explanation from Stern and Granik. There was none other than total confusion. Stern assured me that Louisville was not out of the equation. An NBA committee would have to sort through the day's decisions. He asked me for a private letter setting forth Louisville's position. For four hours, I developed the letter. It was FedExed to Stern the next day.

The "Swap"

It took awhile to figure out why the Hornets would knowingly apply for transfer to the same city as the Grizzlies. From the outside looking in it seemed ridiculous. But it wasn't.

Heisley had been upset upon learning in early March that Wooldridge was intruding on his opportunity in Memphis. But, in fairness, Wooldridge had been considering Memphis for months longer than Heisley so actually the reverse was true—Wooldridge felt that Heisley was intruding on his opportunity.

Somewhere along the line in early-mid March, the idea of a swap had been floated, where both Heisley and Wooldridge would pick the same city and then swap ownership, with the Heisley-owned Hornets staying in Charlotte and Wooldridge taking the Grizzlies to the new city. In some measure, a swap was a good deal for everyone:

Heisley would obtain an immediate title contender with the Hornets, the league would have new ownership in Charlotte and Wooldridge could get out of Dodge (Charlotte). I recalled the notion of UNCC President, Dr. Woodward, that the only way the Hornets would stay in Charlotte was with new ownership. So, the idea of a swap was a win-win-win for everybody. Heisley had even quietly slipped into Charlotte to scout out the Hornets predicament there and Meadows had done some due diligence, but in the end the swap idea was far too iffy. Heisley had a sure shot in either Louisville or Memphis, and if the arena referendum didn't pass in Charlotte he was confined to a city with an outmoded arena for years to come. Heisley needed more certainty in his personal estate planning and a financially solid minority partner situation. I remembered his earliest comment, "When you see me you'll understand, I'm too fat."

So Heisley rejected the swap idea, but Wooldridge was still trying his best to cooperate with the NBA. He hoped that Stern would intervene and somehow effectuate the swap, despite Heisley's rejection of the concept. This hope was further emboldened because Stern had ruled that only one city could be selected by each franchise—but Heisley would go first. So, Wooldridge saw his opportunity—he would select whatever city Heisley selected.

These are my beliefs, based upon no admission from Heisley, Wooldridge or Stern. But it is the only scenario that makes any sense. If Heisley had chosen Louisville, so would have Wooldridge.

That weekend my dear teenaged granddaughter, Anna, came to Louisville. Her mom, Alexis, knew I was deeply hurt—the visit and a dinner with her and Norma at Darryl's (our old stomping ground) was wonderful. The next night the T-Man paid a visit to Barner's house. As I looked at his wonderful big green eyes and his hope for the future, I could only wish— only if! Tristan, Barner and I awakened on Sunday morning, April 1st— April Fool's Day. How appropriate.

For the third time in my life, I had seen Louisville lose the NBA Derby, once by a length with the Rockets and twice by a neck with the Buffalo Braves and now the Grizzlies. For the third time in my life, Kennedy's quote following the Bay of Pigs disaster came to mind: "Victory finds a hundred fathers, but defeat is an orphan." For the third time in my life Louisville had flirted with the NBA and remained Waiting for Godot.

CHAPTER TWELVE

It's Not Over 'Til It's Over

Wasn't it really over? How much national awareness of failed local leadership could Louisville take? How much frustration could I and the Pursuit Team take? They were good questions, and they required answers.

For whatever it was worth, dozens upon dozens of people had thanked me for the effort. The phone rang off the hook. All manner of Joes and Jills —the kind of people that made America great—were upset that Louisville had lost. Each, in their own way, sought to express their appreciation for the endeavor and their wish that Louisville would awaken. Those expressions meant a great deal to me and they still do today.

The editor of *The Courier-Journal* had captured the real essence of the problem, one of unmitigated duplicity and failed leadership. Mayor Armstrong was positioning himself to run for Metro Mayor, and the newspaper opined: "Armstrong again failed to lead forcefully in one direction or the other on the NBA arena proposal. In fact, while supporting it publicly, he also privately assured opponents that he would make sure it wouldn't happen. In the last round of negotiations, he managed within 24 hours both to blindside his supposed allies with an 11th hour press conference in opposition and then to take credit for the terms of the final bid. A neat trick? Yes. Good leadership? No."

But did it really make any difference at this point? In mid-April, Stern and I revisited by phone. I expressed regret for my anger on the evening of the March 26 franchise transfer decisions. My friend was never more magnanimous, saying, "I would have been surprised if you weren't angry." After observing that Louisville's misfortune had been illogical, he noted that shortly the Hornets would be withdrawing their application to Memphis and Charlotte will go through with the June 5 referendum. The point was that it might be too early to quit.

April in Louisville became May, but the healing hadn't set in. As Stern had said several weeks prior, on May 3, Wooldridge withdrew his transfer application to Memphis. A few days later Monarchos won the Derby in the second fastest time in history. The favorite, Point Given, was 7th, proving once again that in the Derby as well as other things favorites can and do lose. Everything was just as it always was in Louisville, slowly moving into the summer, after the rousing Derby festivities.

I hadn't spoken with The Wagman in several months. On Tuesday afternoon May 8, he called. In his judgment the Charlotte referendum would fail and if it did, under no circumstances would the Hornets remain in Charlotte. He bemoaned his client's predicament. It was difficult to be charitable, as I noted we weren't the idiots that chose Memphis—it was his client. The Wagman wasn't surprised with my blunt statement; he knew that I didn't have a habit of mincing words. He agreed his client had made a bad decision. Was Louisville still interested in the Hornets, if the referendum failed? Answer: "How many times do we have to go through this, Craig?" The Wagman's answer, "Only one more time if the referendum fails."

Like a bad penny, the NBA wouldn't go away. The next day at 3:30 in the afternoon a voice from the past called—Mike Goldberg from Houston. He and Carol had watched the Derby on television, thought about us and just wanted to say hello. After the difficulties he and I had experienced, the thoughtfulness of his call and his advice that followed was appreciated: "Stay the course if the Charlotte referendum fails. Don't forget how far down the road Louisville is."

Goldberg's point was well taken—Louisville was far down the road. That was always the view of those directly involved with the NBA. The problem wasn't the NBA, it was Louisville, and it was exceedingly difficult to help Louisville understand the extent and importance of the enormous NBA economic opportunity. Louisville just couldn't seem to take that one last step and join the elite cities that are the world's economic hub, by rejecting its ingrained fear of the unknown and embracing change and its challenges.

On March 26, I had asked Heisley if I would hear from him again and he promised, "Yes." At 5:00 PM on May 15, I did.

He was exasperated with the lack of progress in Memphis, professing, "I've made a terrible mistake in selecting Memphis. I should have listened to you and Agnes." Then he asked, "Could Louisville handle sloppy seconds?" I responded, "I don't know, but we'd try, only if it was absolutely for sure." I asked if he wanted me to call Blum, and he responded, "Not, yet, but maybe soon." I encouraged Mike to call me anytime, morning, noon or night.

Within two days *The Courier-Journal's* Chris Poynter told me his reporter friends in Memphis were concerned—Memphis was getting scared and "...word was beginning to leak that they're going to lose it to Louisville." I couldn't reveal Heisley's call to Poynter, but maybe Yogi Berra was right. Within a few more days, there was worse news for Memphis. Stern had overruled FedEx's desired name change to the Memphis Express. Things got progressively worse. A lawsuit had been filed against the Memphis financing proposal and the local court had ruled that the deal was unconstitutional. To make matters worse, a substantial grassroots anti-NBA yard-sign campaign had begun, which was receiving considerable publicity. Stern and the NBA owners committee had gone to "the City by the Big Muddy" and delivered the message—an arena deal had to be in place in two weeks, or else. Was this the interregnum or was it over?

Hopeless in Charlotte

After months of unrestrained bellicosity, warring factions and vituperative political intrigue, on Tuesday, June 5 the Charlotte voters went to the polls to vote on the referendum package that by then had been increased to $342 million of capital projects, including the Hornets arena. The bundled projects were trounced by a 57-43% landslide. It was a resounding defeat for Wooldridge and Shinn.

Only a week prior to the referendum the Hornets pro-arena advertising campaign seemed to have been well-received. Polling data was predicting up to a 13 point approval margin. Additionally, the Hornets had made a spirited run in the NBA playoffs, which re-kindled the city's past pride of the team. However, as a result of an incredible set of events, within a week the polling margin had evaporated despite the opposition being outspent 30-to-1.

When the Charlotte mayor vetoed a higher minimum wage for city workers, previously approved by the City Council, African-American voters were offended. As a result, the voter turnout in predominantly black precincts was less than 20%. It was reported that 61% of the African-American voters cast ballots against the arena.[291] Just as UNCC's President Dr. Woodward had told us at the Broecker's dinner several months prior, the state legislators were aggravated over the Charlotte in-fighting, the Governor was uninterested, and the Hornets had fully financed the public referendum at the price of $349,000. Further, Mecklenburg County officials opposed the arena and had voiced that opposition in the week before the referendum by voting to acquire the proposed arena land as a public park. As one pundit was quoted in *The Charlotte Observer*, "...for the arena opponents it was as if the planets all lined up at once."

The coup de grace was incredibly poor political leadership from Charlotte's mayor. In a day-after article entitled, "McCrory criticized for lack of leadership, passiveness on arena issue,"[292] a lengthy description was offered of the Republican three-term mayor's passive and vacillating participation. Many didn't know whether he was for or against the referendum. The article contained a particularly incisive observation (which sounded disturbingly familiar): "The mayor has to articulate a vision for the city. He doesn't seem to have a whole lot of interest in this issue. He never took the lead. He never identified why the arena was so important for the community. He never engaged the community in the process. He was a mere passive observer."

In the subsequent summer months the Charlotte mayor's lack of simple leadership would serve to form the basis for Wooldridge's position with Stern that it was hopeless in Charlotte. From several conversations with Wooldridge, it was abundantly clear that he now realized political leadership was the critical factor in the success of an arena debate. Wooldridge would look for such leadership, wherever the Hornets were to transfer.

By 8:00 that evening calls about another Louisville NBA opportunity began to arrive from everywhere. The Pursuit Team was summoned and a meeting was scheduled for 9:30 the next morning. Caution was determined to be the immediate best course of action. Blum volunteered to contact Wooldridge, but the Hornets beat Blum to the punch. At 3:45 that afternoon The Wagman called to report that Wooldridge was to meet with Stern on Thursday, June 7. The meeting's motif—"I've done this your way and lost, now I'm going to do it my way." It was described by The Wagman as a "declaration of independence." Later that evening Wooldridge confirmed his intentions to Blum.

Here we go again.

Two days after the Charlotte referendum, *The Charlotte Observer* carried a major headline: "Eager Louisville already tapping at Hornets door." Pursuit Team member Ed Glasscock had been quoted as saying, "We're interested in opening negotiations, but we have to get first a green light from Charlotte that they're interested, and then the blessing of the NBA commissioner." Ed had gotten a little too excited and spoken out of school. The Wagman called that morning, reiterating Wooldridge's request to begin negotiations but (referencing the day's headline) they had to be out of the press.

To initiate the discussions, The Wagman requested a copy of our Grizzlies proposal. After another Pursuit Team meeting, that afternoon an e-mail was sent to The Wagman in which the Pursuit Team faithfully promised to avoid negotiating in the press.[293]

With the approach to the upcoming negotiations being agreed upon, immediate attention was given to delivering the Grizzlies proposal to The Wagman. Glasscock made private contact with the Governor's office. There was no objection to re-energizing the Grizzlies offer for the Hornets, although there was the continuing concern about local political leadership and a new, but very subterranean concern—the rumor-mill of a Pitino Factor.

Grizzlies proposal offered to Hornets

On Saturday, June 9 the Grizzlies proposal was sent to The Wagman with a major caveat: "Pursuant to our 06/08/01 phone conversation, the following is a bullet point list for your client's consideration. This is 'framed' based upon the assumption that your clients are considering an immediate transfer to Louisville for the immediate 2001-02 season as opposed to a subsequent year, because with the elapse of 1/2 year, criteria and public positioning can change in many ways."

Wooldridge was satisfied with the Grizzlies proposal. We were off to a pretty good start. There was one remaining question.

Will the Hornets transfer now or wait a year?

This was the immediate question. A summer transfer made perfect sense from the Hornets standpoint. With the referendum loss and the subsequent diatribe in Charlotte, the Hornets were on the verge of losing millions of dollars if they played another whole season in Charlotte. It was the Pursuit Team's notion that an immediate transfer of the Hornets would be more achievable and far more preferable in Louisville than another prolonged negotiation with a transfer occurring the following year. From Louisville's standpoint, we already had a politically-approved proposal that had been offered to the Grizzlies. Any delay would afford the opportunity for another city to get involved and for the Ruppians to effectively organize.

A flurry of work followed over the next several weeks, culminating in The Wagman's call on Tuesday, June 19. Wooldridge's preference was a transfer to Louisville for the upcoming season, but there was genuine concern that the Commissioner's office wasn't satisfied the Hornets were hopeless in Charlotte. The next day, in a conversation with the deputy commissioner, the only evidence offered that the Hornets might need one more year in Charlotte germinated from his personal witness of passionate support from the, albeit, small crowds that attended the playoff games in Charlotte. That evening Wooldridge called Blum directing his thoughts to us being ready in Louisville next year. Realizing it was most likely, in view of the extremely short time-frame, Stern would not approve the Hornets mid-summer transfer to Louisville

On June 30 Wooldridge agreed on a one-year lease for the upcoming season with the Charlotte Coliseum, at a price of $400,000. Profits from parking and concessions were to be split evenly between the team and the arena with the Hornets getting 20% of the first $2 million in Coliseum profits and 80% of any profit over $2 million. With the hope of the Hornets transfer to Louisville in the upcoming season dashed, the penultimate question became precise. Could Louisville successfully circumnavigate yet another prolonged delay of an NBA owner's decision-making to transfer his team?

My thoughts went back to that phone conversation with Heisley on February 27 when he said if he had to make the transfer decision on March 1, he would have chosen Louisville. Clearly, Louisville had lost the Grizzlies because of the extra twenty-six days the NBA had given Heisley. I couldn't help but recall the trauma of the ensuing four weeks in March. All the planning and preparation, all the work, meetings, the Vincenzo's dinner that was such a success — and Mayor Dave's repeated fumbles. Then there was the eruption of previously-secret Memphis and the two Kentucky state legislators giving it all away by revealing the Tricon naming-rights offer.

My thoughts invariably returned to the continuing concern about Louisville and its fear of the unknown. How would this diabolical fear be ridden around the track in another episode of the odyssey?

Weren't we riding down the same slippery slope all over again? But then, as so many times in the odyssey, thoughts would turn to the T-Man and all the little Tristans whose bright eyes yearned for a future in a progressive and dynamic city. In large measure, that was at stake, which made the stakes high.

Then there's the ever-present Robert F. Kennedy refrain, borrowed from Samuel Ullman's 1934 prose entitled "Youth":

"Youth [is] not a time of life, but a state of mind....a predominance of courage over timidity, of the appetite for adventure over the love of ease." There was no choice — we had to try again, no matter how foolhardy it seemed.

So what do we do? Anything. Something. So long as we just don't sit there. If we screw it up, start over. Try something else. If we wait until we've satisfied all the uncertainties, it will be too late.

Lee Iacocca

CHAPTER THIRTEEN

The End of Louisville's NBA Odyssey

Lonesome in Queens

On September 18, 1952, five days before Richard Nixon's "Checkers" speech, thirteen months after Alex Groza and Ralph Beard were arrested for bribery in Chicago, and a few months after Adolph Rupp was excoriated by New York Supreme Court Justice Saul Streit, the third son of second generation Sicilian immigrant Rosario "Sal" Pitino and his wife Charlotte was born. His name was Rick Pitino.

Of his early years little has been reported, but what has reveals a profound similarity with Adolph Rupp's childhood in Kansas. The Cambrian Heights, Queens Pitinos were a dual-income family, Sal a building super and Charlotte a hospital administrator (Bellevue). Both commuted to work into Manhattan on the early train before dawn, returning home on the late train, after dark. Their two other sons were much older than Rick, Robert by ten years, Ron by eight. They were seldom at home. So, in Queens, Rick Pitino, like Adolph Rupp in rural Kansas a half-century earlier, grew up lonely "...and alone as he ate breakfast in the morning, alone as he walked to grade school in the winter and frightened as he walked home in the dark to an empty house."[294] For years this little and lonesome latch-key kid lived his childhood in quiet solitude, learning to do most everything for himself and by himself. Like Rupp, this aloneness would have both an enormous positive and negative influence upon his life—it would make him single-minded yet self-absorbed, determined yet angry, and wiley yet duplicitous. By the age of 14, Pitino had found a second family (as had Adolph Rupp)—the basketball team at Oyster Bay's St. Dominick High. This family would become his life, his very reason for being. He envisaged, from the early dawn until the late night, his future through the prism of a basketball. The game became a life-long obsession in which he had to succeed.

Along with his intense single-mindedness was an equally intense and latent anger that embraced this feisty point guard as he enrolled in the University of Massachusetts with a basketball scholarship the same year Dan Issel became a Kentucky Colonel. By his sophomore year that anger boiled over. He was dismissed from the team for an uncontrollable temper that culminated in a fight with senior guard Mike Pagliara. Pitino couldn't accept the fact that Pagliara had been chosen as the team's starting point guard. After this disruption, Pitino's coach began toying with and ignoring him. He was required to be "...always last in line to eat, to board the bus, to run the mile...."[295] In the process he stoically began to realize the coach was "pushing his button" and from that life's lesson it has been written that he would learn how to play other people off against each other, a character trait "...he would draw upon time and time again to motivate players"[296] once his own coaching career began.

After a year's suspension, he returned to the UMass team and, with the promise of greater self-control, he oriented his play to more of a team style. By his senior year he had become the team's scoring leader and by his teammates was awarded the moniker, "Slick Rick."

Upon graduation and with the avowed intent on becoming a head coach before his 25th birthday, his first job was a graduate assistantship at the University of Hawaii. It began with considerable flash and dash. Around the time the High Priest and I were having dinner at Mr. A's in San Diego (discussed in Chapter 5) he had wowed the islanders by successfully recruiting three of the top high school players from New York City to attend college in Hawaii, 12,000 miles from home. This overnight success raised a few eyebrows within the coaching fraternity. Pitino's head coaching goal seemed within reach.

The first big success in his career game was short-lived, being rudely interrupted by a television commercial for a Honolulu car dealership, featuring several of Pitino's recruits. Soon thereafter, the lightning bolt that had flashed across Hawaii's sunny skies brought Adolph Rupp-like storm clouds into Slick Rick's young life. When the inevitable NCAA investigation began, Hawaii's head coach "...asserted Pitino had betrayed him by going to the university president and angling for the head coaching job while the investigation was still going on."[297]

But the University's approach to his in-your-face, Rupp-like determination was far different from that demonstrated by UK when Adolph Rupp returned from the criminal proceedings in New York. Hawaii's dissatisfied university officials encouraged Pitino to move on after the NCAA uncovered 68 rule violations resulting in a two-year probation for the university's basketball program.

After moving on, Pitino's *mea culpa* began with his marriage to Joanne, his high school sweetheart, quickly followed by employment from new Syracuse coach Jim Boeheim. For Rick Pitino, virtually everything in his career became bells and whistles for the next nineteen years.

At the same time John Y. Brown and I were endeavoring to transfer the Buffalo Braves to Louisville and Kentucky's governor and I were meeting with NBA Commissioner Larry O'Brien to facilitate the Braves transfer to Louisville, Rick Pitino was named head coach of Boston University in 1978. Five years later he became an assistant coach to Hubie Brown at the New York Knicks. There he stayed for two years until being selected head coach at Providence College in 1985. After Providence's stirring run in the NCAA he was selected *The Sporting News* Coach of the Year in 1987. Pitino's biographer, Billy Reynolds, noted that he "...manipulated players all the time while at Providence."[298] Immediately he seized upon another opportunity for advancement, becoming head coach of the New York Knicks in 1987. Instead of remaining in New York to finish his Knick's revampment, he accepted the challenge to clean up a beleaguered and NCAA-penalized program as head coach of the University of Kentucky in 1989.

As had occurred at Hawaii nearly fifteen years prior, his first impact recruit at UK, Jamal Mashburn, came from the streets of New York City, being signed almost immediately on November 8, 1989. His next half dozen years at UK were meteoric. He became a rock star in Lexington. After turning down reported (some not confirmed and presumed rumored) NBA head coaching offers from the Los Angeles Lakers, Atlanta Hawks, Indiana Pacers, Los Angeles Clippers and the New Jersey Nets, his UK team won the NCAA championship. A year later, after producing a best-selling book entitled *Success is a Choice*, on May 7, 1997, he bolted UK for the presidency and head coaching position with the Boston Celtics. In little more than twenty years, Sal and Charlotte's youngest son had reached the apex of basketball—head coach and president of the most fabled basketball program in the world—the Boston Celtics. It seemed the little latchkey kid's dream had come true.

Contrary to the title of his book, with the Celtics success wasn't a choice for Pitino, nor was it destined. Like Rupp, Pitino's career had always been about Rick Pitino, and wherever he has coached, the cult of his personality had become more important than anything else. But at the helm of the Celtics, the cult of personality wasn't nearly as important as were the players, the Celtic tradition, or the game itself, none of which he had anything to do with. After a 102-146 record in 3 1/2 seasons and after being slashed to ribbons by the Boston press, the Celtics fans and the players, on January 8, 2001 Rick Pitino quit, cold turkey. This was the very day after Ray Wooldridge honored his prior commitment to me and publicly announced he intended to apply for transfer of the Charlotte Hornets on March 1. Rick Pitino had miserably failed in the greatest opportunity of his life. He couldn't command center stage amid the imposing Celtic tradition and his efforts to do so had made him the laughingstock of the NBA.

The mandated return to collegiate coaching was accompanied by much fanfare and self-promotion. Featured was the daunting question—where would Rick Pitino go? Would he rescue the illicit collegiate program at Las Vegas (UNLV)? Would he rehabilitate the Wolverine's days of glory at Ann Arbor? Was the Los Angeles pond too big for him to receive the requisite fame by returning UCLA to its Wooden-era greatness? Would he be accorded a helicopter ride to his first press conference at UCLA, amid the competing sports stories of the Dodgers spring training camp or the Lakers march to another NBA World Championship?

When the decision was made, the helicopter ride would occur in Louisville, Kentucky. Whatever the fun and joy of that helicopter ride, it was all lost on UK fans, who despised him for leaving Lexington and that hatred had doubled upon his acceptance of the UofL position. But it was a dramatic stage upon which to walk, a perfect glove for Rick Pitino's hand —the return of UofL to its national collegiate basketball preeminence.

Rick Pitino, like Adolph Rupp, was an obsessed individual who was unrelentingly determined to achieve personal success and fame. A most poignant examination of Rick Pitino the person was carried in the February 26, 1996 issue of *Sports Illustrated*. It was entitled, "A Man Possessed." An equally appropriate title might have been, "Unbridled Ambition." All those involved with the Pursuit Team and Louisville's NBA odyssey should have read and re-read this article. None, to my knowledge, did. As the events of the next eight months would unfold, the unbridled personal ambition of that driven former latchkey kid was to play a large role in the sinking of Louisville's NBA odyssey, preventing Louisville from becoming the 29th American city in the central hub of the world's economy.

The inside story of what happened is astounding.

The Pitino Factor

The Pursuit Team directed immediate attention to UofL's president John Shumaker. At 4:00 PM on June 19, 2001 Blum, Glasscock, Blue and I met with Dr. Shumaker and UofL Board of Trustee's chairwoman, Jessica Loving. It was a good meeting, made better by Shumaker's pronouncement of his willingness to and excitement about initiating discussions with the Hornets ownership. At the meeting's inception it seemed as though the UofL president was going to assume control of the University's negotiation with the Hornets and its public positioning for a new downtown arena.

But as the meeting progressed and the discussion gravitated to Rick Pitino, Dr. Shumaker appeared perplexed. Believing that Pitino would probably oppose the Hornets transfer to Louisville, he felt we needed to develop a structure around which his opposition could be neutralized. He asked for our thoughts and suggestions about his self-described "Pitino Factor" and how it could best be handled by him. As the discussion developed, Dr. Shumaker's favored idea was to form a joint, ad hoc committee of the Board of Trustees and the Athletic Association, which he would chair for the purpose of bringing the deal home for the university and the city. The Pursuit Team agreed with the idea and offered its assistance on an as requested basis.

Upon reflection it was painfully obvious—during the June 19 meeting, Dr. Shumaker was less than confident of his ability to exert the required executive leadership vis-a-vis the potentially-burgeoning Pitino Factor. Indeed, there was abundant evidence that he was still bewildered by the jock mentality pervading the university, something that hadn't been a factor in his previous collegiate management experience. The Pursuit Team collectively agreed that Shumaker's doubts were of concern. If Pitino was going to oppose the NBA, the possible delay of their decision to transfer until March, 2002 would provide a full opportunity for him to lead the Ruppians into effective opposition. Time was not our ally. Plus, the Board of Aldermen would be gearing up for the Metro Council election in 2002. The politicization of the process replete with the requirement of campaign contributions, as had occurred in Charlotte's referendum, was of even deeper concern.

As had been done so many times over the past several years, on the evening of June 19, 2001, I occupied my office chair in deep thought. Of all the confusing exigencies in all the years of Louisville's NBA odyssey, the most confounding was The Pitino Factor. Was Dr. Shumaker right? Was Rick Pitino really going to oppose the Hornets transfer to Louisville? The questions abounded: How could a man who had experienced his own immense personal and financial success in the profession of basketball be opposed to others doing the same thing with their lives in Louisville? It made no more sense than it would for Louisville's pre-eminent heart surgeon, Laman Gray, to oppose Dr. Michael DeBakey relocating from Houston to Louisville.

How was it possible for a man who had publicly dedicated his collegiate coaching career to teaching and inspiring young men to excel in their own lives and reach for their life's dream of playing in the NBA be opposed to an NBA team transferring to Louisville? It made no more sense than it would for UofL's medical school dean to be opposed to world-renowned hand and heart surgeons practicing medicine in downtown Louisville.

How was it possible for Rick Pitino to trash the Charlotte Hornets or their ownership when their All-Star, Jamal Mashburn, and their swiftly-improving center, Jamal Magloire, were recruited and taught by him at UK? It made no sense. Weren't they examples he could show to recruits, right in downtown Louisville, of his ability to prepare a collegiate player for the NBA? By opposing the NBA, wouldn't he be damaging his ability to recruit such future stars at UofL and providing unnecessary cannon-fodder for other collegiate coaches who would assert that after Pitino's failure at the Celtics, he had "burned his NBA bridges?"

Surely a man like Pitino, with both collegiate and professional experience, realized the magnitude of the economic benefit NBA basketball had brought to America's mid-sized cities during his coaching career. Surely he would be aware of the economic spin-off of an NBA franchise in Louisville and how it would increase local financial streams which, if effectively negotiated with the Hornets and the local government, could be of significant financial help to UofL.

These were only a few of the multitude of thoughts occupying my mind as the Colgate factory clock across the river approached midnight. To gain a better understanding of Rick Pitino, earlier that day I had purchased his books, *Lead to Succeed* and *Success is a Choice*. They were sped-read that evening. You can't read those books and reach a conclusion that Pitino would oppose what the Pursuit Team was about to accomplish. If he believed what he wrote (assuming he wrote it) about selfless leadership and the importance of the group effort over the individual effort for oneself, it just couldn't happen. That evening I wrote a personal letter to Pitino, requesting a private meeting to discuss the NBA effort. There was never, ever, a response. Nor would there be a response to a half-dozen efforts, through mutual friends, to create a Pitino-Miller meeting.

Like so many other things in Louisville's NBA odyssey that made no sense, Rick Pitino's upcoming negative involvement in the odyssey didn't, either. But, in reaching that observation, overlooked had been the depth and extent of Rick Pitino's ego and personal ambition. It was difficult to believe that, at the turn of the Millennium, Rick Pitino's arrival in Louisville would represent a resurrection of a 1930-40s Adolph Rupp-like ego in Kentucky, where a university basketball coach was personally determined to be more important than almost anything, including the future economic well-being of the university's city, in which he lived. Hadn't Louisville advanced enough to avoid the diabolical temptations of a personality cult? Regardless of what made sense and regardless of logic, we were all about to witness it.

Several days later, in a near hour-long call, I stressed to The Wagman that it was essential for Wooldridge to make a positive and final decision on the Hornets transfer to Louisville and do so immediately, so attention could be directed to the best way to create the Hornets favorable matriculation into Louisville. It was believed if the Hornets could publicly establish they were going to be a good and solid corporate citizen, much of the anti's fervor would be dispelled, including the now-expected eruption of The Pitino Factor. Such an immediate decision would also provide Wooldridge a lengthy opportunity to work with Dr. Shumaker in creating a productive UofL and Hornets working relationship. The Wagman agreed with the idea and promised he would get my thoughts to Wooldridge.

Meanwhile, in Elvis' city on the Big Muddy, Heisley and his Grizzlies continued to experience every difficulty imaginable. In the litigation filed against the arena financing plan, a local judge had ruled in favor of the protesters. The case had been taken to an appellate state court. Finally, after three months of confusion and a favorable appeals decision, on July 3, it was announced that the Vancouver Grizzlies were officially the Memphis Grizzlies. Within a few days, Heisley called to reiterate his appreciation for our efforts in Louisville and to encourage us not to give up. Mike Heisley is a real class act.

Now, if Louisville was to have an NBA future, total attention needed to be directed toward the Charlotte Hornets.

Blum meets with Wooldridge/The Deal's Done

Beginning with July, 2001, the next two and a half months became the most important months in Louisville's 30-year NBA odyssey. The intentions of the Hornets ownership to transfer the franchise to Louisville would become a public reality, as would the continued double-speak of Jurich, the confounding personal ambition of Pitino and the abysmally failed leadership of Dr. Shumaker and Mayor Dave. Nothing was going to be easy.

Over the Fourth of July pause Wooldridge decided he preferred to finalize the negotiations for the Hornets transfer to Louisville in a private meeting with Jonathan Blum. This was fine with the Pursuit Team. To make sure Blum was fully prepared, several days were spent collating material for the upcoming dinner meeting. Sunday evening, July 15, was the magic date and the Four Seasons restaurant in New York City was the site. At that time and in that location, Louisville would learn whether it had an NBA franchise. At 10:00 PM sharp on Sunday, July 15, Blum called my residence. The normally even-keeled Blum was uncharacteristically ecstatic. At the Four Season's dinner Wooldridge had affirmed his oral commitment to accept the Grizzlies proposal and further committed to notify Commissioner Stern on July 23 that he intended to move the Hornets to Louisville.

I'll remember that evening and that phone conversation for the rest of my life. It was one of those marvelous and special times in a person's life, like an adult child's announcement to a parent over the phone that he or she had become engaged to marry. A time when something very wonderful happens, but you're separated by distance and unable to express your face-to-face joy with the good news. I couldn't help but think it was important not to get too happy, because there was still a long way to go with many pitfalls ahead. Boy, was I right about that.

A week or so later, on July 24, early in the morning, I received the best telephone call I'd ever received in Louisville's NBA odyssey—from David Stern. Later in the day, at 1:45 PM Blum called (reaffirming my prior call) to report that Wooldridge's desire to transfer the Hornets to Louisville had been given thumbs up by Commissioner Stern. Of even greater significance was Wooldridge's decision to advance the timing of his transfer application filing to December 31, 2001, so that formal approvals could be received by late March, thereby providing the Hornets sufficient time to prepare for the start of the WNBA season in Louisville on Memorial Day, 2002. [As an aside, there was a note entered in my Daytimer for Wednesday, July 25, 2001 — "Pres. Bush appears to be slipping badly, he may not be up to the job." In 48 days this observation would be dispelled and deposited in the dust heap of history.]

August, 2001: The Hornets move closer

August 2001 began on a positive note with a major change in UofL's positioning. Dr. Shumaker announced UofL was placing the on-campus arena issue on the back burner.

This news was greeted by Wooldridge as an enormous plus and by the Pursuit Team as significant movement. It signalled the initiation of university presidential leadership that was desperately needed. Now, there would be an ability to develop a cooperative working relationship between the Hornets ownership and the university, because Shumaker had decided to assert his leadership responsibilities. There is very little that takes the place of leadership when the object is a half-billion dollar economic enhancement for a city. I wrote a thank-you letter to Shumaker.[299]

The Shumaker announcement so encouraged Wooldridge that he quickly requested an all-day meeting with the Pursuit Team in Atlanta on August 13. The positives kept rolling in as the Sunday, August 5 edition of *The Courier-Journal* carried a major article surveying the considerable economic impact of a new downtown arena. Now, Wooldridge's attention (affirmed by The Wagman) was directed upon Louisville, exclusively. A brief phone discussion with the vacationing Stern, confirmed Wooldridge's decision.

Wooldridge also requested that I begin the preparation of a Memorandum of Understanding, to be discussed in more detail during the Atlanta meeting. The drafting effort began that evening. Every exemplar of such memoranda I possessed was assimilated, with the intent being to pick the best of all the templates. The Pursuit Team activated to the 100% level.

It was vitally important at this juncture to again touch base with UofL's major financial supporter, Owsley Brown Frazier. His family was the founding family and majority shareholder of Brown-Forman Distillery, headquartered in Louisville. The family's interest level in UofL had been substantially enhanced during the 1990s, and it was always deemed essential to have Frazier involved in the Hornets discussions. Blum and Glasscock met with him on Thursday, August 9. The meeting was reported to be positive, further cementing the growing cooperative spirit with the university. It was the precursor to a major breakfast meeting that had been scheduled for Friday, August 10 at Glasscock's law firm. That meeting's goal was to be the segue for Wooldridge's face-to-face negotiation with Dr. Shumaker. The attenders were to be Dr. Shumaker, athletic director Jurich, president-elect of the Board of Trustees, Jessica Loving, and the Pursuit Team. Rick Pitino had been invited, but regrettably on the morning of the meeting it was learned he would be absent, preferring instead Saratoga's race track.

With a full understanding of the meeting's importance, for several weeks our paralegal, Brevin Gaw, had been assigned the task of preparing a document that surveyed the previous thirty-one years of NCAA Final Four participants. With the assumption that the achievement of Final Four participation represented the ultimate success of a collegiate basketball program, the purpose of Gaw's work was to empirically determine whether an NBA/ABA team's existence within the market area of a collegiate team had an adverse impact upon the college team's success. In other words, did the NBA/ABA team inhibit the collegiate teams ability to achieve the coveted Final Four. When completed, the chart listed every Final Four team since 1970 and whether an NBA/ABA team existed within the primary (50 miles), secondary (100 miles) or tertiary market (150 miles) of the collegiate team. UofL's and UK's Final Four appearances were not considered, nor were UNLV (because of its hometown location in Las Vegas). The conclusion was clear and precise—excluding the NCAA Final Four participation of UofL, UK and UNLV, 72.6% of the home town market-area of all Final

Four teams since 1970 had existed within an NBA/ABA market area.[300]

I was pleased with Gaw's work, but felt that it needed to be further refined with an effort to statistically determine whether an NBA/ABA team adversely affected the attendance of a Final Four collegiate program within the NBA/ABA market area. It was believed that if a Final Four collegiate team played to a full or near full arena capacity, despite existing within an NBA/ABA market, it would lessen Dr. Shumaker's concern. This was a far more difficult task, because it required research as far back as 1970 to ascertain the capacity of the collegiate arenas (some of which no longer existed) and the reported attendance figures of the colleges. Working in conjunction with the NCAA headquarters in Indianapolis, Gaw succeeded and the results of his work were enlightening. Since 1970 each Final Four participant that played within an NBA/ABA market area averaged 92.37% of its home arena capacity during its Final Four season.[301] With the required information being gained, Gaw carefully finalized these studies and graphically produced them on an Excel computer program for my presentation to the August 10 breakfast meeting.

When we convened that Friday morning, the agenda provided for my presentation during the breakfast portion of the meeting. Gaw's work was distributed and the presentation began. Dr. Shumaker listened intently, closely examining each chart during the presentation. My contemporaneous notes of the meeting reflect Shumaker was satisfied that an NBA team in Louisville was not a danger to the university's basketball team, provided a sound working relationship was created. Loving, as the Chairperson-to-be of the Board of Trustees, was equally positive. The favorable attitude, among the UofL contingent abruptly ended there.

Athletic Director Jurich was forcefully and vocally negative. Doubting Gaw's month-long research (although producing none of his own), he insisted on being far more familiar about the interference of professional athletics with collegiate athletics than were we or anyone else at the table. Dr. Shumaker became visibly stonefaced. His authority over the university's affairs was being openly and directly challenged in the meeting by the university's athletic director. Periodically as the meeting progressed, Shumaker endeavored in various ways to encourage positive thought from Jurich about the issue, to no avail. Upon leaving the meeting Jurich was overheard by Glasscock at the elevator expressing to Dr. Shumaker his absolute refusal to cooperate with any NBA team or play in a downtown arena.

Later in the day Glasscock reached Pitino by cell phone. His response about the NBA was shocking. He was diametrically opposed to the Hornets transfer to Louisville. According to Glasscock, a litany of negatives were reeled off, to-wit: that the NBA was a terrible product played before half-full arenas, full of lazy players who cared little or nothing about their team's city and he had absolutely no interest, whatsoever, in UofL's joint participation with any NBA team. The stunned Glasscock and I spoke on the phone that evening for nearly an hour about the day's events.

There was no question now: we had one remaining problem and it was going to be generated and led by Pitino and/or Jurich and/or someone on their behalf, unless Dr. Shumaker was capable of asserting himself as the university's president by establishing, leading and directing the school's community priorities.

Atlanta meeting with Wooldridge

Still with considerable hope and anticipation, Blum, Glasscock and I met at the airport on Monday morning, August 13 and joined Blue on his company plane to Atlanta. It was essential to come out of this meeting with a plan of action and some decisions by Wooldridge. The meeting resulted in a continuation of the positive move forward.

Since Wooldridge had made his decision to transfer the Hornets to Louisville, much time was spent discussing the best and most efficient way to effectuate the transfer, which inescapably centered around The Pitino Factor. Wooldridge was confident he could deal, mano-e-mano, with Pitino because the Hornets franchise player was Jamal Mashburn, Pitino's first UK All-American.

Discussion turned to what Wooldridge and the Hornets could do to publicly reflect their intention to enter the Louisville market as a good corporate citizen. Multiple ideas were discussed. Upon learning that Muhammad Ali's dream of building an international center in Louisville to house his memorabilia and provide a forum for dispute resolution was experiencing stalled fundraising, Wooldridge lit up like a Christmas tree. He considered Ali a personal hero whom he admired immensely. Wooldridge expressed his willingness to consider a large financial contribution to the Ali facility upon learning more about its purposes. Discussion was entertained about the timing of Wooldridge's announcement of such a financial commitment. One could easily see Wooldridge's clear-thinking and expansive business mind operating as he explored aloud how the Ali facility could save millions of dollars in cost duplication if it could be built adjacent to the arena utilizing the same telecommunications system. As his thoughts germinated, they became even more intriguing. It was posited that the NBA might be convinced to utilize the facilities for negotiation of player/league disputes. He foresaw that the NBA Players Association might be interested in an involvement with Ali and might even be willing to fund its ongoing work by donating the multi-million dollar NBA fine pot, expenditures from which the players controlled.

Immediately upon our return to Louisville, Ina Brown, who was in charge of the Museum's fundraising, expressed considerable interest in the potential. Later in the day, she reported that Lonnie Ali was equally enthused. Her primary question being, how much money would Wooldridge contribute? Progress was now cascading like the Niagara River over Niagara Falls.

Ellerbe-Becket was the nation's premier modern arena architecture firm, whose list of facilities included Conseco Arena in Indianapolis. Wooldridge had retained them to design an arena for Charlotte. On Thursday, August 16 The Wagman made arrangements, at the Hornets expense, for a team of Ellerbe-Becket architects to evaluate the Blue site. A Gateway Group meeting was held and its members were informed of the progress, specifically that the Hornets were little more than a signature away from making the formal commitment to transfer. Then, on Friday, August 17 interesting news was received by the Pursuit Team.

Louis Katz was the owner of the New Jersey Nets and a member of the NBA committee that reviewed franchise transfers. Todd Blue's father had recently met Katz at a San Diego wedding celebration and he had said the Hornets were moving to Louisville and Stern had no objection. It was now apparent that the NBA infrastructure was in sinc with Wooldridge's decision—the Hornets were moving to Louisville.

This news reinvigorated the financial gurus who were fast about their work of developing the final plans for arena bond financing. On Monday, August 20 the PNC Capital Markets financial planners spent the entire day in Louisville working with Glasscock's law firm and the Governor's office.

As the continuing drafts/re-drafts of the Memorandum of Understanding were worked through, on Wednesday, August 22, a major decision was made by the Pursuit Team—both Wooldridge and Shinn would be required to sign the Memorandum of Understanding. The Pursuit Team wasn't going to go any further without both owners signatures. The next draft of the Memorandum included the joint signature requirement.

After nearly a month of success, our family was hit with a peculiar sucker-punch. In the early 1990s, my son, Jamie, along with his friend Steve Flesch, had experienced some success on pro golf's mini-tour, and later Jamie had worked as assistant professional at the Louisville Country Club. These experiences had been coupled with the responsibility for organizing, operating and managing a group of golf facilities and courses around the country called Different Strokes that were owned by Dan Jones, (whose father had co-founded Humana). Now, he was the head golf professional at a nice 18-hole layout in Pinehurst, North Carolina, called The Bayonette at Puppy Creek.

Out of St. Xavier High School, Jamie had received several golf scholarship offers, but had been convinced by UofL's golf coach John Dromo to stay home. During his entire four-year golf career at UofL, he had been the team's number one golfer, and while I'm sure to be prejudiced, I felt he was broadly qualified for the position of head professional at UofL's new Cardinal Club golf course. Jamie had been among the first applicants for the position. Among his recommenders were the nationally-known golf instructor, Jim Flick, Tommy Smith, the longtime head golf professional at the prestigious Louisville Country Club, and the head of Arnold Palmer Golf, which was to manage the Cardinal Club. Then an inconceivable thing happened.

On Thursday, August 23, 2001, when the applications were delivered to Arnold Palmer Golf by athletic director Tom Jurich, Jamie's wasn't included. Palmer Golf immediately inquired of Jamie why his application was missing and Jamie was stunned. That night he called me in a state of confusion. While there had been no promise of employment, the absence of his application obviously prevented his consideration. Needless to say I, as any father would be, was upset. Surely Jurich's negative attitude about the NBA and my involvement with the effort wasn't going to adversely impact my son's career. I had planned on dealing directly with Dr. Shumaker and Jurich about this, but Jamie requested that I wait. I honored his request. It turned out to be a really good decision on his part.

Within a short period of time Jamie received a far better offer than the

Cardinal Club could have ever possibly represented in his career; actually, it was the opportunity of a lifetime — the general managership and head golf pro responsibility for a three-golf-course facility, one of which had been designed by Arnold Palmer in the golf capitol of America, Pinehurst (called Woodlake Country Club and The Carolina), complete with a clubhouse, boating and lake facility and subdivision complex. Now, four years later, his career has advanced to the next stage with his retention by the New York Stock Exchange Company, IntraWest, to manage the development of a major real estate investment in Roscommon, Michigan including the Tom Weiskopf-designed golf course, Forest Dunes, chosen in 2003 by Golf Digest as the best new upscale golf course in America

However, the nagging question still remained and, while it makes no difference, has never been resolved.

August 2001 ended with Wooldridge and Shinn sending a public letter to the mayor of Charlotte literally pleading for his help. The letter was written with Stern's approval. The results from this letter were to be decisive. If Charlotte's mayor stepped forward and exhibited leadership, then the NBA might require the Hornets to seek a second arena referendum in Charlotte. If not, the Hornets would leave Charlotte. The letter ended with the following entreaty: "For the Hornets to remain long term in Charlotte, we desperately need your help. We cannot allow the New Arena issue to simply "die" because of the failed Referendum. We want to keep the Team in Charlotte, but we cannot make this happen on our own. There must be a community-wide consensus that keeping the Hornets in Charlotte is in the best interest of Charlotte. Affirmative steps must be taken immediately to show support (both financial and otherwise) for the Hornets and discussions must start again to make the New Charlotte Arena a reality. We respectfully request your assistance in our efforts to keep the Hornets and Sting in Charlotte and we look forward to your response to this request at your earliest possible opportunity."

Within a week the mayor of Charlotte publicly acknowledged the receipt of the letter, but observed that the arena situation was not on his plate. He publicly-expressed far more concern about U.S. Air's economic plight and the ongoing status of its Charlotte hub. While that situation was clearly of primary importance, the Charlotte mayor's abject dismissal of the Hornets was unacceptable within the NBA. There was no mistaking the fact that now the Hornets were gone from Charlotte, period.

It had been an incredible August. Louisville was closer than it had ever been to joining the urban world's economic hub. The Hornets were unquestionably leaving Charlotte and the owners were considering no city other than Louisville. They had accepted the Grizzlies proposal, which the Governor of Kentucky was prepared to re-offer and the decision had been made—the Hornets owners would make a private announcement at the NBA Board of Governors October meeting in Dallas that the Hornets transfer application to Louisville would be filed on December 31, 2001.

There were three remaining stumbling blocks: (i) the wording of a mutually agreeable Memorandum of Understanding containing the Grizzlies offer; and (ii) Stern's agreement on the Kentucky Colonels logo, the players' uniform design and the team's renaming to the Kentucky Colonels; and (iii) the impact of The Pitino Factor.

September 1-15, 2001
Labor Day Weekend is usually a bittersweet occasion, sweet as a weekend for family relaxation and anticipation of the upcoming football season, yet bitter signifying the end of summer, the beginning of winter's diminished sunlight and its biting cold. But there would never, ever, be a September like September, 2001. It would be the worst September in my life. It would be a month that changed my life, the life of my city, and irrevocably changed the life of our nation.

After three weeks of negotiation, the Memorandum of Understanding remained unsigned. The Pursuit Team was insisting on a lengthy and definitive document, while the Hornets preferred a less lengthy and more general one. At the Labor Day juncture, The Wagman was in the re-drafting mode and major progress was still being made.

Gov. Patton had agreed to privately meet with Wooldridge and Shinn, and Glasscock was obtaining the governor's time availability. By Friday, September 7, the date and place had been set—the Governor's office on Monday, September 17 at 2:00 PM.

On Saturday, September 8, the Pursuit Team met for a late lunch at Louisville's Azalea restaurant. The purpose was to make definitive plans for the September 17 governor's meeting, to further plan the Ali/Wooldridge arrangements and to determine, with finality, whether we were to continue insisting upon both owner's signatures on the Memorandum. It was a long weekend. There was unanimous agreement: the signatures of both owners would be required, period. The Wagman was informed and the remainder of the weekend was spent sending revised e-mailed versions of the Memorandum back and forth to him.

The final draft of the Memorandum, pending any revisions I felt necessary, was unanimously approved by the Pursuit Team on the evening of September 10, 2001. That evening, I put coffee on and pored over the final draft, line-by-line, making sure that there was absolutely nothing in it that Louisville couldn't live with, financially or otherwise. It was e-mailed to The Wagman at 2:00 AM on September 11. The idea was to sleep in awhile in the morning. As I dozed off, little did I know that three or so hours later a bunch of Islamic religious fanatics were boarding planes in several American airports, bent on commandeering the planes and slamming them into the World Trade Center, the Pentagon and (probably) the U.S. Capitol, killing as many of us as possible.

September 11, 2001: One of those few days that will "live in infamy," forever becoming a chapter, by itself, in Tristan's high school history books. As I enjoyed a relaxing morning coffee and watched the Don Imus Show, the unspeakable happened. From 9:00 AM until noon I, like every American, stared at the television in utter and complete disbelief. Each American had their own thoughts that morning—many were the same—many were different—all were angry. Angry about our nation's lost innocence. Angry over what had happened. Angry about our inescapably changed America. A new America had been born that terrible morning, one that would never be the same for the rest of my life. I wrote in my Daytimer: "This has been the most traumatic day in the life of this country since JFK's assassination. The USA as we knew it was forever changed at 9:00 AM today. Our grandchildren will be as far removed from the America we once knew as I am from the 1900 life of my grandparents." There was one prediction. "We're going to bomb the hell out of somebody by my birthday, October 7." We did, on that day, too.

That evening the saddened but determined President of the United States asked America not to be cowered by the disaster. He asked Americans to stand tall and go about our business, opining that if we shutter and change our life we will be allowing the terrorists an unwarranted victory. In a next morning conference call, the Pursuit Team agreed to heed the President's request of the nation; we would continue to move forward. The Hornets ownership team agreed, too.

Signed, sealed, and soon to be delivered

After years of work, VE and VJ day for the NBA in Louisville had arrived. On Thursday, September 13 exactly at 3:45 PM, The Wagman called to report that both Wooldridge and Shinn had signed the Memorandum of Understanding. A copy of the signed document was being faxed and the original sent by express mail for receipt and our signatures on Friday, September 14. Wooldridge and Shinn would come to Louisville on Sunday, September 16, by the Hornets private jet (the airline schedules were severely reduced as a result of 9/11). They would stay at the Camberly Brown Hotel and requested a dinner meeting on Sunday evening at 8:00. They were prepared to meet the Governor at 2:00 PM on Monday and we would fly in the Hornets plane the next day to meet with Ali in Barren Springs, Michigan and personally make their financial commitment, the extent of which had not yet been decided.

Our friends the Broeckers and the DeWeeses joined Norma and me for dinner at our home on Friday evening. As it did across America that night, the 9/11 horror and what it meant for our nation occupied the dinner conversation. In an effort to see into the future and its hope for goodwill, our seeming success with the Hornets was toasted. Brad Broecker was prepared to contact top officials of SFX Entertainment, should the Hornets and the city desire an independent and private management of the new arena.

Sunday, September 16, 2001. What an incredible week has just ended, warranting a day of reflection about so many things.

My mother had been gone since that day in 1973. After Dad had committed suicide in 1965, she had desperately tried to find happiness. It had been elusive, but the birth of my children had provided the beginning of some healing. She (like I, through Tristan) was beginning to see the future through the eyes of her grandchildren. She loved it when Jamie, Alexis and Sarah called her "Big Gaw Gaw." Her mother, Artie Loebig, was always called Gaw Gaw by my sister Barbara and me. As a matter of fact, I probably had never referred to her as Artie. Mom was taller than Gaw Gaw, hence the moniker. It was endearing.

Mom had gone back to work at the bank, where she had worked when she met Dad. That, together with the grandchildren, seemed to be providing a path along which to find some happiness and that long-lost smile. She was proud of her grandchildren, even dusting off her enormous crocheting, knitting and sewing skills.

Then, just as things began turning around for her, there was that fateful summer day in 1968 when she was diagnosed with leukemia. Mom was a quiet fighter. She didn't quit. Every three months for the next five years she would have a blood transfusion. They would do wonders for her. As the years progressed, her doctor began to believe she was in remission. Then in the mid-summer of 1973, she was feeling weak and went in for a routine transfusion. What had been routine was no longer. Her white corpuscle count was through the roof. Chemotherapy followed, massively. In early September the leukemia was in remission but in the process her kidneys were rendered non-functioning. She fought to the end. The last time I saw her was at the old Baptist Hospital. On that morning, September 16th, we held hands, her eyes were glazed. I kissed her cheek and she said, "Bruce, your Dad and I are very proud of you. He told me that last night. Be a good son, we'll be looking down at you soon." A team of white-smocked doctors interrupted. I insisted on staying, but they insisted I leave, claiming the need to run some tests. Reluctantly, I left. Upon returning at noon Mom was resting easily.

At dinner time, returning for the third time that day, I was met with consummate reality—Mom had just joined Dad in heaven. I hated myself, because I had been a couple of minutes too late. As she lay there, a wonderful smile radiated from her tired face. Mom was back with Dad—and happy. I was utterly devastated.

Despite the thirty years since her death, I still miss her very much. Mom had been an orphan, growing up in Louisville's Masonic Widows & Orphans Home with Gaw Gaw and her youngest sisters, Margaret and Carol (called "Toots" by Gaw Gaw's second husband, Grandpa George because when Toots was little, she did a lot of it) and her brother, Thomas. Mom, as the oldest, always had to be responsible. She had lost Tom at Pearl Harbor, within a year of my birth. It always seemed that she never experienced any sustained period of life's pleasures. Like the NBA odyssey, there was always either work to do or a nail in Mom's road. The happiness of my law school graduation and my sister's success at Vanderbilt undergraduate school had been interrupted by Dad's death. Then in only three years leukemia had hit. She should have had a happier life; good and decent people deserve that.

That day I thought how peculiar it was that I always had remembered Mom's birthday (October 10th) rather than her death day. I never knew why. But whatever, like most people, I had always wanted to make her proud to have been my mother. Maybe now, as she and Dad looked down upon us, a real achievement could be accomplished for the city she lived in and loved all her 63 years of life's trials and tribulations.

On that Sunday thoughts also turned to the enormity of the three years of work on the Millennium edition of Louisville's NBA odyssey. I couldn't help but spend some time that Sunday afternoon reflecting about where we'd been and where we were going. The long ago days of the Kentucky Colonels; the traumatic efforts to transfer the Buffalo Braves; the Rockets; the Grizzlies; and now, finally, it seemed not only likely, but for sure that the Charlotte Hornets team, a legitimate NBA title contender, was transferring to Louisville.

Now, finally, a dream would come true. Louisville would join the 28 other NBA cities whose combined gross metropolitan product was the equivalent of the second-most productive nation in the world. It had been a long journey, but the end was in sight.

Now, our little grandson, the T-Man, would live in a city which was an official member of the central economic hub of world cities. There would be countless opportunities for him, and he, unlike my son Jamie and daughter Alexis, wouldn't have to leave Louisville to find life's opportunity.

Despite the temptation to celebrate, there remained a peculiar and daunting feeling—could Louisville actually deliver, even if everything was signed and sealed?

On Sunday evening at 8:00, the Seelbach's Oakroom corner big table was filled. The Pursuit Team contingent was present and accounted for. The Hornets contingent had expanded by two.

In addition to Wooldridge, The Wagman, and their financial guru, Dan Barrett, were John Stuckey and Richard L. Cass. We had met Stuckey in the August Atlanta meeting. He was a gray-haired political pro who was a longtime friend of Wooldridge — one of those pleasant and interesting guys who easily trods the halls of Congress as well as the the tables at the local corner bar. It was good to see Stuckey again, but Cass was a most significant new addition. Having decided to leave Charlotte, Wooldridge had requested Stern's recommendation of the most talented and available attorney in America with professional athletic team experience to shepherd the Hornets' final move. Cass was Stern's recommendation — a law partner at Washington, D.C.'s prestigious and powerful 576-lawyered Wilmer Cutler & Pickering. Cass was a pro's pro, among the best I've ever seen. Obviously, Wooldridge now meant big-league business, and Louisville was in big-league business with big-league players.

The dinner began by Wooldridge ordering his (and Blum's) favorite wine, Opus One, and his offering of a toast — Louisville and the Hornets were "now a team." The plans and agenda for the next several days were discussed and outlined. But there was other, equally important, news.

Wooldridge announced he would offer Muhammad Ali $15 million to complete his museum and dispute resolution center. It would be contingent only upon Ali agreeing to revise the construction plans to build it adjacent to the arena on the Blue property. Wooldridge's analysis reflected that the two buildings should be synergistic and function inter-dependently, which would reduce the construction costs for the Ali facility by between $7-10 million. This being done and together with his donation, the Ali Center would receive a net cash infusion and construction savings that approached $25 million. His conclusion: "The Hornets will take Ali off the money-raising market and assure him and Louisville that his museum will be a reality." The Pursuit Team, to a man, was happier than it had ever been. This contribution was far more than the Alis had anticipated, quadrupling the value of any other private donation to the Ali Center.

The next morning, I met the Hornets contingent at the Brown Hotel and drove them to Tricon's world headquarters. There they were to meet with Ina Brown and Michael Fox, the impresarios of the Ali Museum fund-raising team. Co-owner George Shinn had flown into town earlier that morning and met us there. The financial commitment to Ali was revealed — $15 million. Ali would be given his preference, $10 million down with $5 million over 5 years, or $5 million down with $10 million over 5 years. Brown and Fox were floored. The Ali Museum was now a reality. They left to notify Muhammad and Lonnie Ali and would join us on the next day's flight to Barren Springs.

Following another Tricon lunch featuring the company's products , we left for Frankfort and the Governor's office.

Upon our arrival, Gov. Patton requested an initial private meeting with the Pursuit Team. He was upset we had not finalized the difficulty with Pitino. More than upset, he was hot. Glasscock and I both opined that we were prepared to do it, but felt the Governor's attendance was required at the ultimate meeting. It was essential for the Governor to remember that we were only private citizens trying to create an opportunity for Kentucky and Louisville. The University of Louisville was his bailiwick—he appointed the Board of Trustees who appointed the president. We could and would facilitate the meeting/s and provide the information needed to make decisions, but it was the governor's job to lead in setting the course for Louisville's and Kentucky's economic development. Then either Glasscock or I (can't remember now) turned it backwards: "Governor, if we had done this all by ourselves, you would have been upset, because you weren't involved and we would have exceeded our authority." He couldn't deny this. The temperature level subsided and, with the Governor saying, "Okay, let's get going with this," the meeting with the Hornets contingent began.

It was an impressive gathering of gubernatorial and Hornets decision-makers: The Pursuit Team, Governor Paul Patton, Chief of Staff Skipper Martin, General Counsel Denis Fleming, Economic Secretary Gene Strong, Crit Luallen, Wooldridge, Shinn, The Wagman, Stuckey and Cass. Some of us sat, others stood, but Shinn and Wooldridge were given the two chairs immediately across from the Governor's desk. The Pursuit Team was anxious and after the obligatory introductions, I recall crossing my fingers (and toes). The results of a 30-year odyssey were beginning to overwhelm me, but I desperately wanted to be alert and remember the moment.

Governor Patton was ebullient. He did what was required and promised, putting the Grizzlies deal on the table for the Hornets and assuring them of his and his office's full and complete cooperation in its implementation. Shaking their hands, he thanked Wooldridge and Shinn for their decision to move their business to Louisville and facilitate its becoming a major league sports city.

Wooldridge and Shinn promised the Governor that they would be responsible corporate citizens in Louisville and take an active role in local and state-wide concerns. The occasion was just like his dinner meeting with

Heisley. When Patton, a former and highly successful businessman, met with other business persons he was in his element. The feelings were mutual. As we left the Governor's office, both Shinn and Wooldridge were completely satisfied, with Shinn commenting, "In all the years in Charlotte we never once met with North Carolina's governor in such a positive environment." There was some high-fiving as we walked to the cars.

"What a revoltin' development this turned out to be!"

After a round of handshakes in the parking lot, we returned to Louisville in two cars, deliberately. Glasscock, Blum and I were in one car and Wooldridge, Shinn and Blue in the other. Blue was to use the opportunity to discuss his arena site and the real estate development deal. Glasscock wanted to call the Mayor to see if we could get Shinn and Wooldridge in to see him. From that point until the end of the evening everything—absolutely everything—went directly south.

Upon reaching Mayor Dave through Glasscock's car phone, he refused to meet. We couldn't believe it. He was quizzed as to his scheduling conflict —there was none. Glasscock requested an option for just a few moments of the mayor's time for Wooldridge and Shinn to merely say hello, and he refused. Finally, Glasscock succeeded in getting Mayor Dave's agreement to provide his staff assistants, Traughber and Driskell, for the following morning. They would meet with Shinn, Glasscock, Glasscock's bond people, Blue, Stuckey and Cass. Wooldridge, Blum, Ina Brown and Michael Fox and I would fly to Barren Springs to meet with Ali. Typically unflappable, Glasscock said, "Let's try Shumaker, maybe we can get in to see him."

Upon reaching Dr. Shumaker, Glasscock promptly explained what we had just accomplished in the governor's office. Shumaker began by apologizing. Audibly down, he admitted complete failure in securing Pitino's support of the Hornets transfer to Louisville. "I've failed," was the bottom line. It was apparent that Dr. Shumaker had given up. This was a virtual 180 degree turnaround from his determination of a month prior to provide solid executive leadership. But his failing wasn't the worst news. More astounding, Shumaker told us that Pitino was now threatening to reconsider his contract and coaching career at UofL. This was appalling. Louisville was now going to be held hostage by a basketball coach who hadn't coached a single game for the university.

As we drove west on I-64 to Louisville, our new and diabolical predicament generated remembrances of my 1950s childhood days back in Schnitzelburg on 1319 Lydia Street as our little family sat on the dining room floor watching the "Life of Riley" TV sit-com. Chester Riley's catch phrase had become famous: "What a revoltin' development this turned out to be!" The president of the University of Louisville was allowing a half-billion dollar investment in Louisville's future economic development be derailed by the ego and unbridled ambition of a 50-year-old basketball coach. It was rather difficult not to reach the conclusion that the university's priorities were more than a bit askew. It seemed like it was operating as some sort of athletic club instead of a university whose mission was to educate students and otherwise assist in enabling the community's future economic and educational advancement. I recalled the August edition of *U.S. News & World Report*, which didn't even rate UofL among the nation's top 150 universities.

What we didn't know at the time, and would learn much later, would have explained it all. Unknown to anyone in Louisville, including the university's trustees, Dr. Shumaker had begun secretly courting numerous university presidential vacancies across the nation, such as Arizona State, Nebraska, Maryland, South Carolina, Purdue, Tennessee and even Vanderbilt. Complicating matters and equally unknown to the UofL family, he was also experiencing considerable marital difficulty. Months later the rumor mill would roar with news that he and the UofL provost were an "item."

Dr. Shumaker was leaving UofL as fast as he could and his heart-throb was quickly exiting, stage left, as well, he to assume the presidency of Tennessee and she the presidency of the University of Alabama at Birmingham. While their departures would both occur several months after the NBA odyssey went aground, the real story wouldn't be learned for over a year. Not only were they an "item," their itemness continued even as Shumaker presided over UT. It was all facilitated by Shumaker's enormous spending spree that included numerous private plane flights (paid for by UT) through Birmingham's airport facilitating the continuing flirtations. The profligate spending didn't stop there. It included over $150,000 for tailgating parties at football games, unbid contracts for friends and nearly a half-million dollars in improvements to the presidential mansion in Knoxville. Within several years, Shumaker would resign as Tennessee's president and have his National Enquirer-esque divorce proceedings spread across the front pages of *The Courier-Journal* and Tennessee's major newspapers.

Upon reflection, it seems Shumaker didn't really give a hoot about the NBA, or Louisville's economic future, or anything else other than getting out of Dodge and resuming life with his secret coquette.

The next morning wheels were up at 9:00 AM on the Hornets' plane for Barren Springs. Ali's estate was exquisite, well-kept, serene and yet exploding with vitality and the aura of a world figure. Ali and Lonnie were most gracious hosts. Their appreciation for Wooldridge's commitments was unrestrained. "The Greatest" was in rare form. His and Lonnie's dreams had been answered. Lonnie indicated the Blue site was always her preference for the Museum location. Lunch was served, a photo and autograph session was accommodated by Ali and everyone returned to Louisville. A report received on the mayor's assistants meeting with the Hornets contingent was marginal, at best. Apparently they appeared befuddled, not knowing what to say. It was described by one in attendance as being totally evident they were out of their league. Not a very good impression to leave with Richard Cass, Wooldridge's new Washington, D.C. attorney. When trying to effectuate change in Louisville, it's difficult to keep all the balls rolling down the bowling alley at the same speed.

Believe it or Not: UofL organizes the Ruppians

As a youngster, the Miller family had regularly attended Douglass Boulevard Christian Church. Its pastor, Dr. Thomas Giltner, was an impassioned, extemporaneous orator whose reputation had expanded throughout the entire region. His message was akin to Paul Harvey's present-day radio commentary, less pious in religiosity and more directed to everyday life. Tom Giltner was spellbinding. There were Sunday services on-the-hour at 8, 9, 10 and 11:00 AM, and the Wednesday night potluck suppers in the church's gynmasium had become community-wide events. It was, truly, an action-oriented place that provided a moral compass on how to live effectively for thousands of people.

Among the regular parishioners were UofL football coach Frank Camp and UofL basketball coach Peck Hickman and their families. They became friends of our family. Peck and Frank were great and dedicated coaches who loved Louisville and dearly wanted to see the city succeed, in every way. They both understood change and had no fear of the unknown. They both integrated their teams long before it was required or fashionable. They were selfless men, far less concerned with their own idolatry than about the greater good of the university, the city and their players. Their lives were as far from a Rupp-like cult of personality as Louisville was from Mongolia. To be sure, with the regeneration of a Rupp-like cult of personality in Louisville, one could unmistakably hear coaches Camp and Hickman roll over in their graves.

On Wednesday morning September 19, we learned three things from Jonathan Blum. UofL had officially backed out of participating in the downtown arena; Malcolm Chancey was to be the circus barker of UofL's opposition; and that Chancey (as a member of the Ali Museum Board) had contacted Ina Brown and was intent upon orchestrating the Ali Board's refusal to accept the $15 million gift from Wooldridge. Dr. Shumaker was nowhere to be found.

The next day's *Courier-Journal* carried only part of the story in an article, entitled "Count UofL out of drive to lure NBA," with the subhead reading, "Pitino swayed change from March stance." The Malcolm Chancey-led opposition to abort the NBA in Louisville by killing the $15 million contribution from Wooldridge to the Ali Museum wasn't mentioned, although it was soon coming. It was obvious. We were in the ultimate and final battle.

So where were we? Absolutely everything had been done and accomplished, but The Pitino Factor, uncontrolled by any university presidential leadership, was unquestionably the final stumbling block, with the triumvirate of Chancey, Pitino and Jurich orchestrating a game-plan to kill the NBA in Louisville. It was clear, precise and without question, and the university president was unable to provide the required executive leadership. Blum joked that maybe he needs to be taken to a Spine Transplant Center somewhere!

That afternoon, Darrell Griffith called with startling news. Pitino was operating in high gear to sabotage the NBA. Griff couldn't believe it. Word, from credible sources, was that Pitino had recently spoken with a select group of UofL athletic contributors and told them that, prior to accepting the UofL job, he met with David Stern and was assured that Louisville

would never receive an NBA team. Reportedly, Pitino went even further —
if an NBA team came to Louisville, he would reconsider his coaching contract
with UofL.

Upon learning of the Stern reference, I spoke with The Wagman about
the information and he agreed to immediately contact Stern, because if it
was true, the Hornets transfer application intentions were dramatically
affected. Within an hour The Wagman returned the call: any such Pitino
statement was untrue *in its entirety.* There was no such statement ever made
to Pitino by Stern.

Now it was abundantly clear: The Pitino Factor and his desire to be the
only big fish in Louisville's small pond was going to hold Louisville and its
university hostage in order to have it his way. There would be no NBA in
Louisville unless Rick Pitino was a personal and direct beneficiary. Ruppdom
was alive, well and kicking in 21st century Louisville, Kentucky. It was to
get worse.

Pursuit Team and Hornets activate to counter the Ruppians

Something had to be done. Louisville was being hamstrung by virtue of
our confidentiality agreement with the Hornets owners. The public didn't
know the Hornets ownership *had actually committed, in writing, to transfer
to Louisville.* We had to be released from it, so we could make public
comment. After two days of intense discussion, on Friday September 20 we
obtained a release from the continually cooperating Wooldridge, and an
immediate meeting was scheduled at Glasscock's offices with Chris Poynter
of *The Courier-Journal.* Poynter was shown the original letter on Hornets
stationery signed by both Shinn and Wooldridge, committing to transfer to
Louisville. Poynter now knew that the NBA odyssey in Louisville was a
reality, and that a signed commitment existed.

The next step was the Ali Board of Directors meeting, where the $15
million Wooldridge gift was to be presented by the Pursuit Team. On Tuesday,
September 25, the Pursuit Team collected at Louisville's Hyatt Hotel and
was invited into the Ali Board meeting. Ina Brown had arranged for a
conference speaker phone enabling Muhammad and Lonnie Ali to hear the
proceedings. The Ali Board was membered by many of Louisville's finest
public-spirited citizens, including among them Dr. Shumaker, John
Schnatter (president and founder of Papa John's Pizza), David Blue (Todd
Blue's father), Larry Townsend, and Mrs. Alice Houston (New York Knicks

star, Allan Houston's, mother). They and a dozen more were present as Jonathan Blum outlined Wooldridge's offer that had been presented to and graciously accepted by the Alis. Chancey and Schnatter sat next to each other audibly kibitzing as the meeting progressed. While not unexpected, it was rude nonetheless. Also present in attendance was another member of the Ali Board of note, an unshaven and otherwise dishevelled Brother Bill Reed, bearing a strong resemblance to a homeless person.

Following Blum's presentation, from the back of the room, stage left, belched a ten-minute diatribe. Sitting directly across the table from Allan Houston's mother, Reed launched into a broadside against the NBA and its players, en masse, describing them as a disgusting collection of greedy, drug-using no-goodnicks, who weren't community-minded and were terrible models for our young people. For some unearthly reason, he wouldn't stop. It went on and on, as his face became redder than a beet. Among the few slurs he didn't utter was the "n-word."

The room was stunned. The question occurred: Has Reed been drinking again? The lovely and demure Mrs. Houston sat impassively, embarrassed and ill at ease. Others shifted their sitting positions, as if suffering from a hemorrhoid or two. Dr. Shumaker quietly bowed his head. A perplexed Ina Brown reached for the chairman's gavel to declare Reed out-of-order, but declined, hoping that sanity would prevail without its gaveled demand. Reed's diatribe was so out-of-order that virtually everyone, whether in favor of the NBA or not, was chagrined. Why would anyone say such offensive things directly across the table from the mother of an NBA All-Star, particularly when her son still returned home and was involved in his home community? What a shame.

There were a few non-relevant questions from the floor. No one even remembers what they were. Shortly the Pursuit Team thanked everyone for the opportunity to make the presentation and left. Before exiting the building, the Pursuit Team sat in the lobby, looking at each other in bewilderment. Within several days after his performance, Brother Bill Reed resigned from the Ali Board.

The next day's *Courier-Journal* offered the most supportive and encouraging of all the numerous editorials to date. Noting the previous across-the-board political agreement to offer the Grizzlies a home in Louisville, and recognizing the 9/11 "watershed", the editor wrote: "Nothing in the interim has changed the rationale for investing in an NBA team as a regional economic magnet for Louisville in general and downtown in particular. Nor has anything changed the NBA's assessment that Louisville is a viable market, capable of supporting a pro team." The editor continued, noting the offer from the Hornets ownership to the Ali Museum, and concluded: "If the community could gain two magnet projects for the price of one, if local businesses could still commit to the steep level of support necessary, and if a cap could be negotiated to limit taxpayers' risk, Louisville might end up with a better deal than the one it was willing to sign last spring. More than ever, what's required is strategic thinking, not knee-jerk reaction."

The *Courier-Journal* writer couldn't have been more right. But just as Coach Rupp refused to hear his old Coach Phog Allen's warnings in 1946, Pitino wasn't listening to anyone in 2001, either.

The Wagman begins to waiver

In the past, sometimes success had been achieved in masking Louisville's fear and aversion to change from NBA owners. However, reality always dictated that such diversion couldn't (and didn't) go on forever. Sooner or later, any masking would become transparent. That time was, again, drawing nigh.

On Tuesday, October 2, the Hornets transfer team was back in town. Barrett, The Wagman and Wilmer, Cutler & Pickering lawyer, Cass, met with the Pursuit Team at Tricon's world headquarters. The subject was the financing of the arena and the bond issue. A lengthy afternoon conference call was conducted with representatives of the State Finance Cabinet, Martin Hanby of PNC Capital Markets Group and Mayor Dave's Bruce Traughber and Jane Driscoll. There was no question that the dollars worked, but— there was the same old story—it required the state and city governments to work together, exerting political and personal leadership. That evening the Hornets team and the Pursuit Team met for dinner at Azalea.

At The Wagman's request, he and I stepped aside for a private conversation. For the first time I began to see waivering on his part. That was, upon later reflection, a major signal. The Wagman simply could not understand what was wrong with Louisville's mayor. He analogized Mayor Dave's attitude to that of the Charlotte mayor, which inevitably meant he was speaking for his client, Wooldridge. The Wagman questioned: "How can we (the Hornets) enthuse him?" The Wagman commented about how upfront the mayor of Norfolk had been recently with Shinn and Wooldridge, with little or nothing to offer in comparison to Louisville. I told The Wagman we'd do our best to get Mayor Dave off his ass, although (in my mind) it would be some heavy lifting.

Mayor Dave enters, again, promising "leadership"

The next morning, Jonathan Blum learned from Wooldridge that Stern had no problems with Louisville's entry into the NBA, describing it as pre-qualified. I had advised Blum the previous night about The Wagman's concerns about Mayor Dave. With these two pieces of information, Blum decided it was time to pull out all stops.

The decision was made to get David Novak, CEO of Tricon, directly involved with Mayor Dave. What was later described as a very demanding phone call from Novak to Mayor Dave was made in the morning of October 4. Armstrong was, in effect, told to "lead, follow or get the hell out of the way." Accordingly, Mayor Dave agreed to lead. When Blum told me about this later in the day, he asked, "Why are you laughing?" Answer: "By now you ought to know—when he leads, my old dog, Teddy, will invent the second theory of relativity." So began Mayor Dave's leadership of the NBA odyssey.

Two days later, Mayor Dave had his first phone conversation with Commissioner Stern. Its results were reported in *The Courier-Journal* the following day. The article began, "While stressing that he's still neutral about the prospect of a National Basketball Association franchise...." This expressed neutrality was damaging in NBA circles particularly in view of Stern's favorable view of the city. There were calls the following day from the NBA offices expressing surprise upon reading of Mayor Dave's neutrality. It had been thought that his conversation with Commissioner Stern had been positive. The NBA officials couldn't and didn't understand Mayor Dave's eccentricity. One of his frequently used angles was the gambit of conflicting signals. If you tell one person one thing and another the exact opposite then you're the only person who knows how you think. It's an angle that works remarkably well in teenage high school dating triads, political campaigning or other ventures. But when adult businesspersons are in the process of making a half-billion dollar business decision, one of the worst things to provide are conflicting signals. Furthermore, after the deal has already been consummated in writing and agreed to by all the decision-makers, from the league Commissioner to the governor, does it really make any sense to be coy?

On October 8, Blum reported that Wooldridge finally had his first conversation with Mayor Dave. More conflicting signals. Mayor Dave told Blum that Wooldridge was willing to cancel the previously required October 15 deadline to receive the Mayor's agreement to support an ordinance authorizing the issuance of arena bonds. When advised of this, Wooldridge told Blum, "I never said that." Then the next day, October 9, Mayor Dave was quoted in *The Courier-Journal* as still being neutral, pending Wooldridge's meeting with him on Monday, October 15. The Pursuit Team was unaware of this pending meeting. Todd Blue and I agreed, at this juncture a one-on-one meeting between Wooldridge and Mayor Dave was a complete disaster for Louisville. Despite this collective belief, Jonathan Blum felt that we had to give the Mayor Dave a chance to lead. The Pursuit Team had a very heated argument about this, probably the most heated argument that occurred in the three-year odyssey. We were split right down the middle — Blum and Glasscock believing the Mayor needed to meet with Wooldridge, while Blue and I felt such a meeting should only occur in our presence.

Blum and his Tricon team went to New York for the purpose of meeting with David Stern on October 15. Blum called after the meeting to report that the Tricon requests for uniform design, logos and other advertising had been approved by Stern and the NBA's advertising and promotion staff.

At nearly the same time Mayor Dave was meeting one-on-one with Wooldridge. At the meeting's conclusion, Mayor Dave was so happy—he was given more time (seven more days) by Wooldridge, until October 22. Wooldridge absolutely had to know on that day whether Mayor Dave was going to support the arena bond issue—the city's part of the Grizzlies offer —because that was the date of the NBA Board of Governor's meeting in Dallas and his signed commitment on September 14 committed the Hornets to tell the Board of Governors on that day of the Hornets intent to transfer to Louisville. Mayor Dave had known of this deadline for an entire month, but had taken no action. Now, he had a week.

Mayor Dave's idea of leadership?

Following his meeting with Wooldridge, Mayor Dave called Blum and insisted the Pursuit Team get out of the press, because he was going to handle it all by himself from now on. When asked by Blum for his plan of action, it was described as consisting of several steps. Mayor Dave's first step was the hiring of outside legal counsel to advise him—an outfit called The Goal Group.[302] This made questionable strategic sense, because it left at the negotiating room's doorstep eighteen months of relationships developed with Wooldridge by the Pursuit Team. His second step was to have Traughber publicly state that the Mayor insisted upon the Louisville Water Company site, knowing full well that Wooldridge preferred the Blue site! His third and most damaging step was the insistence that the Governor guarantee that the state would return a minimum of $5 million from the state's tax increment financing to Louisville. As a former state attorney general, Mayor Dave knew that such a guarantee required state legislative action, which was impossible to obtain in the remaining seven days, but he also knew it didn't make any difference, because the governor had the statutory authority to make the commitment.

With only a week to act in order to preserve our written commitment with Wooldridge, Mayor Dave had set upon a revised course that was impossible to accomplish in a week—probably even in half a year. Within three days of his leadership's initiation, Mayor Dave had arranged for a series of dominos to fall that effectively reversed months and months of progress toward the Hornets transfer to Louisville.

On October 16, Blum was quoted in *The Courier-Journal*, saying that Tricon's commitment with the Hornets was finalized and, "Now, it's up to our mayor to make a commitment to build an arena." Predictably, state senator Tim Shaughnessey, who had been unusually quiet of late, got his name in the newspaper again by prognosticating considerable opposition among the state legislators, and aldermanic president Magre was reporting that the aldermanic head count was moving like a lava lamp—now 6-6!

With Louisville's publicly displayed confusion, one can easily guess what happened, next. The Hornets ownership began looking elsewhere for a home. Wooldridge went back to Norfolk with Shinn, to again meet its mayor and check out arena sites. Wooldridge called Blum from Norfolk endeavoring to find out what Mayor Dave was doing—indicating that there had been no contact for several days and he had to have the mayor's decision by no later than October 22.

Recognizing Mayor Dave's latest ploys, the Pursuit Team determined to encourage the Governor to widen the tax increment financing district, to make up for the Mayor's $5 million guarantee demand. A larger district would leave no question that there would be at least $5 million returned to Louisville. Internally, Traughber was telling Blum that he was now confident that Wooldridge preferred the Water Company site. A check with Wooldridge ascertained this was incorrect; and that the Water Company was not his preference but would be acceptable if it would get the Mayor 'off the dime.'

The Board of Governors meeting was in Dallas on Monday October 22. According to his signed September 14 commitment, at this meeting Wooldridge was to make his presentation that the Hornets would file application to transfer to Louisville on or before December 31. On that day, Blum got word that Stern had approved the renaming of the Hornets to the Kentucky Colonels. With that, everything had been done privately that could be done. If my then nearly four-year-old grandson, Tristan, had been the mayor, he could have carried the ball across the goal line at that point.

But Louisville was in a state of mass confusion. As a result, Wooldridge reported to Blum that he was going to tell the NBA Board of Governors that the Hornets were transferring, but not necessarily to Louisville. He did. Several participants in the meeting inquired about what had happened to Louisville's position of favorite in the Hornets pursuit. It was difficult to explain, but an effort was made to be positive. Now, Louisville would have competition from other cities. Mayor Dave's botched leadership had succeeded in negating a definitive, written commitment from the Hornets ownership that was satisfactory to the NBA, and in doing so he had succeeded in pushing Louisville away from the table.

The next day, Tuesday, October 23, Wooldridge gave an interview to *The Courier-Journal's* Chris Poynter. It was his first with the Louisville press. Wooldridge said, "I think Louisville is a very attractive place, and the state of Kentucky is very attractive." He observed that "Louisville is very well ahead (of any city) as far as the financial plan, arena site, the arena construction and the support of the community and political and business leaders."

He was saying everything he could to encourage a positive attitude from Mayor Dave.

You have to know when to hold 'em and know when to fold 'em

A wag once said that the problem with the present is that the future is always changing. That wag was right, but the problem with the present in

Louisville was that the future wasn't going to change. But it would change in the other cities with whom we were now competing for the Hornets NBA franchise.

Mayor Dave's insistence that he take over the NBA pursuit inescapably meant that for the third time in three years Louisville was going to blow it. To accomplish something like this required teamwork and the specific individuals who had created the opportunity over the course of several years' work. That teamwork was unacceptable to Mayor Dave; he was going to do it all himself, even though he had no idea what he was doing. I recalled the information I had received several years prior from some of Armstrong's "supporters"—he was a loner, on a gigantic ego trip, being driven by a very light truck. After having spent so much time and energy in the odyssey and after having finally succeeded, the thought of all this was deeply depressing.

Another long evening was spent on October 23, contemplating the situation. The question was: Do I sit on the sidelines, as Mayor Dave had demanded, and watch the NBA odyssey be decimated with Louisville becoming nationally embarrassed all over again? Was it possible on the sidelines to remain hopeful, all the while fighting the incredible frustration of watching everything go down the chute? Was there any valid reason to do it, anyway? A yellow pad with a line down the middle of the pages separated the issues: "Ignore Mayor Dave—Stay and Fight" was on one side; "Depart Mayor Dave's Goofy Scene" was on the other. Page after page was filled as thoughts turned into words and phrases. As hard as I tried to find a silver lining anywhere, the reality was inescapable and as obvious as the nose on one's face. Louisville was going to lose its fourth NBA opportunity and its third in less than three years.

On Wednesday, October 24, 2001, I advised the Pursuit Team, that I was required to dock my boat and leave the odyssey for the sidelines. There were two primary reasons. Our law firm, my only source of income, had been severely damaged. After nearly two years of devoting 2,500 uncompensated hours to the NBA odyssey, the firm's revenue stream had been reduced to a trickle. To meet payroll and expenses, I had borrowed all the money I could from banks and credit cards. It was in excess of a half-million dollars and now it was all lost. The firm's lawyers had families whose financial stability was now endangered by the continuation of this effort. I simply had to get back to the active practice of law to try to salvage the firm's stability and my family's financial future. Of near equal significance was the fact that the anti-forces were going to take advantage of the mayor's demanded silent period to exploit Louisville's fear of the unknown and otherwise confuse the Hornets opportunity. They would throw heaps of dung at the wall in the hope that some of it would stick. Since Mayor Dave didn't want our involvement or participation, there was no reason to waste more time. I agreed to stay in contact with the Commissioner's office and to daily speak with the Pursuit Team, as the process continued. It was a sad meeting, but essential.

Little did I, nor the Pursuit Team, know that this Shakespearean tragedy would reach a new, lower level the next day.

Pitino leads the Naysayers

On Wednesday, October 24, Rick Pitino met with Mayor Dave at 11:00 AM. It was all over the evening news. The next day *The Courier-Journal* headline read, "Pitino urges public vote on NBA arena plan." The article began: "Coach Rick Pitino yesterday blasted efforts to bring a National Basketball Association franchise to Louisville, saying that his University of Louisville team would never share a downtown arena with an NBA team unless voters approved building it first."

Pitino didn't offer whether he would support the arena if it was put to a referendum. Nor did he indicate any consideration of Martin Luther King's pungent observation, "A genuine leader is not a searcher for consensus, but a molder of consensus." That wasn't enough. With the microphone in hand, The Pitino Factor went even further with an ad hominem attack on the NBA: "You're probably going to have a team here where no one lives here and the owners probably won't live here. It's something I feel very strong about that the people have to make that decision."

But *The Courier-Journal* saw through everything. The nail was hit directly on its head by its Thursday, October 25 editorial: "Louisville's furious full-court press to land an NBA franchise appears on the verge of victory. But instead of pushing ahead to put the game away, Mayor Dave Armstrong has opted to slow it down. He's put off this month's deadline for negotiating an agreement with the Charlotte Hornets until the end of the year."

Citing the need for immediate action to help the taxpayers understand the commitment, the editor concluded: "The best strategy is to do it sooner, in an off-year, rather than later, in an election year. The risk of slowing down a team's offense too soon is that it can end up icing its momentum instead of the score."

Mayor Dave's response to the editorial was that he would have an arena plan ready in two weeks. Another mayoral brain implosion. An arena plan wasn't to be produced in two weeks. As a matter of fact, it wasn't ready for over a month. In the meantime, Wooldridge went to St. Louis for further negotiations with Bill Laurie and back to Norfolk to receive that city's commitment, all the while still hoping and waiting for positive public statements from Mayor Dave. *The Courier-Journal* opined again on November 1: "The University of Louisville's transformation from a potential partner to an active foe of a downtown basketball arena is now complete. Last spring, UofL wisely cooperated in the city's bid for an NBA team, remaining open to moving downtown and sharing the state-of-the-art facilities and higher revenues a new arena would bring. Now, it not only has nixed any partnership, but seems to be doing what President John Shumaker said it wouldn't: torpedoing even an NBA arena. Last week basketball coach Rick Pitino warned of potential damage to his program and publicly accused Mayor Dave Armstrong of misleading him. This week, UofL reactivated a committee to explore building its own arena, as part of what Athletics Director Tom Jurich described as 'our own little sports mecca.' But it's not understandable that UofL's board and administration, at this very late date, would participate in thwarting a major and broad-based community development project. Especially without having any realistic plan for achieving something better."

The newspaper's common-sense, bulls-eye observation made no difference at all. When you're a determined anti-progressive, whose lack of confidence manifests itself in a psychotic fear of the unknown which propels you toward an aversion to change so you can protect your hegemony within a picket-fence environment, you keep moving on no matter how nonsensical your actions. UofL's athletic club had done its part. There was more to come.

On November 7, Malcolm Chancey made his first public appearance in the picture, announcing his formation of an ad hoc group called the "Special Projects Taxpayer Review Committee." Its purpose—to question and challenge the economics of the downtown arena. To further edify the lack of common sense with this taxpayer committee's formation, one needed to go no further than a cursory examination of its chairman, Malcolm Chancey. He had spent his Louisville business years weaving through the banking circles of Liberty Bank. Two predecessors as bank president, Billy Joe Phelps and Frank Hower, had guided the bank's merger with Bank One. Upon their retirement Chancey was left, to take credit for it all. Then after becoming active with the UofL Board of Trustees, he sidled-up to Owsley Brown Frazier, who routinely shied away from publicity generated by his community philanthropy. Chancey was left, again, to take credit for it all.

Malcolm Chancey is a Louisville phenomenon. That is, his success could have only occurred in Louisville. In a city with more skilled and dynamic leadership, "Meddlin' Malcolm," as some call him, wouldn't have advanced past the vice-presidential level of a bank. But in Louisville he did, even becoming an award-winning citizen with a school named for him. No bigger ego, with less reason, existed in Louisville, with a duplicitousness to rival the ego.

To further complicate matters, according to a conversation with Magre on November 19, the aldermanic coalition was slipping. Apparently, one alderman's son, previously an NBA supporter, had been given free tuition to Pitino's summer basketball camp, and Magre wasn't sure where that alderman stood. Additionally, Chancey had financially sponsored an alderman's fortieth birthday party along with making significant political contributions to other aldermen, serving in several instances as chief fundraiser. Just as had been predicted months ago, the whole thing was becoming politicized. Magre also felt that the aldermen were not going to support Mayor Dave's request of a personal services contract for The Goal Group. Didn't take long for that dispute to hit the airwaves, because that's the way things were handled in City Hall. By November 22, Mayor Dave was publicly stating that the lack of aldermanic support was slowing down his arena plan progress. The competing cities loved it. Wooldridge scratched his head in utter disbelief.

Finally, on November 28, Mayor Dave announced an arena plan— primarily generalities with few specifics. His plan brought Wooldridge back to Louisville. Trying his best to be open and above-board, Wooldridge held a free-flowing press conference on Thursday, November 29, announcing he had decided to meet one-on-one with each alderman to personally answer their questions. Wooldridge believed that he could dispel Chancey's under-the-table tomfoolery by openness and forthrightness. Nice thought, probably right when common sense is applied, but common sense wasn't given a seat at the table. Those meetings occurred on Friday, November 30—my Dad's death day. That November 30 didn't turn out too well, either. Several of the aldermen were so rude they refused to meet. How do you explain that? I couldn't to David Stern.

With Wooldridge in town, on November 31, the Chancey committee brought forth an old canard for another parade around the block—it was examining plans for the enlargement of half-century-old Freedom Hall.

Louisville's final shot—another embarrassing airball[303]

To facilitate maximum public exposure, the aldermen found a way to get the entire thing on live TV. On the morning of Saturday, December 1, the Board of Aldermen met in a specially-called and televised town meeting to consider the city's construction of a new downtown arena. Again hopeful of a common sense approach by the decision-makers, Wooldridge was pleased with the opportunity. Blum and Glasscock explained the importance of the opportunity for Louisville's future and Ray Wooldridge praised the city, offering his personal promise to be a responsible corporate citizen.

The five-foot six-inch Chancey and his fellow taxpayer's committee member, Bill Stone, whose attachment with UofL is so tight that he's been called "Barnacle Bill," offered the anti-position. Of particular repugnancy was Chancey's opening comment that he had spoken with the retired president of a bank in Charlotte, who had nothing good to say about Wooldridge—an opening remark resembling one made by a high school kid during in a fraternity black-ball session. Thus began Chancey's litany of untruths and his appeal to Louisville's lowest common denominator—the fear of the unknown.

He stated that no bank would purchase the 30-year bond proposed for the arena, because such a lengthy bond term was financially irresponsible. Within several days Barry Smitherman of Bank One Capital Markets (Chancey's own bank from which he had retired!) opined that 30-year bonds are the normal financing vehicle for arena and stadium construction projects. Smitherman observed that Marion County (Indianapolis) had issued 30-year bonds to finance the new Conseco Fieldhouse in downtown Indianapolis. They were rated AAA and were issued by First Chicago, Bank One (Chancey's bank), and Morgan Stanley. Other cities had also issued 30-year bonds to finance arenas and stadiums, including Nashville (for the construction of Adelphia Stadium), Houston (for the construction of a new arena for the NBA Houston Rockets), Chicago (for a renovation of Soldier

Field) and Phoenix (for the construction of the America West Arena, home of the Phoenix Suns, and a separate new stadium for its NFL Arizona Cardinals). Even more amazingly, one didn't even have to look outside Jefferson County. Two years earlier, in December 1999, the Louisville Metropolitan Sewer District issued $300 million in 30-year bonds to finance capital projects.

The problem with Chancey's fabrication and Smitherman's subsequent rebuttal/correction was that while a falsehood told one day is corrected by the truth the next day, the truth rarely receives equal publicity. The lie prevails in the public's mind.

Unfortunately, one falsehood wasn't enough. More fear was imparted as Chancey claimed that the new metro government's bond rating would suffer with the issuance of such a bond, because the more bonded indebtedness, the lower the bond rating. But as usual with Chancey, facts never got in the way of his story. While Jefferson County had $303 million in bonded indebtedness and Louisville had only $64 million, Jefferson County's bond rating of Aa2 was higher than Louisville's of Aa3!

Chancey still wasn't finished with his prevarication. Next, there was the averment that the proposed arena bonds were fiscally irresponsible because they were back-end loaded, meaning there were larger payments in the out years than the near years. Totally ignored was the fact that all the bonding for stadiums and arenas was back-end loaded, including UofL's Papa John's Stadium, and *Chancey didn't reveal he was involved with the bond funding for Papa John's Stadium.* Then there was the usual negative that NBA tickets were too expensive. A simple examination of the Hornets ticket structure in Charlotte would have found that nearly 83% of the seats were priced lower than the NBA average of $55 each. The tickets prices were $9, $15, $21, $29, $39, $45, and $55.

It was just like we knew: Chancey, Barnacle Bill and the other anti's would say anything, regardless of its truth, to kill the NBA in Louisville. And Mayor Dave and his leadership were nowhere to be found. He, conveniently, wasn't present that Saturday morning.

As Wooldridge sat impassively and watched these proceedings in the aldermanic chambers, with each succeeding prevarication you could see his already diminished interest level decline even further. Chancey had deliberately undertaken an effort to publicly and personally savage

Wooldridge, exactly like the Charlotte anti's had done, making him feel unwelcome, unwanted and unworthy.

That evening Dave Novak, CEO of Tricon, had a sumptuous Christmas party for hundreds of Louisville businessmen and women. The honored guest was Ray Wooldridge. Novak was trying to replicate what had been previously done with the dinner parties for the Rockets management and Mike Heisley. That evening, as before, Louisville's business community gave its best effort. Many came forward and apologized for Meddlin' Malcolm's astonishingly embarrassing performance and tried to encourage Wooldridge by reminding him that Chancey was one of those small-of-stature guys who longed to remain a big fish in a small pond. They offered their support, promised advertising and suite/seat purchases, gave business cards hoping to persuade Wooldridge to help Louisville become a big league sports city. It was a wonderful occasion replete with a lot of really talented people doing their best to make up for Chancey's exhibition of perfidy. But it was too late; the party was over.

Toward the evening's end, Norma and I spent some quiet time with Wooldridge. It was one last chance to try to assure him of Louisville's capability. He knew Louisville's market was fully capable of supporting major league sports, but he was looking for something in addition to that. He yearned to be part of a city that would appreciate his contribution to its well-being and future. There was no way that Louisville had effectively given evidence of that.

Ray Wooldridge left Louisville the next morning, never to return. Shortly thereafter, Malcolm Chancey, really proud of himself for having successfully protected his big guppy status by maintaining Louisville's small and shallow pond, shortly left thereafter for his tax haven in Florida, to return in the spring when the weather got better.

On December 2 came *The Courier-Journal* headline, "Arena plan faces hurdle in tax-wary legislature." The sub-headline was, "Opposition to ticket surcharge is strong." The next day, on Monday, December 3, the Board of Alderman voted 6-5 to approve The Goal Group's contract, with Alderman Bentley (now the President of the Board) abstaining. Magre's political leadership had completely evaporated.

On Tuesday, December 11, in a conference call with the Pursuit Team, Blum reported that, "The owners don't think we can do this, politically." Early that evening The Wagman called to tell me that it didn't look good for

Louisville. His client was in New Orleans, and unless Mayor Dave could make chicken salad out of chicken (you know what), the Hornets transfer to Louisville was history.

New Orleans seizes the reins[304]

Doug Thornton was the very insistent and determined general manager of the New Orleans Arena (and the Superdome). Its financing and construction had been authorized by the Louisiana state legislature in 1993. For a variety of reasons, the arena remained uncompleted in the summer of 1999. Thornton's persistence was equalled by Stephen Perry, Chief of Staff for Louisiana's Governor Foster. Following the 1999 referendum loss in Houston, Thornton and Perry had orchestrated a press conference the day after, affirmatively asserting that New Orleans was going to purloin the Rockets. Having been quietly rebuked by the NBA offices, they quieted down, completed the arena construction and waited their next opportunity. But in 2001 that opportunity was being severely challenged by another problem. The Saints were considering leaving New Orleans, because the Superdome had not been maintained to the requirements of their lease. Agreeing that this situation was damaging the city's national image, there began a concerted effort to bring the disparate coalitions in New Orleans and Louisiana governments together into a unified force. While the effort to lure the Vancouver Grizzlies to New Orleans had failed, it provided the needed occasion and impetus for the cooperative effort.

Until the Hornets referendum failure in Charlotte, the only Hornet-Wooldridge-New Orleans interactions that had occurred were a Hornets exhibition game there in October 2000 and a chamber of commerce-type document that had been delivered by Thornton to Wooldridge's financial analyst, Dan Barrett, in March, 2001. The intrepid Thornton had religiously continued his contact with Wooldridge and kept him advised about the eventual resolution between the state and the Saints in September, 2001. At that time, however, Wooldridge and Shinn had signed a commitment on September 14 to transfer the Hornets to Louisville and New Orleans wasn't even being given a passing thought. But at that time Mayor Dave hadn't taken over the leadership of the NBA effort, either!

Then, the "big call" came. On December 4, 2001, the day after the 6-5 Louisville aldermanic vote, Wooldridge called Thornton and inquired about the Hornets opportunities in New Orleans. Thornton determined to keep any re-invigorated effort under the radar screen. Wooldridge and his Washington, D.C. lawyer, Dick Cass, went to New Orleans on December 11.

Thus began the first steps by New Orleans to facilitate Louisville's loss of the Hornets.

Thornton and the Governor's Chief of Staff, Perry, were fully aware of Louisville's work with Wooldridge for nearly 18 months, as well as Tricon's $100 million offer. They wanted to make sure that Wooldridge wasn't using them for further leverage in Louisville. Having heard from Wooldridge's own mouth about the political leadership disaster in Louisville, their comfort level increased, and they left Wooldridge's hotel room for a dinner at Commander's Palace. Perry explained the Governor's economic development plans for New Orleans. The party of four closed down Commander's Palace (just as Wooldridge, The Wagman, Blum and I closed down Lilly's in Louisville in September, 2000, fifteen months prior).

The next day Perry and Thornton began privately speaking with New Orleans businesses. Knowing they couldn't match Tricon's $100 million offer, they still believed a reasonable effort was possible. After four days of continuous effort (and some success), the opportunity was brought to the attention of New Orleans Mayor Marc Morial on December 15. At the same time a key Democratic state legislator, John Alario, from Westwego, a suburb of New Orleans, got involved. Westwego isn't a traditional city suburb. Some of Louisiana's bayous are found on its outskirts. It serves as the launching point for many swamp tours and bayou excursions. It's also just a short distance away from several plantation homes along the Mississippi River. Hard to picture a legislator from a swampy plantation region of Louisiana taking the lead to bring the primarily African-American NBA to New Orleans. But Alario, unlike certain of Louisville's state legislators, wasn't interested in his newspaper clippings, nor was he fearful of change or being a positive leader. He was a man with vision.

Alario met at Bell South's New Orleans offices with business leaders and began fashioning a tax plan to salvage the Saints. The plan involved re-directing several taxes; namely the hotel/motel tax in the Orleans and Jefferson parishes and the City of New Orleans, which had been previously dedicated solely to education and economic development. The critical issue was whether some of these taxes could and should be diverted to salvage the Saints NFL franchise. At this meeting the Governor's Chief of Staff not only encouraged the planned diversion of the tax revenue to salvage the

Saints, but further encouraged an additional stipend designed to entice the Hornets to New Orleans. Meeting with favorable encouragement, Perry asked Alario to put together the tax package to include the Saints and the Hornets. To be sure there were entities and concerns whose proverbial oxen were being gored by the redirection of the taxes, but there was a growing consensus that it had to be done to salvage the New Orleans position as a progressive city, which in turn had enormous benefits for the state as a whole.

After a Britney Spears concert at the New Orleans arena on December 16th, the mayor, Perry, Thornton and several other business leaders examined the same bullet point list of Hornets requirements that the Louisville Pursuit Team and the governor had worked with for 13 months and Mayor Dave knew of for months. Mayor Morial was advised about the efforts underway among the state legislative delegation. He agreed to support them. Of course, none of this had happened in Louisville.

Daily reports of progress in New Orleans were delivered between Thornton and Wooldridge. Political and business leaders of both New Orleans and Louisiana worked in unison to have everything ready within a month for Wooldridge's return to New Orleans on January 9, 2002.

Upon his return, the stage was set. Wooldridge would be the featured speaker at the normally staid New Orleans Business Council. To his complete surprise and distinct pleasure, Wooldridge received a prolonged standing ovation—there it was, the appreciation he had been seeking for years— after being demeaned in Charlotte, making the wrong decision in Memphis and being pulled in every-which-direction by Louisville. The Louisiana state legislative delegation was impressed with Wooldridge, who was later quoted as saying, "It was really a great meeting. You really started to feel that this move had broad support in the community and it was important for us to have that support."

From the standing ovation forward, Wooldridge's heart never left New Orleans. During the time that Louisville Mayor Dave was supposedly speaking with Wooldridge (and wasn't), he was being wined and dined by the apex of the New Orleans and Louisiana business and political communities. They became regulars in the French Quarter restaurants. George Shinn joined the New Orleans festivities on January 11 and, after a private dinner at the House of Blues with the powers-that-be, went house-hunting the next day.

About the time of Shinn's house-hunt, Mayor Dave presented his $300 million dollar plan, with every bauble UofL ostensibly wanted. It really didn't make any difference; it was dead on arrival. Mayor Dave had let the fish off the hook and, most unfortunately, in the process had totally embarrassed the city all over again, and had singlehandedly sabotaged Louisville's bright and shiny future among the elite cities in America.

CHAPTER FOURTEEN

The Tale of Two Cities

We began several hundred pages ago recalling the events of a particular date—January 18, 2002—the day that featured a flower-bedecked parade through New Orleans' Vieux Carre culminating in Ray Wooldridge's announcement that his Charlotte Hornets NBA franchise would transfer to New Orleans (instead of Louisville). It was a moment of utter frustration with my city's political climate and its inability to understand the concept of change and growth.

At that point, Louisville's opportunity to lure an NBA franchise had severely hemorrhaged. The only possibility of medical relief was remote, requiring a massive injection of that old, time-worn, yet essential quality known as leadership to be administered by the family doctor immediately. Louisville's Marcus Welby, M.D. was on an extended multi-year vacation, so it didn't happen. But it did, elsewhere.

"Goin' to Kansas City, Kansas City here I come...."

Kansas City, Missouri. A city in a state with many historical similarities to Kentucky. Both states have experienced state legislatures quarrelling between their rural and urban populations and the relationship between the two major cities in each state is fraught with considerable animosity. Both were savagely-split Civil War border states contributing equally to both the Confederate and Union armies. Internal fratricide has been further compounded by too many counties vying for too little. (Kentucky with 120, only six more than Missouri's 114.) Like Kentucky's limestone-based bluegrass region, Missouri's northern tier, where the last Ice Age ended, is rich agricultural land. Missouri's southern tier of the Ozark Mountains was settled by Tennesseans and Kentuckians who migrated from the Appalachian Mountains, bringing with them all manner of inertia, suspicion and aversion to progress. Societal irony abounded in both states. While they were home to nationally renowned newspapers with reputations for journalistic excellence, both enjoyed their fair share of desperados like Missouri's Jesse James gang, which flourished amid a strong religious bent.

But in the mid-1940s, as Kentucky became increasingly mesmerized by the stubborness of Adolph Rupp, a changing event happened in Missouri that would quickly move it to a level of progress far beyond Kentucky. It replaced an outmoded and decrepid 1875 constitution with a new one that included a host of progressive reforms, among them the encouragement of urban home rule, the non-partisan selection of its judiciary and the depolitization of its education system. The results enabled Missouri and its major cities to effectively compete in the last half of the 20th century. Kentucky, with its equally-decrepid 1890 constitution still in place today, didn't change and its cities didn't effectively compete, economically.

Like Louisville, Kansas City (early on called "Westport") was born next to a river on the extreme edge of a state. The infancy period of both cities share much in common—Lewis & Clark and Daniel Boone (Westport businessman Albert Gallatin Boone, was a grandson of Daniel) and both were starting blocks for 19th century western adventurers (Westport being the embarkation and destination point for the Santa Fe, California and Oregon Trails). Both cities experienced enormous 19th century growth, fired by this adventurism. With the nation's western expansion complete, the Depression/Prohibition era for both cities became an inglorious period of unrestrained political corruption. Kansas City featured a boss-mogul, Tom J. Pendergast, and Louisville, the Whalen Brothers and the later Fourth Street Machine. While bossism dulled the innate adventurism of both cities well into the mid-20th century, Kansas City's continuing ties to the dramatically growing American west and its cattle industry railroad hub coupled with the state's modern urban-inspired constitution gave it advantages it over Louisville.

Capitalizing on its continuing economic growth, in the mid-1960s

Texan Lamar Hunt placed an AFL football franchise in Kansas City. It was named the Chiefs. With their Hall of Fame coach, Hank Stram, and quarterback Len Dawson, the team became a premier franchise in the NFL. Kansas City had previously experienced the aura and impact of the major leagues by the arrival of the Philadelphia Athletics in 1956, along with the Cincinnati Royals NBA team (renamed the Kings). By the early 1970s Kansas City had become a genuine major league sports city. At that time the only cities between the Mississippi River and the Pacific Ocean with three major league franchises were Houston, Los Angeles, San Francisco and Kansas City.

But for various reasons Kansas City, like Louisville, suffered the loss of its basketball franchise when their Kings were sold for $10.5 million to Sacramento investors in 1984 and moved to California the next year.

During the last several decades of the 20th century, Kansas City retrogressed, joining other cities like Louisville that were struggling to find their place and identity. The struggle became even greater when one of its remaining stars, the national headquarters of the NCAA, left for newer and zippier digs in burgeoning Indianapolis. Convention after convention left Kansas City for Denver, Dallas, Houston and San Antonio. Kansas City was in a downward spiral with its downtown area beginning to stagnate. It was a condition normally found only in rust-belt cities. Both Louisville and Kansas City experienced multiple failed downtown redevelopment schemes. Louisville seemed incapable of rejuvenating the turn-of-the century splendor of its Fourth Street, and in the mid-1990s Kansas City experienced penultimate failure with the collapse of a downtown entertainment scheme called the Power & Light District Plan.

At the same time, May 2000, Louisville, with the encouragement of NBA Commissioner David Stern, was courting the ownership of the Houston Rockets Kansas City's business leadership, with the support of the city's new mayor, Kay Barnes, announced the hiring of a consultant to study and recommend downtown development projects, including a new sports arena. The work continued, but at a snail's pace.

As time passed, Mayor Barnes became increasingly intrigued with redeveloping the city's downtown business district by the focal point of a state-of-the-art arena. Barnes sought help with her vision. She found a Pursuit Team, comprised of an investment banker, Jack Holland, and a lawyer, Herb Kohn, and empowered it to act. Things began happening.

Meanwhile in July, 2001, to great public accolade, Louisville Mayor

Dave Armstrong announced a $13 million financing "deal" with Baltimore developer The Cordish Company. It called for the city to acquire its failing downtown Galleria from Oxford Properties for $4 million and sell it to Cordish for $1, which would redevelop the Galleria with a $9 million grant from the City—all being funded by a city bond issue. Cordish had done a similar thing in Houston, but had combined it with a major league baseball stadium as the central focus. Although the same opportunity was available, there was no interest of the part of Louisville's mayor to tie the Cordish plan into a downtown arena for an NBA team. The vision was limited.

In December, 2001, shortly after the Louisville Board of Aldermen roundly rebuffed the Charlotte Hornets owner, Mayor Barnes unveiled the drawing of a new downtown arena prepared by the Kansas City-based and nationally-recognized arena architecture firm. Her plan was a mere "drawing," while the Hornets owner actually possessed an arena blueprint ready-made for Louisville that he paid millions of dollars to create. Soon thereafter, the importance of Kansas City's downtown arena drawing grew exponentially. It lost the Big 12 collegiate basketball tournament to Dallas. While it had been played in Kansas City since 1946, the aging Kemper Arena (like Louisville's Freedom Hall) was rapidly growing non-competitive. Dallas won by offering its new $400 million American Airlines Arena (home of the NBA Dallas Mavericks).

A year later, in December, 2002, the Kansas City Sports Commission recommended the construction of a new downtown arena. Realizing time was fleeting, Mayor Barnes quickly authorized her Pursuit Team to determine an arena site and create a financing package, all to be completed by March 31, 2003. But vestiges of the past in the form of political infighting delayed the process for a year, when they only recommended a site, not the financing. Then in the early spring of 2004, a monumental lightning bolt of planned public leadership struck Kansas City.

While Louisville and Cordish were completing the $13 million, bonded, one-block-long "Fourth Street Live," Mayor Barnes and her Pursuit Team announced a $536.4 million redevelopment of the seven-square-block South Loop of Kansas City's downtown. H&R Block would build an eighteen-story, glass-sheathed $308.4 million world headquarters building, in conjunction with a $44.1 million renovation of the historic President Hotel and the $183.5 million redevelopment of 425,000 square feet of retail space in the South Loop to be called "Kansas City Live" and built by

The Cordish Company! Kansas City had copied Louisville's Cordish development, even down to the name, but it was 14 times larger than Louisville's "Fourth Street Live."

This $536.4 million redevelopment was in addition to previously-announced plans in the same seven-block South Loop area of Bartle Hall's $197 million overhaul, the Kansas City *Star's* $200 million production facility, a $304 million Performing Arts Center and the $100 million redevelopment of the historic art-deco Power & Light Building into a condominium showpiece. One culminating piece that would tie together this incredible series of announcements remained.

Within a month that piece was announced. Kansas City would build a $250 million downtown state-of-the-art arena within the South Loop. For $50 million in naming rights it would be called the Sprint Center, for the company headquartered in Kansas City. It would be managed by Anschutz Entertainment Group, a wholly-owned subsidiary of the Anschutz Corporation headquartered in Denver and owned by reclusive billionaire Philip Anschutz, who *Forbes Magazine* lists as being worth $5.2 billion. AEG, whose annual revenue from its entertainment offerings exceeds $1 billion, controls the largest movie exhibition company in the world with nearly 5,000 movie screens, owns the Kings NHL team in Los Angeles along with 30% of the Los Angeles Lakers and is the builder/operator of the Los Angeles Staples Center (which in five years has hosted over 1,000 events that attracted 18.5 million people through its turnstiles). The Sprint Center would be managed by Anschutz's right-hand-man and AEG's president, Tim Leiweke, whose career began years ago as the general manager of the Kansas City Comets.

The battle wasn't over. A referendum was required to approve a $4-a-day tax on rental cars and a hotel tax addition of $1.50-a-day to fund the arena's bonding. It was scheduled for August 3, 2004. The anti's, called The Coalition Against Arena Taxes, rallied. They were funded by entities who thought they would be damaged by the change. Pre-eminent among them was Enterprise Leasing, a national rental-car business headquartered in Kansas City's long-hated archrival, St. Louis. Over the remaining two months, Enterprise funded a half million dollars in opposition television ads. It was countered by pro-television ads costing another half-million dollars gained from contributions by Kansas City's Sports Commission, the Anschutz Entertainment Group, the Chamber of Commerce, Sprint, H&R

Block, DST Systems and local contractors.

The vituperative battle reached its zenith a week prior to the referendum, when an African-American councilwoman seized her moment of fame by reversing her position to the anti side (obtaining, as a result, maximum publicity). Then the chairman of the Civic Progress Group of St. Louis stated, "If Kansas City builds this new arena, our chances of landing an NBA team are vastly diminished, and that would be disastrous, especially for Bill, here"[305]—pointing to Bill Laurie, owner of the St. Louis Blues, the Savis Center, husband of a Wal-Mart heir, and a long-time NBA courtier with whom Louisville's path had crossed. Mayor Barnes, with her leadership being challenged from everywhere, declined to attend the Democratic National Convention, remaining in Kansas City to personally lead the final battles of "the war." The last two weeks were dramatic.

Similar to the Louisville anti's, the Kansas City anti's grouched, "What will happen to our old and wonderful Kemper Arena, where the All-Americans played?" The Mayor Barnes answer was quick and precise—a consultant would be hired to study how to turn the aging arena into a year-round equestrian and agricultural center. The visionary Barnes was quoted saying, "There is a whole industry called agri-entertainment that involves a much broader range of activities than we've seen at Kemper."[306] Former NHL owner, Howard Baldwin, announced he would seek a major league hockey team for Kansas City. The family of Orlando Magic owner, who originally had a minor league hockey team in Kansas City, expressed potential interest in Kansas City for their NBA team. The city's labor unions announced support, as did Kansas City Chiefs owner, Lamar Hunt, and Kansas City Royals owner, David Glass. Golden Peak, president of a Kansas City-based entertainment and marketing company, publicly promised he would pursue a major league arena football team. The National Association of Basketball Coaches, the only remaining vestige of the NCAA in Kansas City, announced it would contribute $10,000 to the Sprint Center to house its offices and the National College Basketball Hall of Fame (something that might have been transportable to Louisville, with a new downtown arena).

With the battle joined, referendum day arrived.

"Mayor hits a home run with this one" was the next morning's headline of an article written by nationally-recognized *Kansas City Star* sports journalist, Jason Whitlock. The referendum had passed with 57.5% of the vote. An elated Mayor Barnes observed, "The opposition to the downtown arena awakened a sleeping giant and a pride and determination that we were going to decide our own destiny. We're doing it."[307]

Kansas City Star columnist, Joe Posanski, said it all: "Well, how about that. Fear strikes out. You know, that doesn't happen much in the real world. Seems like most of the time, scare tactics work, mud gets in people's eyes and someone simply screaming, "TAXI" at the top of his lungs can be enough to halt dreams....I happen to believe that we have drifted a little bit, that there was a time when leaders dreamed big and Kansas City saw itself as a player. Shoot, Kansas City was a player, and this town pulled in big-time sports, built two stadiums that changed the landscape of sports architecture, brought home the biggest conventions, built an airport that is still the easiest in-and-out in America. For some reason, people always seem to talk about those as the good old days, as if we can never get back to it. I happen to believe we can, and will."[308]

Two cities in two states with considerable similarity. One chose to dream because if you don't have a dream, you can't make a dream come true. With the lowest bonding interest rates in 40 years, one chose to reach beyond its grasp and, *in one fell-swoop,* invested $1.5 billion into its downtown's future, thereby honoring its heritage by leaving hope and the platform of progress for the real stakeholders in the future—its younger citizens. The other chose the easier path of a more limited investment —a path where dreams are realized an inch-at-a-time. There, the comfort zone was found in the middle-of-the-herd. One demanded and received leadership. The other was satisfied with the political spin of a wonderfully small project, enabled with not a single word being uttered or written in the media about Kansas City's dwarfing of Louisville's effort.

A big question remains for Kansas City—can the velocity of this $1.5 billion capital infusion and the leadership of the NBA-respected Anschutz Entertainment Group attract the transfer of an NBA team? Ironically, in Louisville it is a question that didn't require answering, because on September 13, 2001, the Charlotte Hornet owners had committed, *in writing,* to transfer their franchise to Louisville.

"Powerful national and international forces are reshaping the American economy. The states and cities that will fare the best will be those that, while mourning the passage of the old, most aggressively prepare themselves and their people to create and capture the new."
—Editorial in *The Courier-Journal*, October 29, 2003

EPILOGUE

Lost Opportunities and Leadership

Isn't life funny (and exciting)? It takes nine months to begin, after which follows a lifetime of twists and turns through both deep and shallow valleys, leading to splendid mountain-top vistas or depressing, cavernous nadirs, all followed by the inexorable question—was it all a success?

Without question, the NBA odyssey you've just read about had a life of its own. Was it successful? No, it clearly failed. Is the odyssey over? *Yes, it's over.* In every individual's life and in the life of every city, there occur openings in the fleecy clouds that hover in the skies above. Those openings represent opportunities to reach beyond an individual's or a city's grasp. But those opportunities are fleeting, not returning for the faint of heart to reconsider. When not grasped, those opportunities are seized upon by other individuals or cities that are always in the wings and more willing to accept the demands of the challenge.

Louisville's NBA opportunity has gone its way. Unlike any other city in America, Louisville had four legitimate opportunities to obtain admission into this exclusive list of world class cities that are home to an NBA franchise. With the international growth of the sport, the NBA's future is, now, transnational. Only cities with a determined, confident and world-focused vision of themselves need apply.

So where does that leave those left behind? Twenty years from now will be the year 2024. If I make it that long, for most of that year I'll be 83 years old. That, for me, will probably be a lifetime. My share of views from mountain-top vistas and cavernous nadirs will have been experienced. Will I have succeeded? An old wag once said, "Success is getting what you want, but happiness is wanting what you get." If that wag was right, while I probably did succeed in my legal career and with my family, I didn't succeed with Louisville's NBA effort. But it was a remarkable journey, made even more resplendent by many new friendships with a truckload of talented and genuine people. Of all the happy things within that journey was the love and support of my wife, Norma. Hopefully in 2024 she and I will still be on the grassy side of planet Earth.

Twenty years from now, my teenage granddaughter, Anna, will be 37. Success in life will undoubtedly be hers, because she enjoys a full understanding of the challenges of change. It has been an integral part of her life. But she probably won't be in Louisville—the horizons are too broad elsewhere and the road is wide.

My grandson, Tristan, the dear and darling little T-man and the absolute apple-of-my-life, will have completed college and be 26 years old. That's hard to fathom right now. But he, too, will be fine, because he's already a happy and proud little people person who knows that people are to love and hold dear, not to be used for ulterior motives. He already is beginning to understand the challenge of life and change. He, too, will find his life's journey taking him elsewhere down an exciting yellow brick road, where greater opportunity and greater challenge abounds.

But what about the city of Louisville and those involved in the odyssey?

In 2024, each of those determined supporters who played a positive role in the odyssey will be twenty years older. Some will still be with us and some won't. Despite the loss, each of them should be proud of their effort and vision. There should be no regret.

For the city of Louisville, if I could rub the genie's bottle and make two wishes, they would be that in 2024 Louisville's remarkable business community would be as responsive, determined and deeply concerned about the city's economic future as it was during the course of the odyssey; and, likewise, that the editors, reporters and columnists of *The Courier-Journal* would be as fair, concerned and responsible as they were during those frenetic times. Those who comprise these two groups have very much about which to be proud. Every single one of those forward-thinking individuals were legitimate champions.

Of the five who shared primary responsibility for scuttling the NBA dream through failed public leadership, one is already long gone — UofL's president, Dr. John Shumaker. It didn't take very long for him to disappear into the chasm of the non-relevant. Within a short year or so, he spent his way into oblivion and disgrace as president of the University of Tennessee.

Mayor Dave isn't gone. He's reportedly teaching "Leadership" to university students at UofL! One would hope if Louisville has learned anything from this process it would be that his form of public leadership should be retired, permanently.

Of the other three who shared responsibility, UofL athletic director Tom Jurich is still in place, and will be approaching his 70s in 2024. Maybe he'll have realized by then that his primary mission as a university athletic director is to assure that its student-athletes are assimilated into the educational process of the university and educated beyond merely graduating, and to be fully prepared to make a positive contribution to their families and community. Maybe UofL will have enjoyed a successful experience in the Big East Conference, into which he has worked so hard to accomplish admission. If it does, that will be nice for the university's athletic program, but the city of Louisville will not have prospered as a result.

Rick Pitino will be 72. Maybe he'll be with us and maybe he won't. Maybe he'll have won an NCAA championship for UofL and maybe he won't. One thing is for sure; even if he wins five NCAA championships, during those twenty years there will be virtually no taxable revenue streams into Louisville's coffers as a result of those championships. Louisville and its school system receive tax revenue primarily from occupational, property and business license taxes. The basketball television revenue received by the university's athletic program isn't taxed, nor is the athletic department. Amateur collegiate players don't receive locally taxable salaries, nor do the players purchase expensive local homes or other such items as would NBA players and front-office personnel with a $65-75 million annual payroll, nor do collegiate players invest money into the local business economy, nor do they create charitable foundations through which to benefit the community's less fortunate.

No major national or international companies are likely to relocate their corporate headquarters to Louisville because Rick Pitino won an NCAA tournament or because UofL's athletic program was admitted into the Big East Conference. Not a single major American city can realistically point to any significant enhancement of its economy or tax base as a result of successful amateur collegiate athletics in the city. There's a simple reason for this. Major businesses are led by highly-trained officers, managers and employees, who have graduated from and have allegiances to a wide variety of universities. This doesn't mean that corporate executives or employees of such businesses aren't interested in or concerned about local universities—it simply means their horizons are generally larger. Those larger horizons become increasingly imbedded into the lives of the cities in which those businesses locate. The natural progression in such cities finds their universities partnering with the local governments and businesses for the purpose of their joint and mutual economic advancement. The universities there participate in the collaborative effort by offering the benefits of their research and intellectual capacity—not their football or basketball team. Nor will the Jefferson County public school system, which is also fueled by occupational and property taxes, have a larger tax base from which to better educate the community's children because of a successful collegiate athletic program at UofL.

And "Meddlin' Malcolm" is still meddling in mediocrity, mostly by long distance from his Florida home. His tiny footprint in Louisville will soon be gone, but the long-term damage he did will live for a long time.

In sum, all those UofL collegiate athletic victories, whether in bowl games or the NCAA tournament, will be represented in the year 2024 by nothing other than warm memories, a yellowed scrapbook, and a bunch of rusting silver or gold cups sitting on a shelf in a city that trails, even further, its competitor cities who have taken progressive steps to enhance their tax base. For sure, Louisville will feel good about itself as a result of UofL's athletic accomplishments, much like Kentuckians did when they marched down the Glory Road with Adolph Rupp, but Louisville as a city will gain no more lasting benefit than a few hotel room stays.

Missing will be the simple realization that a city only advances past its competitors by virtue of developing a tax base that expands more rapidly than theirs. It's not any more complicated than that.

Simple local political leadership would have allowed this to be understood by Louisvillians — but it didn't occur.

Leadership and Action

Leadership and Action. For centuries, observations by great leaders about these two concepts have served as inspiration for many. Chrysler's savior, Lee Iacocca, once observed, "So what do we do? Anything. Something. So long as we just don't sit there. If we screw it up, start over. Try something else. If we wait until we've satisfied all the uncertainties, it's probably going to be too late."

The famed and elegant British Prime Minister Margaret Thatcher's observation about leadership (previously noted in the beginning of Chapter Eleven) is particularly relevant to Louisville's predicament. When being challenged by doubters following her decision to send British troops to the Falkland Islands, she observed: "Lack of consensus is no reason for lack of leadership."

John F. Kennedy's *Profiles in Courage* chronicles the stories of eight former U.S. Senators who exhibited enormous political courage, often at the risk of their reputations and careers. Their busts in Statutory Hall of the nation's Capitol Building are silent reminders that among the largest challenges of public life is the requirement for political leaders to do what is right and to make difficult choices. Kennedy referred to it as possessing grace under pressure, which can be otherwise defined as having the moral courage to lead, despite the political consequences, political pressures or obstacles.

Niccolo Machiavelli wrote *The Prince* while in exile. His book offered advice to the Medici family, hoping they would release him from exile and permit him to resume his political career. Among the many prescient things he wrote 550 years ago is something particularly applicable to Louisville's NBA odyssey: "There is nothing more difficult to carry out, nor more doubtful of success, nor dangerous to handle, than to initiate a new order of things. For the reformer has enemies in all those who profit by the old order, and only lukewarm defenders in those who would profit by the new order...."

A new order of things

The NBA odyssey about which you have read primarily involved a new order of things in five American cities—Houston, Charlotte, Memphis, New Orleans and Louisville. At the conclusion of the odyssey, four of them are now included on the list of the (now) 29 American cities whose combined gross metropolitan product qualifies them, collectively, as the world's second largest nation. In other words, they are each home to an NBA team (including Charlotte which, subsequent to the odyssey, has been granted an expansion franchise after it lost the Hornets). The city excluded from this world economic hub is Louisville. It was done in by its own hand.

In each of these cities there existed, at one point or another, political dissension about whether to retain or acquire an NBA franchise. Each city and its political leadership was confronted with same or similar arguments for and against the proposition. Each city in its own way has been historically subjected to peculiar political leadership, none more constricting or debilitating than the infamous Boss Crump political machine in Memphis or the Long family and parish politics of Louisiana. The cities of Houston, Charlotte and Memphis each experienced the peculiar vicissitudes of Republican-dominated county government and a Democratic-dominated city government, as had Louisville. Each of these five cities was southern in its geography and had experienced social difficulties during the twentieth century that were primarily attributable to that southernness. There were deleterious busing issues in Charlotte that led to rancorous civil rights litigation, appealed all the way to the U.S. Supreme Court. Racial disruption had been intense in Houston, and for decades Martin Luther King's assassination had cast a pall over Memphis, its image and its future. The state legislatures of each state comprising these five cities had routinely provided less than adequate K-through-12 public education funding. Each city possessed a nationally-prominent local newspaper with significant local and regional influence. And at various stages in the process, each city's newspaper, including Louisville's, editorially supported the economic importance to the city of its attracting or retaining an NBA team.

While many of the arguments of the anti's in each city were similar, there is one particularly noteworthy distinction between the anti-arguments in Louisville and the four other cities of Houston, Charlotte, New Orleans and Memphis. In Houston a new arena for the Rockets wasn't opposed because of a latent fear that the team's success would endanger the Houston arts or its baseball Astros or its new NFL team. In Charlotte, the Hornets were never accused of being hurtful or damaging to other local entertainment such as NASCAR or its arts or its local university. In Memphis, the university's new and exciting young collegiate coach (unlike Pitino) supported the city's NBA pursuit as an economic boost for the city. In New Orleans, the city's other entertainment venues were en masse in support of the NBA in New Orleans, believing it provided a necessary and essential economic boost to the city. This was believed in the Crescent City, even to the extent of the state legislature's willingness to redirect hotel/motel tax revenues from other particular interests to the Saints and the Hornets. Generally, in each of these cities, there was an all-encompassing belief, encouraged by visionary political leadership, that a rising tide raises all boats.

But in Louisville, the debate content was far different. There was the ever-present, inexplicable, and well-publicized fear that an NBA team would result in a major economic detriment to every conceivable existing organization, from soup kitchens, to the Crusade for Children, to Churchill Downs, to the arts, to the public library, to the local university. In Louisville this doubt and fear was seized upon by a certain ilk of people who, for their own personal reasons, chose to exaggerate the danger of change and the fear of the unknown.

But each of the other cities, after all the dissension and in spite of it, found a way to effectively and deftly apply local political leadership and vision to understand their destiny, allowing them to avoid the triple threats of short-sightedness, aversion to change, and fear of the unknown—each city, except Louisville.

Each southern state in which these five cities exist has had citizens during the twentieth century who have retarded the development of each state and city. But none of these states other than Kentucky have deliberately set upon a course of conduct to thwart the progressive development of its largest city. Further, none of these states except Kentucky has experienced a dominating individual like Adolph Rupp, who spent 42 years successfully ingraining into the fabric of the state an intractable disdain of big city life, coupled with an aversion to change and fear of the future. None of these four other southern cities have had their elan, their spirit or their economic importance circumscribed for over a century by their state governmental, legislative and political process, as has Louisville.

Want an example of what I mean? During the odyssey some said Freedom Hall was "fine." But is it? When Freedom Hall was opened on September 10, 1956, Dwight Eisenhower was President, and Alaska and Hawaii weren't even states yet. In this era, Louisville's grandiose Freedom Hall was one of the nation's largest and most spectacular arenas. The NCAA played its national championship there six times in a dozen years —*but never returned again after 1969.* By the year 2000 there was <u>no major city in America whose primary arena was 46 years old</u>. During those 46 years Indianapolis constructed a downtown arena, then demolished it and built a new one that became the pride of the city, as did San Antonio, Denver, Atlanta,

Philadelphia, Portland, Phoenix, Salt Lake City, Dallas and Cleveland.

The decline of Freedom Hall over those years was not better exhibited than in the December 31, 2000 issue of *Pollstar* Magazine. It was reported that the year of 2000 found the list of the Top 25 indoor concert venues, in terms of concert tickets sold, to be comprised of twelve NBA arenas. The twenty-fifth ranked arena was the Savis Center in St. Louis, which sold 191,252 concert tickets. Freedom Hall was not listed. Well hidden in its annual report were Freedom Hall's statistics. In 2000, Freedom Hall sold only 129,133 non-State Fair concert tickets. Upon being asked, Pollstar officials estimated that Freedom Hall would have ranked between 75th and 100th in the nation in concert attendance.

Simply stated, by the year 2000, Louisville's Freedom Hall was an old, unkempt, uninviting, non-relevant entertainment and economic-generating venue, *from which the city gained virtually no taxable revenue.* But some still said Freedom Hall was "fine." As Rick Pitino observed, "It's where the All-Americans played"—completely ignoring the fact that All-Americans played in the Boston Garden, Chicago Stadium, the Salt Palace in Salt Lake City, the Hemisphere in San Antonio, Reunion Center in Dallas, the War Memorial Auditorium in Phoenix and Market Square Arena in Indianapolis —all of which had been replaced in the 1990s.

Its age and physical deterioration weren't the only problems Freedom Hall presented for Louisville. Its ownership by the state prevented any direct economic benefit by the city, because the state pays no local property tax and the rental receipts, sales taxes and parking fees from its usage belonged to the state. However, the modern NBA arenas were all built in downtown areas and were financed through bonding vehicles that permitted and encouraged tax revenues for their cities. The downtown location of these modern NBA arenas also became centerpieces for other development in the city's center core, which added additional revenue streams for the NBA cities. All of this was available during Louisville's NBA odyssey and the bonding vehicle would have provided for the city's ownership of the arena.

It was all so simple. In the midst of its fear of the unknown Louisville didn't comprehend the simplicity of the matter, and the Kentucky state legislators weren't willing to relinquish their direct control over Freedom Hall and Louisville's future.

What happens when a city passes up an opportunity for growth and development? Often its political leaders entertain a process of self-analysis, hoping to find excuses for their failure. In their self-analysis since World War II, often Louisville leaders have excused its failure to effectively compete with other cities because:

•it isn't the state capitol. Neither are Charlotte, Portland or San Antonio.

•in the 1950s it was faced with a rust-belt economic base driven by declining industries such as tobacco and whiskey. Yet Indianapolis was a major rust belt city; Charlotte's economy was confronted with torturous furniture and tobacco declines; Portland was affected by the two-decade-long logging industry recession; Denver by decline in mining (the original reason for the city); and San Antonio was constantly subject to the annual whim and caprice of federal military spending.

•the socio-economic difficulties the city experienced with busing. Yet Denver and Charlotte each had similar problems that exploded to the extent of being litigated in federal courts; Denver, Charlotte and San Antonio each experienced socio-economic disorientation due to enormous recent increases in their Latino population.

In reality, and try as a Louisvillian can to find one, there are no acceptable excuses for Louisville's 50-year snooze.

Nothing, not a single thing in the entire NBA odyssey, is more indicative of Louisville's absolute incapacity to understand its ability to grasp beyond its reach than a piece of data obtained during the odyssey. Virtually everyone involved in the NBA industry across the nation believed from an economic standpoint that, despite its century-long problems, Louisville was still the single most logical available NBA market. That information unquestionably established that there was absolutely no real or economic excuse for Louisville's failure to perform.

This most utterly amazing (and unreported) fact was SportsEconomics, Inc.'s study completed and released in March 2001 by Dr. Daniel Rascher.[305] The study was previously discussed in these pages but not fully obtained until recently. It was a detailed "Financial Success Model" utilizing a data set of nineteen variables, whose purpose was to determine the best potential city for NBA expansion from an economic standpoint. The study clearly showed that Louisville was more economically capable of maintaining a financially-successful NBA franchise *than any other city in the competition*. The following table, contained in the appendix to the study, is instructive as it summarizes the findings. The cities without an NBA team are bolded, with Memphis, Norfolk, St. Louis and New Orleans (the cities then in competition for the Grizzlies) underlined and bolded.

Forecast Results for Location Model Predicting Best NBA Cities

City	Forecast Rating	City	Forecast Rating
Boston	1.000	Miami	0.575
Chicago	1.000	San Antonio	0.503
Dallas	1.000	**Norfolk**	**0.426**
Detroit	1.000	**Las Vegas**	**0.406**
Houston	1.000	Milwaukee	0.385
Los Angeles	1.000	**Baltimore**	**0.379**
Minneapolis	1.000	**St. Louis**	**0.294**
New York City	1.000	**Pittsburgh**	**0.282**
Philadelphia	1.000	Cleveland	0.273
Washington, D.C.	1.000	**Memphis**	**0.245**
Atlanta	0.999	Sacramento	0.191
Portland	0.999	**Hartford**	**0.135**
Seattle	0.992	**Austin**	**0.118**
Phoenix	0.984	**Nashville**	**0.094**
Salt Lake City	0.954	**Kansas City**	**0.024**
Charlotte	0.900	**Cincinnati**	**0.002**
Indianapolis	0.889	**Columbus**	**0.002**
San Diego	**0.850**	**New Orleans**	**0.002**
Orlando	0.845	**Jacksonville**	**0.000**
Denver	0.688	**Albuquerque**	**0.000**
Louisville	**0.649**	**Buffalo**	**0.000**

Unbelievable! But it is even worse now. In the August 2004 issue of the *Journal of Sports Management*, Dr. Rascher has revised his 2001 research. Louisville has vaulted past San Diego and is given a rating of 0.740.[306]

Where does Louisville go from here? The answer centers around one simple question: To whom does Louisville's future belong?

Does it belong to those who fear the future and change, whose first answer to any risk proposition is "No," or "We can't do it"? Does it belong to those who, when the chips are down, will deliberately deceive the public and appeal to Louisville's fears? The odyssey you've just read reveals the names of many of these people—and there are more. Those people are never hard to find; they are everywhere and fully capable of finding something wrong with virtually anything and everything. Did this ilk of people ever direct progress in the history of mankind? Never. When will this kind of people ever direct progress in the future? Never.

Louisville's future does not belong to them. Louisville's future, as have Houston's, Charlotte's, Memphis' and New Orleans', belongs with a completely different group: men and women of vision, courage, persistence, confidence, conscience, integrity, creativity, enthusiasm and character. Men and women who, no matter their age, have the ability to think big, think young, think positive, think proud and think growth, development and change. Men and women who are prepared to think in terms of the common good for all, believing that, in this process, the city will progress, and they will not be hurt or endangered by progress. These are the people possessive of the extraordinary ability to ignore the chaos, confusion and negative impulses that surround them. These are the people who are able to share their vision and impart it to others by their actions and life. They are the leaders. They are the people who live by Robert Kennedy's thought: "Some men see things as the are and say why; others see things as they should be and say why not." Or heed Teddy Roosevelt's advice: "Far better it is to dare mighty things, to win glorious triumphs even though checkered by failure, than to take rank among those timid souls who neither enjoy much nor suffer much, because they live in the gray twilight that knows not victory nor defeat."

Those are the people who will have to step up and lead if the young people here are going to find their bright future in Louisville. It cannot continue to be the anti's or vacillators or fools about whom you've just read, whose guiding principle in life is to protect their turf by closing the door to any opportunity that might challenge their hegemony.

Each year as election days approach, every Louisvillian should ask him or herself: Down which path do the present local political leaders dare to lead? It's *the* critical question for Louisville and its future.

To be sure, the leadership platform is there, as it is in every city. A lot of young people in Louisville are waiting, hopeful that the next book's title will be "Swish!", not "Airball."

Has Louisville learned anything from this process I've called "the NBA odyssey"? Time will tell. But we end just as we started, with a quote from

Will and Ariel Durant: "When the group or a civilization declines, it is through no mystic limitation of a corporate life, but through the failure of its political or intellectual leaders to meet the challenges of change."

A final aside

I finished the first draft of this book on Mother's Day, 2003, and the next draft on Father's Day of that year. On that Father's Day, the San Antonio Spurs won the NBA championship in San Antonio for the second time in five years. The victory occurred in San Antonio's brand-new $250 million arena before an international television audience of several hundred million people. It was a fitting victory for an old ABA city—a city whose team in those Long Ago Days of Magic couldn't hold a candle to Louisville and its Kentucky Colonels, but a city that became big-league because its political and civic leadership was determined to renounce the fear of the unknown. It was all done while Louisville slept.

ENDNOTES

AUTHOR'S NOTE

1. Seattle, Portland, Sacramento, Phoenix, Dallas, Houston, San Antonio, Salt Lake City, Denver, New Orleans, Memphis, Orlando, Miami, Atlanta, Charlotte, Indianapolis and Milwaukee.
2. Gunther, John, *Inside U.S.A.*, p. 693

CHAPTER ONE: When the Saints Come Marchin' In

3. Chris Poynter, *The Courier-Journal*, January 19, 2002.
4. (See chart page 391)
5. Street & Smith's, *Sports Business Journal*, Vol. 6, Issue 44, March 1-7, 2004.
6. In the 2003-4 playing season NBA teams possess contracts with 87 foreign players from 36 nations of the world. *Ibid.*, at p. 35. Additionally in November, 2003 the NBA reported that 51.2% of the 58 million hits on its website during the month of November were placed from foreign countries., *Ibid*, Vol. 6, Issue 33, p. 9.
7. Street & Smith, *Sports Business Journal*, Vol. 6, Issue 27, p. 26
8. Ibid., p. 35.
9. U.S. Bureau of Census, Table 18, *100 Largest Urban Places: 1950*

CHAPTER TWO: Louisville Becomes Infected With Kentucky

10. Many books have been read and studied in the development of this chapter's thesis. They are listed in the Bibliography. Certain of these books offer analysis about what happened to Kentucky between 1800-1930. There are various excuses offered for its economic regression. Some blame it on the continued westward migration — however, that doesn't explain Missouri's 20th century economic success nor that of St. Louis or Kansas City. Others blame it on the Civil War, which doesn't explain the economic emergence of Atlanta or Nashville or Charlotte in the 20th century. From this study, I will offer my analysis and conclusion/s/. The reader is invited to agree or disagree.
11. Clark, Dr. Thomas D., *A History of Kentucky*, p. 477. Dr. Clark is Kentucky's Historian Laureate for Life and has been awarded the American Historical Association's Award for Scholarly Distinction. He has written over 30 monographs and books, among them: *The Rampaging Frontier* (1939), *Frontier America* (1959), *The Emerging South* (1961) and *The South Since Appomattox* (1967).
12. Gunther, John, *Inside U.S.A.,* p. 693.
13. Harrison, Lowell H. & Klotter, James C., *A New History of Kentucky*, p. 102.
14. *Ibid.*, p. 152.
15. *Ibid.*, p. 136.
16. *Ibid.*, pp. 100-02.
17. *Ibid.*. p. 90.
18. *Ibid.*, p. 102.
19. Klein, Maury, *History of the Louisville & Nashville Railroad*, p. 1.
20. Harrison, Lowell H. & Klotter, James C., *A New History of Kentucky*, p. 153.
21. *Ibid.*, p. 102.
22. *Ibid.*, p. 102.
23. *Ibid.*, p. 130.

Source: Global Insight (formerly DRI [Data Resources, Inc.] and WEFA [Wharton Econometric Forecasting Associates]) study done for National Conference of Mayors, Spring 2003. The study records the following Gross Product of Countries and Metro Areas, with cities containing an NBA franchise underlined.

Rank City	US$ (in billions)	Rank City	US$ (in billions)
1. USA	10,208.00	61. Riverside	91.12
2. Japan	4,145.00	62. Iran	89.00
3. Germany	1,849.00	63. Tampa/St.Pete	88.78
4. Britain	1,431.00	64. Egypt	88.00
5. France	1,307.00	65. Malaysia	87.50
6. China	1,160.00	66. Singapore	85.60
7. Italy	1,089.00	67. Cleveland	84.53
8. Canada	700.00	68. Pittsburgh	83.73
9. Mexico	594.00	69. Colombia	80.60
10. Spain	585.00	70. New Haven	79.72
11. India	507.00	71. Miami	76.77
12. Brazil	505.00	72. Portland	73.64
13. New York City	461.01	73. Philippines	71.40
14. South Korea	423.00	74. Puerto Rico	70.30
15. Los Angeles	389.72	75. Kansas City	69.35
16. Netherlands	380.00	76. Charlotte	67.91
17. Australia	355.00	77. Hartford	67.90
18. Chicago	348.61	78. Sacramento	66.75
19. Russia	310.00	79. Fort Worth	65.70
20. Taiwan	282.00	80. Middlesex	64.92
21. Argentina	260.00	81. Chile	64.90
22. Boston, MA.	256.06	82. United Arab Em.	64.20
23. Switzerland	246.70	83. Columbus	63.85
24. Wash. D.C.	228.30	84. Cincinnati	63.16
25. Belgium	228.30	85. Orlando	62.77
26. Sweden	209.80	86. Indianapolis	61.03
27. Houston	190.04	87. Bergen/Passaic	60.78
28. Philadelphia	188.59	88. Las Vegas	58.97
29. Austria	188.10	89. Pakistan	57.50
30. Poland	177.00	90. Milwaukee	57.11
31. Atlanta	175.28	91. San Antonio	56.95
32. Saudi Arabia	169.60	92. Czech Republic	56.40
33. Dallas	169.58	93. Peru	55.90
34. Norway	163.90	94. Algeria	55.10
35. Denmark	162.40	95. Norfolk/Va.Beach	53.26
36. Hong Kong	161.60	96. Hungary	51.10
37. Detroit	159.84	97. Ft.Lauderdale	50.08
38. Indonesia	145.30	98. Greensboro	49.96
39. Orange Co.	142.59	99. Austin.	49.80
40. Turkey	142.00	100. New Zealand	49.60
41. Minneapolis	128.06	101. Buffalo	49.55
42. Venezuela	124.90	102. Salt Lake City	49.10
43. Seattle	124.41	103. Nashville	46.26
44. Finland	121.10	104. Raleigh/Durham	47.83
45. Phoenix	119.32	105. Rochester	46.92
46. Greece	115.50	106. New Orleans	46.26
47. South Africa	113.30	107. Bangladesh	46.20
48. Thailand	113.20	108. Jacksonville	45.61
49. San Diego	113.14	109. Richmond	45.49
50. San Francisco	112.58	110. GrandRapids	43.83
51. Nassau/Suffolk	111.89	111. Memphis	42.17
52. Israel	109.40	112. Louisville	40.25
53. Portugal	105.20	113. Romania	39.70
54. Ireland	103.60	114. Albany/Schnec.	39.67
55. Baltimore	100.32	115. Ukraine	39.00
56. Oakland	99.46	116. Nigeria	38.80
57. Newark	98.40	117. WestPalmBch	36.08
58. Denver	95.99	118. Kuwait	35.20
59. St. Louis	92.77	119. Honolulu	35.01
60. San Jose	91.53	120. Morocco	34.10

24.Clark, Thomas D., *A History of Kentucky*, p. 184.

25. Harrison, Lowell H. & Klotter, James C., *A New History of Kentucky*, pp. 102-03.

26. *Ibid.*, p. 132.

27. *Ibid.*, p. 132.

28. Clark, Thomas D., *A History of Kentucky*, p. 187.

29. Klein, Maury, *History of the Louisville & Nashville Railroad*, p. 94.

30. Clark, Thomas D., *A History of Kentucky*, pp. 185-87.

31. U.S. Bureau of Census, Table 8, *100 Largest Urban Places: 1850*

32. New Albany, Indiana — 8,181 and Indianapolis, Indiana — 8,091. See: U.S. Bureau of the Census, Table 8, *Population of 100 Largest Urban Places: 1850.*

33. Harrison, Lowell H. & Klotter, James C., *A New History of Kentucky,* pp. 161-2.

34. Clark, Thomas D., *Agrarian Kentucky*, p.128

35. Harrison, Lowell H. & Klotter, James C., *A New History of Kentucky*, p. 118.

36. *Ibid.*, p. 141.

37. Clark, Thomas D., *Agrarian Kentucky*, p. 129

38. Harrison, Lowell H. & Klotter, James C., *A New History of Kentucky*, p. 130.

39. Klein, Maury, *History of the Louisville & Nashville Railroad*, p. 5.

40. *Ibid.*, pp. 12-14.

41. *Ibid.*, p. 6.

42. 150 years later, during the upcoming NBA odyssey the question would present itself —Could Louisville's mayor and board of aldermen exhibit similar political courage, vision and determination?

43. Harrison, Lowell H. & Klotter, James C., *A New History of Kentucky*, p. 132.

44. Klein, Maury, *History of the Louisville & Nashville Railroad*, p. 17.

45. *Ibid.,* p. 17.

46. *Ibid.*, p. 17.

47. "Few, if any, of the southerners were cognizant of the fact that the railroad was becoming the most important factor in the economic life of the Mississippi Valley." Clark, *A History of Kentucky*, p. 382.

48. Klein, Maury, *History of the Louisville & Nashville Railroad,* p. 42.

49. *Ibid.*, pp. 90-1.

50. Harrison, Lowell H. & Klotter, James C., *A New History of Kentucky*, p. 141.

51. Clark, Thomas D., *A History of Kentucky*, p. 382.

52. U.S. Bureau of Census, Table 10, *100 Largest Urban Places: 1870.*

53. Harrison, Lowell H. & Klotter, James C., *A New History of Kentucky*, p. 247-50.

54. *Ibid.*, p. 340.

55. *Ibid.*, p. 219.

56. *Ibid.*, p. 240.

57. *Ibid.*, p. 235.

58. *Ibid.*, p. 244.

59. Kentucky's ratification of the Thirteenth and Fifteenth Amendments occurred in 1976, with the written notation— "...this Bicentennial Year is an appropriate time to erase this shadow on Kentucky's history." Harrison, Lowell H. & Klotter, James C., *A New History of Kentucky*, p. 180.

60. *Ibid.*, p. 212.

61. *Ibid.*, p. 220.

62. *Ibid.*, p. 212.

63. Klein, Maury, *History of the Louisville & Nashville Railroad*, pp. 104-05

64. *Ibid.*, p. 95.

65. *Ibid.*, pp. 95-6.

66. *Ibid.*, p. 108.

67. Dr. Thomas Clark best described this inter-city economic warfare as: "Behind this movement to build efficient rail connections to the south was a life and death struggle to strangle Cincinnati's southern trade." Clark, Thomas D., *A History of Kentucky*, p. 384.

68. Klein, Maury, *History of the Louisville & Nashville Railroad*, pp. 92-3.

69. Harrison, Lowell H. & Klotter, James C., *A New History of Kentucky*, p. 230-31.

70. U.S. Bureau of Census, Table 10, *100 Largest Urban Places: 1870*

71. U.S. Bureau of Census, Tables 8 *100 Largest Urban Places: 1850* and Table 10, *100 Largest Urban Places: 1870*.

72. Clark, Thomas D., *A History of Kentucky*, p. 386.

73. Klein, Maury, *History of the Louisville & Nashville Railroad*, p. 109 "It became apparent early that bribery and other chicanery would be tolerated, *even approved*; the only morality on the subject pertained to the source of the money. Most of the lobbyists agreed that the war chest should come from private contributors rather than from the public coffers."

74. *Ibid.*, p. 110.

75. Tapp, Hamilton & Klotter, James C., *Kentucky: Decades of Discord 1965-1900*, p. 58.

76. Klein, Maury, *History of the Louisville & Nashville Railroad*, pp. 171-87.

77. *Ibid.*, p. 251.

78. *Ibid.*, p. 252-54.

79. *Ibid.*, p. 256.

80. *Ibid.*, p. 295.

81. Clark, Thomas D., *A History of Kentucky*, p. 397.

82. Harrison, Lowell H. & Klotter, James C., *A New History of Kentucky*, p. 272.

83. U.S. Bureau of Census, Table 13, *100 Largest Urban Places: 1900*

84. *Ibid.*

85. King, Moses, *King's Handbook of the United States*, p. 645.

86. *Ibid.*, p. 278.

87. *Ibid.*, p. 285.

88. *Ibid.*, p. 290.

89. *Ibid.*, p. 290.

90. *Ibid.*, p. 279.

91. *Ibid.*, p. 280.

92. *Ibid.*, p. 289.

93. Tapp, Hamilton & Klotter, James C., *Kentucky: Decades of Discord 1965-1900*, p. 204.

94. *Ibid.*, p. 190.

95. *Ibid.*, p. 191.

96. *Ibid.*, p. 63.

97. Harrison, Lowell H. & Klotter, James C., *A New History of Kentucky*, pp. 274-77. In

Frankfort, Percy Haly ran the town, Lexington was Billy Klair's domain, western Kentucky was controlled by Tom Rhea and 'Doc' Beachamp; central Kentucky was led by 'Boss' Ben Johnson and J. Dan Talbott and eastern Kentucky was daily under the thumb of the Morehead Manipulator, Albert 'Allie' Young.

98. Clark, Thomas D., *A History of Kentucky*, p. 474.

99. *Ibid.*, p. 474.

100. The Southern Intercollegiate Athletic Association, as formed, and in addition to Kentucky A&M, was comprised of: Alabama Polytechnical Institute (Auburn), Georgia Tech, the University of the South (Sewanee), Vanderbilt, Alabama, Georgia, North Carolina, Central, Clemson, Cumberland, L.S.U., Mercer, Mississippi A&M, Nashville, Southern Presbyterian, Tulane, Tennessee and Texas. Betsy Boles Ellison, *Kentucky's Domain of Power, Greed and Corruption*, Writer's Club Press, 2001, p. 5.

101. Betsy Boles Ellison, *Kentucky's Domain of Power, Greed and Corruption*, Writer's Club Press, 2001, at pp. 5-7.

102. "The older we get the more set in our ways we become. We've found out what our comfort level is, and we all want to stay with it. We don't want to be risk takers anymore, because risk frightens us, and simply not changing seems easiest." Rick Pitino, *Success is a Choice*, p. 27.

CHAPTER THREE: Rupp Creates, Then Becomes "The Religion"

103. Rosen, Charley *The Scandals of '51*, at pp. 10-12.

104. Fitzpatrick, Frank, *And the Walls Came Tumbling Down*, p. 91-2.

105. "His word was law. And if you forgot it, he'd be there with a lash." Frank Fitzpatrick, *And the Walls Came Tumbling Down*, p. 92.

106. *Ibid.*, p. 92.

107. Rice, Russell, *Adolph Rupp, Kentucky's Basketball Baron*, p. 5.

108. Frank Fitzpatrick, *And the Walls Came Tumbling Down*, p. 93.

109. Rice, Russell, *Adolph Rupp, Kentucky's Basketball Baron*, p. 6.

110. *Ibid.*, p. 10.

111. Fitzpatrick, Frank, *And the Walls Came Tumbling Down.*, p. 91.

112. Rice, Russell, *Adolph Rupp, Kentucky's Basketball Baron*, p. 17

113. Harrison, Lowell H. & Klotter, James C., *A New History of Kentucky*, p. 358.

114. *Ibid.*, p. 303.

115 *Ibid.*, p. 320.

116. Stoll and his *Herald-Leader* would refuse to print stories about civil rights issues as late as the 1960s. Harrison, Lowell H. & Klotter, James C., *A New History of Kentucky*, p. 320. Ironically, in mid-2004, *The Lexington Herald-Leader* devoted their entire first page to an "apology" for this conduct.

117. *Ibid.*, p. 320.

118. *Ibid.*, p. 361.

119. "The sheer power of the Baron's personality rapidly propelled the game of basketball throughout the state. It wasn't long before basketball was Kentucky's official sport." Charley Rosen, *The Scandals of '51*, p. 85.

120. Fitzpatrick, Frank, *And the Walls Came Tumbling Down*, p. 19.

121. *Ibid.*, p. 21.

122. Billy Reed, *The Louisville SportsReport*, May 22, 2002, pp. 16-17.

123. Harrison, Lowell H. & Klotter, James C., *A New History of Kentucky*, p. 385.

124. A classic example of the "fruity myth" that has developed around Adolph Rupp is found in Russell Rice's book, *Adolph Rupp, Kentucky's Baron of Basketball*, where it is written, "The Original Celtics had taught Rupp all he knew about the New York style of play....featuring players like Dutch Dehnert, Nat Holman, and Joe Lapchick. They had come to Alumni Gym....Rupp said there was much to learn from the Celtics and I would stay until the wee hours of the morning talking to them." (*Ibid.*, p. 54.) In reality, Nat Holman didn't play for the Original Celtics during Rupp's tenure as UK coach.

125. *Scientific Basketball* (1921); *Winning Basketball* (1933); *Championship Basketball* (1942) and *Holman on Basketball* (1950). [See: Nat Holman biography in Naismith Basketball Hall of Fame website, www.hoopball.com]

126. Charley Rosen, *The Scandals of '52*, p. 52

127. *Ibid.*, p. 54.

128. *Ibid.*, pp. 16-7.

129. Fitzpatrick, Frank, *And the Walls Came Tumbling Down*, p. 57.

130. *Ibid.*, p. 57.

131 "Our boys are under constant and absolutely complete supervision while they're on the road. Especially in New York." Charley Rosen, *The Scandals of '51*, p. 86.

132. Frank Fitzpatrick, *And the Walls Came Tumbling Down*, p. 134.

133. Charley Rosen, *The Scandals of '51*, p. 165.

134. *Ibid.*, p. 188-89.

135. Fitzpatrick, Frank, *And the Walls Came Tumbling Down*, p. 100.

136. Gunther, John, *Inside U.S.A.*, p. 693.

137. "...he had played football for the University of Kentucky from 1945 to 1947." Charley Rosen, *The Scandals of '51*, at p. 157; and Fitzpatrick, Frank, *And the Walls Came Tumbling Down*, p. 157.

138. Martin Fennelly, "A mistake that changed a life", *Tampa Tribune*, March 26, 1999.

139. Charley Rosen, *The Scandals of '51*, p. 191.

140. *Ibid.*, p. 191.

141. At least two particular games have been ascertained and reported: the Alabama v. Kentucky game (Charley Rosen, *The Scandals of '51*, p. 170) and the Xavier v. Kentucky game (Frank Fitzpatrick, *And the Walls Came Tumbling Down*, p. 101).

142. Charley Rosen, *The Scandals of '51*, p. 202.

143. Fitzpatrick, Frank, *And the Walls Came Tumbling Down*, p. 101.

144. "In the gambling world, Curd was the equivalent of the man who invented the wheel. Because of point spread betting, illegal gambling grew into a multi-billion dollar a year business." Billy Reed, *Louisville SportsReport*, May 22, 2002.

145. Billy Reed, *The Louisville SportsReport*, May 22, 2002, pp. 16-17.

146. Confirmed at Charley Rosen, *The Scandals of '51*, p. 170; and Frank Fitzpatrick, *And the Walls Came Tumbling Down*, p. 101.

147. A classic example of the continuing obfuscation of Adolph Rupp's attitude is exemplified by Earl Cox's rendition in his latest book that constantly extols the virtues and ignores the foibles of Rupp: "I can remember when sports was fun and games. We

didn't have our athletes suspended for a year for drunken driving and others getting their names in the paper and on television for drinking and fighting....At the University of Kentucky when Adolph Rupp was coach, the manager charged with making bed checks knew better than to catch stars. Harry Lancaster, Rupp's trusted sidekick, once told me about being out with Rupp to get a drink. The first nightspot they entered, Lancaster said that Rupp exclaimed, 'Good gawd, Harry, let's get out of here. There's Haig (Cliff Hagan) and (Frank) Ramsey!' Both were All-Americans and Rupp didn't want to know if they were having a little fun." Earl Cox, in *Calling It Like I See It* (Butler Books, 2002)

148. Of the 190 games Rupp lost in 42 years at Kentucky, 153 of them (or 80.5%) were on the road—an inordinately high percentage for the nation's most dominant collegiate basketball program.

149. C. Harvey Gardiner, *Coach Diddle/Mister Diddle*, p. 135.

150. The well-coached Rupp's grand jury testimony on this point was deliberately not forthcoming:

> Q: Were you familiar with the point spread while your team played?
> A: When we played New York, I was acquainted with it, yes, sir.
> Q: Weren't you acquainted with it outside of New York?
> A: Well, you would be but then sometimes we would go six, seven or eight ball games and never know what the games were, when we played in Lexington....
> Q: Did you ever call Ed Curd and ask him what the point spread was?
> A: I did once, yes sir.
> Q: What was the reason for that?
> A: Well, we were sitting out in the athletic office one day and I didn't—I don't remember if I called him or called his office.

151. Transcript of Judge Streit's April 29, 1952 hearing at p. 52. This transcript was very difficult to acquire. It had to be done through the good offices of the archives section of the New York State Library. The passage of time and the reverence for Adolph Rupp has allowed the sworn facts in this trial transcript to become obscured. The entire transcript is so revealing and amazing that it should be preserved for posterity in order to temper the idol worship of Adolph Frederick Rupp.

152. Stuyvesant High School's website reflects that among its graduates have been New York Supreme Court Justices: Thomas Chimera, Samuel DiFalco, Harry B. Frank, Edward Greenfield, Harold T. McLaughlin, Irving Saypol, Ernst Rosenberger and Robert J. Trainor; and U.S. District Court Judges, Denny Chin and Herbert J. Stern. Not bad for an engineering school in Brooklyn.

153. Gunther, John, *Inside the U.S.A.,* pp. 692-3.

154. Donovan was quoted as saying that Justice Streit's Opinion was little more than a "...harangue filled with misrepresentation. According to Judge Streit, all the culprits live in Kentucky. The judge forgets that one of the rottenest gambling joints in the world, Madison Square Garden, is in his own bailiwick." Charley Rosen, *The Scandals of '51*, at p. 203.

155. Charley Rosen, *The Scandals of '51*, p. 203-204.

156. *Ibid.*, p. 206.

157. *Ibid.*, p. 206.

158. *Ibid.*, p. 206.

159. Frank Fitzpatrick, *And The Walls Came Tumbling Down*, p. 101.

160. Russell Rice, *Adolph Rupp: Kentucky's Basketball Baron*, Sagamore Publishing (1994), p. 135.

161. Harrison, Lowell H. & Klotter, James C., *A New History of Kentucky*, p. 384.

162. "The older we get, the more we must change. Change is what keeps us fresh and innovative. Change is what keeps us from getting stale and stuck in the mud. Change is what keeps us young." Rick Pitino, *Success is a Choice*, p. 27.

163. Fox, Larry, *Illustrated History of Basketball.*, pp. 43-58.

164. *Ibid.* pp. 155-56.

165. *Ibid.*, p. 156.

166. *Ibid.*, p. 159.

167. The original members of the BAA were the New York Knickerbockers, Boston Celtics, Providence Steamrollers, Philadelphia Warriors, Washington Capitols, Toronto Huskies, Chicago Stags, St. Louis Bombers, Cleveland Rebels, Detroit Falcons and the Pittsburgh Ironmen. Hollander, Zander, *The NBA's Official Encyclopedia of Pro Basketball*, p. 43.

168. Fox, Larry, *Illustrated History of Basketball*, p. 158-59.

169. *Ibid.*, p. 160.

170. Fitzpatrick, Frank, *And the Walls Came Tumbling Down*, p. 56.

171. Fox, Larry, *Illustrated History of Basketball*, p. 161.

172. Halberstam, David, *The Fifties*, p. 692-94.

173. *Ibid.*, p. 694.

174. *Ibid.*, p. 694.

175. *Ibid.*, p. 694.

176. Wolf, Dave & Bruns, Bill, *The Great Moments in Pro Basketball*, Random House, New York, 1968.

177. Statistics compiled from: Hollander, Zander, *The NBA's Official Encyclopedia of Pro Basketball*, pp. 75-108.

178. Ellison, Betty Boles, *Kentucky's Domain of Power, Greed and Corruption*, p. 65.

179. *Ibid.*, p. 65.

180. *Ibid.*, p. 64.

181. Fitzpatrick, Frank, *And the Walls Came Tumbling Down*, p. 24 and 46.

182. "There is no age limit on transforming your life. No rule that says that after a certain age you are simply the way you are and that's it. Change not only is possible, any time, but is essential." Rick Pitino, *Success is a Choice*, p. 41.

183. *Ibid.*, p. 63.

184. Carey Spicer (twice), Paul McBrayer, Forrest "Aggie" Sale (twice), Ellis Johnson, John DeMoisey, Bernard Opper, Lee Edwards (twice), Bob Brannum, Jack Parkinson, Ralph Beard (3 times), Alex Groza (3 times), Wallace Jones, Bill Spivey, Cliff Hagan (twice), Frank Ramsey (twice), Bob Burrow, Vernon Hatton, Johnny Cox, Cotton Nash (3 times), Pat Riley, Louie Dampier and Dan Issel (twice).

185. Red McCrocklin, Carlyle Towery, Oran McKinney, Dee Gibson, Don Ray, Odie Spears, Johnny Oldham, Bob Lavoy, Rip Gish, Art Spoelstra, Tom Marshall, Bobby Rascoe and Darel Carrier.

186. Charlie Tyra, Don Goldstein, John Turner, Wes Unseld and Alfred "Butch" Beard.
187. Fitzpatrick, Frank, *And the Walls Came Tumbling Down*, p. 37.
188. Rice, Russell, *Adolph Rupp: Kentucky's Basketball Baron*, p. 34.
189. Lancaster, Harry & Caywood Ledford, *Adolph Rupp, As I Knew Him*, Lexington Productions, Inc., 1979, p. 88.
190. Flem D. Sampson (R), Ruby Lafoon (D) , A.B. "Happy" Chandler (twice) (D), Keen Johnson (D), Simeon S. Willis (R), Earle C. Clements (D), Lawrence W. Wetherby (D), Bert T. Combs (D), Edward T. Breathitt (D), Louie B. Nunn (R) and Wendell H. Ford (D).
191. Frank Fitzpatrick, *And the Walls Came Tumbling Down*, p. 20-21.

CHAPTER FOUR
Long Ago Days of Magic — The Incredible Story of the Kentucky Colonels
192. The "life" of the ABA was never fully or adequately chronicled. Several efforts have been made, which are noteworthy and form some of the source information used in this chapter. Most noteworthy are Terry Pluto's book, *Loose Balls: The Short, Wild Life of the American Basketball Association*, Simon & Shuster, 1990, and the website, www.remembertheaba.com. Anyone interested in exploring the history and dynamics of the ABA should examine these sources. Much of the information in this chapter, however, is derived from my own recollection, notes, documents and records resulting from my legal representation during the relevant time frame of a number of ABA and NBA players as well as in person and phone interviews with certain of the individuals involved. Each such living player that I represented has provided his permission to use any reference that I've made to him in this chapter.
193. A retired public relations executive and former mayor of Buena Vista, California, and, reputedly, a voracious Los Angeles Lakers fan.
194. A New York promoter and president of Professional Sports Management Co.
195. The "first" franchise awards were given for varying amounts reported to be from $5,000-30,000 each to: *Anaheim Amigos* (Art Kim and James Ackerman); *Minnesota Muskies* (L.P. Shields & Fred Jefferson); *New Jersey Americans* (Arthur J. Brown and Mark Binstein); *Indiana Pacers* (the DeVoe family and a large group of Indy business-men, including Dick Tinkham); *Houston Mavericks* (William Whitmore, Charles Frazier and Cloyce Box [of Detroit Lions fame]); *New Orleans Buccaneers* (Morton Downey, Jr., Charles G. Smither and a group from New Orleans); *Oakland Oaks* (singer Pat Boone, Ken Davidson and Dennis Murphy); *Dallas Chaparrals* (John Klug and James Peters); *Pittsburgh Pipers* (Gabe Rubin); and the *Kentucky Colonels* (Don Regan).
196. Reportedly, the name, American Basketball Association, was the idea of Murphy's friend and Boston Celtic great, Bill Sharman, as was the 3-point shot.
197. The NBA's immediate answer to the ABA's founding was an expansion to twelve teams by including Seattle and San Diego and realignment of the league for the 1967-68 season.
198. Between the February 2, 1967 formation meeting and the March 31, 1967 formal announcement several ownership changes had already occurred: Houston Mavericks (Cloyce Box sold his interest to T.S. Morrow and Bud Adams [owner of the Houston

Oilers]); Dallas Chaparrals (Klug and Peters sold their interests to a group led by Robert S. Folsom, Jr. [worth a reported $500 million]); and Kentucky Colonels (Don Regan sold his interest to Maime and Joe Gregory and their attorney, William C. Boone [a highly-successful young Louisville attorney who represented Kentucky Fried Chicken and touring PGA golf professionals Frank Beard and Bobby Nichols, from Louisville]).

199. Maime Gregory was the daughter of Senator Robert Reynolds of North Carolina. Her mother was the granddaughter of John R. McLean, who made a fortune mining gold in Colorado and (at one time) owned the Hope Diamond.

200. By the 1968-69 Playing Season: the *Minnesota Muskies* moved to Miami, becoming the *Miami Floridians*; the *Houston Mavericks* were sold to a group led by James Gardner and moved to North Carolina to become the *Carolina Cougars*; the *Oakland Oaks* were moved to Washington, D.C. to become the *Washington Capitols*, for one year, then the *Virginia Squires*; the *Pittsburgh Pipers* were sold to Bill Erickson and moved to Minneapolis as the *Minnesota Pipers* — and when Erickson defaulted, the team moved back to Pittsburgh; the *Anaheim Amigos* were sold to Jim Kirst and moved to Los Angeles to become the *Los Angeles Stars*; and the *New Jersey Americans* moved to Long Island, New York.

201. Bobby Rascoe, Darrel Carrier and Wayne Chapman of Western, Dampier, Cotton Nash and Tommy Kron from UK, Sam Smith and Bud Olsen of UofL. The first coaches, Johnny Givens and Gene Rhodes, were Diddle protégés from Western.

202. This "spurning" is subsequently discussed in the section entitled, "ABA Goes a-Courtin.'"

203. In his first ABA year, Haywood led the league in scoring and rebounding, was chosen as the Rookie of the Year and the league's Most Valuable Player. During his 2-year stint in the ABA he averaged 30 points and 19.5 rebounds per game.

204. These attendance figures were obtained from a combination of sources; namely, the NBA archives and records, the writer's files and newspaper clippings and the www.remembertheaba.com website.

205. The Gregory's retained 3% interest in the Colonels.

206. Eventually, Extendicare sold its nursing homes, bought many more hospitals, changed its name to Humana and became the world's largest hospital company by the mid-1980's. Now, Humana, still headquartered in Louisville, is one of the nation's largest publicly-traded health benefits companies.

207. Eventually, this new law firm was to grow from a dozen lawyers to become one of the region's largest law firms—Greenebaum Doll & McDonald. Grissom's career continued to skyrocket. Leaving the law firm he became the Chairman of Citizens Fidelity Bank & Trust Company, which he merged into PNC Bank, and is now serving as the Chairman of a major Louisville-based venture capital firm known as Mayfair Capital, Inc.

208. Doyle played games home games in Miami Beach, but regionally in Jacksonville, Tampa/St. Petersburg and West Palm Beach.

209. The Cougars played in Greensboro, Winston-Salem, Charlotte and Raleigh, North Carolina.

210. Norm Drucker, Joe Gushue, John Vanak and Earl Strom.

211. Terry Pluto in *Loose Balls* has written that Issel's contract provisions were: a bonus of $72,000 paid out in 10 annual and equal installments; a car, college tuition for his children, a Dolgoff Plan paying him $12,000 a year for ten years beginning in 1989, with owner personally-guaranteed salaries:

1970-71:	$52,000 cash, with $40,000 deferred
1971-72:	$62,000 cash, with $50,000 deferred
1972-73:	$72,000 cash, with $60,000 deferred
1973-74:	$87,000 cash, with $75,000 deferred
1974-75:	$87,000 cash, with $75,000 deferred
1975-76:	$132,000 cash, with $100,000 deferred
1976-77:	$152,000 cash, with $100,000 deferred
1977-78:	$182,000 cash, with $100,000 deferred
1978-79:	$212,000 cash, with $100,000 deferred
1979-80:	$237,000 cash, with $100,000 deferred.

The deferred payments to begin in 1974, ending in 1983 and paid in 216 equal semi-monthly payments. See: Terry Pluto, *Loose Balls*, p. 199.

[**Due to the attorney-client privilege, the author cannot confirm or deny this rendition of Issel's initial contract, other than to say that it was the largest professional athletic contract entered into, at that time.**]

212. See: Endnote #204.

213. Including Wes Unseld, who the Colonels' had lost to the Baltimore Bullets.

214. Cincinnati Sports, Inc. was comprised of William O. DeWitt, Sr., William O. DeWitt, Jr., Albert E. Heekin, III, Lawrence H. Kyte, Jr., Brian E. Heekin, James J. Rammacher, Robert D.H. Anning, Charles L. Heekin, Philip S. Smith, J.R. Williams, Columbia Oldsmobile Company, and George E. Heekin.

215. Julius Erving, Dan Issel, Artis Gilmore, George Gervin, Moses Malone, Mel Daniels, George McGinnis, Bobby Jones, Ralph Sampson, Marvin 'Bad News' Barnes, Roger Brown, Mack Calvin, Connie Hawkins and James Silas.

216. This section is a summary of 31 pages of contemporaneous notes that were taken by me during the period between September 19, 1975 and October 11, 1975. Since I trusted no one at this point other than Dan and Cheri Issel, the purpose of these notes was to accurately chronicle my representation of Issel during this period.

217. 1/2 interests in Fly-by-Venus, Herbager, Indian Nurse and Gleaming. He and Gentry had just sold two thoroughbreds (one by High Echelon and the other by Silent Screen) at the famed Keeneland Summer Sales.

218. While the following several-page, detailed rendition of chronological events could easily be lengthened to a half dozen pages, it is hoped that this shortened version reflects the utter absurdity of the unnecessary events surrounding Issel's sale/trade and sets the stage for the soon-to-occur tragic consequences of those events upon Louisville's first NBA odyssey. It is deemed important for the reader to understand the frustration and utter senselessness of the occasion.

219. TAMS standing for Tennessee, Arkansas and Mississippi!

220. The Baltimore Claws had folded on October 20, 1975; the San Diego Sails were dispersed on November 12, 1975 and the Utah Stars disbanded, selling their players to the Spirits of St. Louis on December 2, 1975.

221. Terry Pluto, *Loose Balls - The Short, Wild Life of the American Basketball Association*, Simon & Schuster, p. 425.

222. *Ibid.* at p. 429.

223. Carl Scheer (Denver Nuggets), Roy Boe (New Jersey Nets), Angelo Drossos (San Antonio Spurs) and Bill Eason (Indiana Pacers).

224. It has been reported that Angelo Drossos's San Antonio ownership group had to borrow $5 million to finance the transaction. *Ibid.* at p. 433. Drossos confirmed this with me at the subsequent Chicago meetings, hereinafter discussed.

225. There is a rendition of the Merger Settlement and the ABA's internal settlement found in Terry Pluto's, *Loose Balls*, at pp. 432-33. It is partially correct. The inaccuracies are noted hereinafter.

226. Terry Pluto has reported in *Loose Balls* at p. 432 that this required payment was $4.8 million. During the course of the evening, I saw the document—the price was $4.5 million. Boe told me that during the evening he had offered Dr. J. to the Knicks for the $4.5 million payment and they had refused.

227. Terry Pluto in *Loose Balls* (at p. 432) reported that the Silna's received $2.1 million plus 4/7ths of the ABA team's TV rights. This is incorrect, as I witnessed the transaction.

228. University of Louisville, Men's Basketball Media Guide, 2002-03, p. 124.

229. Wes Unseld, Alfred "Butch" Beard, Jim Price, Ulysses "Junior" Bridgeman, Allen Murphy and Darrell Griffith.

230. *Ibid.* at p. 136.

231. Billy Knight (Pacers), David Thompson (Nuggets), Dan Issel (Nuggets) and George Gervin (Spurs).

232. Larry Brown.

233. Julius Erving, Bobby Jones and George McGinnis (Philadelphia 76'ers,); Dan Issel and David Thompson (Denver Nuggets); Don Buse, and Billy Knight (Indiana Pacers); George Gervin (San Antonio Spurs); Maurice Lucas (Portland Trailblazers); Artis Gilmore(Chicago Bulls); and Rick Barry (Golden State Warriors).

234. Portland: Maurice Lucas, Dave Twardzik; and Philadelphia: Julius Erving, George McGinnis and Caldwell Jones.

235. George Mikan (ABA Commissioner), Alex Hannum (Coach, Oakland Oaks), Billy Cunningham (Carolina Cougars), Alex English (Denver Nuggets), Julius Erving (New Jersey Nets and Virginia Squires), George Gervin (San Antonio Spurs), Connie Hawkins (Pittsburgh Pipers), Dan Issel (Kentucky Colonels and Denver Nuggets), Frank Ramsey (coach, Kentucky Colonels), Cliff Hagan (Dallas Chaparrals), David Thompson (Denver Nuggets), Moses Malone (St. Louis Spirits), and Larry Brown (Player, Carolina Cougars and Coach, Denver Nuggets).

CHAPTER FIVE: Dinner With the High Priest

236. Rice, Russell, *Adolph Rupp, Kentucky's Baron of Basketball*, at p. 38.

237. Adolph Frederick Rupp died on December 10, 1977.

CHAPTER SIX: Saving The Kentucky Colonels

238. October 2, 1977 Cleveland Cavaliers v. Detroit Pistons; October 5, 1977 Atlanta

Hawks v. Indiana Pacers; October 6, 1977 Cleveland Cavaliers v. Buffalo Braves; October 14, 1977 (doubleheader) Kansas City Kings v. Buffalo Braves and Atlanta Hawks v. New Orleans Jazz and January 19, 1978 Atlanta Hawks v. Chicago Bulls.

239. These net proceeds were used to cover the game expense of programs, publicity and to reimburse the NBA teams' travel expenses. The only teams that required a fee to play were the New Orleans Jazz and the Chicago Bulls. The Hawks originally required one, but it was waived, *personally*, by Ted Turner. The balance was used to fund the Boosters' Club activities. There was no net profit, in the end.

240. Despite the animus that existed in the final meeting of the ABA between John Y. Brown, Jr. and the owners of the four (4) ABA teams that merged with the NBA, invaluable assistance was provided by Gary Antonoff and Carl Scheer of the Denver Nuggets (and their head coach Larry Brown), Angelo Drossos of the San Antonio Spurs (and their head coach Doug Moe and Drossos' assistant, Bob Bass, who would later be the general manager of the Charlotte Hornets during their upcoming foray with Louisville), Roy L. M. Boe of the New Jersey Nets and Jim Walker of the Pacers (and their head coach Bob "Slick" Leonard).

241. Assistance came here from assistant coach, Joe Roberts, who played on the great Ohio State teams of the early 1960s that included: Jerry Lucas, John Havlicek, Larry Siegfried, Mel Nowell and Bobby Knight (a reserve forward) each of whom understood the basketball religion in Kentucky.

242. With the help of their coach, Jerry West (who also understood the basketball religion in Kentucky), and assistant coach Stan Albeck, who was assistant coach to Hubie Brown of the Kentucky Colonels, when they won the ABA championship.

243. As was earlier discussed, Block and Sun's treasurer, Donald Pitt (and the Sun's General Manager, Jerry Colangelo), had made an effort to entice Dan Issel of the Colonels to jump leagues after his rookie season. They were all very familiar with the basketball religion in Kentucky.

244. With advice from Elgin Baylor, the Jazz coach, who had played for Seattle University against Rupp's 1958 team at Freedom Hall for the NCAA championship and fully understood the religion in Kentucky.

245. While Terry Pluto in *Loose Balls* has reported this—and it certainly was a rumor at the time—it was directly and in person denied by Wirtz.

246. Another coach, Bill Fitch of the Cavaliers, was of considerable help in advising his owner (Mileti) about Louisville's value as an NBA market.

247. And re-affirmed by his then-general manager, Stan Kasden.

248. I was never convinced that Pollin would vote for Louisville. Just didn't feel right.

249. Buffalo and Miami-8 pps, Dallas-17 pps, Minneapolis-11 pps and Toronto-12 pps.

250. Source: Coopers & Lybrand, Louisville, Kentucky, September 10, 1976.

251. COMPARATIVE BALANCE SHEETS 1975-76 SEASON

ITEM	BRAVES	COLONELS
ASSETS		
Cash	$179,640	$136,717
Accounts Receivable	196,480	304,956
Receivables from Partners	54,000	
Prepaid Expenses	10,773	12,771
Total Current Assets	386,893	508,444
Equipment, at cost	340,884	61,658
Less Accum.Depreciation	(93,068)	(22,337)
Investments required by players contracts		321,703
Player Acquisition Costs	223,000	676,983
Franchise (less Depreciation)	399,800	296,099
Organization costs		6,641
Other assets		88,723
Total Assets	**$1,346,292**	**$1,849,191**
LIABILITIES		
Current:		
Notes Payable, bank	$500,000	$300,000
Notes Payable, individual	20,000	505,150
Notes Payable, general partner	0	1,219,125
Current installments: long term debt	283,096	0
Deferred players' compensation	99,363	0
Automobile Installment loans		8,340
Accounts Payable	102,414	255,301
Lease cancellation expense (1st year)		33,188
Accrued Expenses (player salaries)	515,606	176,530
Advanced season ticket sales	406,081	0
Total Current Liabilities	**$1,926,560**	**$2,497,634**
Long Term:		
Long-Term debt, excluding current	2,546,039	0
Lease cancellation expense		119,533
Automobile installment loans		12,697
Deferred compensation	1,866,163	357,472
Total Long-Term Liabilities	**4,412,202**	**489,702**
Total Liabilities	**$6,338,762**	**$2,987336**
Deficit:		
Assets vs. Liabilities	**($4,992,470)**	**($648,443)**
EQUITY		
Common Stock w/out par value	2,070,000	
Accumulated deficit	(7,062,470)	
Stockholder's equity	(4,992,470)	
Partners' capital (deficit)		(1,138,145)

252.   COMPARATIVE STATEMENTS OF OPERATION 1975-76 SEASON
       BUFFALO BRAVES, INC. VS. KENTUCKY COLONELS, LTD.

Item		Braves	Colonels
Revenue:			
Regular Season Ticket Sales, Net			
Of Direct Costs (**See Note 1**)			
Gross Sales	1,610,763		
Less: Game Exp.	459,404		
Net Gate Receipts		$1,151,359	$532,270
Playoff Ticket Sales, Net Of			
Direct Costs		170,597	51,219
Television/Radio (**See Note 2**)		679,050	12,703
Game Programs, Net Of			
Direct Costs		68,402	28,441
Concessions		125,703	0
Other, Net		45,738	10,427
Total Revenue		**$2,240,849**	**$635,060**
Operating Expenses:			
Team & Game		2,048,559	$1,264,445
General & Administrative		499,502	559,554
Promotion & Publicity		145,329	59,335
Provision For Lease Cancellation			
(**See Note 2**)			187,721
Depreciation Of Improvements			
And Equipmt		21,232	0
League Assessments			
(**See Note 2**)		411,291	0
Total Operating Expenses		**$3,125,913**	**$2,071,055**
Loss From Operations, Before			
Amortization And Loss (Gain)			
On Disposition Of Players		**($885,064)**	**($1,435,955)**
Amortization And Loss On Disposition			
Of Players:			
Amortiz. Player Acquis. Costs		0	$ 194,328
Amortiz. Franchise Costs		0	-8,003
Loss/Gain On Disposition			
Of Players		0	+117,168
Loss From Operations		**($885,064)**	**($1,461,118)**
Interest Expense (Net)		-306,932	-106,653
Net Net Loss From Operation		**$1,191,966**	**$1,567,711**

Note 1: The difference between the average net ticket price in the '75-76 playing season, between the Braves and the Colonels was of major concern. It was my contention that it could only be explained as a result of the sale of Issel to the Baltimore Claws prior to the '75-76 Colonels' season. The '75-76 Colonels had experienced a 20.5% decrease in attendance, even though they had won the ABA championship the previous year. As the attendance statistics reflect, prior to that time, the Colonels' attendance had exceeded the Braves' attendance.

	Braves	Colonels
Net Gate	$1,151,359	$532,270
Av. Gate Per Game	$27,413	$ 12,673
Av. Attendance Per Game	7,972	6,937
Av. Net Ticket Price	$3.44	$1.83

Note 2: In comparing the NBA Braves vs. the ABA Colonels, the NBA television package must be added to the Colonels' figures, the Colonels' lease cancellation provision must not be deducted from the Colonels' figures and the NBA's league assessment must be included

in the Colonels' figures. When doing so, the following is the net result:

NetNet Loss From Operations	($1,317,699)	($1,627,811)
Add In NBA Television Monies	0	+679,050
Add In Colonels' Lease Cancellation		+187,721
Deduct NBA League Assessment		(411,291)
Correct Net/Net Loss	($1,317,699)	($1,172,331)

253. *Forbes Magazine*, February 17, 2003: Indiana Pacers = $248 million; San Antonio Spurs = $242 million; New Jersey Nets = $218 million and the Denver Nuggets = $209 million.

254. *Ibid.*: Dallas Mavericks = $304 million; Miami Heat = $250 million; Indiana Pacers $248 million; San Antonio Spurs = $242 million; Utah Jazz = $226 million; New Jersey Nets = $218 million; Denver Nuggets = $209 million; Memphis Grizzlies = $198 million and the New Orleans Hornets = $172 million.

CHAPTER EIGHT: Remember My Friends—It All Began With A Mouse

255. Wyatt, Wilson W., *Whistle Stops: Adventures in Public Life*, University of Kentucky Press, 1985., pp. 14.

256. *Ibid.*, pp. 28-30

257. *Ibid.*, pp. 113-144.

258. *Ibid.*, p. 31.

259. Chris Poynter, *The Courier-Journal*, "Alderman's tenacity led to shot at an NBA team", March 18, 2001.

260. *Ibid.*

261. First, the Task Force believes that the Board of Aldermen should pursue the arena project. There are still a large number of uncertainties and a number of difficult issues to work through. However, the general consensus was that a new arena located in downtown Louisville would be a significant plus for the community as a whole. The Task Force clearly believes that it is well worth the effort to take further steps to develop the project. Second, there is a general consensus that an entity needs to be created to spearhead the project. The Task Force did not articulate the nature of the entity, but suggests that the Board of Aldermen either create an arena authority or a not-for-profit corporation to further the arena development. This entity should have support from the entire community and should not only be a vehicle of the City of Louisville. This entity should be empowered to develop the public/private partnership necessary for success. Third, the arena project should seek not only to enhance entertainment opportunities of the greater Louisville community, but should be part of an overall strategy for enhancing travel and tourism within the community and to enliven Louisville's downtown neighborhood. **Professional sports franchises should be pursued** as should major amateur tournaments and championship events.

CHAPTER NINE: The Rockets Rocket Into Louisville

262. A $387 million bond issue for Port of Houston improvements and a $119 million bond issue for a new downtown Civil Justice Center.

263. "Contrary to the recent public statements and actions of the Governor of Louisiana and the Mayor of New Orleans, you can be assured that there will be absolutely no public statement/s/ from me or anyone else in Kentucky about the Houston situation or the opportunity that it presents for Louisville and Kentucky, because neither you, the Rockets nor the City of Houston deserves that at this point. It is our feeling that the "stability of the League" demands and requires that such discussions must take place privately and not be battered by such publicity as has been created by the public officials of Louisiana. However, I don't want the "lack of publicity" to cause any doubt as to Louisville's interest; and in that regard, I do want you to personally know that I am exceedingly interested in privately meeting with you at any time and any place, to discuss the concepts of such a "transfer."

264. Dr. Shumaker's educational and university employment background being: a Masters (1966) and Ph.D. (1969) degree from the University of Pennsylvania; post-doctoral work at the University of Toronto, Oxford University and the University of California at Irvine (mid-1970s); dean of Humanities/Fine Arts at S.U.N.Y. In Albany, N.Y. (1977-1987); and from 1987 to 1995 as the president of Central Connecticut State.

265. The $200 million leveraged recapitalization of the YankeeNets, LLC; the refinancing of the Phoenix Suns; the City of San Diego's $250 million in tax-exempt financing for the new Padres ballpark; a $126.9 million refinancing to construct BankOne Ballpark in Phoenix; the $100.3 million refinancing of Giants Stadium; Continental Airlines Arena and Monmouth Park in New Jersey; the $400 million American Airlines Arena in Dallas; the $334.9 million tax-exempt bond financing of Paul Brown Stadium in Cincinnati—and the list went on.

266. While not yet on the University's "horizon," of Endnote interest here is a quote from Rick Pitino's book, *Lead to Succeed*: "The other thing I have come to know is that leaders must be selfless. It can't be just about you. Your career, your record. Your advancement, your success." [The reader can reach his/her own conclusion about the 'selflessness' of the University's actions—particularly in light of its ostensible mission to serve the community as a whole.

CHAPTER TEN: The First Sting of the Hornets

267. The information in these prior paragraphs on the last several pages was gained from various articles in *The Charlotte Observer*, general internet sources and from numerous personal discussions between September, 2000 and December, 2001 with Wooldridge and his counsel, "The Wagman."

268. The *Houston Chronicle* reported that Rockets owner Les Alexander was its largest contributor, pouring $965,000 into the campaign. The subsequently infamous Enron, whose chairman and CEO, Ken Lay, was co-chairman of the pro-arena campaign and loaned the campaign $400,000 and contributed $195,441. Reliant Energy, Alexander's law firm (Baker & Botts) and nine other Houston companies donated between $75-100,000 each.

269. *The Courier-Journal*, "Experts to draft NBA arena plan", Thursday, November 16, 2000.

270. Dear Dr. Shumaker: It's been a "jammed up" day (as you might imagine), but I

wanted to get in touch w/you before it closes; because I dearly want to reiterate what I discussed w/you at the Schusterman's home several months ago — i.e. that our efforts regarding the transfer of an NBA franchise to Louisville and the construction of an arena to accommodate same are going to be done in a manner which specifically includes the University of Louisville's programs, should that be U/L's desire. As I told you that evening, while I didn't receive either of my degrees from the University, I have been an enthusiastic supporter of its programs since my return to Louisville from Vanderbilt in 1965. My only son is a proud graduate of UofL and led its golf team for four (4) years in the late 1980s. Please know that the last thing I would ever want to do or participate in would be something that would harm the University. As this matter goes forward, privately, I will endeavor to keep you apprised. There will probably be a date in late November or early December when the owner of a particular team will be coming to Louisville. During a previous visit, he has personally committed to me that, if he transfers his franchise to Louisville, he wants to make it a "win-win" situation for both his franchise and the University. I've expressed to him that such a win-win situation would not only be advisable, it would also be necessary. In the meantime, I would hope that we all could keep an open mind about this project. It's my dedicated intention to make sure that Louisville's future will be enhanced by an expanded and successful University and its programs and a dynamic presence in the national/international business community as the home to a NBA/WNBA franchise. There's no reason why we can win across the board on this.

Looking forward to our future discussions, I remain Yours with personal regards, J. Bruce Miller.

271. Dizney originally began working for Humana's predecessor, Extendicare, in 1966, formed his own medical company (United Medical Corporation) relocating its headquarters to Orlando's Atlantic Bank Building in 1977 and by the early 1980s owned/operated dozens of acute care and psychiatric hospitals throughout the southeastern United States.

272. David Williams, Memphis *Commercial Appeal,* "NBA Worth Look, Consultant Says" June 25, 1998.

273. Geoff Calkins, Memphis *Commercial Appeal,* Sunday, April 23, 2000.

274. This information is gained from David Williams, *The Memphis Commercial-Appeal,* "Secret Pursuit, Two Came Calling", October 7, 2001; and from various conversations with Craig Wagner, Ray Wooldridge and Michael Heisley.

275. David Williams, *Memphis Commercial-Appeal,* "Secret Pursuit, Two Came Calling", October 8, 2001.

CHAPTER ELEVEN: Grizzled By Graceland

276. David Williams, *Memphis Commercial-Appeal,* "Secret Pursuit, Two Came Calling." October 8, 2001. This story was never confirmed by Meadows; however Heisley did tell me in a long call, much later, that Meadows' initial meeting in Memphis was of little value in the beginning.

277. *Ibid.*

278. Brad Ziemer, *Vancouver Sun,* February 24, 2001.

279. There wasn't a single *Fortune 500* company in New Orleans, as the only one,

Entergy, was scheduled to leave for Tampa in April.

280. David Williams, *Memphis Commercial Appeal*, "Secret Pursuit, Two Came Calling."

281. The *Los Angeles Times* reported that free land, a buy-out of the Grizzlies four-year lease in Vancouver and lease concessions from Disney that owned The Pond (where the Grizzlies would have to play in Anaheim) were offered to Heisley. However, it was still clear that the NBA was unhappy with the idea of a third team in the Los Angeles market area. Howard Tsumura, *The Vancouver Province*, February 28, 2001.

282. Bill: Well, as Ronald Reagan said to Mondale once, "there you go again." The 'flash words' you've used—'"idiotic", "irresponsible", "unconscionable"—are amazing. All so totally unnecessary. I, as I've said before, have no problem with your adversary position to what we're trying (and about) to accomplish. If you knew and understood what we're doing, how we're doing it and what it would mean to Louisville, the University of Louisville and Kentucky, I think you would be surprised. I simply don't understand (and never will) after all the time we've shared together for the last 20+ years, after all the fun we've enjoyed, after all the 'trials and tribulations' that we've gone through and shared together, why it is necessary for you to continue to use 'flash words' that have no seeming purpose other than to endeavor to 'impeach' me and my integrity (which I prize). Billy, as I view the obituary columns and realize that, virtually every week, one of our 'collective' acquaintances or friends leaves us, it seems to me that life's too short and too precious to take this approach. So much for the thought. Best wishes.

283. Chris Poynter, *The Courier-Journal*, March 8, 2001.

284. The correctness of his beliefs was later proven and is discussed in "The Swap," hereinafter.

285. Chris Poynter, *The Courier-Journal*, "UofL open to playing downtown", March 12, 2001.

286. Members of this committee were: Sonny Altman, managing partner, Deming Malone Livesay & Ostroff; businessman Larry Hayes; Jim Gaunt, CEO Fifth/Third Bank; Len Spalding, Chairman St. Catharine College; Dee Maynard; Kevin Hable, managing partner Wyatt Tarrant & Combs; attorney, Christy Ames; Charlie Clephas, president Louisville Central Labor Council; businessman, Greg Fischer; realtor Sandy Metts [David Snowden's wife]; businessman Junior Bridgeman; Kelly Downard, president Louisville Community Development Bank; Kim Burse, Community Development Bank; Jerry Parham, African-American Venture Capital Fund; and Malcolm Chancey.

287. Which included the city's portion of the occupational taxes on player and other Grizzlies personnel of $1.2 million; a $2 dollar ticket surcharge on all tickets sold and there was no way (at that point) to estimate the collateral income the city would derive from the arena operation that would be taxable and could be contributed to assist in bond retirement.

288. Chris Poynter, *The Courier-Journal*, March 15, 2001, headline (front page immediately below the masthead)—"Hoop Dreams...the NBA/Executives woo team's owner/ Armstrong faults finance plan."

289. Of interest is that "certain" of the Mayor's "blue-ribbon" committee (listed in Endnote 286) had rather unusual interests: the Memphis office of Wyatt, Tarrant &

Combs (represented in the meeting by Kevin Hable) handled the bonds for the city of Memphis and the Grizzlies, when they eventually moved to Memphis; Malcolm Chancey would play the lead anti role in the final chapter of the NBA odyssey, <u>after</u> a written commitment, signed by the Hornets' owners, was obtained; and Sandra Metts was David Snowden's husband, who had been opposed to the NBA in Louisville from the very beginning. Of other interest is that the majority of these individuals, were *actually* supportive of the NBA in Louisville and several of them, including Jim Gaunt and Junior Bridgeman actively and publicly supported the Grizzlies—attended the Heisley meeting with the Gateway Group <u>the very next evening</u> and fully supported the final chapter of the NBA odyssey.

290. Chris Poynter, *The Courier-Journal*, "City plans new arena for Grizzlies, UofL", March 16, 2001.

CHAPTER TWELVE: "It's Not Over 'Til It's Over"

291. *The Charlotte Observer*, "Voters' distrust, disgust doomed arena package" by Bruce Henderson, June 7, 2002.

292. June 7, 2001 *The Charlotte Observer*, Jim Morrill and Lauren Markoe.

293. Craig: Following discussions last night and this morning, in accordance with your client's request of Blum last night and in accordance with our discussions of yesterday afternoon, from this point forward "everyone here" will categorically and specifically deny any suggestion or question about on-going discussions with your client OR the extant city; until such time as any such comment is mutually-agreed upon. Everyone here includes "everybody." The derivation of this morning's story in the extant city did not come from this office as is obvious from the attribution in the story. However, EVERYONE is now on the "same page." Your client does need to understand how, UTTERLY EXCITED, everyone is here about the possibility. It's understandable that he doesn't understand that, because of the long-standing and continuing wholesale lack of appreciation he has received in the extant city. Exuberance, sometimes (particularly as it relates to this subject in Louisville), leads to "over-action." Looking forward to working with you, I remain Yours personally, Bruce Miller.

CHAPTER THIRTEEN: The End of Louisville's NBA Odyssey

294. Nack, William, *My Turf*, DeCapo Press, 2003, at p. 324

295. *Ibid* at p. 326.

296. *Ibid* at p. 327.

297. *Ibid* at p. 328.

298. *Ibid* at p. 327.

299. Dear Dr. Shumaker: This morning I read, with considerable interest, the article on the sports page of the *Courier-Journal*. I wanted to offer my sincere and deep congratulations. From our standpoint, this decision is certainly in the University's short/long-term financial interest; and certainly makes clear that the University's overarching goal is the primary utilization of its financial wherewithal for education of young men and women. And further, to be sure, this decision now would appear to provide your team and ours an opportunity to fully consider an integration of the arena construction planning and financing, with the ultimate goal being to provide

financial stability for the University's basketball programs for the long-term, with the least possible drain on University resources. I look forward with great anticipation to the opportunity to further entertain these discussions with you, and offer My warm personal regards to you and your family

300.

	ANALYSIS OF LAST 31 YEARS OF FINAL 4 TEAMS VS. NBA TEAM IN COLLEGE MARKET AREA				
COLUMN 1	COLUMN 2	COLUMN 3	COLUMN 4	COLUMN 5	COLUMN 6
Year	Final Four Teams	NBA Team Primary Mkt 50 miles	NBA Team Secondary Mkt 100 miles	NBA Team Tertiary Mkt 150 miles	* by Final 4 Team w/in NBA mkt area
2001	Duke			Hornets	*
	Arizona			Suns	*
	Maryland	Wizards			*
	Mich. St.			Pistons	*
2000	Mich. St.			Pistons	*
	Florida		Magic		*
	N.Carolina			Hornets	*
	Wisconsin			Bulls	*
1999	Connecticut	Celtics			*
	Duke			Hornets	*
	Mich. St.			Pistons	*
	Ohio St.		Cavaliers		*
1998	*Kentucky*				not considered
	Utah	Jazz			*
	N.Carolina			Hornets	*
	Stanford	GoldenState			*
1997	Arizona			Suns	*
	Kentucky				not considered
	Minnesota	Timberwlves			*
	N.Carolina			Hornets	*
1996	*Kentucky*				not considered
	Syracuse				
	U.Mass.	Celtics			*
	Miss. St.				
1995	UCLA	Lakers			*
	Arkansas				
	N.Carolina			Hornets	*
	Okla.St.				
1994	Arkansas				
	Duke			Hornets	*
	Arizona			Suns	*
	Florida		Magic		*
1993	N.Carolina			Hornets	*
	Michigan	Pistons			*
	Kansas				
	Kentucky				not considered
1992	Duke			Hornets	*
	Michigan	Pistons			*
	Cincinnati				
	Indiana	Pacers			*
1991	Duke			Hornets	*
	Kansas				
	UNLV				not considered
	N.Carolina			Hornets	*
1990	*UNLV*				not considered
	Duke			Hornets	*
	Arkansas				
	Ga.Tech	Hawks			*
1989	Michigan	Pistons			*
	SetonHall	Nets			*
	Duke			Hornets	*
	Illinois	Bulls			*

	ANALYSIS OF LAST 31 YEARS OF FINAL 4 TEAMS VS. NBA TEAM IN COLLEGE MARKET AREA				
COLUMN 1	COLUMN 2	COLUMN 3	COLUMN 4	COLUMN 5	COLUMN 6
Year	Final Four Teams	NBA Team Primary Mkt 50 miles	NBA Team Secondary Mkt 100 miles	NBA Team Tertiary Mkt 150 miles	* by Final 4 Team w/in NBA mkt area
1988	Kansas				
	Oklahoma				
	Arizona			Suns	*
	Duke			Hornets	*
1987	Indiana	Pacers			*
	Syracuse				
	UNLV				not considered
	Providence			Celtics	*
1986	*Louisville*				not considered
	Duke				
	Kansas				
	LSU				
1985	Villanova	76ers			*
	Georgetown	Bullets			*
	St. Johns	Knicks			*
	Memphis				
1984	Georgetown	Bullets			*
	Houston	Rockets			*
	Kentucky				not considered
	Virginia			Bullets	*
1983	NCState				*
	Houston	Rockets			*
	Georgia		Hawks		*
	Louisville				not considered
1982	N.Carolina				
	Georgetown	Bullets			*
	Houston	Rockets			*
	Louisville				not considered
1981	Indiana	Pacers			*
	N.Carolina				
	Virginia			Bullets	*
	LSU	Jazz			*
1980	*Louisville*				not considered
	UCLA	Lakers			*
	Purdue			Bulls	*
	Iowa				
1979	Mich. St.			Pistons	*
	Indiana St.			Bulls	*
	DePaul	Bulls			*
	Pennsylvania	76ers			*

ANALYSIS OF LAST 31 YEARS OF FINAL 4 TEAMS VS. NBA TEAM IN COLLEGE MARKET AREA					
COLUMN 1	COLUMN 2	COLUMN 3	COLUMN 4	COLUMN 5	COLUMN 6
Year	Final Four Teams	NBA Team Primary Mkt 50 miles	NBA Team Secondary Mkt 100 miles	NBA Team Tertiary Mkt 150 miles	* by Final 4 Team w/in NBA mkt area
1978	*Kentucky*				not considered
	Duke				
	Arkansas				
	Notre Dame		Bulls		
1977	Marquette	Bucks			*
	N.Carolina			Cougars/ABA	*
	UNLV				not considered
	UNCC				
1976	Indiana	Pacers/ABA			*
	Michigan	Pistons			*
	UCLA	Lakers			*
	Rutgers	Nets/ABA			*
1975	UCLA	Lakers			*
	Kentucky				not considered
	Louisville				not considered
	Syracuse				
1974	NCState			Cougars/ABA	*
	Marquette	Bucks			*
	UCLA	Lakers			*
	Kansas				
1973	UCLA	Lakers			*
	Memphis	Tams/ABA			
	Indiana	Pacers/ABA			*
	Providence			Celtics	*
1972	UCLA	Lakers			*
	Florida St.				
	N.Carolina			Cougars/ABA	*
	Louisville				not considered
1971	UCLA	Lakers			*
	Villanova	76ers			*
	Western Ky.				not considered
	Kansas				
1970	UCLA	Lakers			*
	Jacksonville				
	NMexSt.				
	St.Bonnevtur			Celtics	*

Analysis of Information

31 years of Final 4's = 124 Final 4 'slots'
Kentucky/Louisville/UNLV/Western Ky. = 18 'slots'
Therefore: Only 106 'slots' are considered.
And: In Column 6 the symbol for 'not' in NBA Mkt Area=

Of 106 slots 29 'slots' were commprised of teams
that were not w/in an NBA/ABA market
area --- or :27.40%
OR
72.6% of ALL Final 4 teams in last 31
Final 4's were w/in an NBA/AVA market area

301.

COLLEGE ATTEND VS. ARENA CAPACITY / NBA TEAM WINNING % W/IN 50 MILES

YEAR	NBA TEAM IN PRIMARY COLLEGE MKT. AREA	WINNING % NBA TEAM	COLLEGE TEAM IN NCAA FINAL 4	CAPACITY OF COLLEGE ARENA	AVERAGE ATTENDANCE OF COLLEGE TEAM	% ATTEND. TO ARENA CAPACITY
2001	Wizards	23.00%	Maryland	14,500	14,058	97%
1999	Celtics	?	Connecticut	16,294	13,345	82%
1998	Jazz	75.60%	Utah	15,000	13,818	92%
	GoldenState	23.20%	Stanford	7,391	6,734	91%
	Jazz	78.00%	Utah	15,000	14,047	94%
1997	Timberw'vs	48.80%	Minnesota	14,300	14,054	98%
1996	Celtics	40.20%	U.Mass	9,493	9,493	100%
1995	Lakers	58.50%	UCLA	12,819	11,400	89%
1993	Pistons	48.80%	Michigan	13,562	13,734	101%
1992	Pacers	48.80%	Indiana	17,357	16,536	95%
	Pistons	58.50%	Michigan	13,562	12,986	96%
1990	Hawks	50.00%	Ga.Tech	10,000	8,930	89%
1989	Pistons	76.80%	Michigan	13,562	12,838	95%
	Nets	31.70%	SetonHall	played in 3 different arenas		
1987	Pacers	50.00%	Indiana	17,357	16,562	95%
1986	Lakers	75.60%	UCLA	12,819	9,927	78%
1985	76ers	70.70%	Villanova	played in 3 different arenas		
	Bullets	48.80%	Georgetown	14,883	19,035	78.20%
	Knicks	29.30%	St.Johns	played in 3 different arenas		
1984	Bullets	41.70%	Georgetown	played in 2 different arenas		
	Rockets	35.40%	Houston	played in 2 different arenas		
1983	Rockets	17.10%	Houston	8,479	7,990	94%
1982	Bullets	52.40%	Georgetown	played in 2 different arenas		
	Rockets	56.10%	Houston	8,479	6,780	80%
1981	Pacers	53.70%	Indiana	17,357	15,965	92%
1980	Lakers	73.20%	UCLA	12,819	11,218	88%
1979	Bulls	37.80%	Depaul	5,300	4,589	87%
	76ers	57.30%	Pennsylvania	played in 2 different arenas		
1977	Bucks	36.60%	Marquette	?	?	
1976	Pacers/ABA	46.40%	Indiana	17,357	16,892	97%
	Pistons	43.90%	Michigan	13,562	?	
	Lakers	48.80%	UCLA	12,819	?	
	Nets/ABA	?	Rutgers	played in 2 different arenas		
1975	Lakers	36.60%	UCLA	12,819	12,384	97%
1974	Lakers	57.30%	UCLA	12,819	12,385	97%
1973	Lakers	73.20%	UCLA	12,819	12,515	98%
1971	Lakers	58.50%	UCLA	12,819	12,625	98%
1970	Lakers	56.10%	UCLA	12,819	12,293	96%

Average NBA Winning ' 49.15%   **Average Attendance vs. Capacity 92.37%**

LEGEND: PRIMARY MARKET AREA FOR COLLEGE IS DEFINED AS BEING WITHIN
50 MILES OF THE NBA CITY.

302. The Goal Group had no significant track record other than their assistance to the City of Memphis in negotiating the arrangement between the City-owned Pyramid and the to-be City-owned NBA arena—not a particularly difficult assignment. Within 2 months they would create a bill in excess of $175,000 (which would never be paid) and within several more months, after the loss of the Hornets to New Orleans, the Goal Group would disband!

303. The facts referenced in this Section refuting Malcolm Chancey's aldermanic oration were subsequently ascertained by a committee called, "Citizens for Action in Greater Louisville" which was formed for the sole purpose of "clarifying" Chancey's misstatements.

304. Portions of this Section have been derived from discussions with The Wagman, Wooldridge and from Steward Yerton's article entitled "The art of the deal," *The Times-Picayune*, January 20, 2002.

CHAPTER FOURTEEN: The Tale of Two Cities

305. Mike Hendricks, *The Kansas City Star*, "Archrivals in cahoots? It's a hoot", July 26, 2004.

306. Lynn Horsley, *The Kansas City Star*, "Study to assess Kemper's fate in case downtown plan wins", July 30, 2004.

307. Lynn Horsley, *The Kansas City Star*, "New downtown arena on the way", August 4, 2004.

308. Joe Posanski, *The Kansas City Star*, "Voters choose hope rather than fear", August 4, 2004.

EPILOGUE: Lost Opportunities and "Leadership"

309. Heather Rascher and Daniel A. Rascher, PhD., *Examining the Viability of Various Cities for NBA Expansion or Relocation.*

310. Table 6, p. 290-91 "Forecast Results for Location Model Predicting Probable NBA Cities, *Journal of Sports Management,* Dr. Daniel Rascher and Heather Rascher, August, 2004.

BIBLIOGRAPHY

A.

Archdeacon, Thomas J., *Becoming American: An Ethnic History*, Free Press, 1983.

B.

Bernstein, Irving, *The Lean Years: A History of the American Worker*, Houghton Mifflin, 1960.

Bernstein, Michael A., *The Great Depression: Delayed Recovery and Economic Change in America, 1929-39*, Cambridge University Press, 1987.

Bjarkman, Peter C., *The Biographical History of Basketball*, Chicago Masters Press, 1998.

Bolin, James Duanne, *Bossism and Reform in a Southern City: Lexington, Ky. 1880-1940*; The University of Kentucky Press, Lexington, Ky. 2000.

Branch, Taylor, *Parting the Waters: America in the King Years (1954-63)*, Simon & Schuster, 1988.

Brown, Gene, *The Complete Book of Basketball*, Arno Press, 1980.

C.

Chandler, Dan/Vernon Hatton, *Rupp: From Both Ends of the Bench*, Basic Books, 1972.

Chandler, David Leon, *The Bingham's of Louisville, The Dark History Behind One of America's Greatest Fortunes*, Crown Publishers, New York, 1987.

The Charlotte Observer

Clark, Dr. Thomas D.; *A History of Kentucky*, Prentice-Hall, 1937.

Clark, Dr. Thomas D.; *Agrarian Kentucky*, The University Press of Kentucky, 1977.

Cox, Earl, *Calling It Like I See It*, Butler Books, 2002.

The Courier-Journal.

D.

Douchant, Mike, *Encyclopedia Of College Basketball*, Gale Research, Inc. 1994.

Durso, Joseph, *Madison Square Garden — 100 Years Of History*, Simon & Schuster, 1979.

E.

Embry, Mike, *Baron Of The Bluegrass*, Cumberland House Publishing Co., 2000.

F.

Fishman, Lew, *The New York Knicks: Pride Of Gotham,* Prentice-Hall, Inc., 1974.

Fitzpatrick, Frank, *And The Walls Came Tumbling Down*, University Of Nebraska Press, 1999.

Fox, Larry, *Illustrated History Of Basketball*, Grosset & Dunlap, 1974.

Frager, Dr. Stanley R., *The Champion Within You*, Champion Press, 1992.

G.

Gailbraith, John Kenneth, *The Great Crash,* Houghton Mifflin, 1955.

Gardiner, C. Harvey, *Coach Diddle/Mister Diddle*, Parthenon Press, 1984.

Giuliani, Rudolph W., *Leadership*, Miramix Books, 2002.

Green, Harvey, *The Uncertainty Of Everyday Life*, Harper-Collins, 1992.

Greenberg, Martin J., *The Stadium Game*, Marquette University Press, 2000

Gould, Todd, *Pioneers Of The Hardwood: Indiana And The Birth Of Professional Basketball*, Indiana University Press, 1998.

Gunther, John, *Inside the U.S.A.*, Harper & Bros., New York, 1951.

H.

Halberstam, David, *The Breaks Of The Game*, Alfred A. Knopf, 1981.

Halberstam, David, *The Fifties*, Random House, 1993.

Harrison, Lowell H. & James C. Klotter, *A New History of Kentucky*, The University of Kentucky Press, 1997.

Heatherly, Charles L., *Mandate for Leadership*, Heritage Found., 1981.

Hollander, Zander, *The NBA's Official Encyclopedia Of Pro Basketball*, The New American Library, Inc. 1981.

Hoover, Herbert, *The Memoirs Of Herbert Hoover: The Cabinet And The Presidency*, Macmillan, 1952.

The Houston Chronicle

The Honolulu Star

I.

Isaacs, Neil D., *All The Moves: A History Of College Basketball*, J.B. Lipincott Co., 1975.

Issel, Dan/Buddy Martin, *Parting Shots*, Contemporary Books, Inc., 1985.

J.

Jackson, V.A., *Beyond The Baron*: A Personal Glance At Coach Adolph Rupp, McClanahan Publishing House, 1998.

Jenkins, William M., Jr., *The Man With The Red Towel*, Jenkins, 2000.

Johnson, Haynes and Broder, David S., *The System: The American Way of Politics at the Breaking Point*, Little-Brown, 1996.

K.

Kahn, Roger, *The Flame Of Pure Fire, Jack Dempsey And The Roaring '20's*, Harcourt Brace & Company, 1999.

Kennedy, David M., *Freedom From Fear: The American People In The Depression And War*, Oxford University Press, 1999.

Kennedy, John F., *Profiles in Courage*.

Kindred, David, *Basketball The Dream Game In Kentucky*, The Courier-Journal and Louisville Times, 1976;

King, Moses, *King's Handbook of the United States*, The Matthew-Northrup Co. and the Moses King Corporation, New York and Buffalo, N.Y., 1890.

Kirby, Jack T., *Rural Worlds Lost: The American South*, Louisiana State University Press, 1987.

Klein, Maury, *History of the Louisville & Nashville Railroad*, The University of Kentucky Press, Lexington, Ky. 2003.

Koppett, Leonard, *Twenty-Four Seconds To Shoot*, Macmillan, 1968.

L.

Lancaster, Harry, (As Told To Caywood Ledford), *Adolph Rupp, As I Knew Him*, Lexington Productions, Inc., 1979.

Lane, Mark, *Plausible Denial*, Thundermouth Press, 1991.

Laudeman, Tev, *The Rupp Years*, The Courier-Journal and Louisville Times, 1972.

Ledford, Cawood, *Heart Of Blue*, Host Communications, Inc. 1995.

Ledford, Cawood, *Six Roads To Glory*, Host Communications, Inc. 1997.

Leuchtenburg, William E., *The Perils Of Prosperity*, University of Chicago Press, 1958.

M.

Maraniss, David, *When Pride Still Mattered*, Simon & Schuster, 1999.

The Memphis Commercial-Appeal

McAvoy, Rogers, *Mr. Basketball: The Clair Bee Story*, Goldenseal (1991).

McGill, John, *Kentucky Sports*, Jim Host & Associates, Inc. 1978.

Mitchener, James, *Sports In America*, Random House, 1976.

N.

Nack, William, *My Turf*, DeCapo Press, 2003.

Nelli, Bert and Steve, *The Winning Tradition: A History Of Kentucky Wildcat Basketball*, The University of Kentucky Press, 1998.

The New Orleans Times-Picayune

Nixon, Richard M., *Six Crises*, Pyramid Boods, 1968.

P.

Pitino, Rick, *Success Is A Choice*, Broadway Books, 1997.

Pitino, Rick, *Lead To Succeed*, Broadway Books, 2000.

Pluto, Jerry, *Loose Balls - The Short And Wild Life Of The American Basketball Association*, Simon & Shuster, 1990.

Powell, Robert A., *Kentucky Governors*, Kentucky Images, 1976.

R.

Reed, Billy, *The Final Four*, Host Communications, Inc., 1988.

Rice, Russell, *Adolph Rupp, Kentucky's Basketball Baron*, Sagamore Publishing, 1994.

Rice, Russell, *Kentucky Basketball's Big Blue Machine*, Strode Publishers, 1987.

Rosen, Charles, *Scandals Of 1951*, Holt, Rinehart & Winston, 1978.

Russell, Fred, *Vanderbilt - A Golden Tradition*, Vanderbilt University, 1991.

Ryan, Bob, *The Pro Game "The World Of Professional Basketball"*, McGraw-Hill Book Company, 1975.

S.

Smith, Hedrick, *The Power Game*, Random House, 1988.

Sobel, Robert, *The Great Bull Market: Wall Street In The 1920's*, Macmillan, 1968.

T.

Tapp, Hambleton and Klotter, James C., *Kentucky: Decades of Discord 1865-1900*, The Kentucky Historical Society, Frankfort, Ky., 1977.

Temin, Peter, *Did Monetary Forces Cause The Great Depression*, Norton, 1976.

Tuell, Gary, *Above The Rim: A Pictorial History Of Basketball At The University of Louisville*, University of Louisville Athletic Association, 1987

V.

Vaught, Jamie H., *Cats Up Close: Champions of Kentucky Basketball*, McClanahan Publishing House, 1999.

W.

Western Kentucky University Website

West Virginia Archives And History Website

Wetzel, Dan & Don Yaeger, *Sole Influence: Basketball, Corporate Greed and the Corruption of America's Youth*, Warner Books, 2000.

Weyand, Alexander M., *The Cavalcade Of Basketball*, Macmillan, 1960.

Wolff, Alexander and Armen Keteyian, *Raw Recruits: The High Stakes Games Colleges Play To Get Their Basketball Stars*, Simon & Schuster, Inc., 1990.

Wolf, Dave, *Foul: The Connie Hawkins Story*, Holt, Rinehart, 1971.

www.remembertheaba.com